STAR WARS®
TALES OF THE JEDI™
The Sith War

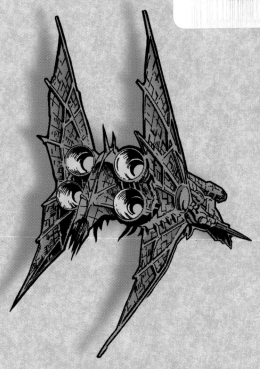

The events in this story take place 3996 years before the Battle of Yavin (as seen in *Star Wars: A New Hope*).

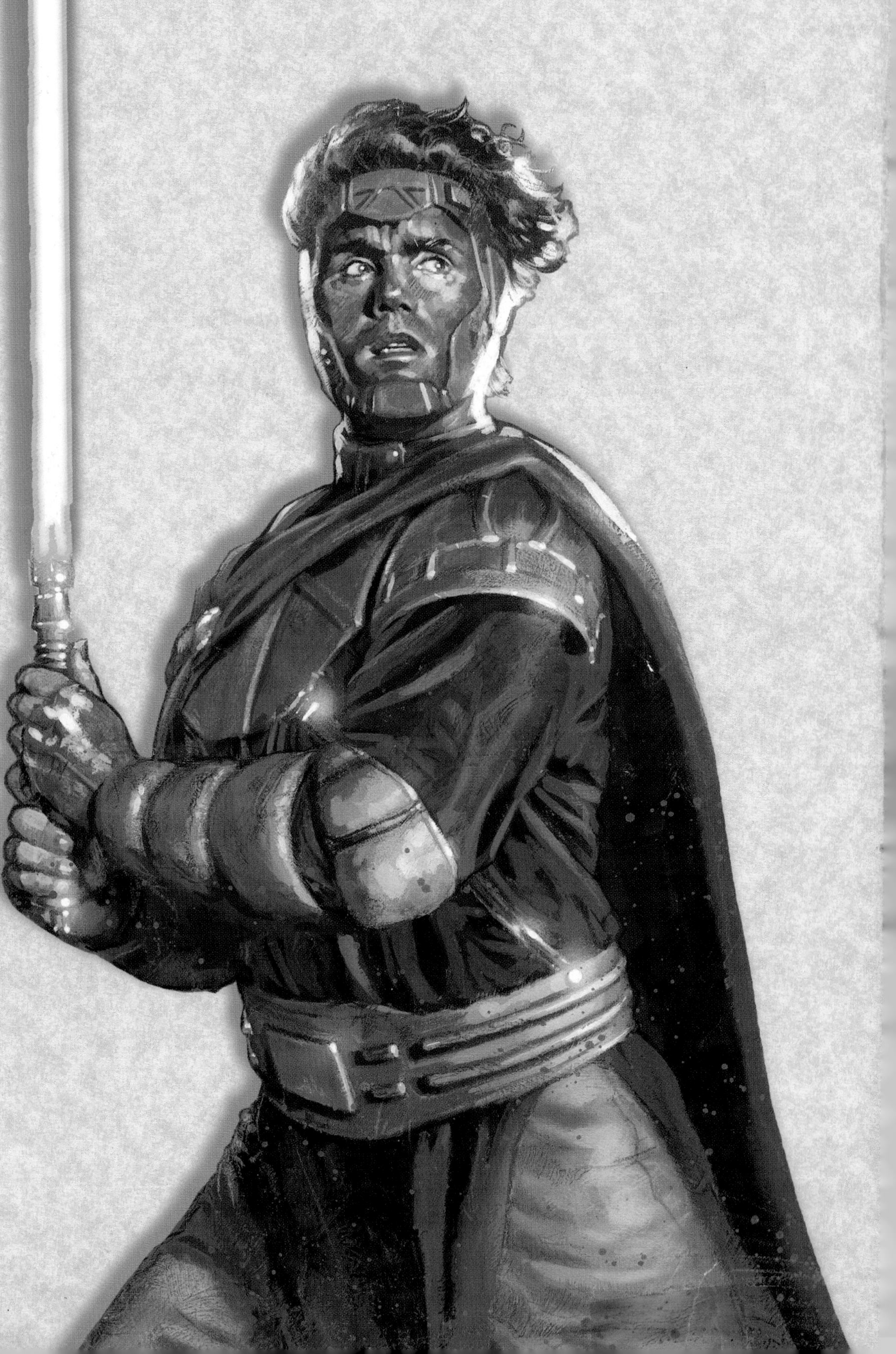

STAR WARS®
TALES OF THE JEDI™
The Sith War

script
Kevin J. Anderson

pencils
Dario Carrasco, Jr.

inks
Jordi Ensign
Mark G. Heike
Bill Black
David Jacob Beckett

colors
Pamela Rambo
Rachelle Menashe

lettering
Willie Schubert

cover art
Mathieu Lauffray

DARK HORSE BOOKS™

publisher
Mike Richardson

series editor
Bob Cooper

collection editor
Lynn Adair

collection designers
Jeremy Perkins and Scott Tice

special thanks to
**Lucy Autrey Wilson and Allan Kausch
at Lucas Licensing**

STAR WARS®: TALES OF THE JEDI™—THE SITH WAR

This volume collects issues one through six of the Dark Horse comic-book series
Star Wars®: Tales of the Jedi™—The Sith War.

Published by Dark Horse Books
A division of Dark Horse Comics, Inc.
10956 S.E. Main Street
Milwaukie, OR 97222

darkhorse.com
starwars.com

First edition: July 1996
ISBN: 1-56971-173-9

7 9 10 8

Printed in China

Edge of the Whirlwind

It has been six months since the former
enemies Exar Kun and Ulic Qel-Droma have
joined forces, forced into a common goal by
hypnotic visions of a reborn Golden Age of
the Sith.

Through his dabbling in forbidden teachings,
Exar Kun has fallen completely under the spell of
the ancient Sith ways, and he knows he must
gain additional disciples to fan the flames of his
planned victory.

Meanwhile, in the iron-walled city of Cinnagar in the
Empress Teta system, Ulic Qel-Droma has stumbled down
the dark path — driven by a distorted need to avenge the
murder of his beloved Master Arca, poisoned by dark Sith
toxins, and seduced and manipulated by his wily lover
Aleema. He has allied himself with Exar Kun to bring about
a new Golden Age, following the dream-images that fog his
mind. His mission is to gather an army awesome enough to
take on even the mighty galactic Republic.

But as their plans proceed, far from the watchful eyes of the
loyal Jedi Knights, other vicious crusaders turn their attentions to
what may seem to be easy pickings while Ulic is preoccupied . . .

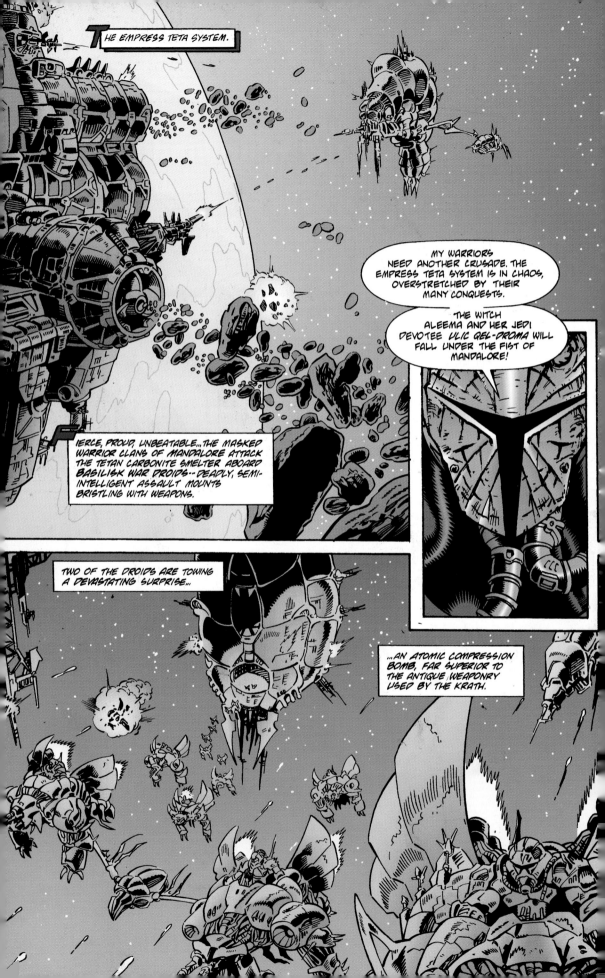

THE EMPRESS TETA SYSTEM.

MY WARRIORS NEED ANOTHER CRUSADE. THE EMPRESS TETA SYSTEM IS IN CHAOS, OVERSTRETCHED BY THEIR MANY CONQUESTS.

THE WITCH ALEEMA AND HER JEDI DEVOTEE *ULIC QEL-DROMA* WILL FALL UNDER THE FIST OF MANDALORE!

IERCE, PROUD, UNBEATABLE...THE MASKED WARRIOR CLANS OF MANDALORE ATTACK THE TETAN CARBONITE SMELTER ABOARD *BASILISK WAR DROIDS*--DEADLY, SEMI-INTELLIGENT ASSAULT MOUNTS BRISTLING WITH WEAPONS.

TWO OF THE DROIDS ARE TOWING A DEVASTATING SURPRISE...

...AN *ATOMIC COMPRESSION BOMB*, FAR SUPERIOR TO THE ANTIQUE WEAPONRY USED BY THE KRATH.

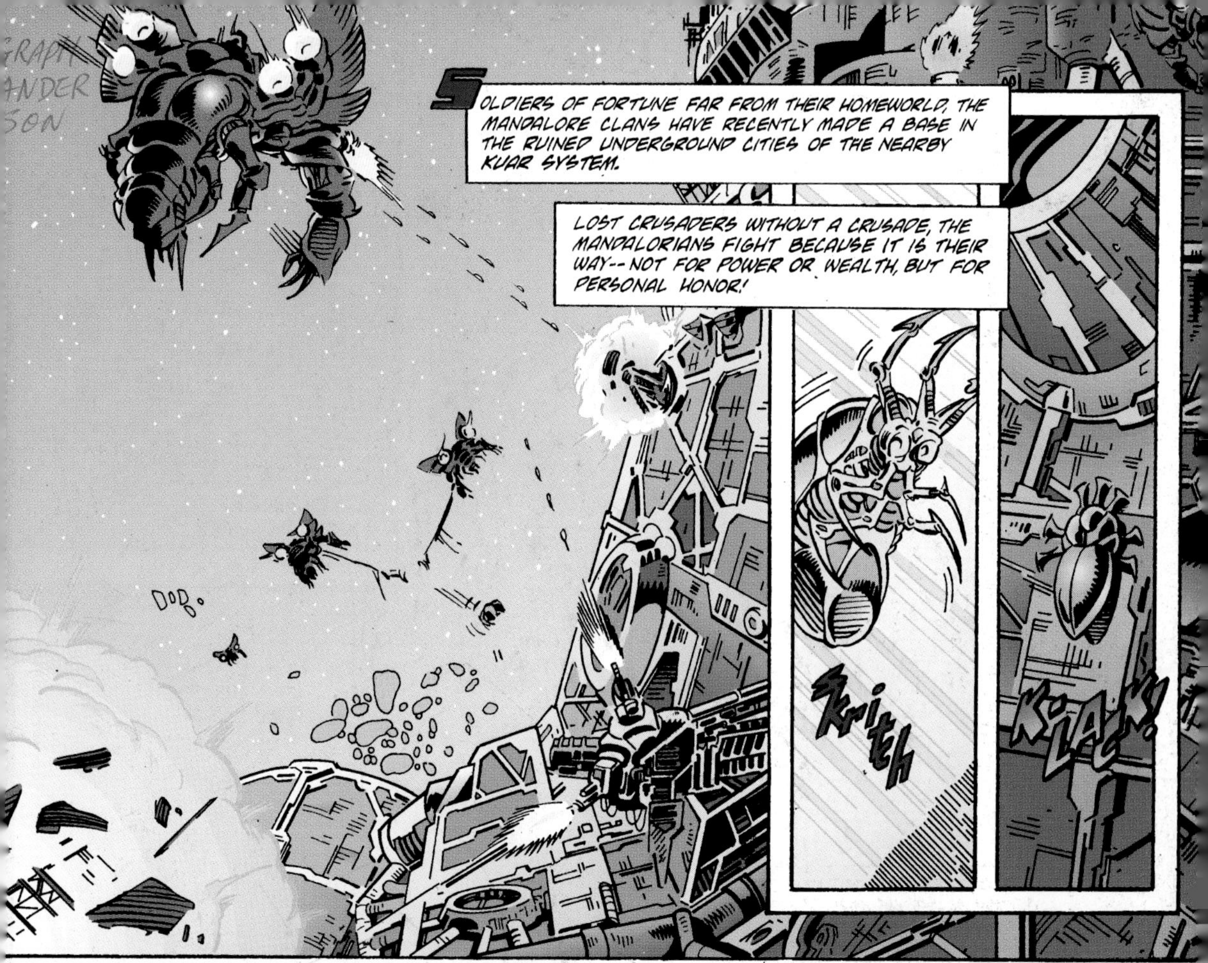
SOLDIERS OF FORTUNE FAR FROM THEIR HOMEWORLD, THE MANDALORE CLANS HAVE RECENTLY MADE A BASE IN THE RUINED UNDERGROUND CITIES OF THE NEARBY KUAR SYSTEM.
LOST CRUSADERS WITHOUT A CRUSADE, THE MANDALORIANS FIGHT BECAUSE IT IS THEIR WAY-- NOT FOR POWER OR WEALTH, BUT FOR PERSONAL HONOR!
SKRITCH
K-LAK!

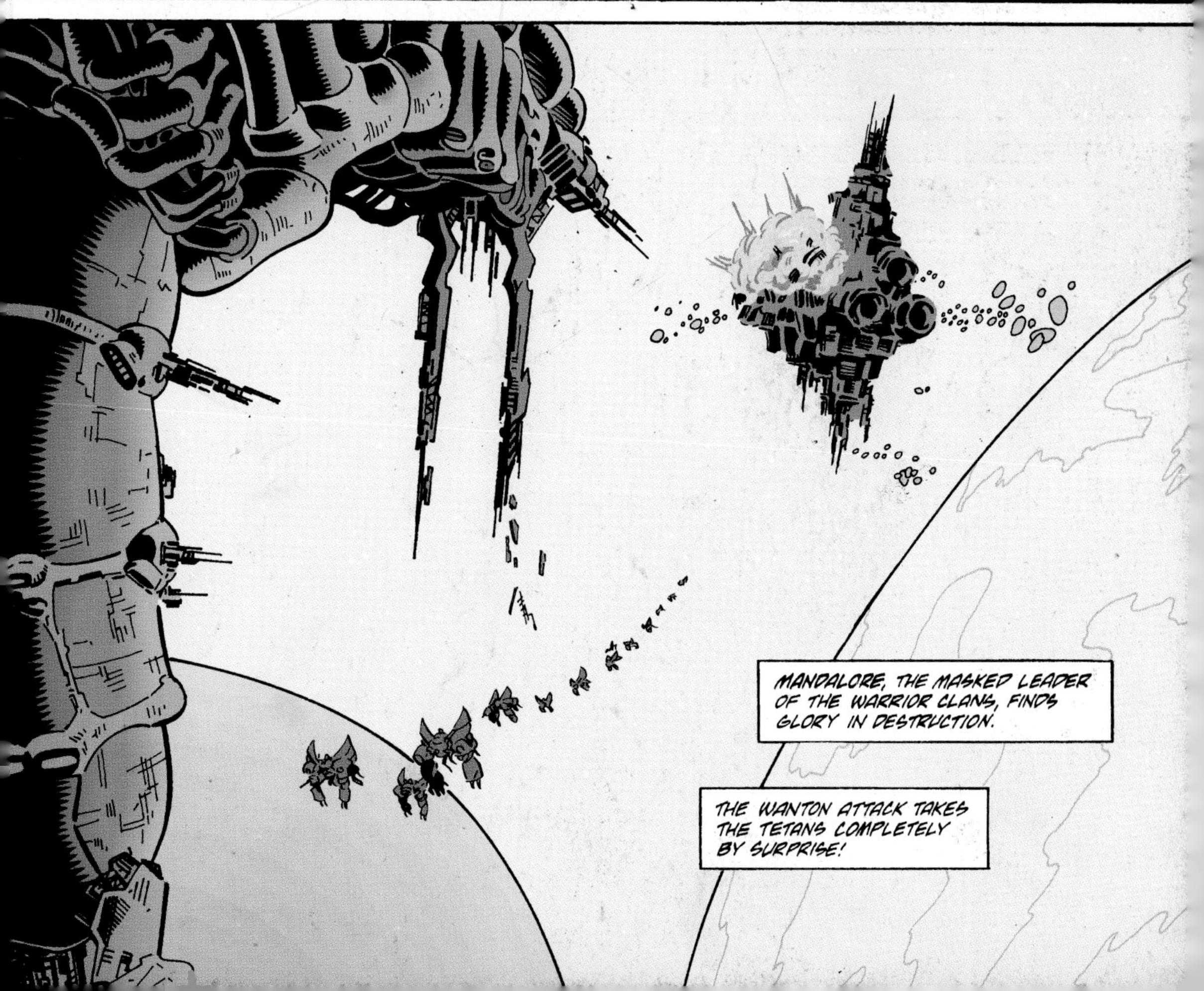
MANDALORE, THE MASKED LEADER OF THE WARRIOR CLANS, FINDS GLORY IN DESTRUCTION.
THE WANTON ATTACK TAKES THE TETANS COMPLETELY BY SURPRISE!

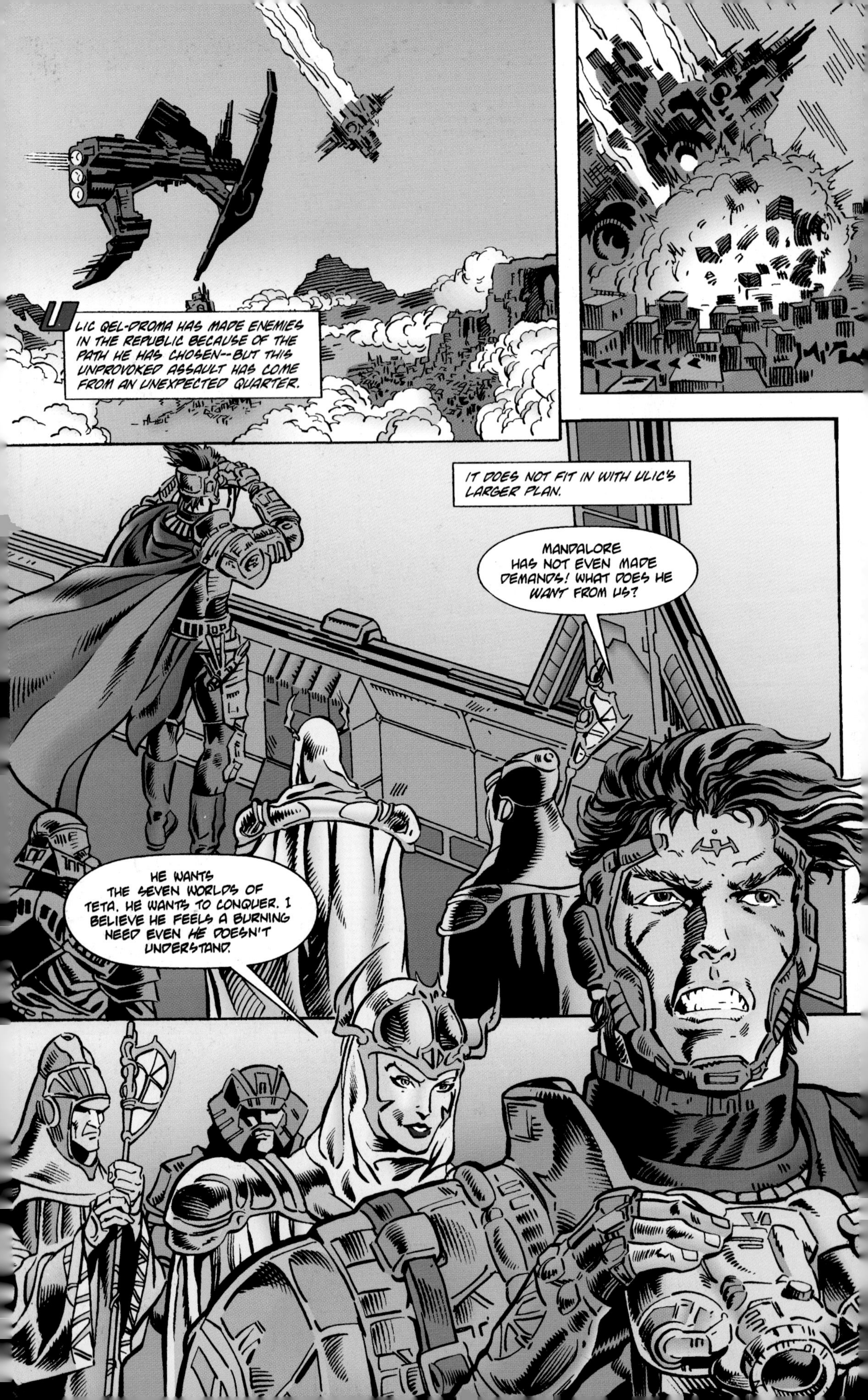
ULIC QEL-DROMA HAS MADE ENEMIES IN THE REPUBLIC BECAUSE OF THE PATH HE HAS CHOSEN--BUT THIS UNPROVOKED ASSAULT HAS COME FROM AN UNEXPECTED QUARTER.
IT DOES NOT FIT IN WITH ULIC'S LARGER PLAN.
MANDALORE HAS NOT EVEN MADE DEMANDS! WHAT DOES HE WANT FROM US?
HE WANTS THE SEVEN WORLDS OF TETA. HE WANTS TO CONQUER. I BELIEVE HE FEELS A BURNING NEED EVEN HE DOESN'T UNDERSTAND.

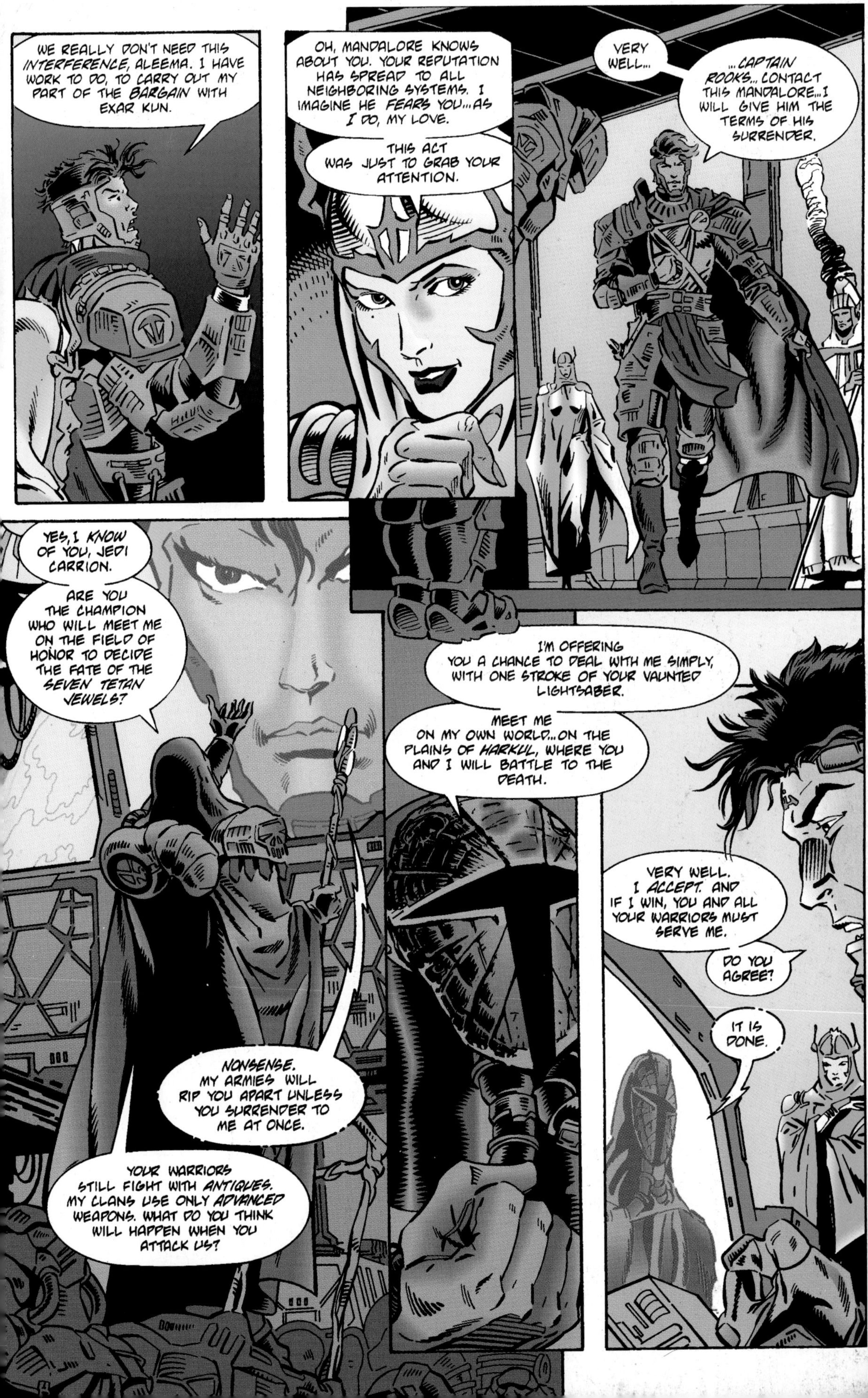
WE REALLY DON'T NEED THIS INTERFERENCE, ALEEMA. I HAVE WORK TO DO, TO CARRY OUT MY PART OF THE BARGAIN WITH EXAR KUN.
OH, MANDALORE KNOWS ABOUT YOU. YOUR REPUTATION HAS SPREAD TO ALL NEIGHBORING SYSTEMS. I IMAGINE HE FEARS YOU...AS I DO, MY LOVE.
THIS ACT WAS JUST TO GRAB YOUR ATTENTION.
VERY WELL...
...CAPTAIN ROOKS... CONTACT THIS MANDALORE...I WILL GIVE HIM THE TERMS OF HIS SURRENDER.
YES, I KNOW OF YOU, JEDI CARRION.
ARE YOU THE CHAMPION WHO WILL MEET ME ON THE FIELD OF HONOR TO DECIDE THE FATE OF THE SEVEN TETAN JEWELS?
NONSENSE. MY ARMIES WILL RIP YOU APART UNLESS YOU SURRENDER TO ME AT ONCE.
YOUR WARRIORS STILL FIGHT WITH ANTIQUES. MY CLANS USE ONLY ADVANCED WEAPONS. WHAT DO YOU THINK WILL HAPPEN WHEN YOU ATTACK US?
I'M OFFERING YOU A CHANCE TO DEAL WITH ME SIMPLY, WITH ONE STROKE OF YOUR VAUNTED LIGHTSABER.
MEET ME ON MY OWN WORLD...ON THE PLAINS OF HARKUL, WHERE YOU AND I WILL BATTLE TO THE DEATH.
VERY WELL. I ACCEPT. AND IF I WIN, YOU AND ALL YOUR WARRIORS MUST SERVE ME.
DO YOU AGREE?
IT IS DONE.

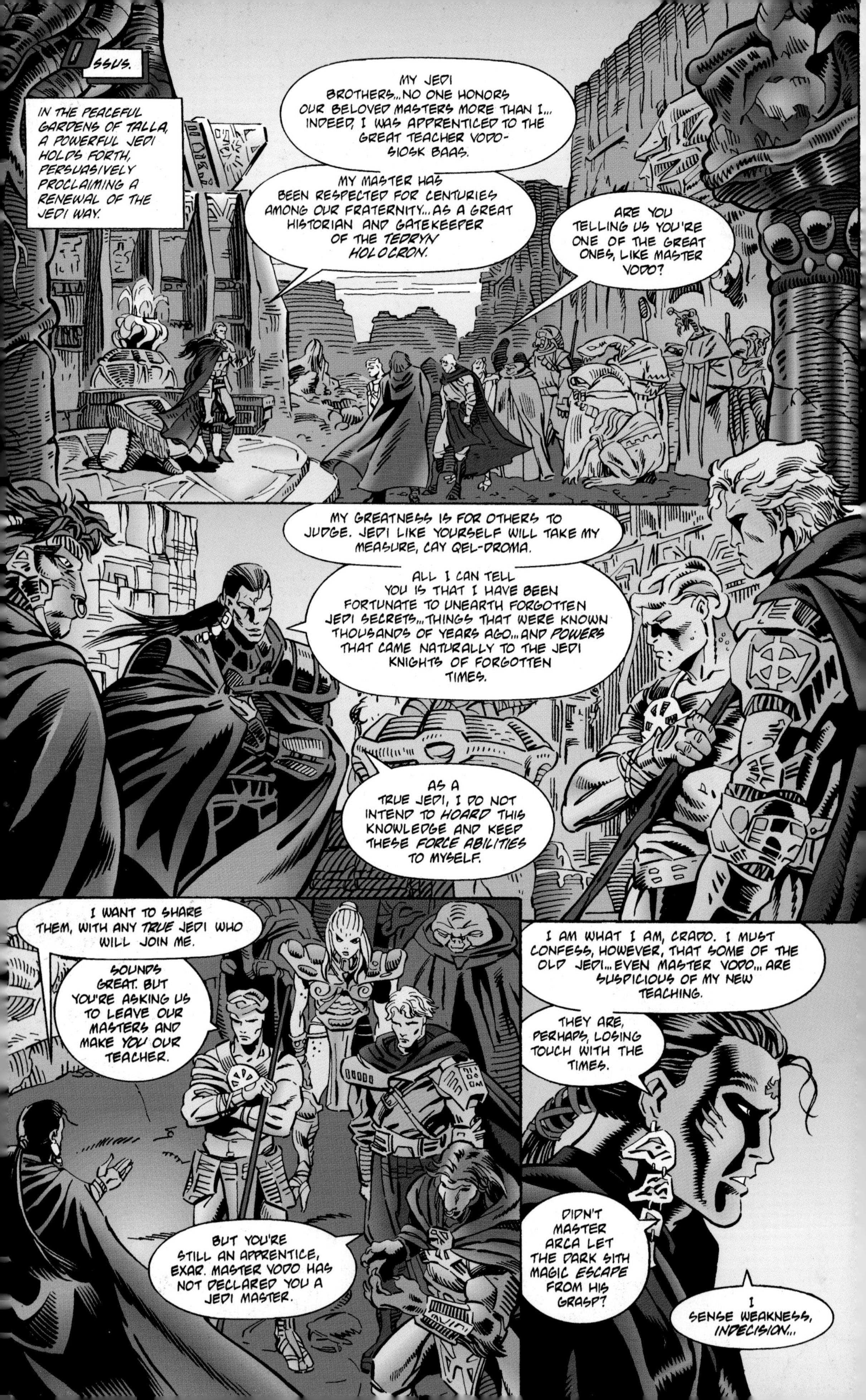
OSSUS.
IN THE PEACEFUL GARDENS OF TALLA, A POWERFUL JEDI HOLDS FORTH, PERSUASIVELY PROCLAIMING A RENEWAL OF THE JEDI WAY.
MY JEDI BROTHERS... NO ONE HONORS OUR BELOVED MASTERS MORE THAN I... INDEED, I WAS APPRENTICED TO THE GREAT TEACHER VODO-SIOSK BAAS.
MY MASTER HAS BEEN RESPECTED FOR CENTURIES AMONG OUR FRATERNITY... AS A GREAT HISTORIAN AND GATEKEEPER OF THE TEDRYN HOLOCRON.
ARE YOU TELLING US YOU'RE ONE OF THE GREAT ONES, LIKE MASTER VODO?
MY GREATNESS IS FOR OTHERS TO JUDGE. JEDI LIKE YOURSELF WILL TAKE MY MEASURE, CAY QEL-DROMA.
ALL I CAN TELL YOU IS THAT I HAVE BEEN FORTUNATE TO UNEARTH FORGOTTEN JEDI SECRETS... THINGS THAT WERE KNOWN THOUSANDS OF YEARS AGO... AND POWERS THAT CAME NATURALLY TO THE JEDI KNIGHTS OF FORGOTTEN TIMES.
AS A TRUE JEDI, I DO NOT INTEND TO HOARD THIS KNOWLEDGE AND KEEP THESE FORCE ABILITIES TO MYSELF.
I WANT TO SHARE THEM, WITH ANY TRUE JEDI WHO WILL JOIN ME.
SOUNDS GREAT. BUT YOU'RE ASKING US TO LEAVE OUR MASTERS AND MAKE YOU OUR TEACHER.
BUT YOU'RE STILL AN APPRENTICE, EXAR. MASTER VODO HAS NOT DECLARED YOU A JEDI MASTER.
I AM WHAT I AM, CRADO. I MUST CONFESS, HOWEVER, THAT SOME OF THE OLD JEDI... EVEN MASTER VODO... ARE SUSPICIOUS OF MY NEW TEACHING.
THEY ARE, PERHAPS, LOSING TOUCH WITH THE TIMES.
DIDN'T MASTER ARCA LET THE DARK SITH MAGIC ESCAPE FROM HIS GRASP?
I SENSE WEAKNESS, INDECISION...

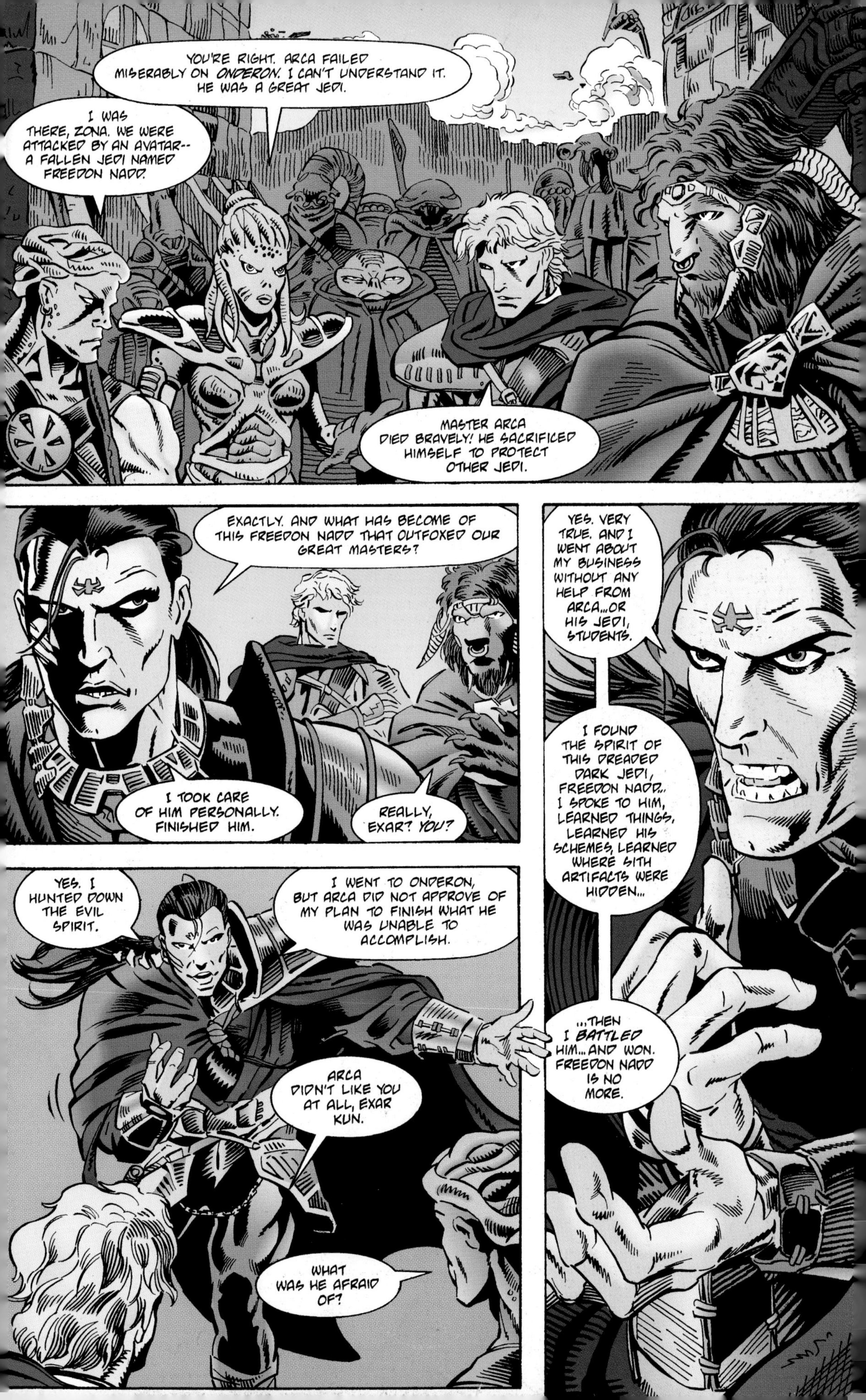
YOU'RE RIGHT. ARCA FAILED MISERABLY ON *ONDERON*. I CAN'T UNDERSTAND IT. HE WAS A GREAT JEDI.
I WAS THERE, ZONA. WE WERE ATTACKED BY AN AVATAR-- A FALLEN JEDI NAMED FREEDON NADD.
MASTER ARCA DIED BRAVELY! HE SACRIFICED HIMSELF TO PROTECT OTHER JEDI.
EXACTLY. AND WHAT HAS BECOME OF THIS FREEDON NADD THAT OUTFOXED OUR GREAT MASTERS?
I TOOK CARE OF HIM PERSONALLY. FINISHED HIM.
REALLY, EXAR? *YOU*?
YES. I HUNTED DOWN THE EVIL SPIRIT.
I WENT TO ONDERON, BUT ARCA DID NOT APPROVE OF MY PLAN TO FINISH WHAT HE WAS UNABLE TO ACCOMPLISH.
ARCA DIDN'T LIKE YOU AT ALL, EXAR KUN.
WHAT WAS HE AFRAID OF?
YES. VERY TRUE. AND I WENT ABOUT MY BUSINESS WITHOUT ANY HELP FROM ARCA...OR HIS JEDI, STUDENTS.
I FOUND THE SPIRIT OF THIS DREADED DARK JEDI, FREEDON NADD.. I SPOKE TO HIM, LEARNED THINGS, LEARNED HIS SCHEMES, LEARNED WHERE SITH ARTIFACTS WERE HIDDEN...
...THEN I *BATTLED* HIM...AND WON. FREEDON NADD IS NO MORE.

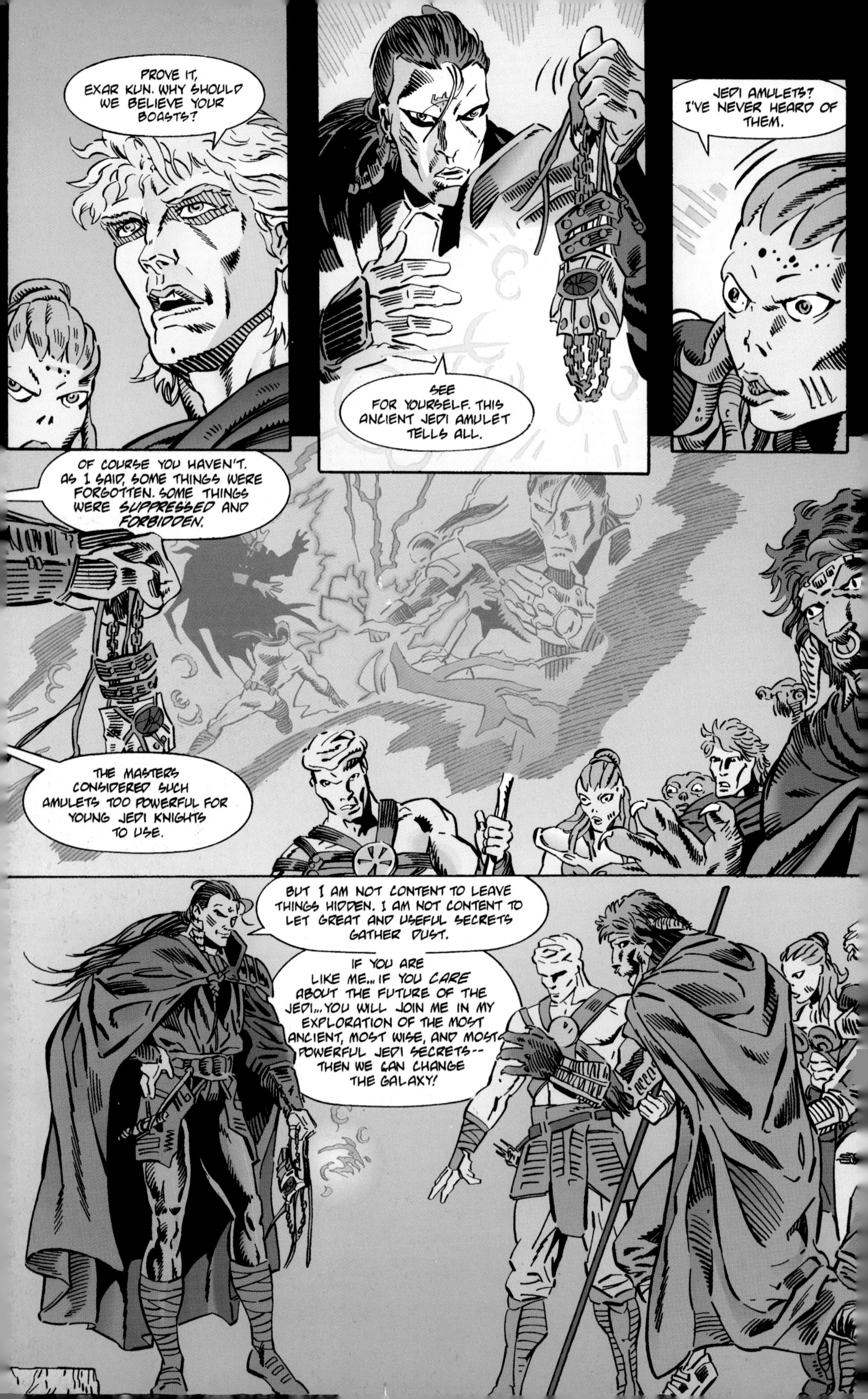
PROVE IT, EXAR KUN. WHY SHOULD WE BELIEVE YOUR BOASTS?
SEE FOR YOURSELF. THIS ANCIENT JEDI AMULET TELLS ALL.
JEDI AMULETS? I'VE NEVER HEARD OF THEM.
OF COURSE YOU HAVEN'T. AS I SAID, SOME THINGS WERE FORGOTTEN. SOME THINGS WERE SUPPRESSED AND FORBIDDEN.
THE MASTERS CONSIDERED SUCH AMULETS TOO POWERFUL FOR YOUNG JEDI KNIGHTS TO USE.
BUT I AM NOT CONTENT TO LEAVE THINGS HIDDEN. I AM NOT CONTENT TO LET GREAT AND USEFUL SECRETS GATHER DUST.
IF YOU ARE LIKE ME... IF YOU CARE ABOUT THE FUTURE OF THE JEDI... YOU WILL JOIN ME IN MY EXPLORATION OF THE MOST ANCIENT, MOST WISE, AND MOST POWERFUL JEDI SECRETS-- THEN WE CAN CHANGE THE GALAXY!

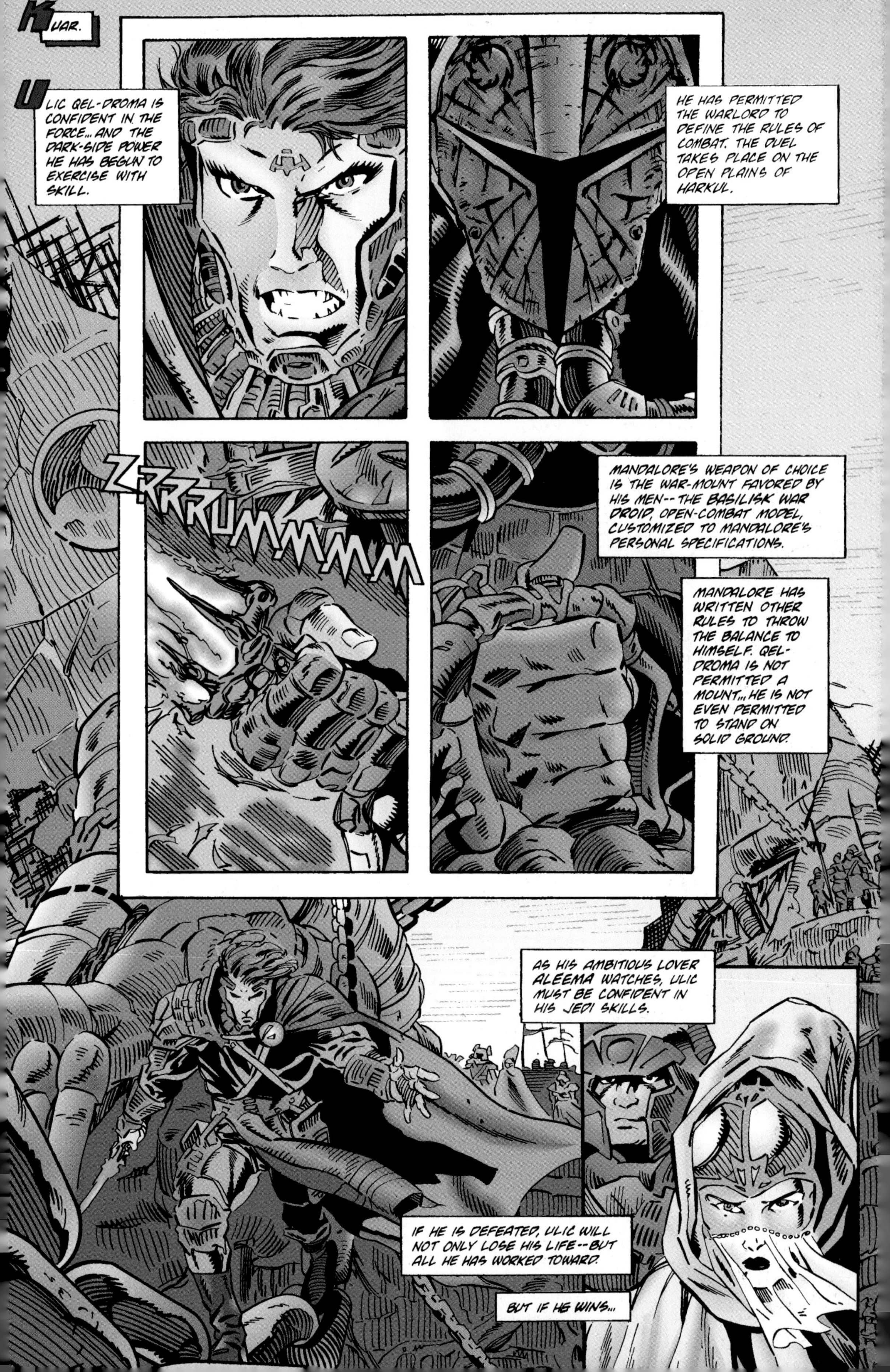
KUAR.
ULIC QEL-DROMA IS CONFIDENT IN THE FORCE... AND THE DARK-SIDE POWER HE HAS BEGUN TO EXERCISE WITH SKILL.
HE HAS PERMITTED THE WARLORD TO DEFINE THE RULES OF COMBAT. THE DUEL TAKES PLACE ON THE OPEN PLAINS OF HARKUL.
ZRRRUMMMMM
MANDALORE'S WEAPON OF CHOICE IS THE WAR-MOUNT FAVORED BY HIS MEN-- THE BASILISK WAR DROID, OPEN-COMBAT MODEL, CUSTOMIZED TO MANDALORE'S PERSONAL SPECIFICATIONS.
MANDALORE HAS WRITTEN OTHER RULES TO THROW THE BALANCE TO HIMSELF. QEL-DROMA IS NOT PERMITTED A MOUNT... HE IS NOT EVEN PERMITTED TO STAND ON SOLID GROUND.
AS HIS AMBITIOUS LOVER ALEEMA WATCHES, ULIC MUST BE CONFIDENT IN HIS JEDI SKILLS.
IF HE IS DEFEATED, ULIC WILL NOT ONLY LOSE HIS LIFE--BUT ALL HE HAS WORKED TOWARD.
BUT IF HE WINS...

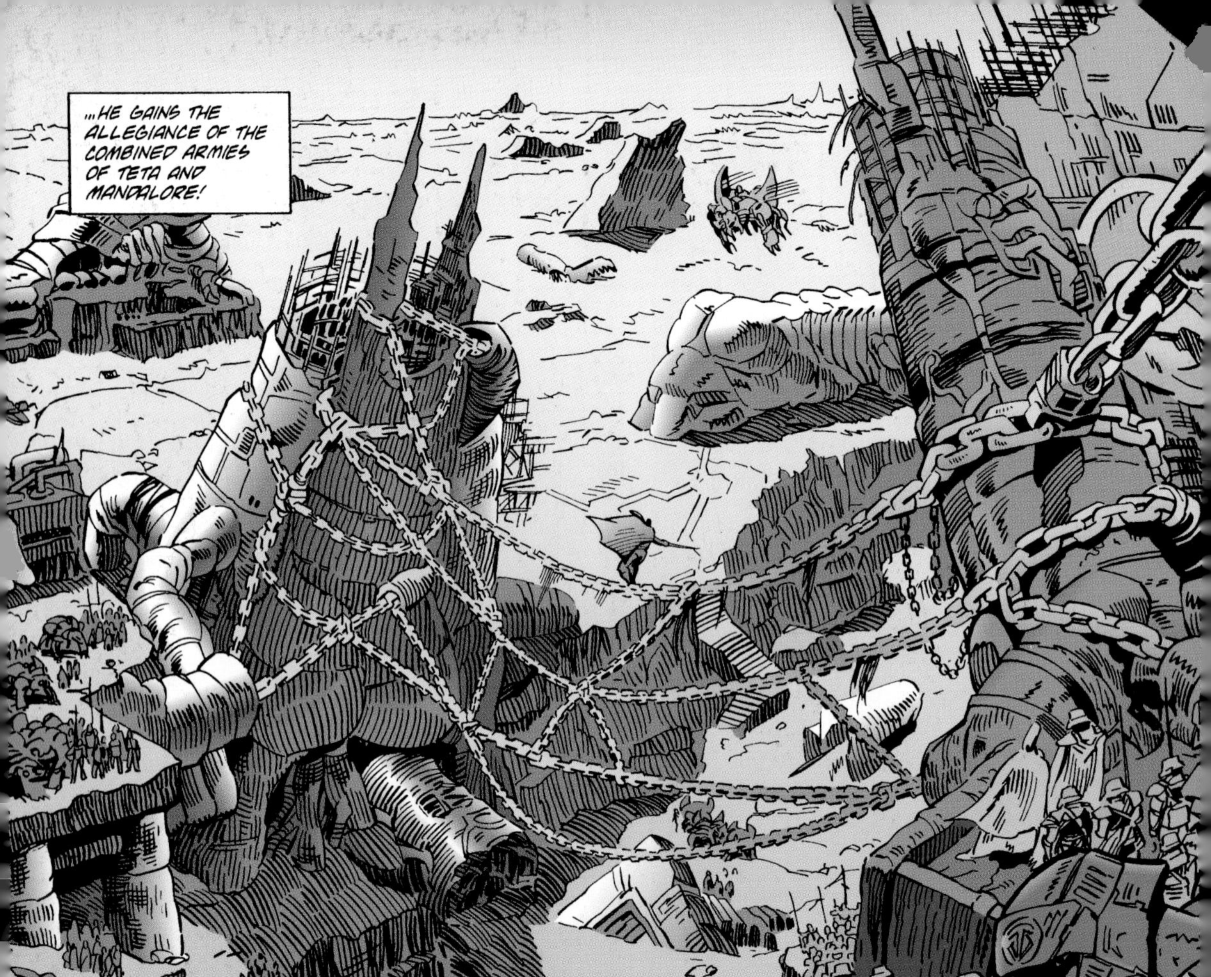
...HE GAINS THE ALLEGIANCE OF THE COMBINED ARMIES OF TETA AND MANDALORE!

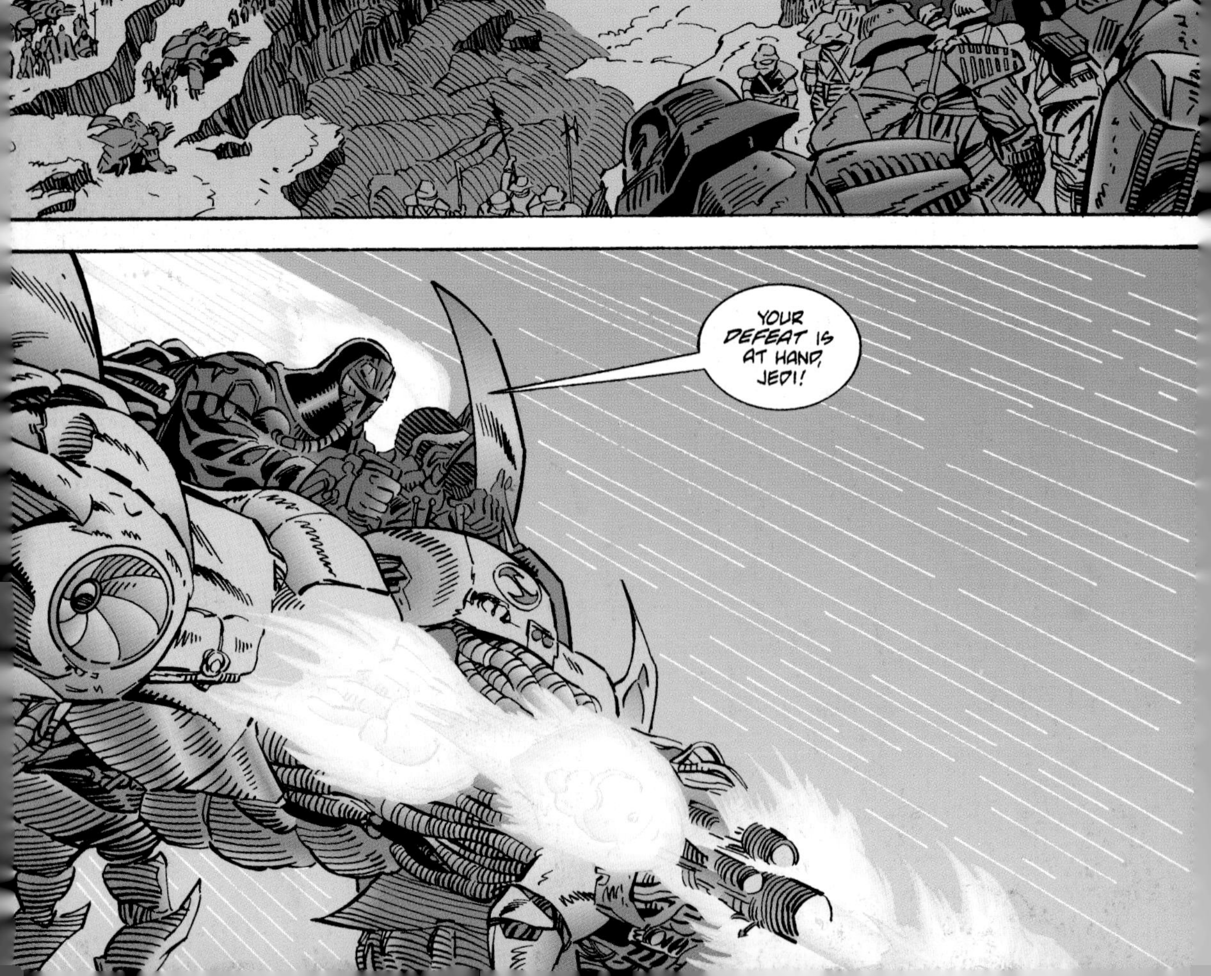
YOUR DEFEAT IS AT HAND, JEDI!

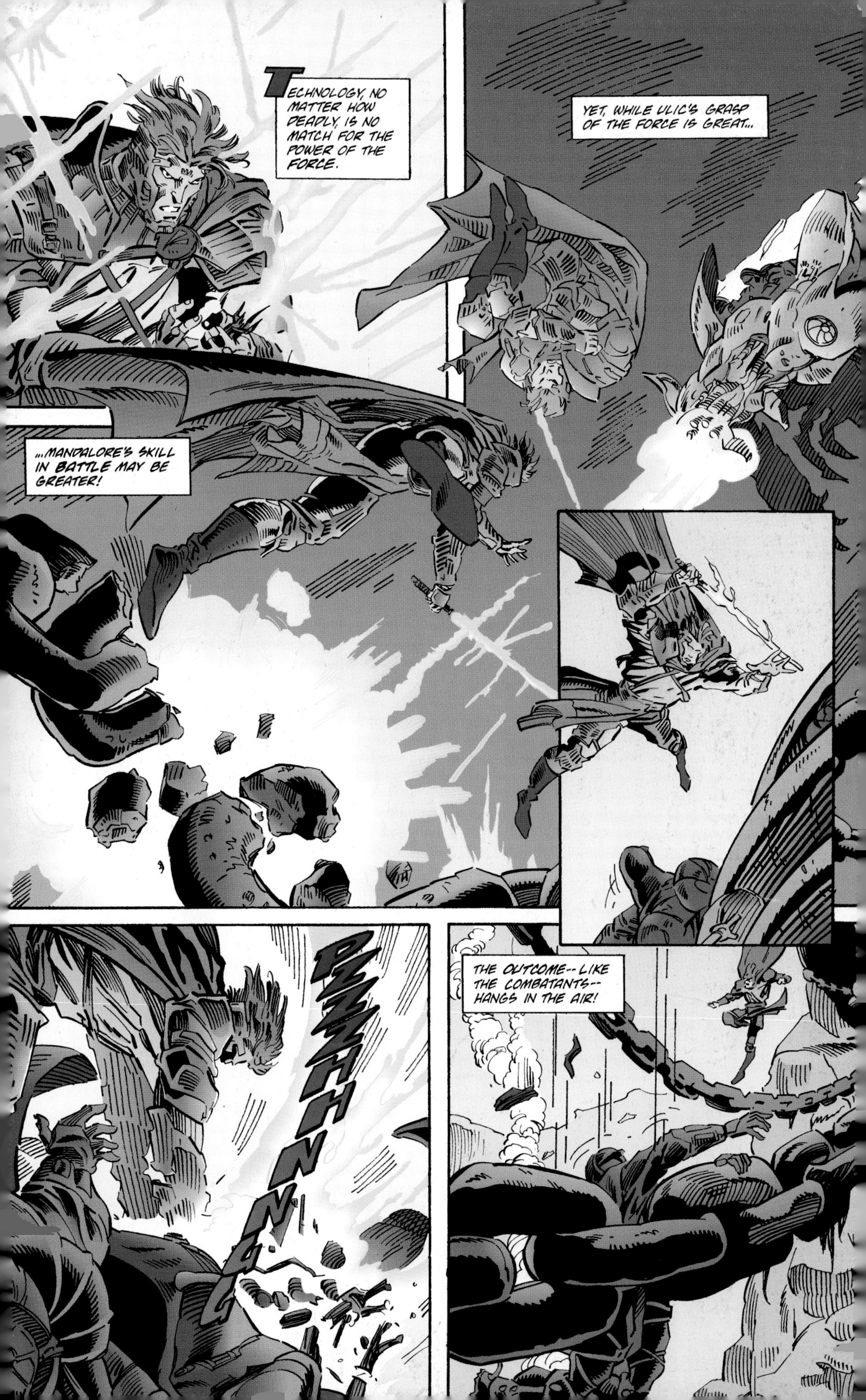
TECHNOLOGY, NO MATTER HOW DEADLY, IS NO MATCH FOR THE POWER OF THE FORCE.
YET, WHILE ULIC'S GRASP OF THE FORCE IS GREAT...
...MANDALORE'S SKILL IN BATTLE MAY BE GREATER!
DWWHHNNG
THE OUTCOME--LIKE THE COMBATANTS--HANGS IN THE AIR!

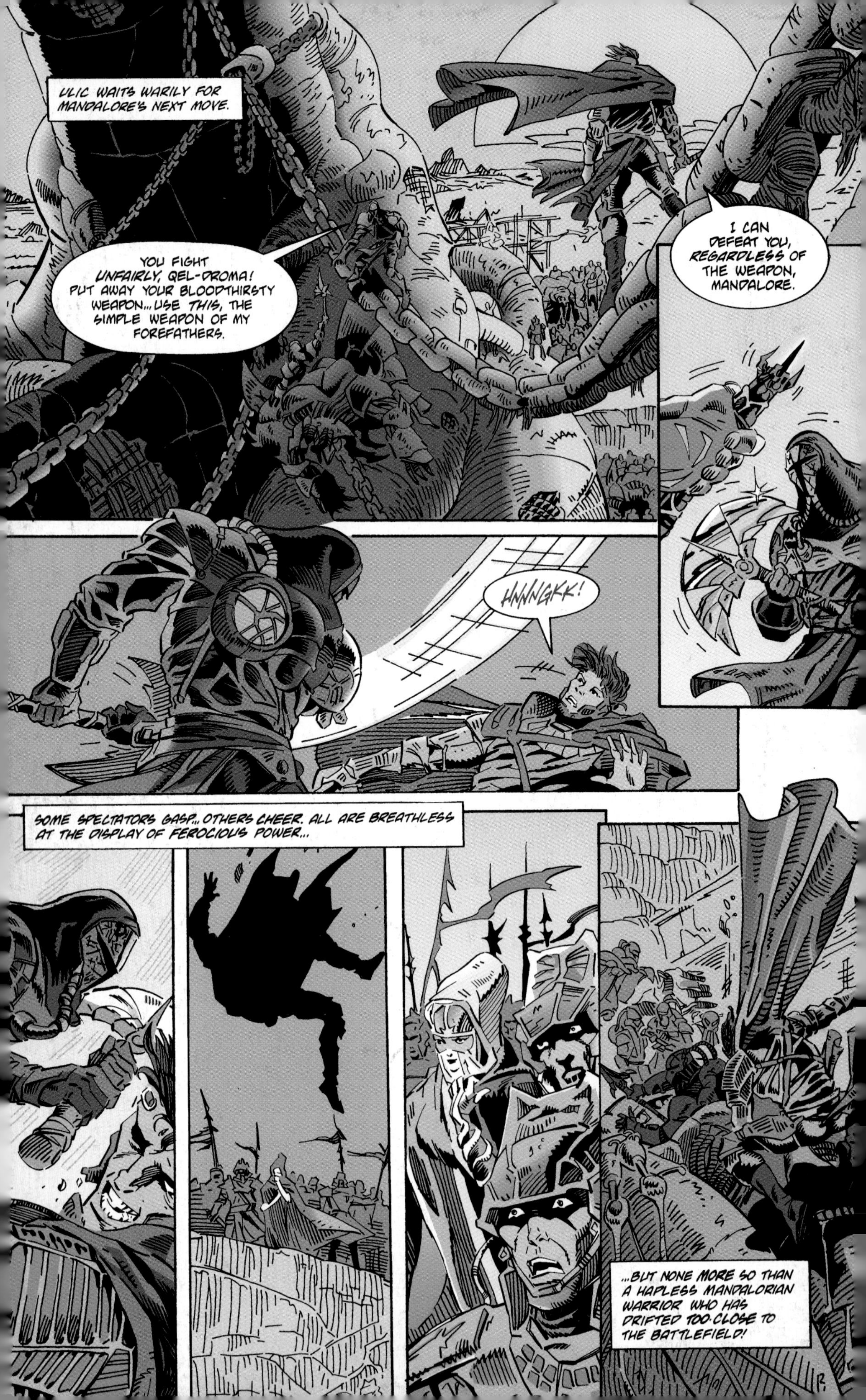
ULIC WAITS WARILY FOR MANDALORE'S NEXT MOVE.
YOU FIGHT UNFAIRLY, QEL-DROMA! PUT AWAY YOUR BLOODTHIRSTY WEAPON... USE THIS, THE SIMPLE WEAPON OF MY FOREFATHERS.
I CAN DEFEAT YOU, REGARDLESS OF THE WEAPON, MANDALORE.
UNNNGKK!
SOME SPECTATORS GASP... OTHERS CHEER. ALL ARE BREATHLESS AT THE DISPLAY OF FEROCIOUS POWER...
...BUT NONE MORE SO THAN A HAPLESS MANDALORIAN WARRIOR WHO HAS DRIFTED TOO CLOSE TO THE BATTLEFIELD!

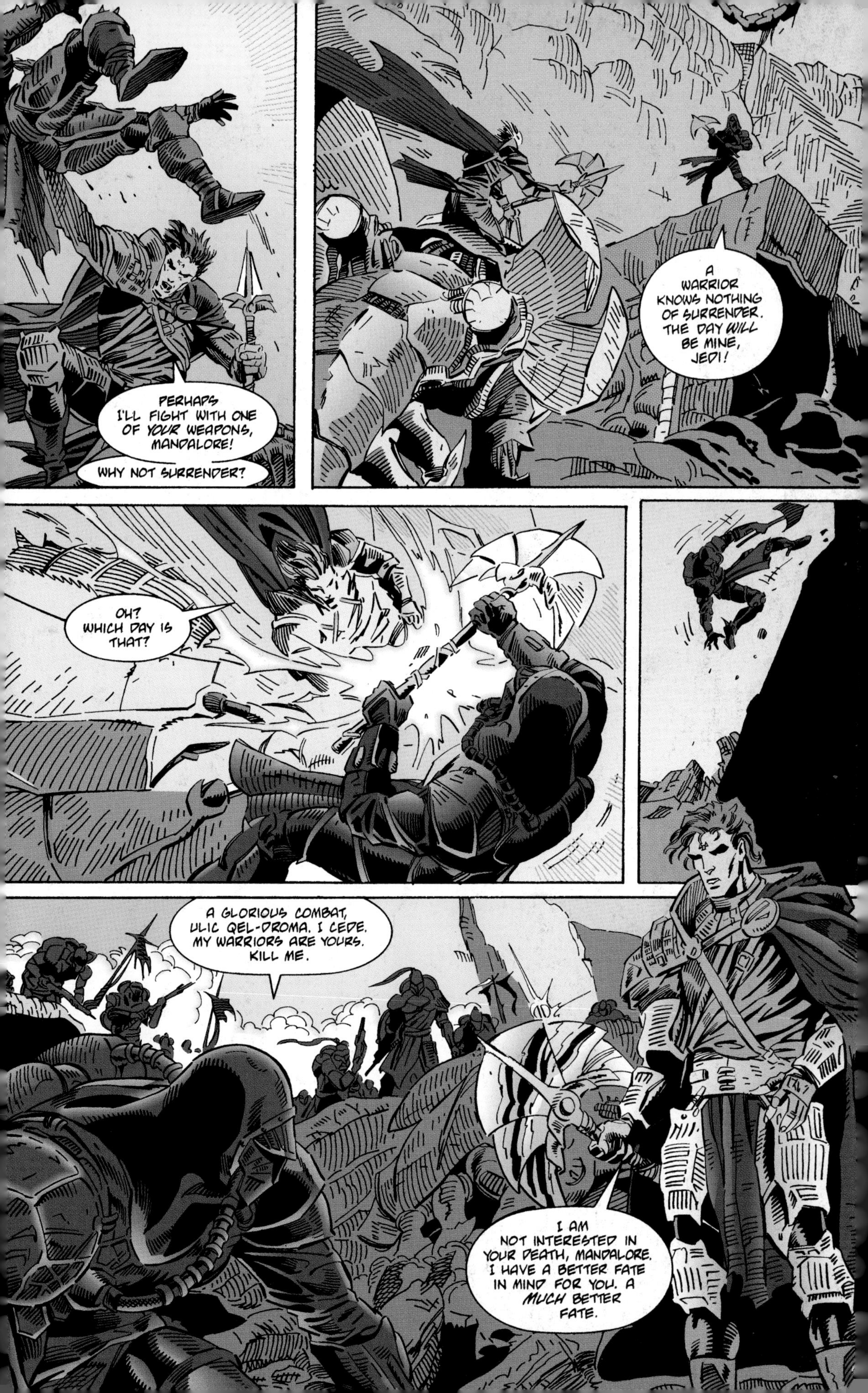
PERHAPS I'LL FIGHT WITH ONE OF YOUR WEAPONS, MANDALORE!
WHY NOT SURRENDER?
A WARRIOR KNOWS NOTHING OF SURRENDER. THE DAY WILL BE MINE, JEDI!
OH? WHICH DAY IS THAT?
A GLORIOUS COMBAT, ULIC QEL-DROMA. I CEDE. MY WARRIORS ARE YOURS. KILL ME.
I AM NOT INTERESTED IN YOUR DEATH, MANDALORE. I HAVE A BETTER FATE IN MIND FOR YOU. A MUCH BETTER FATE.

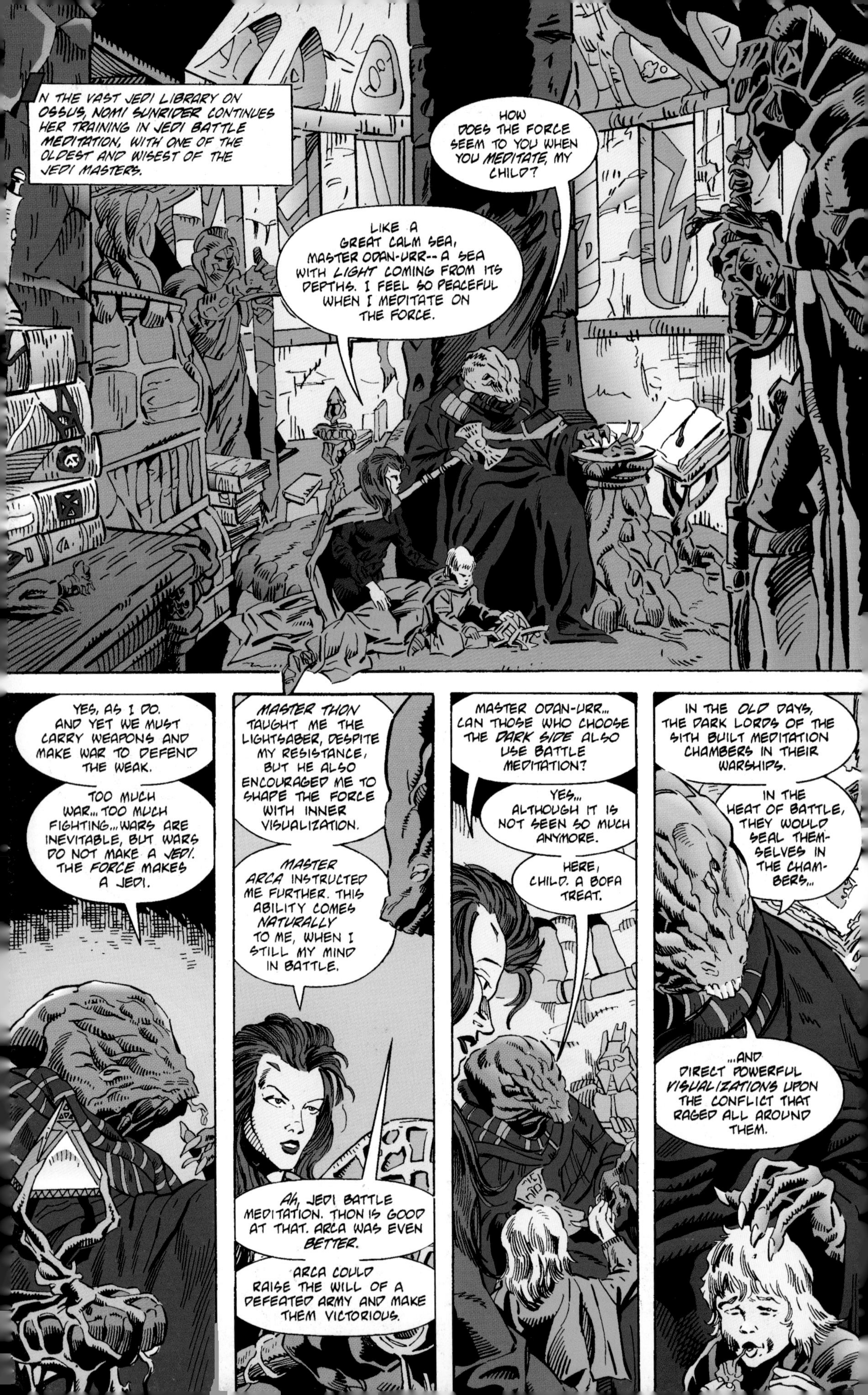
N THE VAST JEDI LIBRARY ON OSSUS, NOMI SUNRIDER CONTINUES HER TRAINING IN JEDI BATTLE MEDITATION, WITH ONE OF THE OLDEST AND WISEST OF THE JEDI MASTERS.
HOW DOES THE FORCE SEEM TO YOU WHEN YOU MEDITATE, MY CHILD?
LIKE A GREAT CALM SEA, MASTER ODAN-URR-- A SEA WITH LIGHT COMING FROM ITS DEPTHS. I FEEL SO PEACEFUL WHEN I MEDITATE ON THE FORCE.
YES, AS I DO. AND YET WE MUST CARRY WEAPONS AND MAKE WAR TO DEFEND THE WEAK.
TOO MUCH WAR... TOO MUCH FIGHTING... WARS ARE INEVITABLE, BUT WARS DO NOT MAKE A JEDI. THE FORCE MAKES A JEDI.
MASTER THON TAUGHT ME THE LIGHTSABER, DESPITE MY RESISTANCE, BUT HE ALSO ENCOURAGED ME TO SHAPE THE FORCE WITH INNER VISUALIZATION.
MASTER ARCA INSTRUCTED ME FURTHER. THIS ABILITY COMES NATURALLY TO ME, WHEN I STILL MY MIND IN BATTLE.
AH, JEDI BATTLE MEDITATION. THON IS GOOD AT THAT. ARCA WAS EVEN BETTER.
ARCA COULD RAISE THE WILL OF A DEFEATED ARMY AND MAKE THEM VICTORIOUS.
MASTER ODAN-URR... CAN THOSE WHO CHOOSE THE DARK SIDE ALSO USE BATTLE MEDITATION?
YES... ALTHOUGH IT IS NOT SEEN SO MUCH ANYMORE.
HERE, CHILD. A BOFA TREAT.
IN THE OLD DAYS, THE DARK LORDS OF THE SITH BUILT MEDITATION CHAMBERS IN THEIR WARSHIPS.
IN THE HEAT OF BATTLE, THEY WOULD SEAL THEMSELVES IN THE CHAMBERS...
...AND DIRECT POWERFUL VISUALIZATIONS UPON THE CONFLICT THAT RAGED ALL AROUND THEM.

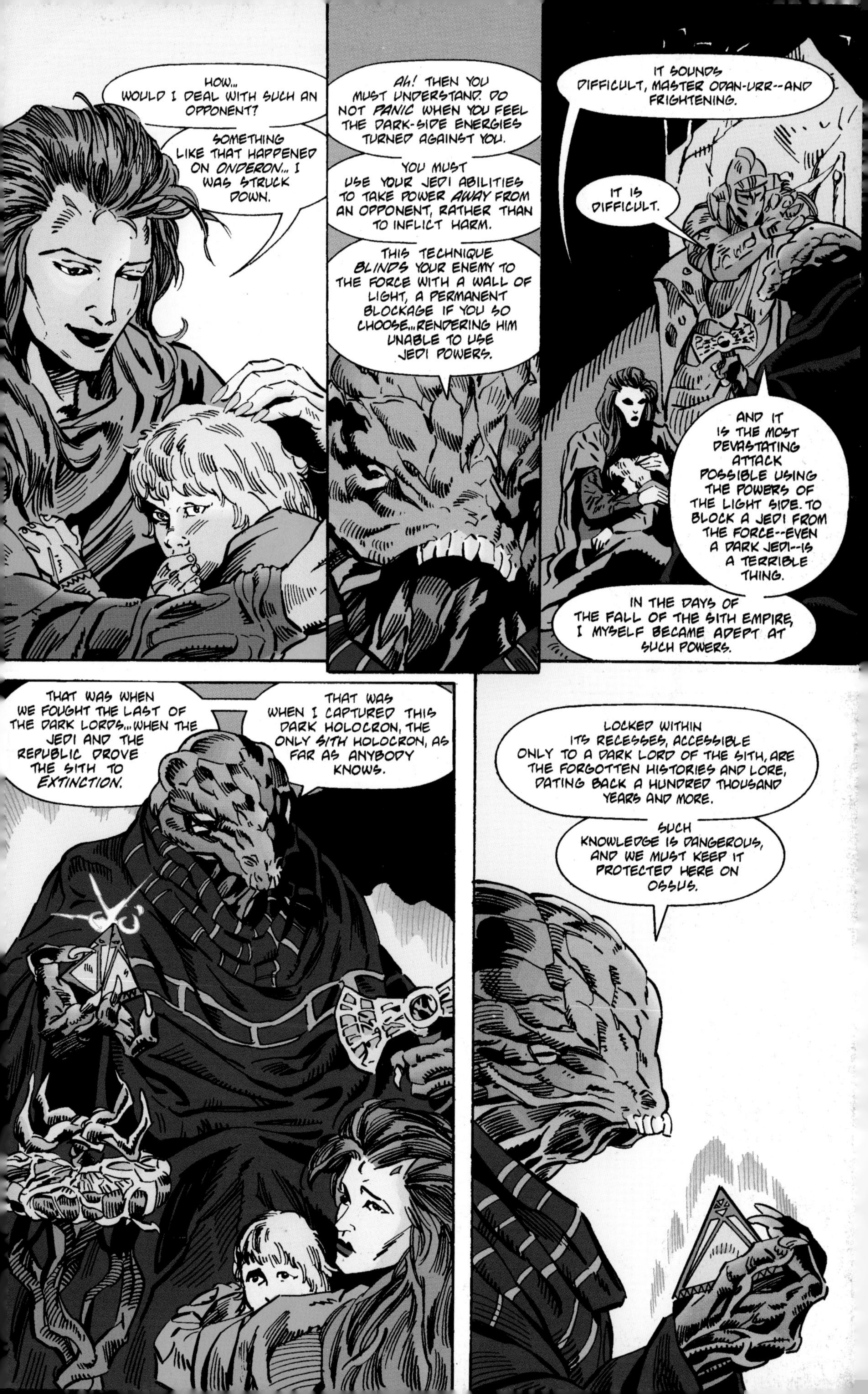

HOW... WOULD I DEAL WITH SUCH AN OPPONENT?
SOMETHING LIKE THAT HAPPENED ON ONDERON... I WAS STRUCK DOWN.
AH! THEN YOU MUST UNDERSTAND. DO NOT PANIC WHEN YOU FEEL THE DARK-SIDE ENERGIES TURNED AGAINST YOU.
YOU MUST USE YOUR JEDI ABILITIES TO TAKE POWER AWAY FROM AN OPPONENT, RATHER THAN TO INFLICT HARM.
THIS TECHNIQUE BLINDS YOUR ENEMY TO THE FORCE WITH A WALL OF LIGHT, A PERMANENT BLOCKAGE IF YOU SO CHOOSE... RENDERING HIM UNABLE TO USE JEDI POWERS.
IT SOUNDS DIFFICULT, MASTER ODAN-URR--AND FRIGHTENING.
IT IS DIFFICULT.
AND IT IS THE MOST DEVASTATING ATTACK POSSIBLE USING THE POWERS OF THE LIGHT SIDE. TO BLOCK A JEDI FROM THE FORCE--EVEN A DARK JEDI--IS A TERRIBLE THING.
IN THE DAYS OF THE FALL OF THE SITH EMPIRE, I MYSELF BECAME ADEPT AT SUCH POWERS.
THAT WAS WHEN WE FOUGHT THE LAST OF THE DARK LORDS... WHEN THE JEDI AND THE REPUBLIC DROVE THE SITH TO EXTINCTION.
THAT WAS WHEN I CAPTURED THIS DARK HOLOCRON, THE ONLY SITH HOLOCRON, AS FAR AS ANYBODY KNOWS.
LOCKED WITHIN ITS RECESSES, ACCESSIBLE ONLY TO A DARK LORD OF THE SITH, ARE THE FORGOTTEN HISTORIES AND LORE, DATING BACK A HUNDRED THOUSAND YEARS AND MORE.
SUCH KNOWLEDGE IS DANGEROUS, AND WE MUST KEEP IT PROTECTED HERE ON OSSUS.

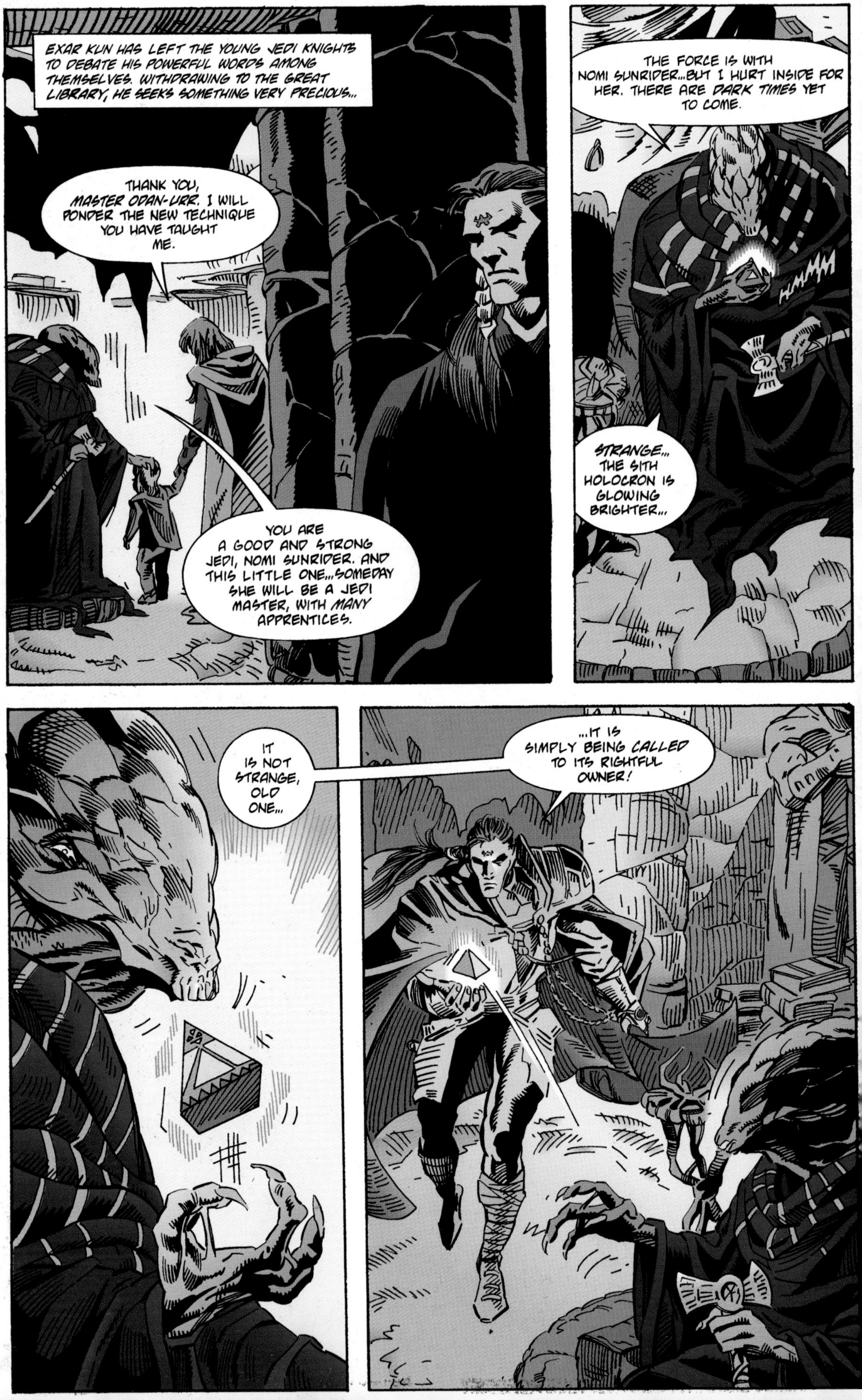
EXAR KUN HAS LEFT THE YOUNG JEDI KNIGHTS TO DEBATE HIS POWERFUL WORDS AMONG THEMSELVES. WITHDRAWING TO THE GREAT LIBRARY, HE SEEKS SOMETHING VERY PRECIOUS...
THANK YOU, MASTER ODAN-URR. I WILL PONDER THE NEW TECHNIQUE YOU HAVE TAUGHT ME.
YOU ARE A GOOD AND STRONG JEDI, NOMI SUNRIDER. AND THIS LITTLE ONE...SOMEDAY SHE WILL BE A JEDI MASTER, WITH MANY APPRENTICES.
THE FORCE IS WITH NOMI SUNRIDER...BUT I HURT INSIDE FOR HER. THERE ARE DARK TIMES YET TO COME.
HMMM
STRANGE... THE SITH HOLOCRON IS GLOWING BRIGHTER...
IT IS NOT STRANGE, OLD ONE...
...IT IS SIMPLY BEING CALLED TO ITS RIGHTFUL OWNER!

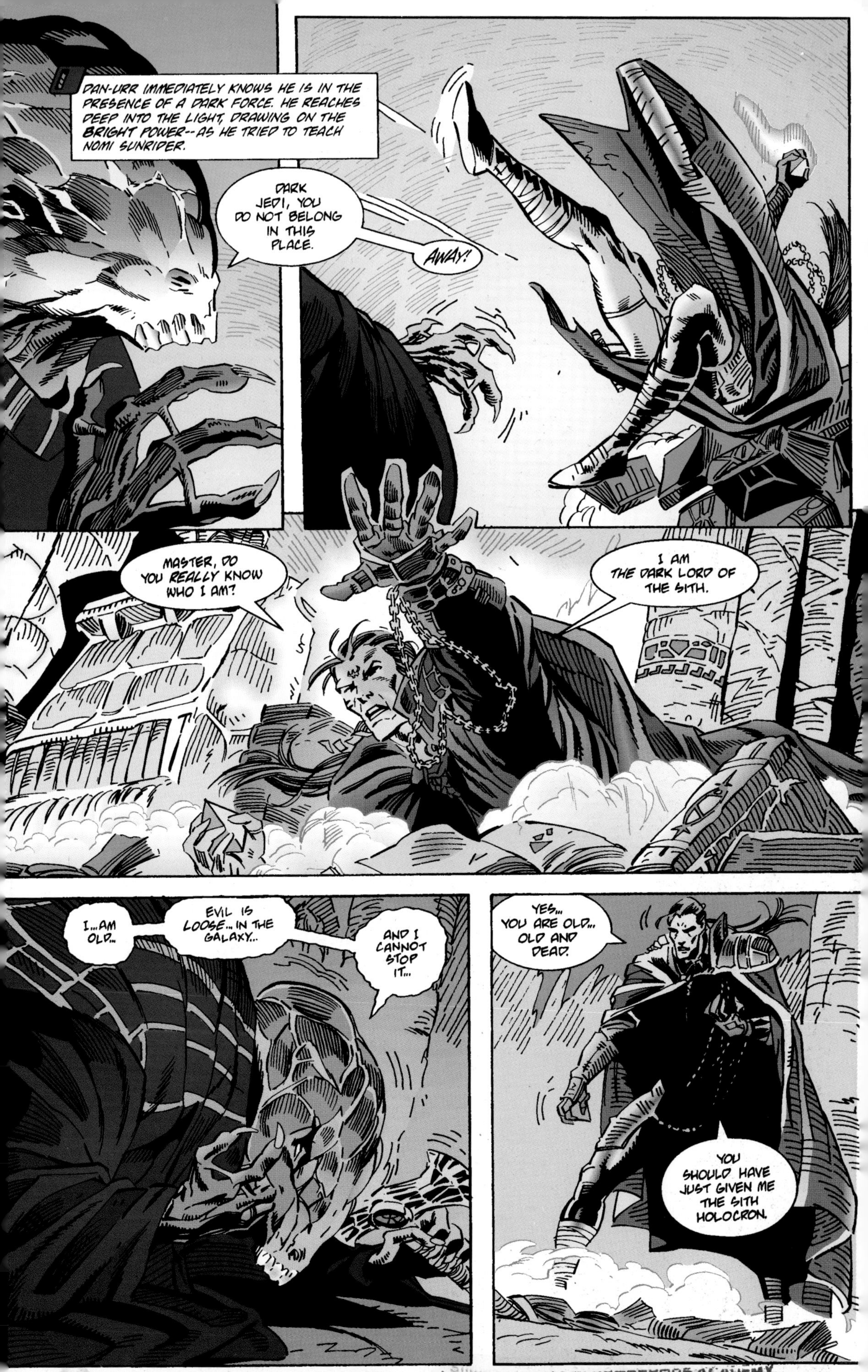
DAN-URR IMMEDIATELY KNOWS HE IS IN THE PRESENCE OF A DARK FORCE. HE REACHES DEEP INTO THE LIGHT, DRAWING ON THE BRIGHT POWER--AS HE TRIED TO TEACH NOMI SUNRIDER.
DARK JEDI, YOU DO NOT BELONG IN THIS PLACE.
AWAY!
MASTER, DO YOU REALLY KNOW WHO I AM?
I AM THE DARK LORD OF THE SITH.
I...AM OLD...
EVIL IS LOOSE... IN THE GALAXY...
AND I CANNOT STOP IT...
YES... YOU ARE OLD... OLD AND DEAD.
YOU SHOULD HAVE JUST GIVEN ME THE SITH HOLOCRON.

SIMMS LIBRARY ALBUQUERQUE ACADEMY

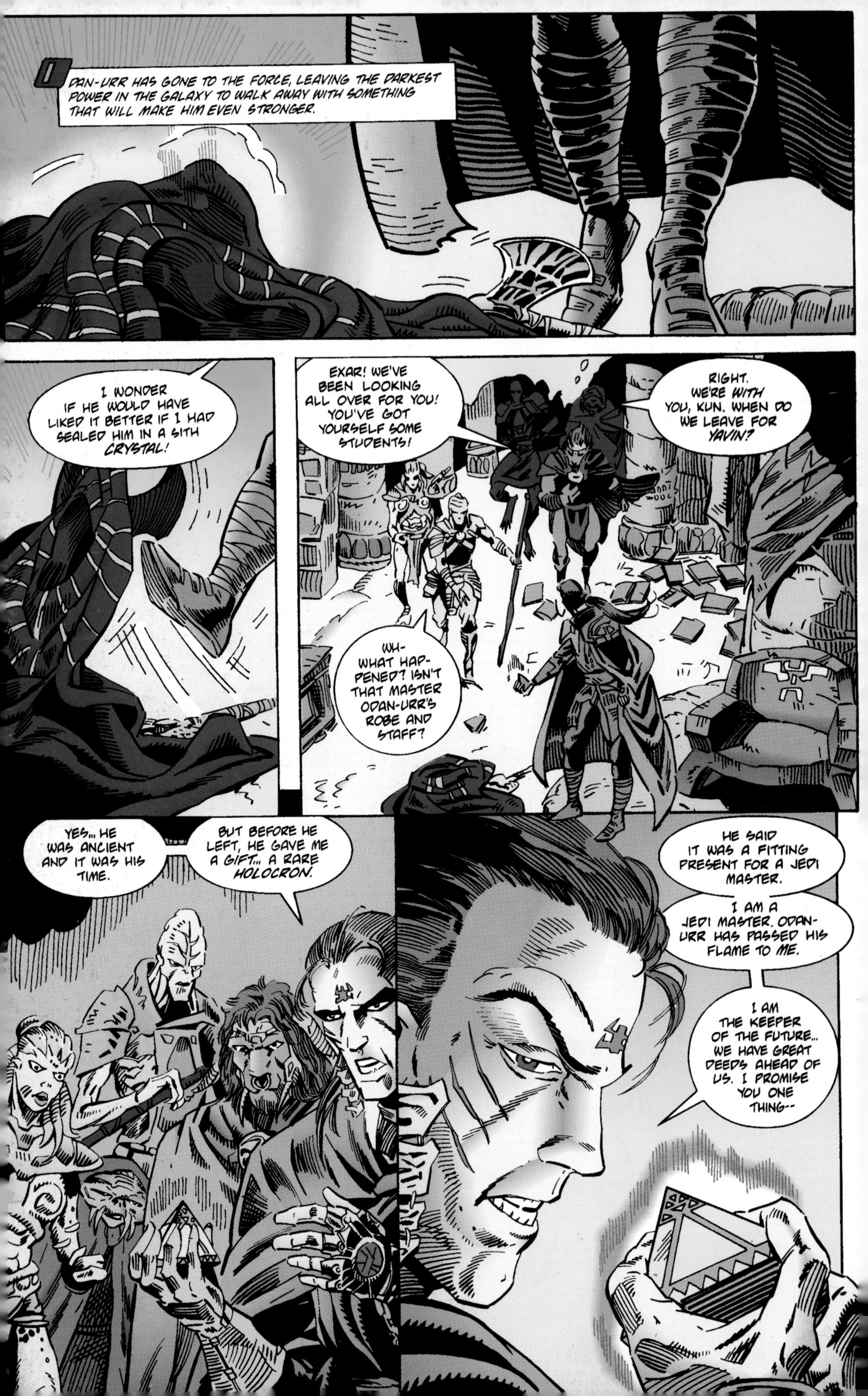
ODAN-URR HAS GONE TO THE FORCE, LEAVING THE DARKEST POWER IN THE GALAXY TO WALK AWAY WITH SOMETHING THAT WILL MAKE HIM EVEN STRONGER.
I WONDER IF HE WOULD HAVE LIKED IT BETTER IF I HAD SEALED HIM IN A SITH CRYSTAL!
EXAR! WE'VE BEEN LOOKING ALL OVER FOR YOU! YOU'VE GOT YOURSELF SOME STUDENTS!
RIGHT. WE'RE WITH YOU, KUN. WHEN DO WE LEAVE FOR YAVIN?
WH- WHAT HAP-PENED? ISN'T THAT MASTER ODAN-URR'S ROBE AND STAFF?
YES... HE WAS ANCIENT AND IT WAS HIS TIME.
BUT BEFORE HE LEFT, HE GAVE ME A GIFT... A RARE HOLOCRON.
HE SAID IT WAS A FITTING PRESENT FOR A JEDI MASTER.
I AM A JEDI MASTER. ODAN-URR HAS PASSED HIS FLAME TO ME.
I AM THE KEEPER OF THE FUTURE... WE HAVE GREAT DEEDS AHEAD OF US. I PROMISE YOU ONE THING--

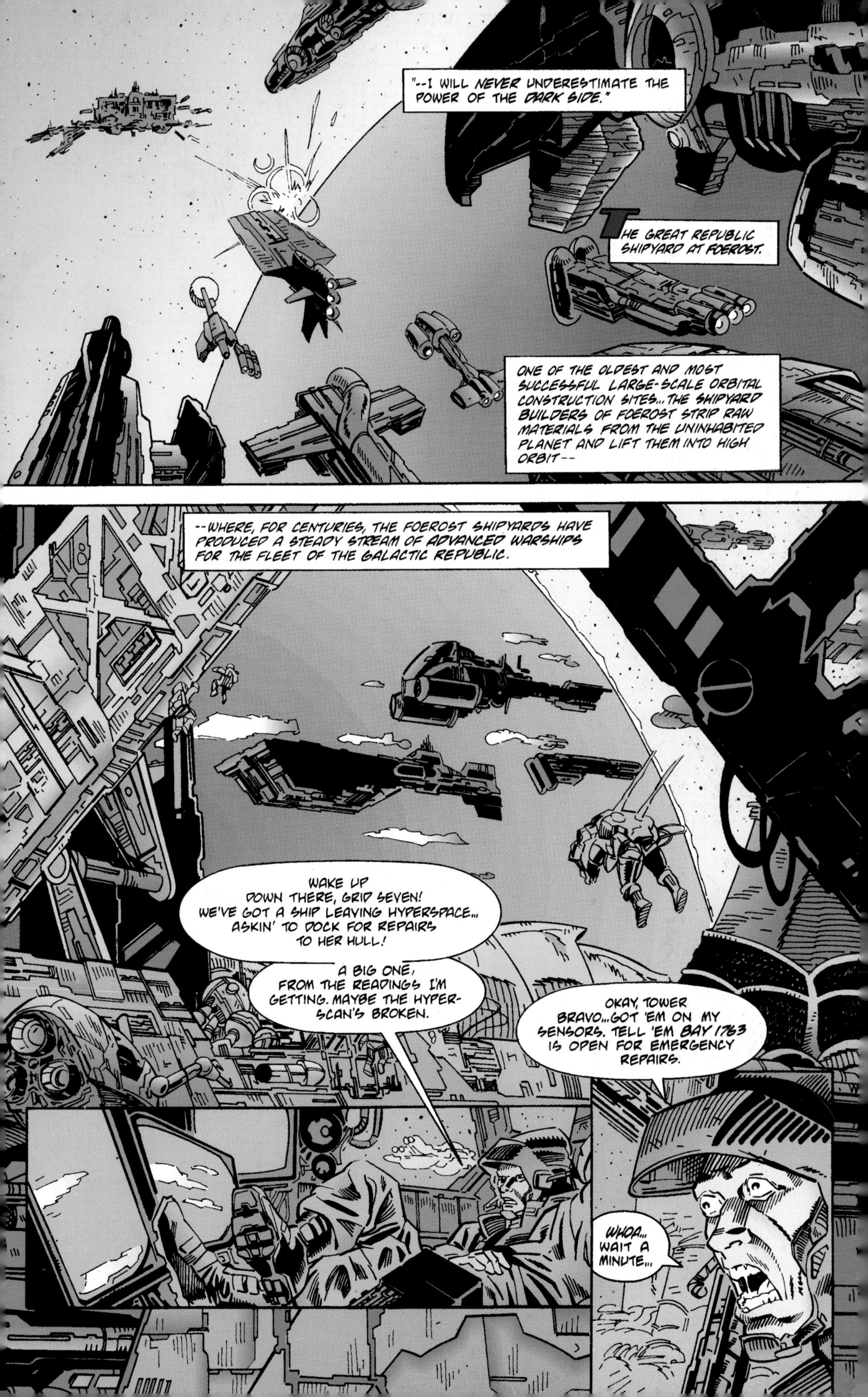
"--I WILL NEVER UNDERESTIMATE THE POWER OF THE DARK SIDE."
THE GREAT REPUBLIC SHIPYARD AT FOEROST.
ONE OF THE OLDEST AND MOST SUCCESSFUL LARGE-SCALE ORBITAL CONSTRUCTION SITES... THE SHIPYARD BUILDERS OF FOEROST STRIP RAW MATERIALS FROM THE UNINHABITED PLANET AND LIFT THEM INTO HIGH ORBIT--
--WHERE, FOR CENTURIES, THE FOEROST SHIPYARDS HAVE PRODUCED A STEADY STREAM OF ADVANCED WARSHIPS FOR THE FLEET OF THE GALACTIC REPUBLIC.
WAKE UP DOWN THERE, GRID SEVEN! WE'VE GOT A SHIP LEAVING HYPERSPACE... ASKIN' TO DOCK FOR REPAIRS TO HER HULL!
A BIG ONE, FROM THE READINGS I'M GETTING. MAYBE THE HYPER-SCAN'S BROKEN.
OKAY, TOWER BRAVO... GOT 'EM ON MY SENSORS. TELL 'EM BAY 1763 IS OPEN FOR EMERGENCY REPAIRS.
WHOA... WAIT A MINUTE...

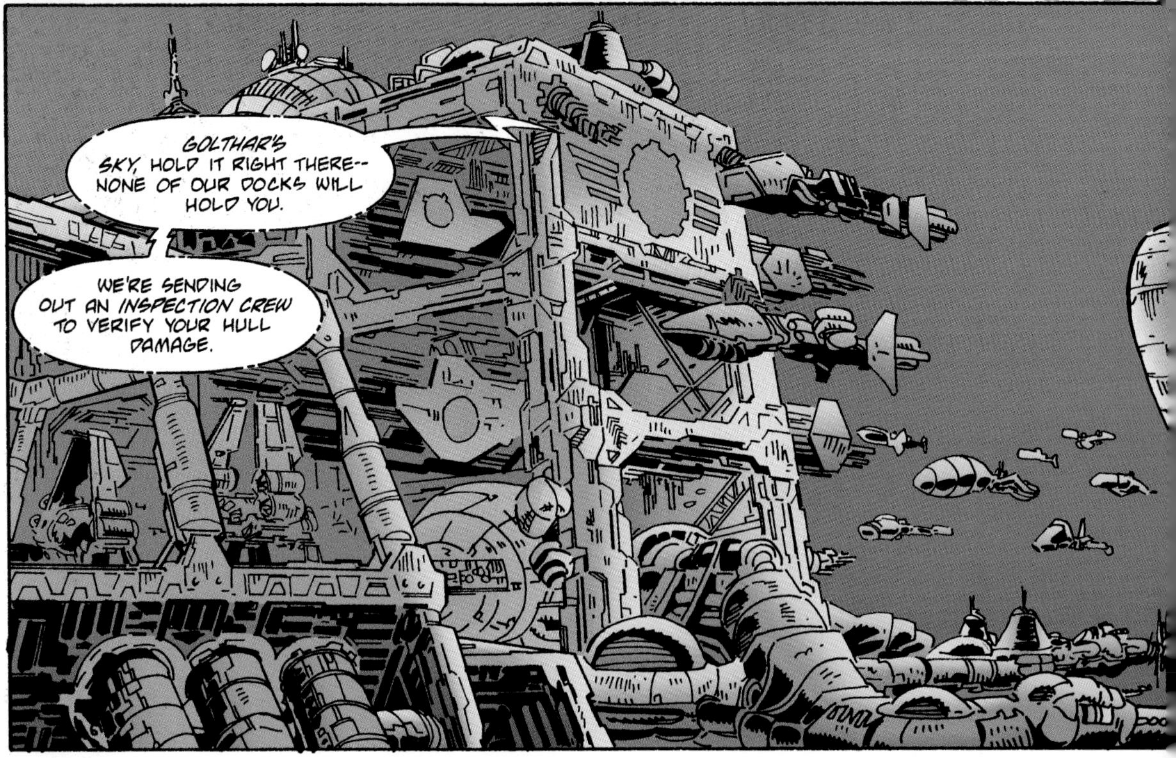
GOLTHAR'S SKY, HOLD IT RIGHT THERE-- NONE OF OUR DOCKS WILL HOLD YOU.
WE'RE SENDING OUT AN *INSPECTION CREW* TO VERIFY YOUR HULL DAMAGE.

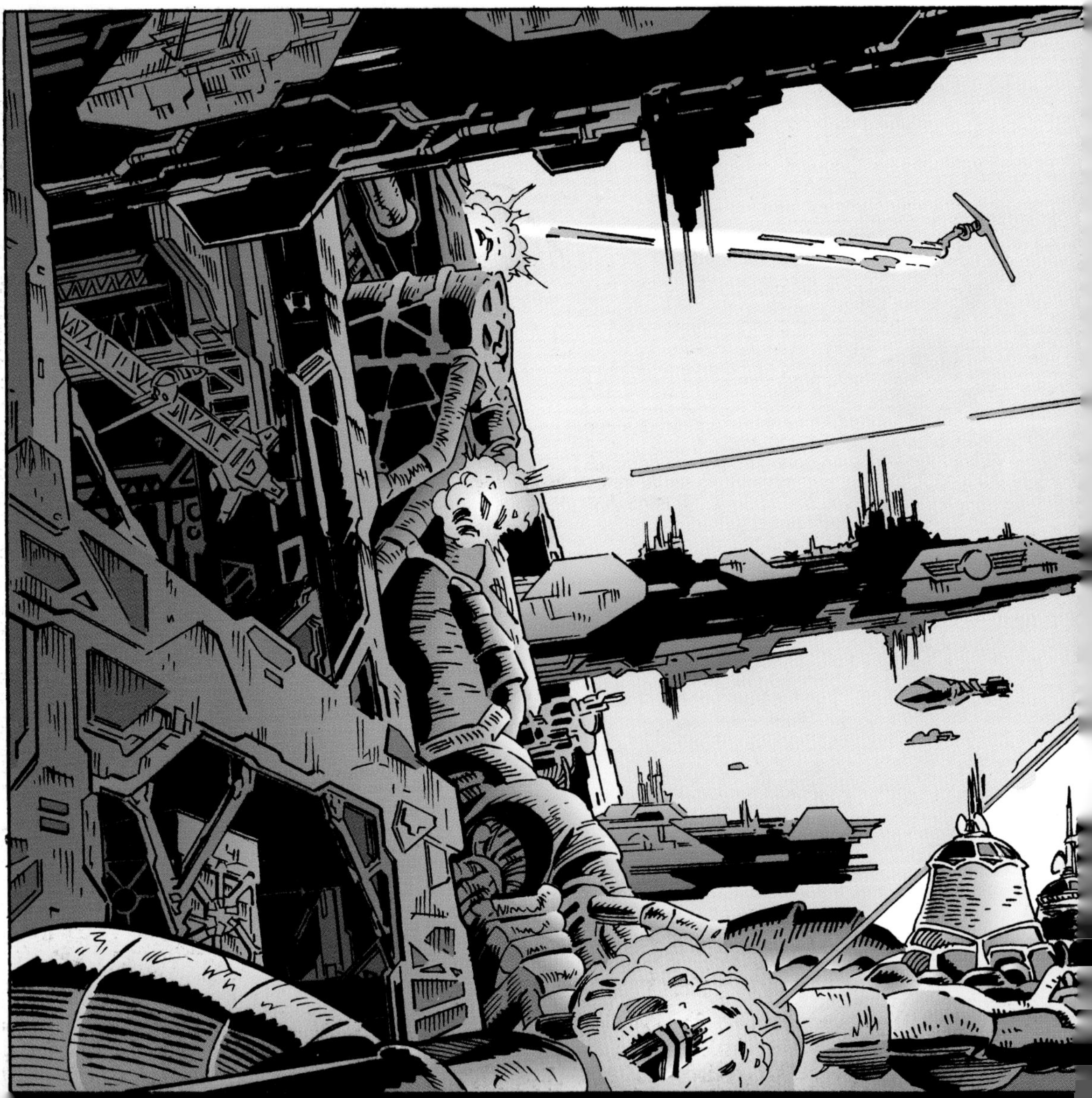

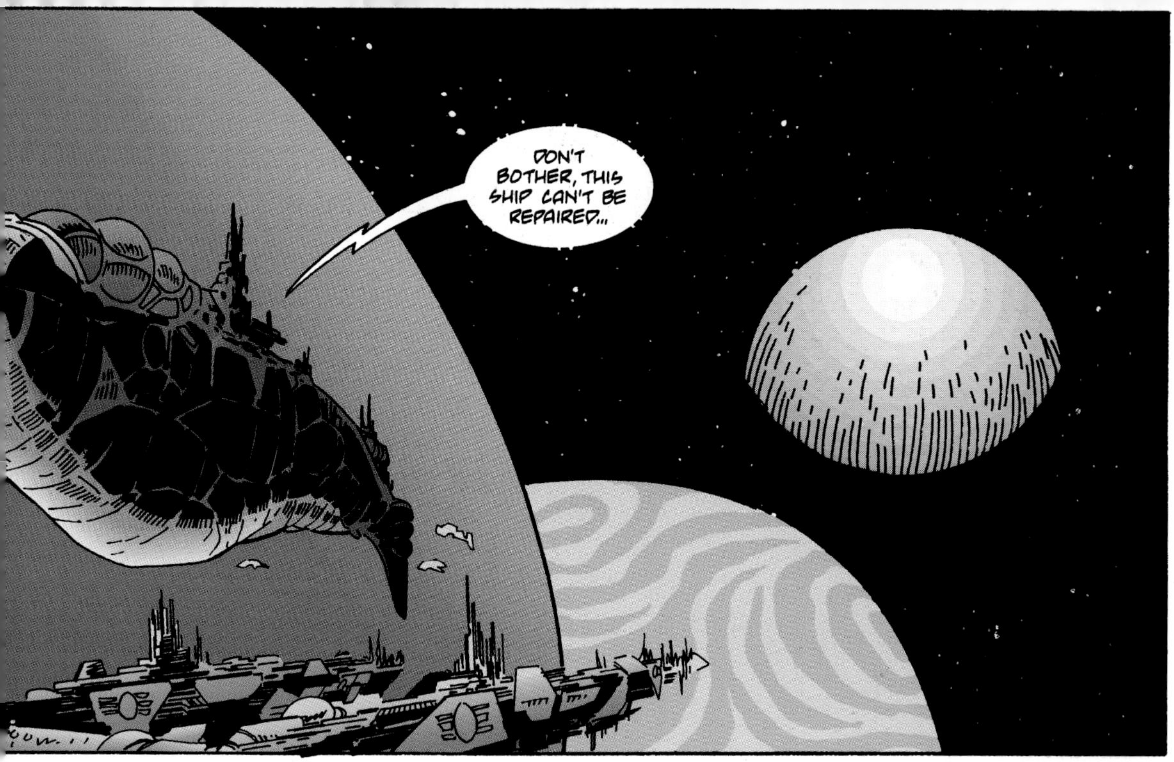
DON'T BOTHER, THIS SHIP CAN'T BE REPAIRED...

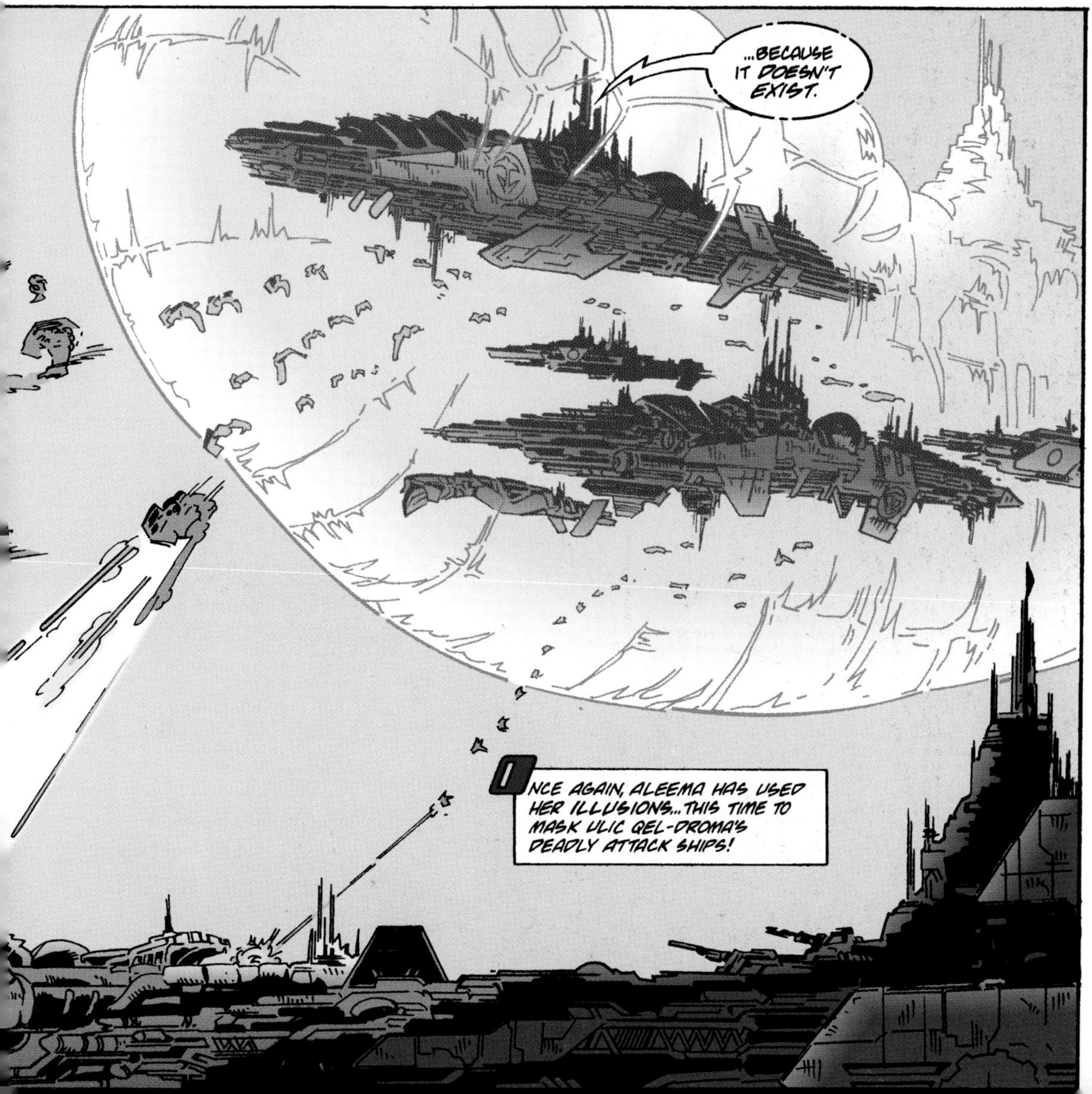
...BECAUSE IT DOESN'T EXIST.
ONCE AGAIN, ALEEMA HAS USED HER ILLUSIONS... THIS TIME TO MASK ULIC QEL-DROMA'S DEADLY ATTACK SHIPS!

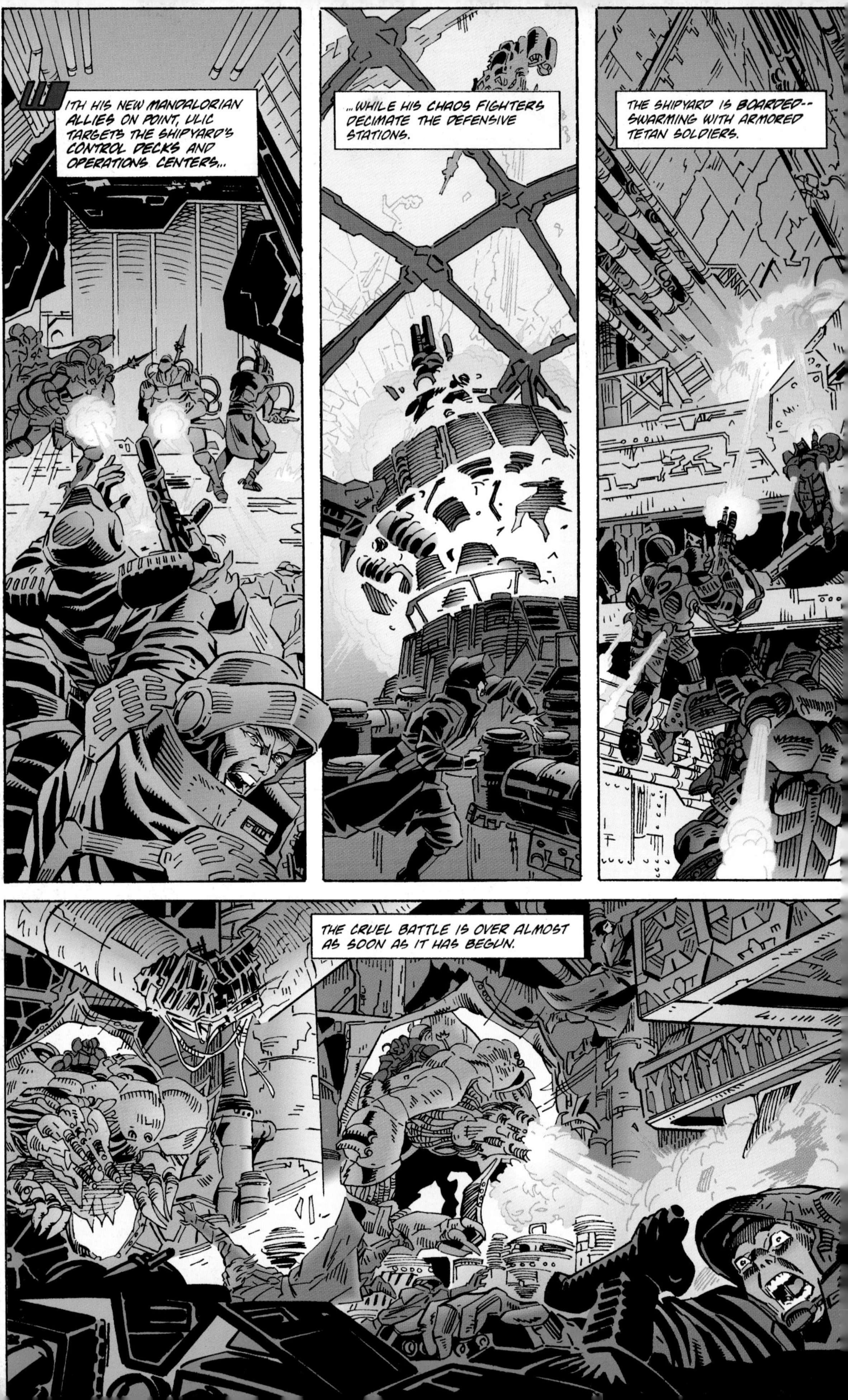
WITH HIS NEW MANDALORIAN ALLIES ON POINT, ULIC TARGETS THE SHIPYARD'S CONTROL DECKS AND OPERATIONS CENTERS...
...WHILE HIS CHAOS FIGHTERS DECIMATE THE DEFENSIVE STATIONS.
THE SHIPYARD IS BOARDED--SWARMING WITH ARMORED TETAN SOLDIERS.
THE CRUEL BATTLE IS OVER ALMOST AS SOON AS IT HAS BEGUN.

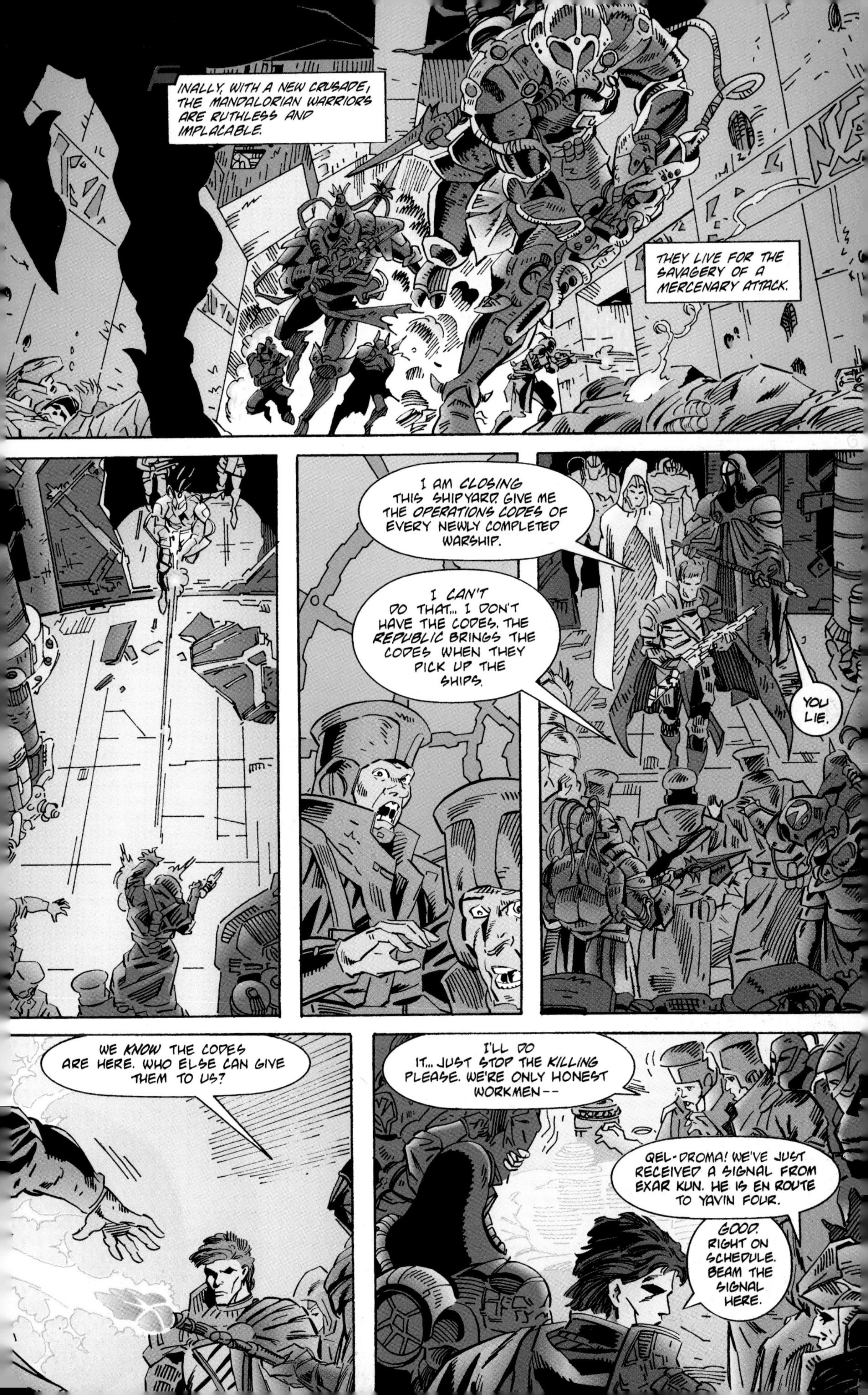
INALLY, WITH A NEW CRUSADE, THE MANDALORIAN WARRIORS ARE RUTHLESS AND IMPLACABLE.
THEY LIVE FOR THE SAVAGERY OF A MERCENARY ATTACK.
I AM CLOSING THIS SHIPYARD. GIVE ME THE OPERATIONS CODES OF EVERY NEWLY COMPLETED WARSHIP.
I CAN'T DO THAT... I DON'T HAVE THE CODES. THE REPUBLIC BRINGS THE CODES WHEN THEY PICK UP THE SHIPS.
YOU LIE.
WE KNOW THE CODES ARE HERE. WHO ELSE CAN GIVE THEM TO US?
I'LL DO IT... JUST STOP THE KILLING PLEASE. WE'RE ONLY HONEST WORKMEN--
QEL-DROMA! WE'VE JUST RECEIVED A SIGNAL FROM EXAR KUN. HE IS EN ROUTE TO YAVIN FOUR.
GOOD. RIGHT ON SCHEDULE. BEAM THE SIGNAL HERE.

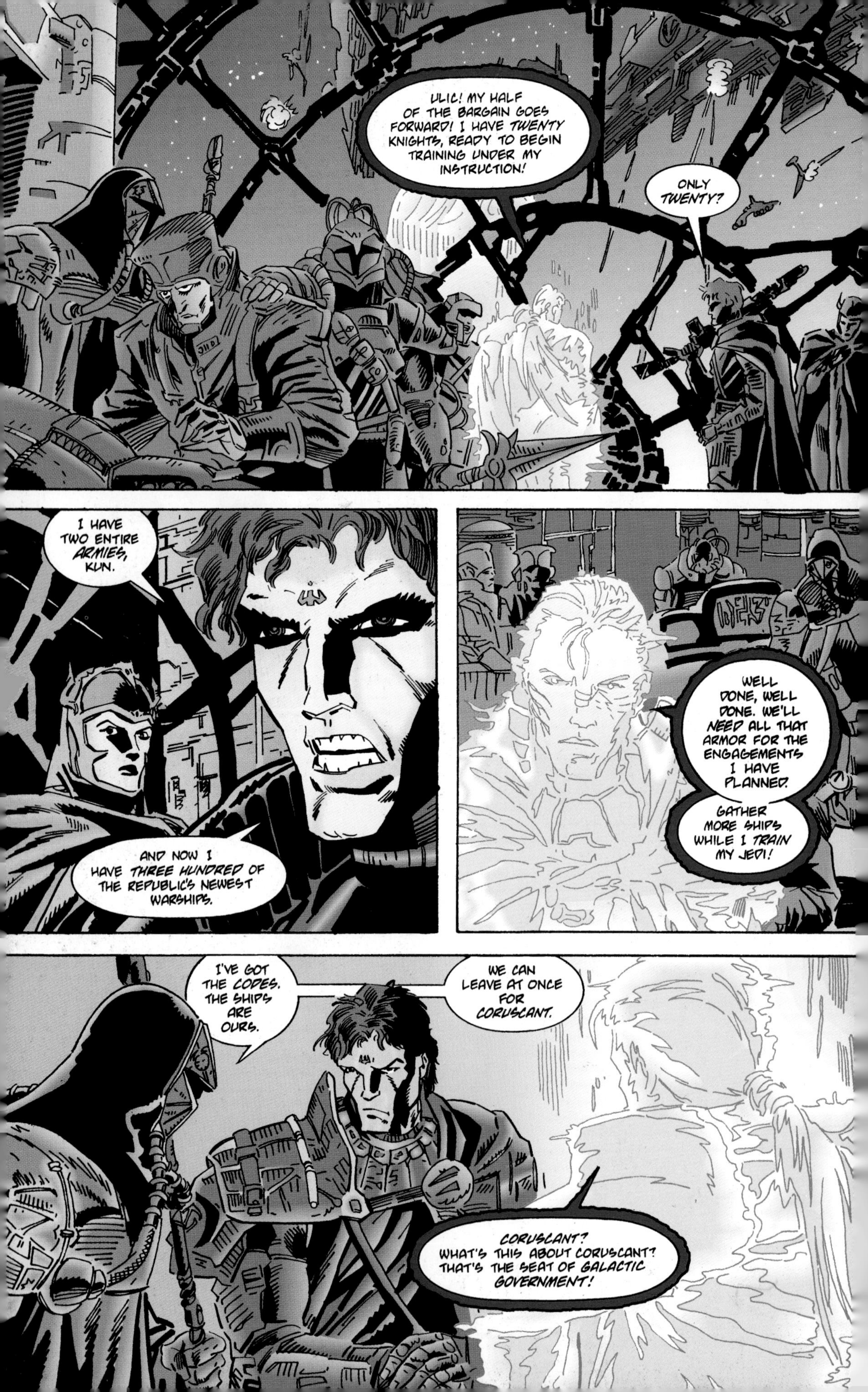
ULIC! MY HALF OF THE BARGAIN GOES FORWARD! I HAVE *TWENTY* KNIGHTS, READY TO BEGIN TRAINING UNDER MY INSTRUCTION!
ONLY *TWENTY?*
I HAVE TWO ENTIRE *ARMIES*, KUN.
AND NOW I HAVE *THREE HUNDRED* OF THE REPUBLIC'S NEWEST WARSHIPS.
WELL DONE, WELL DONE. WE'LL *NEED* ALL THAT ARMOR FOR THE ENGAGEMENTS I HAVE PLANNED.
GATHER MORE SHIPS WHILE I *TRAIN* MY JEDI!
I'VE GOT THE *CODES*. THE SHIPS ARE OURS.
WE CAN LEAVE AT ONCE FOR *CORUSCANT*.
CORUSCANT? WHAT'S THIS ABOUT CORUSCANT? THAT'S THE SEAT OF GALACTIC *GOVERNMENT!*

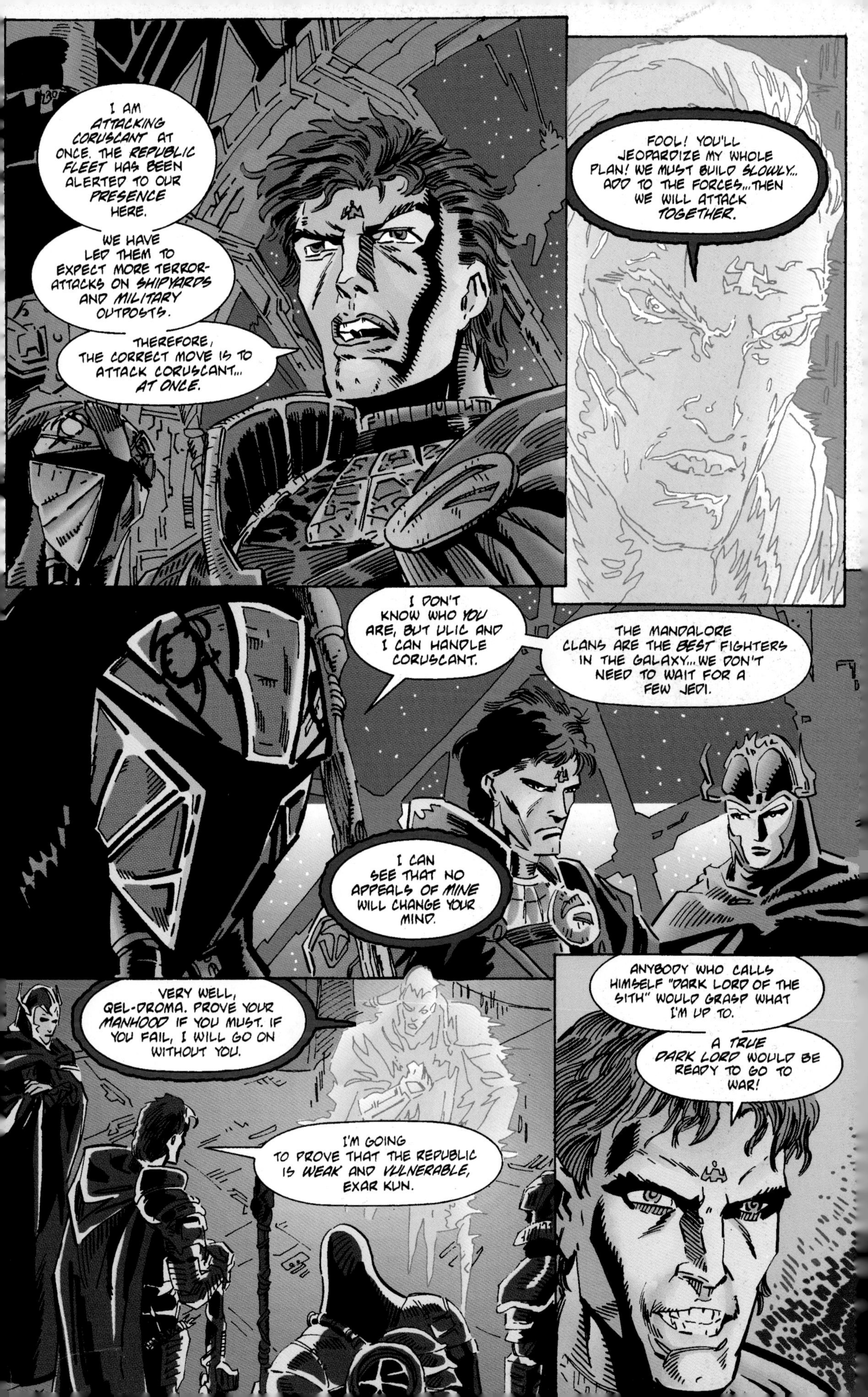
I AM ATTACKING CORUSCANT AT ONCE. THE REPUBLIC FLEET HAS BEEN ALERTED TO OUR PRESENCE HERE.
WE HAVE LED THEM TO EXPECT MORE TERROR-ATTACKS ON SHIPYARDS AND MILITARY OUTPOSTS.
THEREFORE, THE CORRECT MOVE IS TO ATTACK CORUSCANT... AT ONCE.
FOOL! YOU'LL JEOPARDIZE MY WHOLE PLAN! WE MUST BUILD SLOWLY... ADD TO THE FORCES... THEN WE WILL ATTACK TOGETHER.
I DON'T KNOW WHO YOU ARE, BUT ULIC AND I CAN HANDLE CORUSCANT.
THE MANDALORE CLANS ARE THE BEST FIGHTERS IN THE GALAXY... WE DON'T NEED TO WAIT FOR A FEW JEDI.
I CAN SEE THAT NO APPEALS OF MINE WILL CHANGE YOUR MIND.
VERY WELL, QEL-DROMA. PROVE YOUR MANHOOD IF YOU MUST. IF YOU FAIL, I WILL GO ON WITHOUT YOU.
I'M GOING TO PROVE THAT THE REPUBLIC IS WEAK AND VULNERABLE, EXAR KUN.
ANYBODY WHO CALLS HIMSELF "DARK LORD OF THE SITH" WOULD GRASP WHAT I'M UP TO.
A TRUE DARK LORD WOULD BE READY TO GO TO WAR!

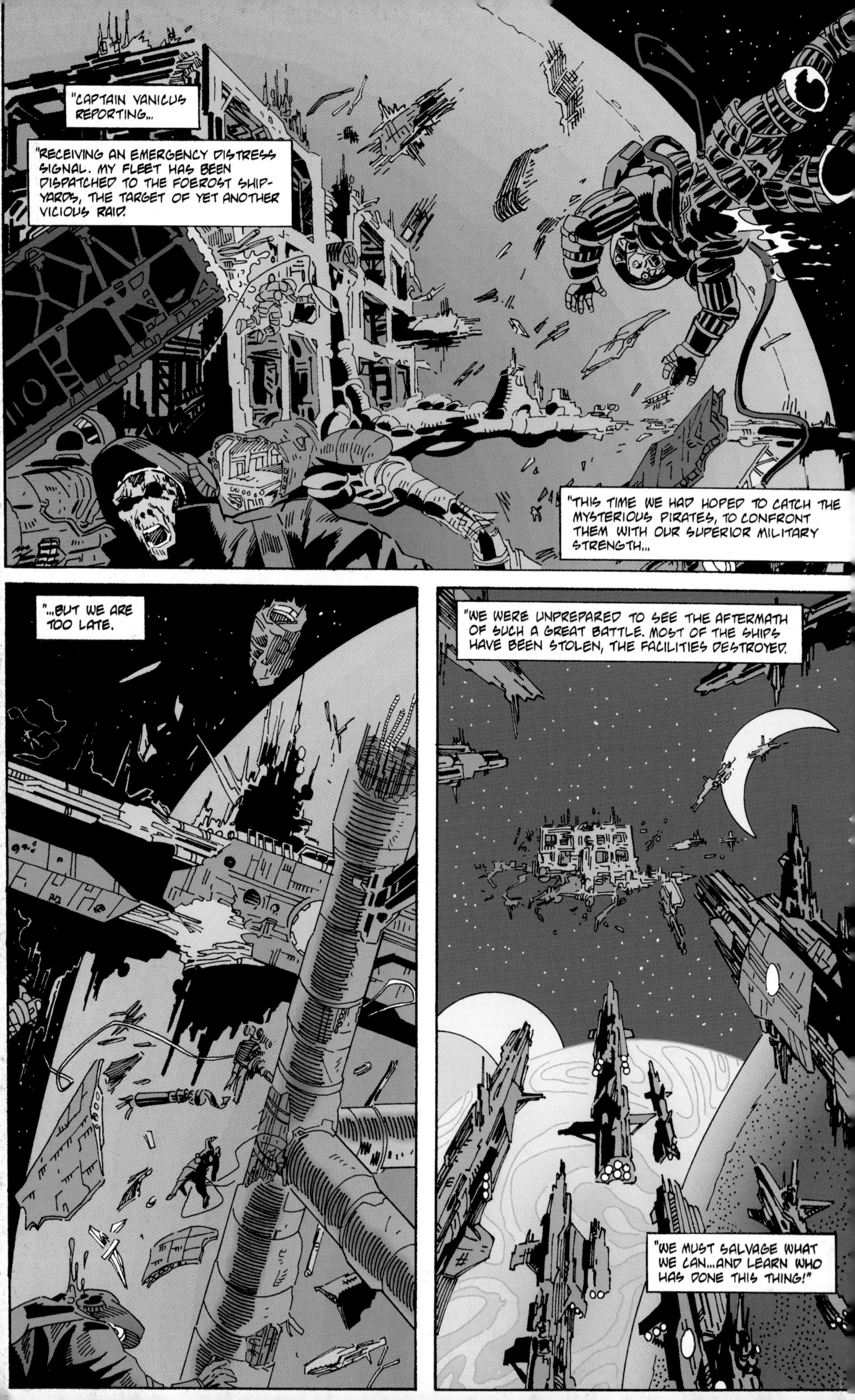
"CAPTAIN VANICUS REPORTING...
"RECEIVING AN EMERGENCY DISTRESS SIGNAL. MY FLEET HAS BEEN DISPATCHED TO THE FOEROST SHIP-YARDS, THE TARGET OF YET ANOTHER VICIOUS RAID.
"THIS TIME WE HAD HOPED TO CATCH THE MYSTERIOUS PIRATES, TO CONFRONT THEM WITH OUR SUPERIOR MILITARY STRENGTH...
"...BUT WE ARE TOO LATE.
"WE WERE UNPREPARED TO SEE THE AFTERMATH OF SUCH A GREAT BATTLE. MOST OF THE SHIPS HAVE BEEN STOLEN, THE FACILITIES DESTROYED.
"WE MUST SALVAGE WHAT WE CAN...AND LEARN WHO HAS DONE THIS THING!"

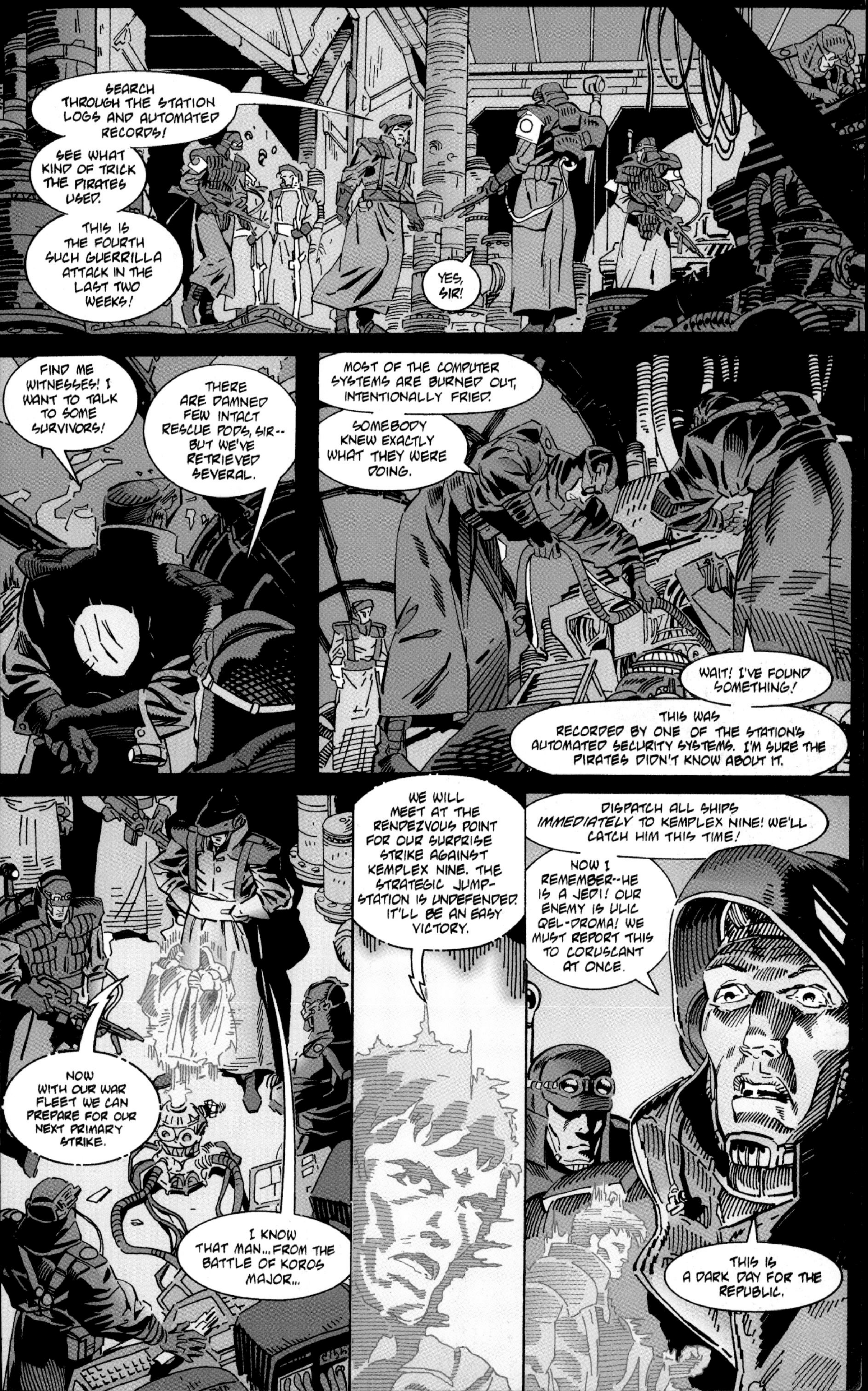
SEARCH THROUGH THE STATION LOGS AND AUTOMATED RECORDS!
SEE WHAT KIND OF TRICK THE PIRATES USED.
THIS IS THE FOURTH SUCH GUERRILLA ATTACK IN THE LAST TWO WEEKS!
YES, SIR!
FIND ME WITNESSES! I WANT TO TALK TO SOME SURVIVORS!
THERE ARE DAMNED FEW INTACT RESCUE PODS, SIR-- BUT WE'VE RETRIEVED SEVERAL.
MOST OF THE COMPUTER SYSTEMS ARE BURNED OUT, INTENTIONALLY FRIED.
SOMEBODY KNEW EXACTLY WHAT THEY WERE DOING.
WAIT! I'VE FOUND SOMETHING!
THIS WAS RECORDED BY ONE OF THE STATION'S AUTOMATED SECURITY SYSTEMS. I'M SURE THE PIRATES DIDN'T KNOW ABOUT IT.
NOW WITH OUR WAR FLEET WE CAN PREPARE FOR OUR NEXT PRIMARY STRIKE.
I KNOW THAT MAN... FROM THE BATTLE OF KOROS MAJOR...
WE WILL MEET AT THE RENDEZVOUS POINT FOR OUR SURPRISE STRIKE AGAINST KEMPLEX NINE. THE STRATEGIC JUMP-STATION IS UNDEFENDED. IT'LL BE AN EASY VICTORY.
DISPATCH ALL SHIPS IMMEDIATELY TO KEMPLEX NINE! WE'LL CATCH HIM THIS TIME!
NOW I REMEMBER--HE IS A JEDI! OUR ENEMY IS ULIC QEL-DROMA! WE MUST REPORT THIS TO CORUSCANT AT ONCE.
THIS IS A DARK DAY FOR THE REPUBLIC.

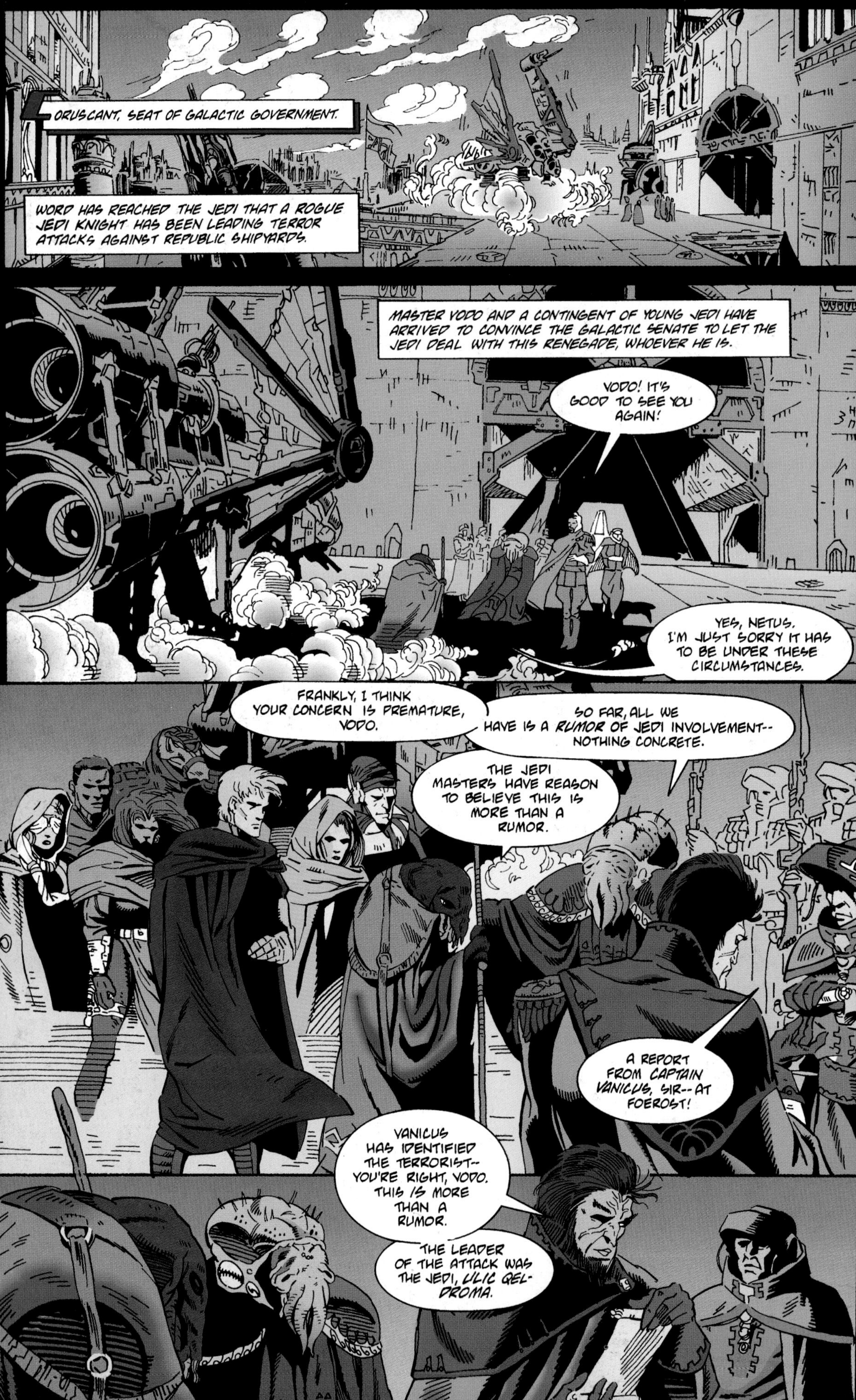
CORUSCANT, SEAT OF GALACTIC GOVERNMENT.
WORD HAS REACHED THE JEDI THAT A ROGUE JEDI KNIGHT HAS BEEN LEADING TERROR ATTACKS AGAINST REPUBLIC SHIPYARDS.
MASTER VODO AND A CONTINGENT OF YOUNG JEDI HAVE ARRIVED TO CONVINCE THE GALACTIC SENATE TO LET THE JEDI DEAL WITH THIS RENEGADE, WHOEVER HE IS.
VODO! IT'S GOOD TO SEE YOU AGAIN!
YES, NETUS. I'M JUST SORRY IT HAS TO BE UNDER THESE CIRCUMSTANCES.
FRANKLY, I THINK YOUR CONCERN IS PREMATURE, VODO.
SO FAR, ALL WE HAVE IS A RUMOR OF JEDI INVOLVEMENT--NOTHING CONCRETE.
THE JEDI MASTERS HAVE REASON TO BELIEVE THIS IS MORE THAN A RUMOR.
A REPORT FROM CAPTAIN VANICUS, SIR--AT FOEROST!
VANICUS HAS IDENTIFIED THE TERRORIST--YOU'RE RIGHT, VODO. THIS IS MORE THAN A RUMOR.
THE LEADER OF THE ATTACK WAS THE JEDI, ULIC QEL-DROMA.

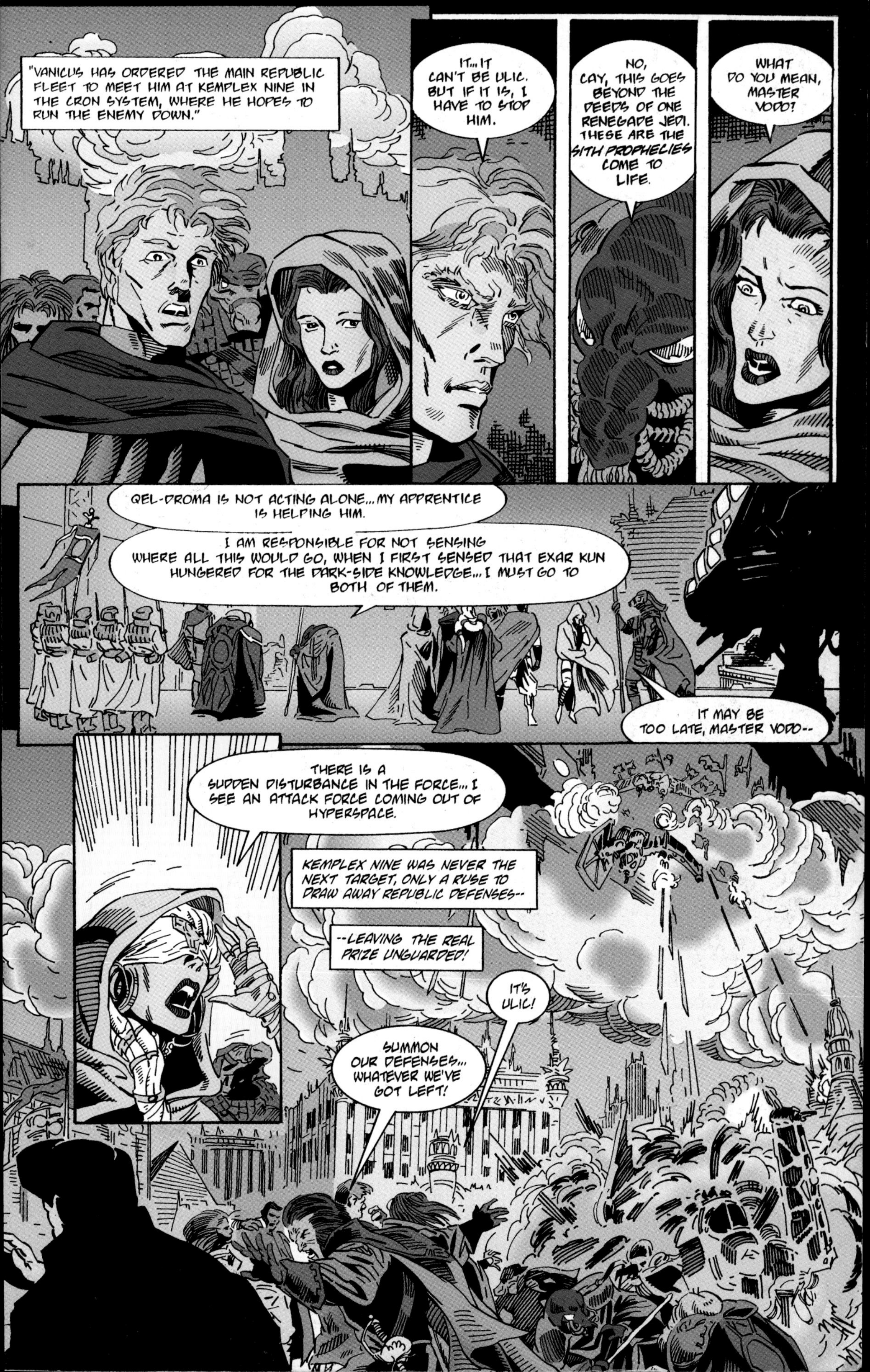
"VANICUS HAS ORDERED THE MAIN REPUBLIC FLEET TO MEET HIM AT KEMPLEX NINE IN THE CRON SYSTEM, WHERE HE HOPES TO RUN THE ENEMY DOWN."
IT... IT CAN'T BE ULIC. BUT IF IT IS, I HAVE TO STOP HIM.
NO, CAY, THIS GOES BEYOND THE DEEDS OF ONE RENEGADE JEDI. THESE ARE THE SITH PROPHECIES COME TO LIFE.
WHAT DO YOU MEAN, MASTER VODO?
QEL-DROMA IS NOT ACTING ALONE... MY APPRENTICE IS HELPING HIM.
I AM RESPONSIBLE FOR NOT SENSING WHERE ALL THIS WOULD GO, WHEN I FIRST SENSED THAT EXAR KUN HUNGERED FOR THE DARK-SIDE KNOWLEDGE... I MUST GO TO BOTH OF THEM.
IT MAY BE TOO LATE, MASTER VODO--
THERE IS A SUDDEN DISTURBANCE IN THE FORCE... I SEE AN ATTACK FORCE COMING OUT OF HYPERSPACE.
KEMPLEX NINE WAS NEVER THE NEXT TARGET, ONLY A RUSE TO DRAW AWAY REPUBLIC DEFENSES--
--LEAVING THE REAL PRIZE UNGUARDED!
IT'S ULIC!
SUMMON OUR DEFENSES... WHATEVER WE'VE GOT LEFT!

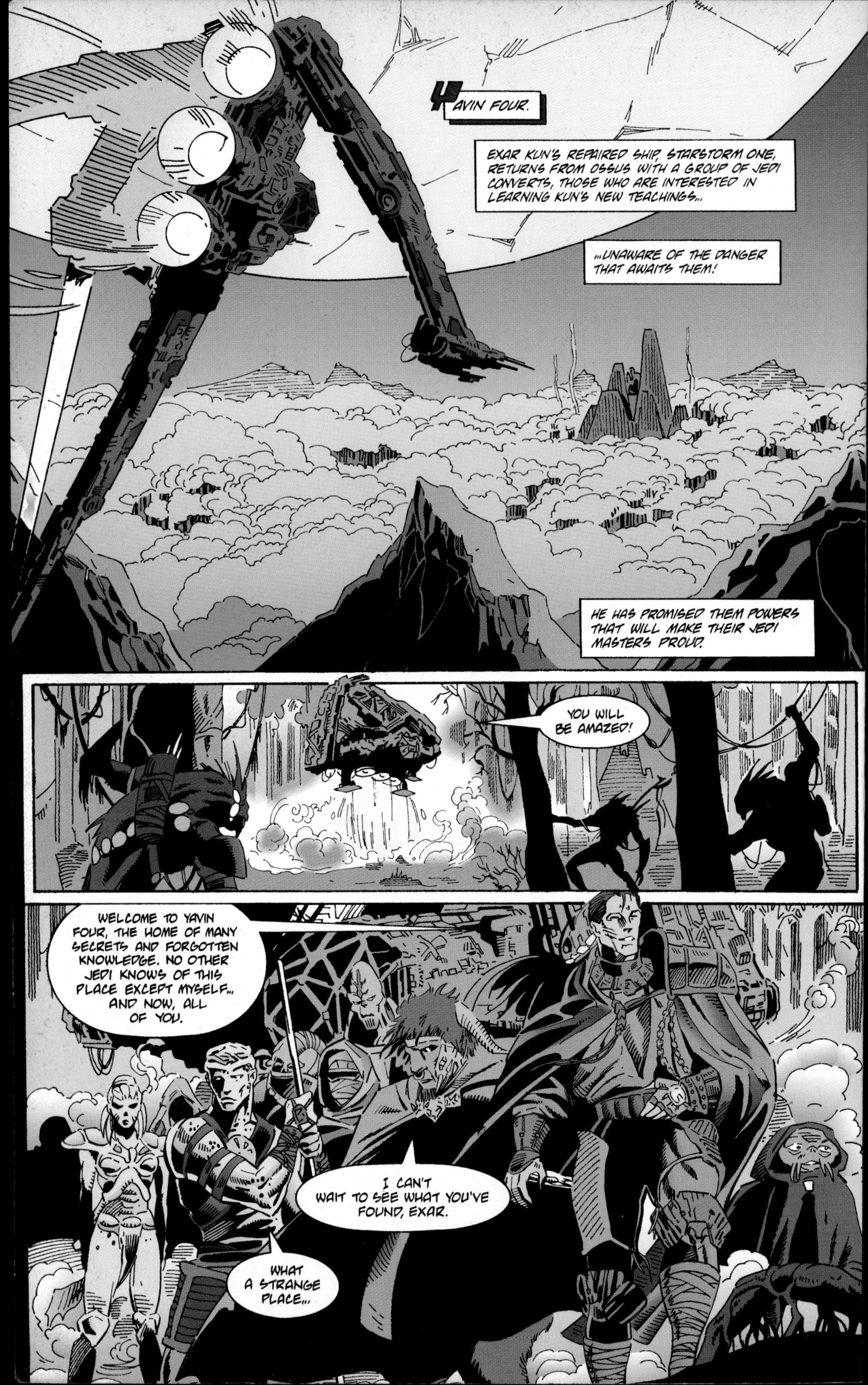
YAVIN FOUR.
EXAR KUN'S REPAIRED SHIP, STARSTORM ONE, RETURNS FROM OSSUS WITH A GROUP OF JEDI CONVERTS, THOSE WHO ARE INTERESTED IN LEARNING KUN'S NEW TEACHINGS...
...UNAWARE OF THE DANGER THAT AWAITS THEM!
HE HAS PROMISED THEM POWERS THAT WILL MAKE THEIR JEDI MASTERS PROUD.
YOU WILL BE AMAZED!
WELCOME TO YAVIN FOUR, THE HOME OF MANY SECRETS AND FORGOTTEN KNOWLEDGE. NO OTHER JEDI KNOWS OF THIS PLACE EXCEPT MYSELF... AND NOW, ALL OF YOU.
I CAN'T WAIT TO SEE WHAT YOU'VE FOUND, EXAR.
WHAT A STRANGE PLACE...

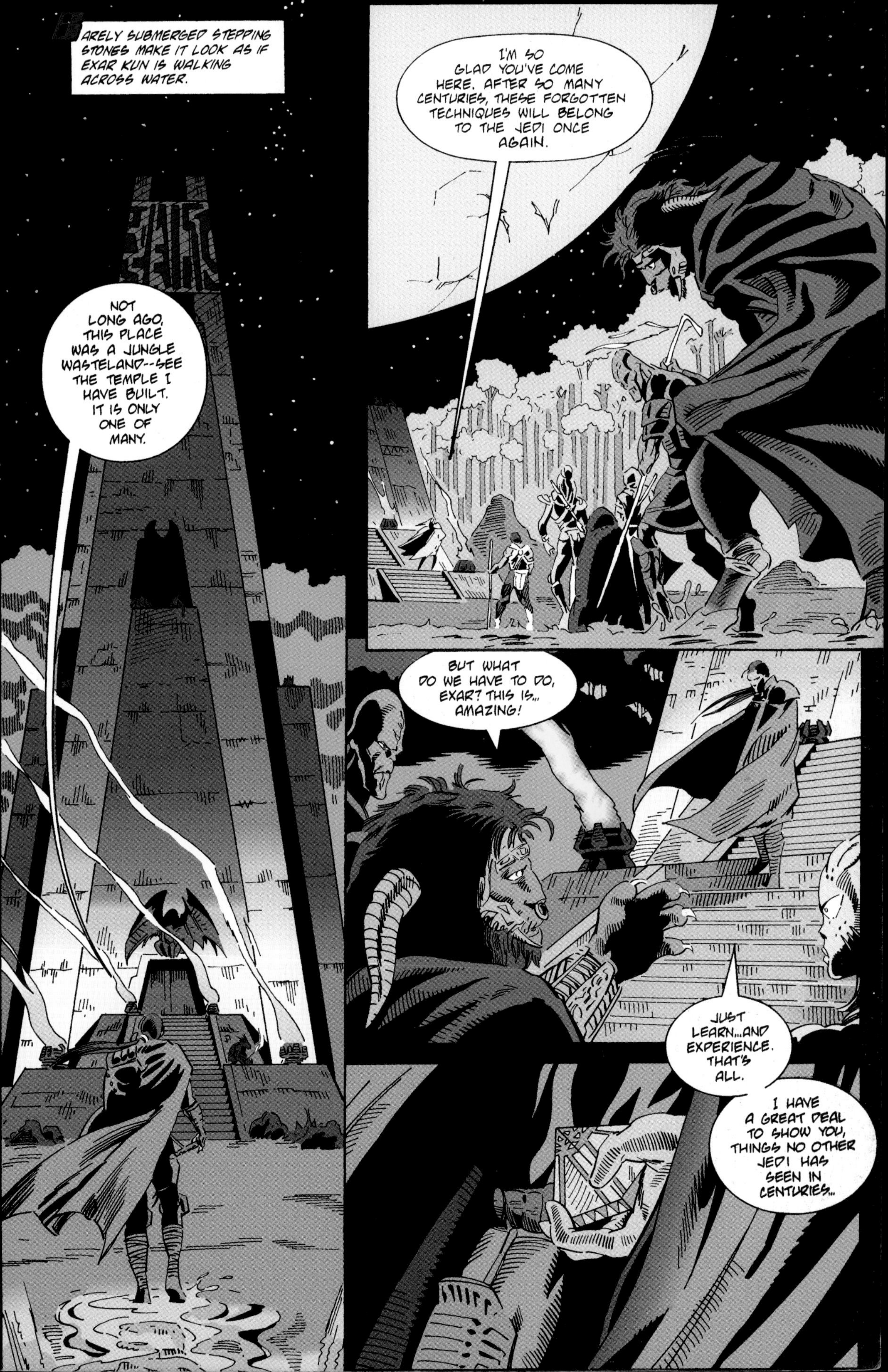
BARELY SUBMERGED STEPPING STONES MAKE IT LOOK AS IF EXAR KUN IS WALKING ACROSS WATER.
NOT LONG AGO, THIS PLACE WAS A JUNGLE WASTELAND--SEE THE TEMPLE I HAVE BUILT. IT IS ONLY ONE OF MANY.
I'M SO GLAD YOU'VE COME HERE. AFTER SO MANY CENTURIES, THESE FORGOTTEN TECHNIQUES WILL BELONG TO THE JEDI ONCE AGAIN.
BUT WHAT DO WE HAVE TO DO, EXAR? THIS IS... AMAZING!
JUST LEARN...AND EXPERIENCE. THAT'S ALL.
I HAVE A GREAT DEAL TO SHOW YOU, THINGS NO OTHER JEDI HAS SEEN IN CENTURIES...

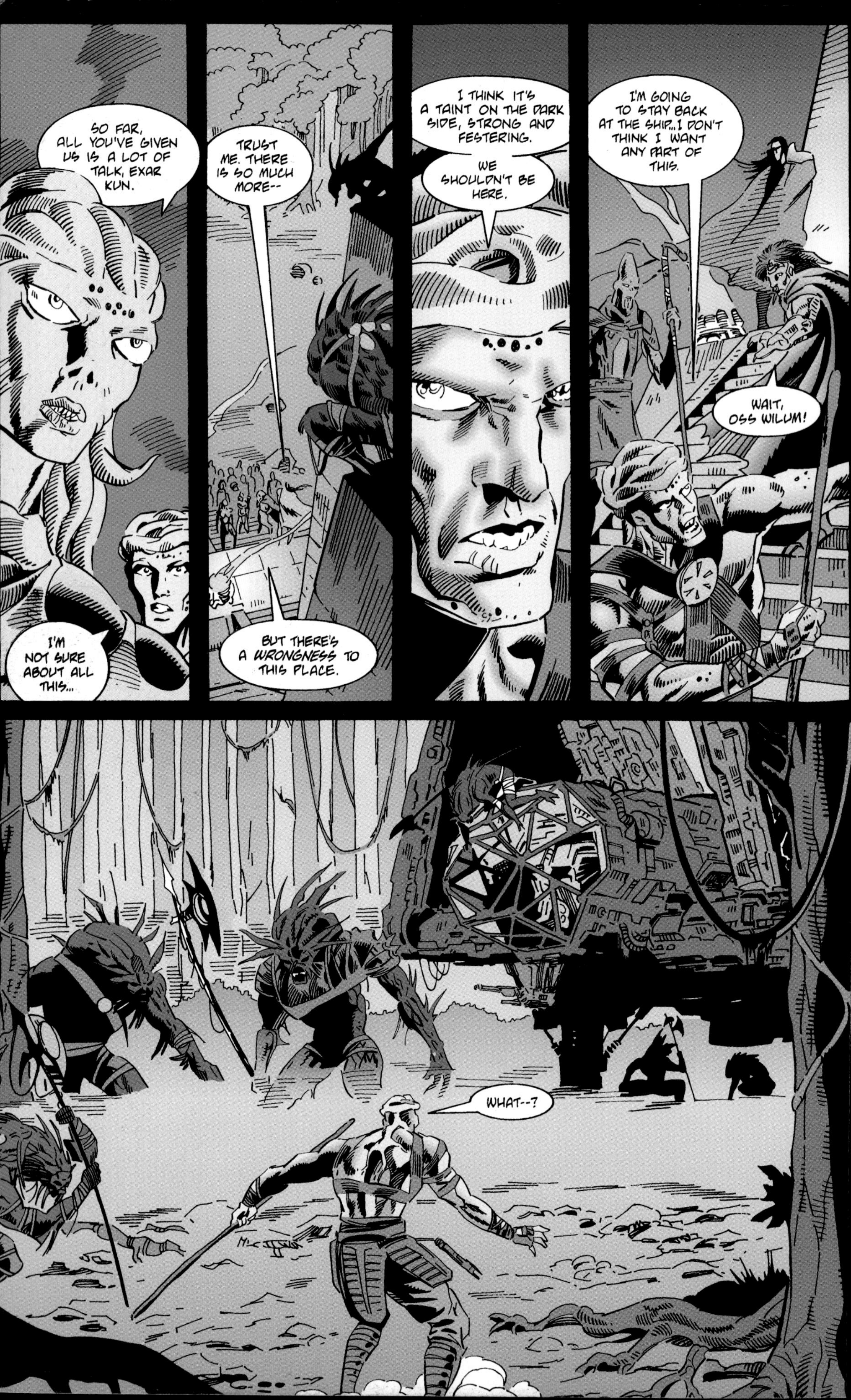
SO FAR, ALL YOU'VE GIVEN US IS A LOT OF TALK, EXAR KUN.
I'M NOT SURE ABOUT ALL THIS...
TRUST ME. THERE IS SO MUCH MORE--
BUT THERE'S A WRONGNESS TO THIS PLACE.
I THINK IT'S A TAINT ON THE DARK SIDE, STRONG AND FESTERING.
WE SHOULDN'T BE HERE.
I'M GOING TO STAY BACK AT THE SHIP...I DON'T THINK I WANT ANY PART OF THIS.
WAIT, OSS WILUM!
WHAT--?

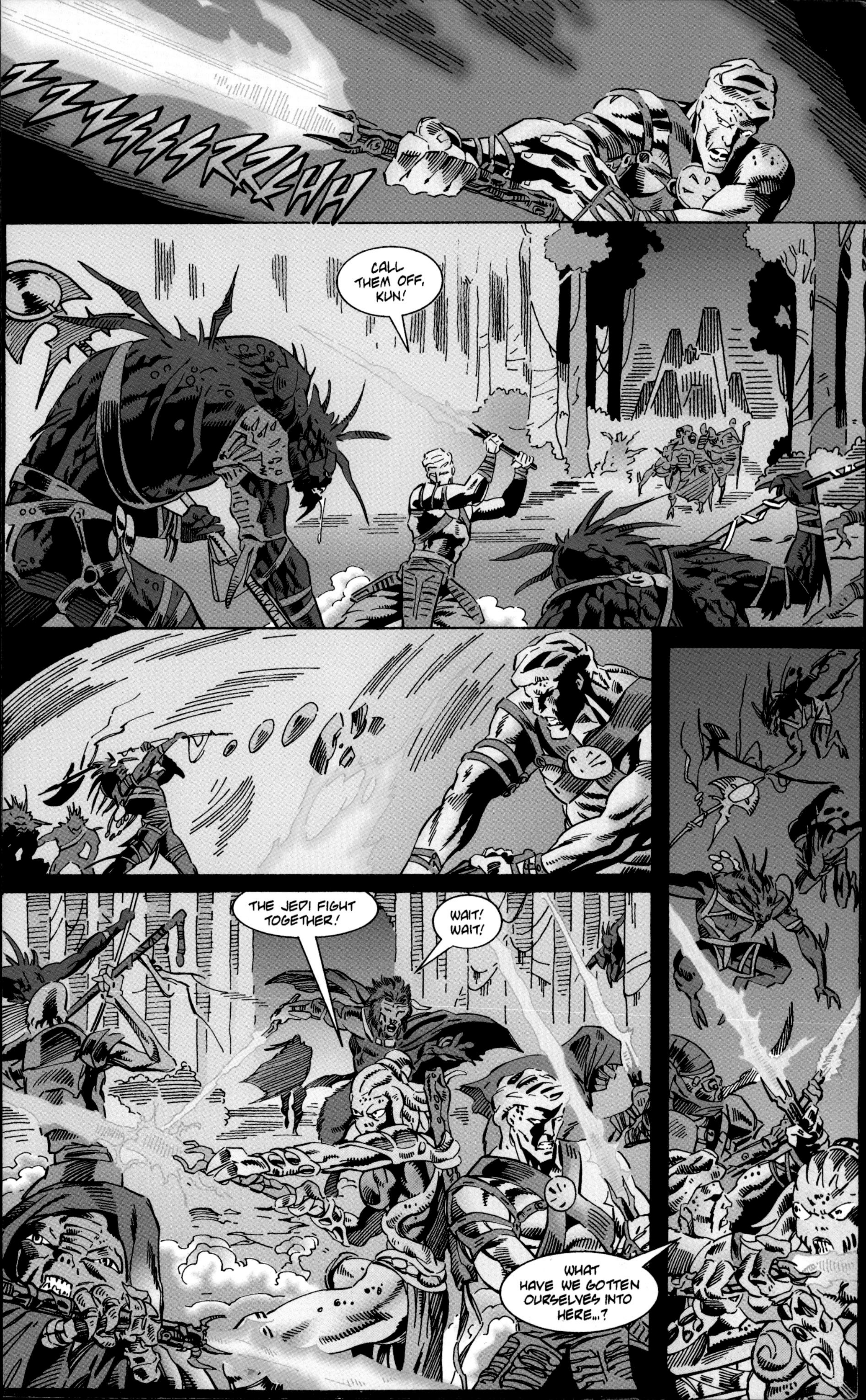
ZZZZZZZZRRZHH
CALL THEM OFF, KUN!
THE JEDI FIGHT TOGETHER!
WAIT! WAIT!
WHAT HAVE WE GOTTEN OURSELVES INTO HERE...?

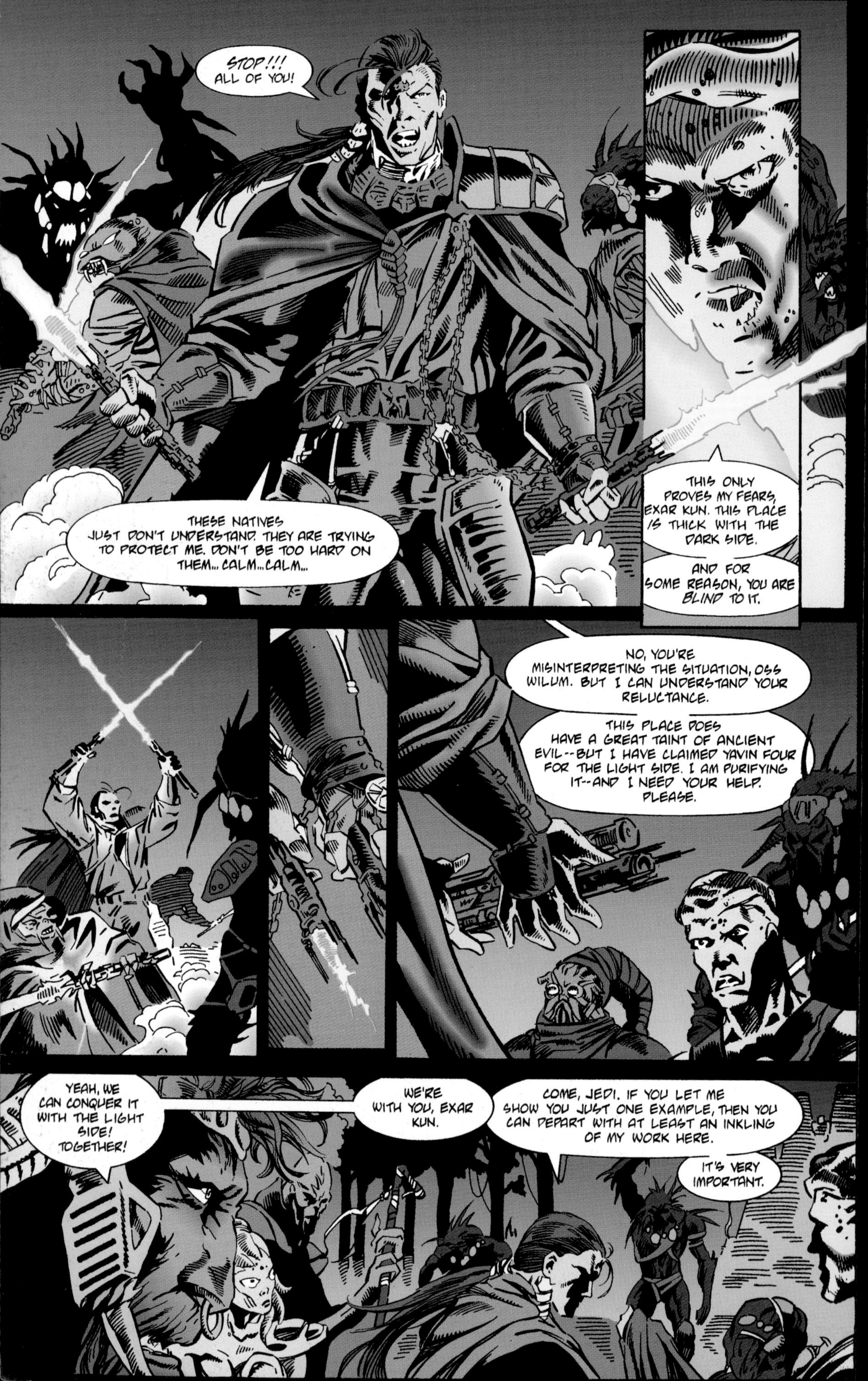
STOP!!! ALL OF YOU!
THESE NATIVES JUST DON'T UNDERSTAND. THEY ARE TRYING TO PROTECT ME. DON'T BE TOO HARD ON THEM... CALM...CALM...
THIS ONLY PROVES MY FEARS, EXAR KUN. THIS PLACE IS THICK WITH THE DARK SIDE.
AND FOR SOME REASON, YOU ARE BLIND TO IT.
NO, YOU'RE MISINTERPRETING THE SITUATION, OSS WILUM. BUT I CAN UNDERSTAND YOUR RELUCTANCE.
THIS PLACE DOES HAVE A GREAT TAINT OF ANCIENT EVIL--BUT I HAVE CLAIMED YAVIN FOUR FOR THE LIGHT SIDE. I AM PURIFYING IT--AND I NEED YOUR HELP. PLEASE.
YEAH, WE CAN CONQUER IT WITH THE LIGHT SIDE! TOGETHER!
WE'RE WITH YOU, EXAR KUN.
COME, JEDI. IF YOU LET ME SHOW YOU JUST ONE EXAMPLE, THEN YOU CAN DEPART WITH AT LEAST AN INKLING OF MY WORK HERE.
IT'S VERY IMPORTANT.

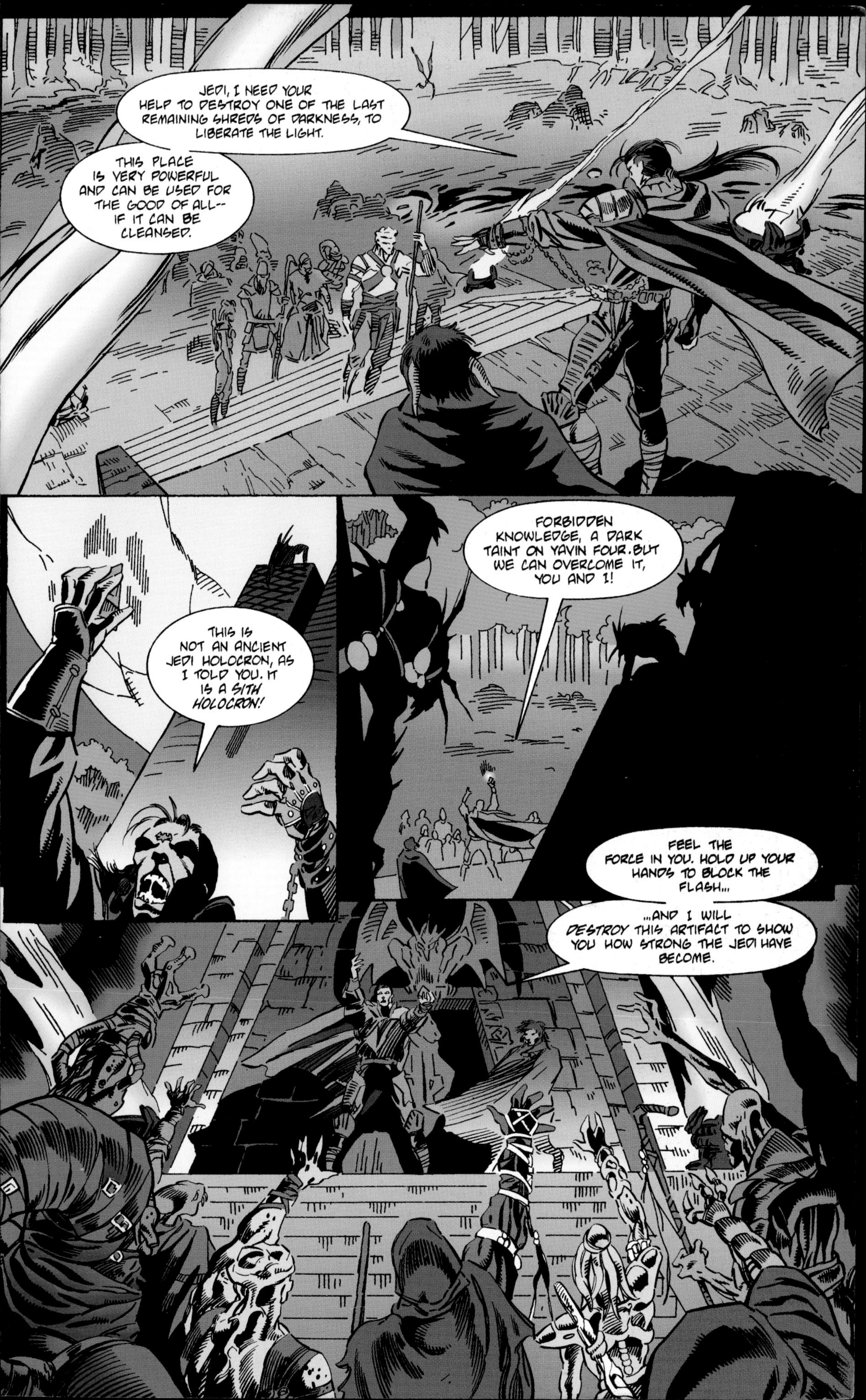
JEDI, I NEED YOUR HELP TO DESTROY ONE OF THE LAST REMAINING SHREDS OF DARKNESS, TO LIBERATE THE LIGHT.
THIS PLACE IS VERY POWERFUL AND CAN BE USED FOR THE GOOD OF ALL-- IF IT CAN BE CLEANSED.
THIS IS NOT AN ANCIENT JEDI HOLOCRON, AS I TOLD YOU. IT IS A *SITH HOLOCRON!*
FORBIDDEN KNOWLEDGE, A DARK TAINT ON YAVIN FOUR. BUT WE CAN OVERCOME IT, YOU AND I!
FEEL THE FORCE IN YOU. HOLD UP YOUR HANDS TO BLOCK THE FLASH...
...AND I WILL *DESTROY* THIS ARTIFACT TO SHOW YOU HOW STRONG THE JEDI HAVE BECOME.

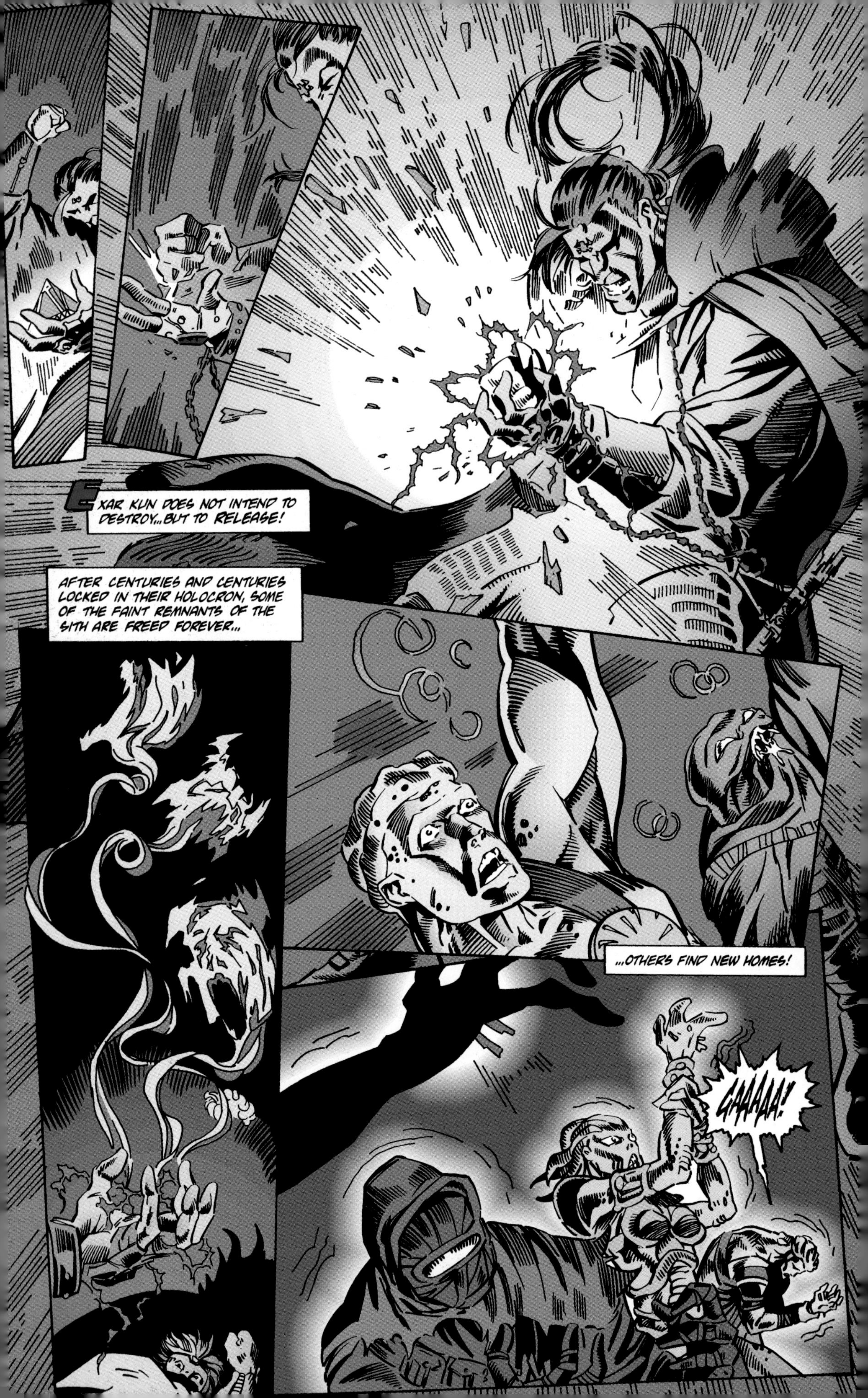
EXAR KUN DOES NOT INTEND TO DESTROY...BUT TO RELEASE!
AFTER CENTURIES AND CENTURIES LOCKED IN THEIR HOLOCRON, SOME OF THE FAINT REMNANTS OF THE SITH ARE FREED FOREVER...
...OTHERS FIND NEW HOMES!
GAAAAA!

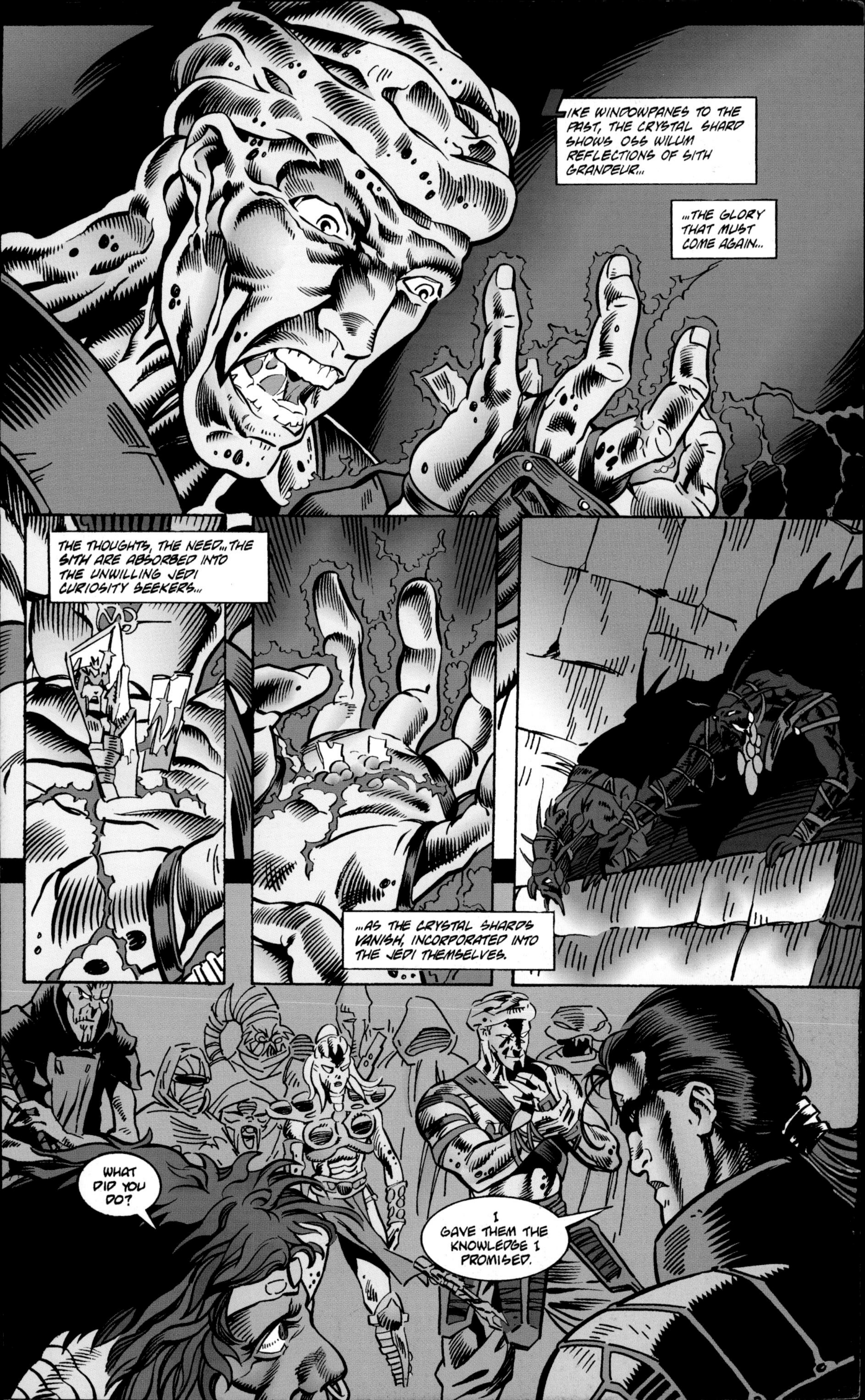
LIKE WINDOWPANES TO THE PAST, THE CRYSTAL SHARD SHOWS OSS WILUM REFLECTIONS OF SITH GRANDEUR...
...THE GLORY THAT MUST COME AGAIN...
THE THOUGHTS, THE NEED... THE SITH ARE ABSORBED INTO THE UNWILLING JEDI CURIOSITY SEEKERS...
...AS THE CRYSTAL SHARDS VANISH, INCORPORATED INTO THE JEDI THEMSELVES.
WHAT DID YOU DO?
I GAVE THEM THE KNOWLEDGE I PROMISED.

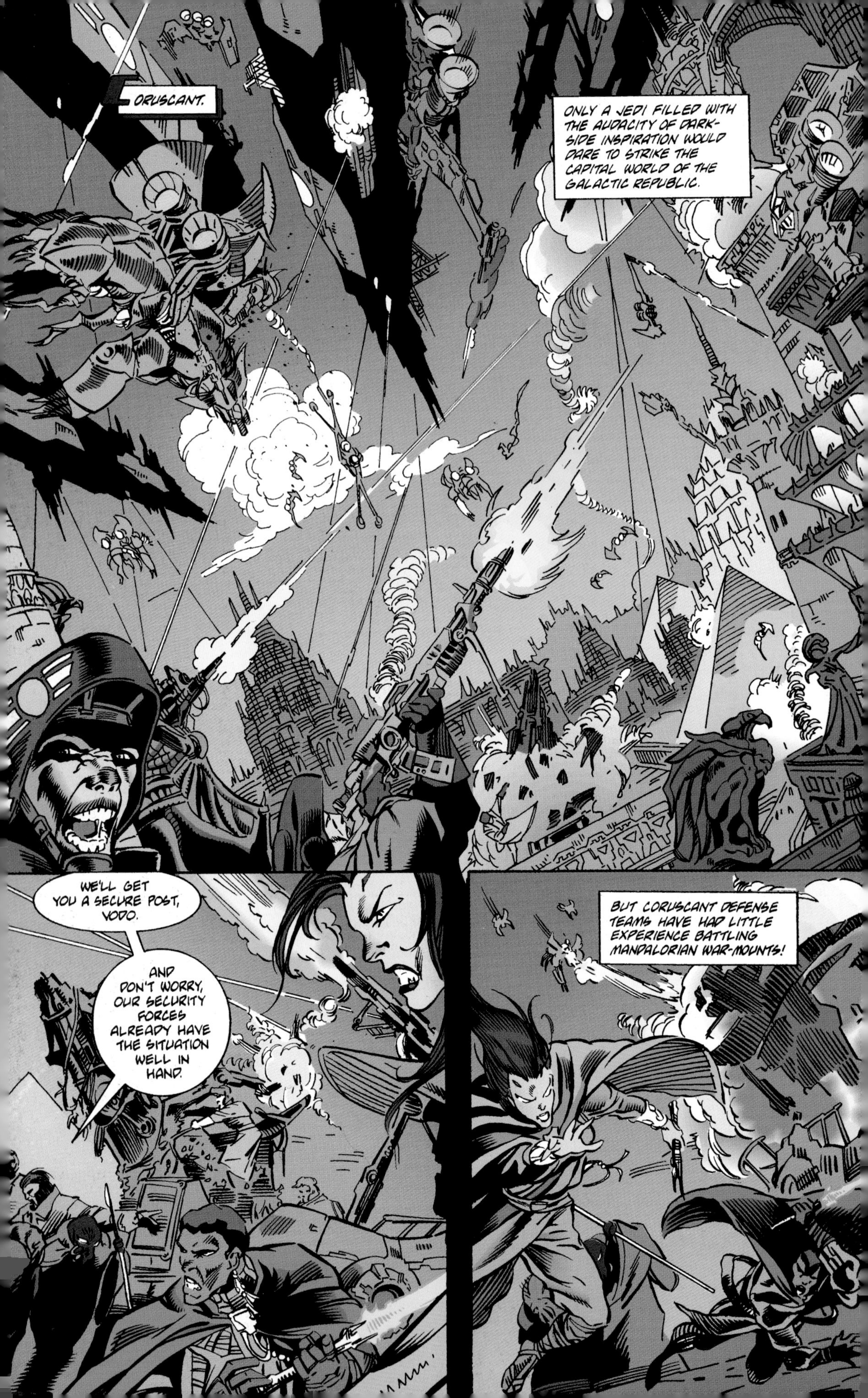
CORUSCANT.
ONLY A JEDI FILLED WITH THE AUDACITY OF DARK-SIDE INSPIRATION WOULD DARE TO STRIKE THE CAPITAL WORLD OF THE GALACTIC REPUBLIC.
WE'LL GET YOU A SECURE POST, VODO.
AND DON'T WORRY, OUR SECURITY FORCES ALREADY HAVE THE SITUATION WELL IN HAND.
BUT CORUSCANT DEFENSE TEAMS HAVE HAD LITTLE EXPERIENCE BATTLING MANDALORIAN WAR-MOUNTS!

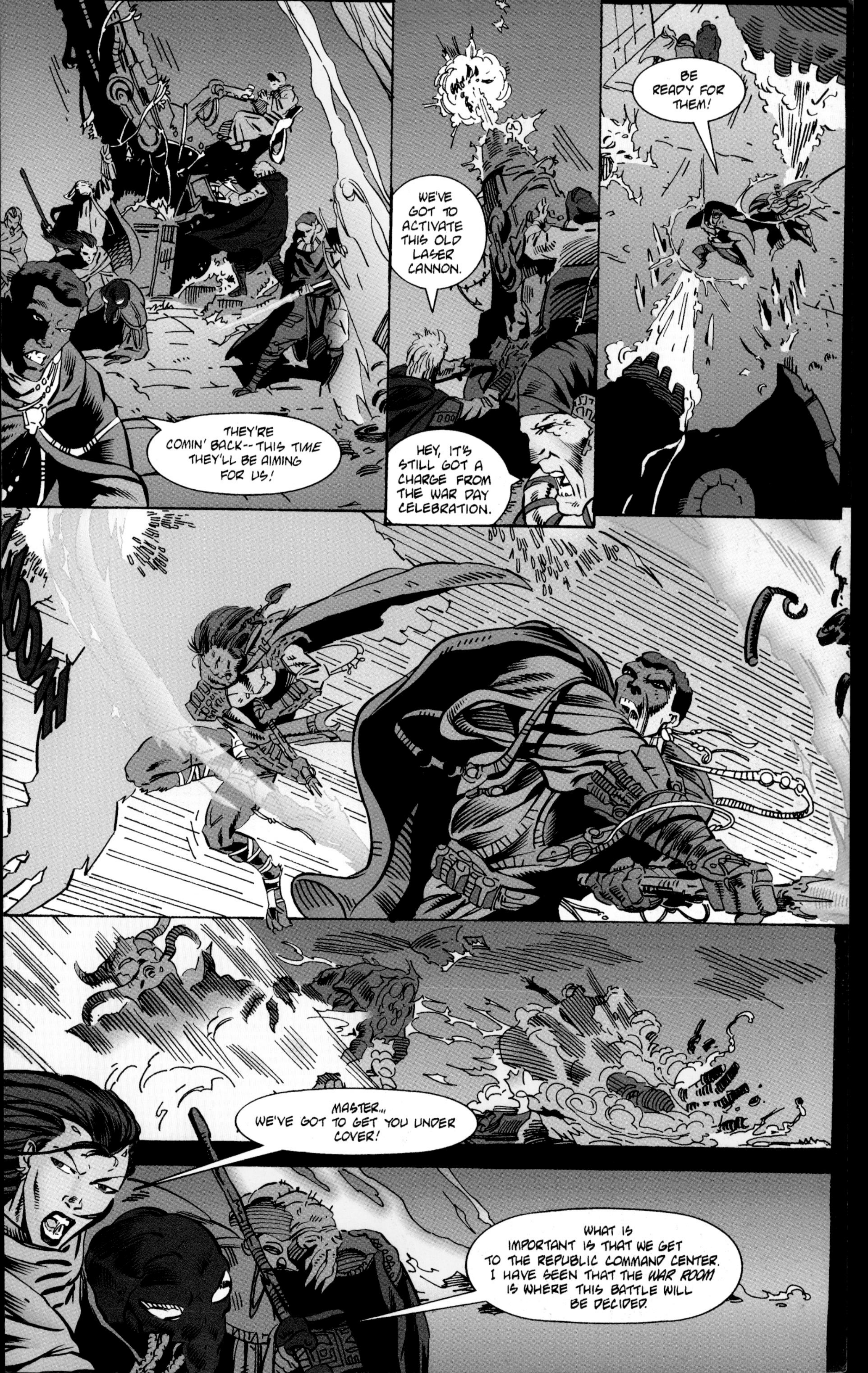
THEY'RE COMIN' BACK-- THIS TIME THEY'LL BE AIMING FOR US!
WE'VE GOT TO ACTIVATE THIS OLD LASER CANNON.
HEY, IT'S STILL GOT A CHARGE FROM THE WAR DAY CELEBRATION.
BE READY FOR THEM!
MASTER... WE'VE GOT TO GET YOU UNDER COVER!
WHAT IS IMPORTANT IS THAT WE GET TO THE REPUBLIC COMMAND CENTER. I HAVE SEEN THAT THE WAR ROOM IS WHERE THIS BATTLE WILL BE DECIDED.

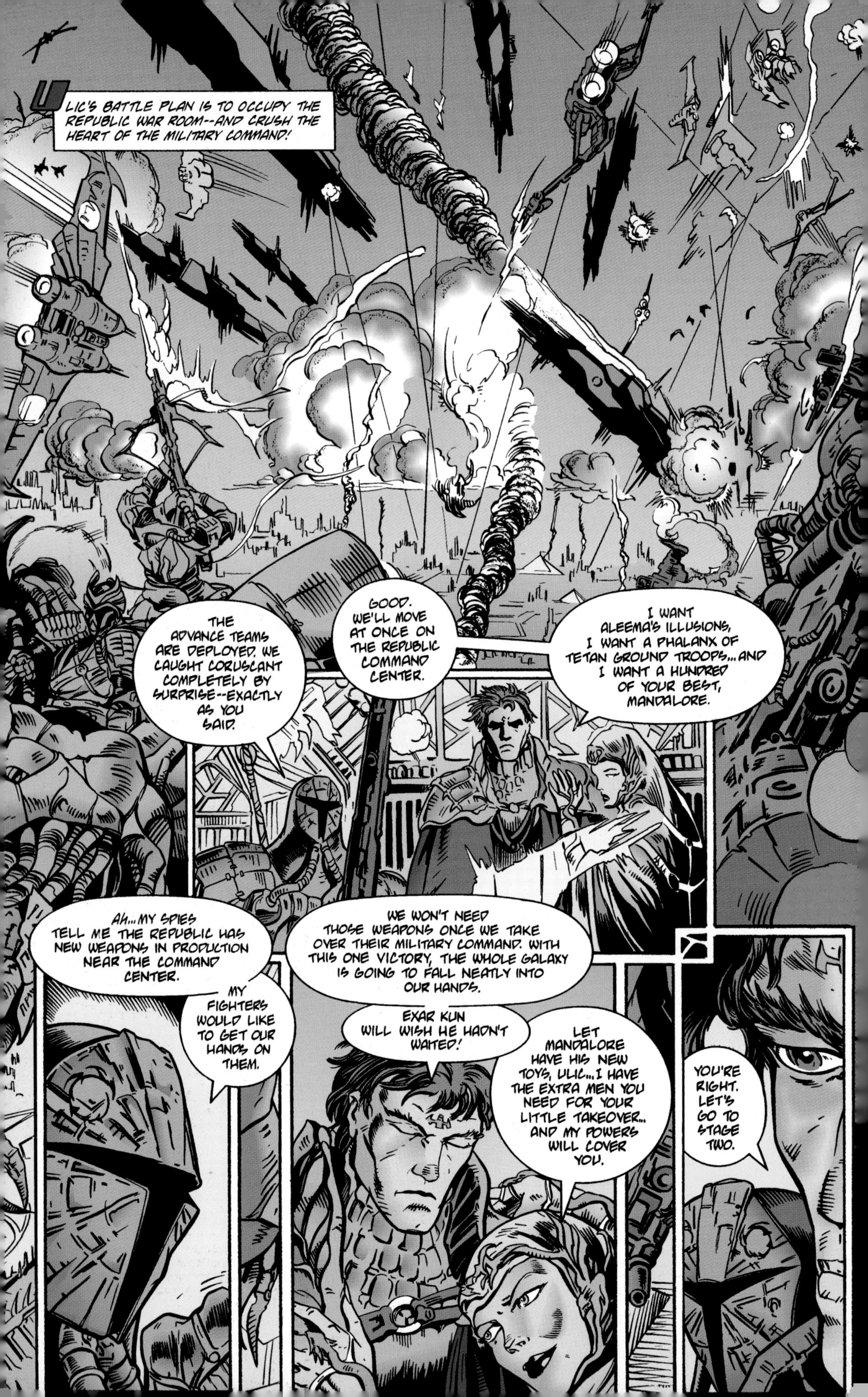

ULIC'S BATTLE PLAN IS TO OCCUPY THE REPUBLIC WAR ROOM--AND CRUSH THE HEART OF THE MILITARY COMMAND!
THE ADVANCE TEAMS ARE DEPLOYED. WE CAUGHT CORUSCANT COMPLETELY BY SURPRISE--EXACTLY AS YOU SAID.
GOOD. WE'LL MOVE AT ONCE ON THE REPUBLIC COMMAND CENTER.
I WANT ALEEMA'S ILLUSIONS, I WANT A PHALANX OF TETAN GROUND TROOPS...AND I WANT A HUNDRED OF YOUR BEST, MANDALORE.
AH...MY SPIES TELL ME THE REPUBLIC HAS NEW WEAPONS IN PRODUCTION NEAR THE COMMAND CENTER.
MY FIGHTERS WOULD LIKE TO GET OUR HANDS ON THEM.
WE WON'T NEED THOSE WEAPONS ONCE WE TAKE OVER THEIR MILITARY COMMAND. WITH THIS ONE VICTORY, THE WHOLE GALAXY IS GOING TO FALL NEATLY INTO OUR HANDS.
EXAR KUN WILL WISH HE HADN'T WAITED!
LET MANDALORE HAVE HIS NEW TOYS, ULIC...I HAVE THE EXTRA MEN YOU NEED FOR YOUR LITTLE TAKEOVER... AND MY POWERS WILL COVER YOU.
YOU'RE RIGHT. LET'S GO TO STAGE TWO.

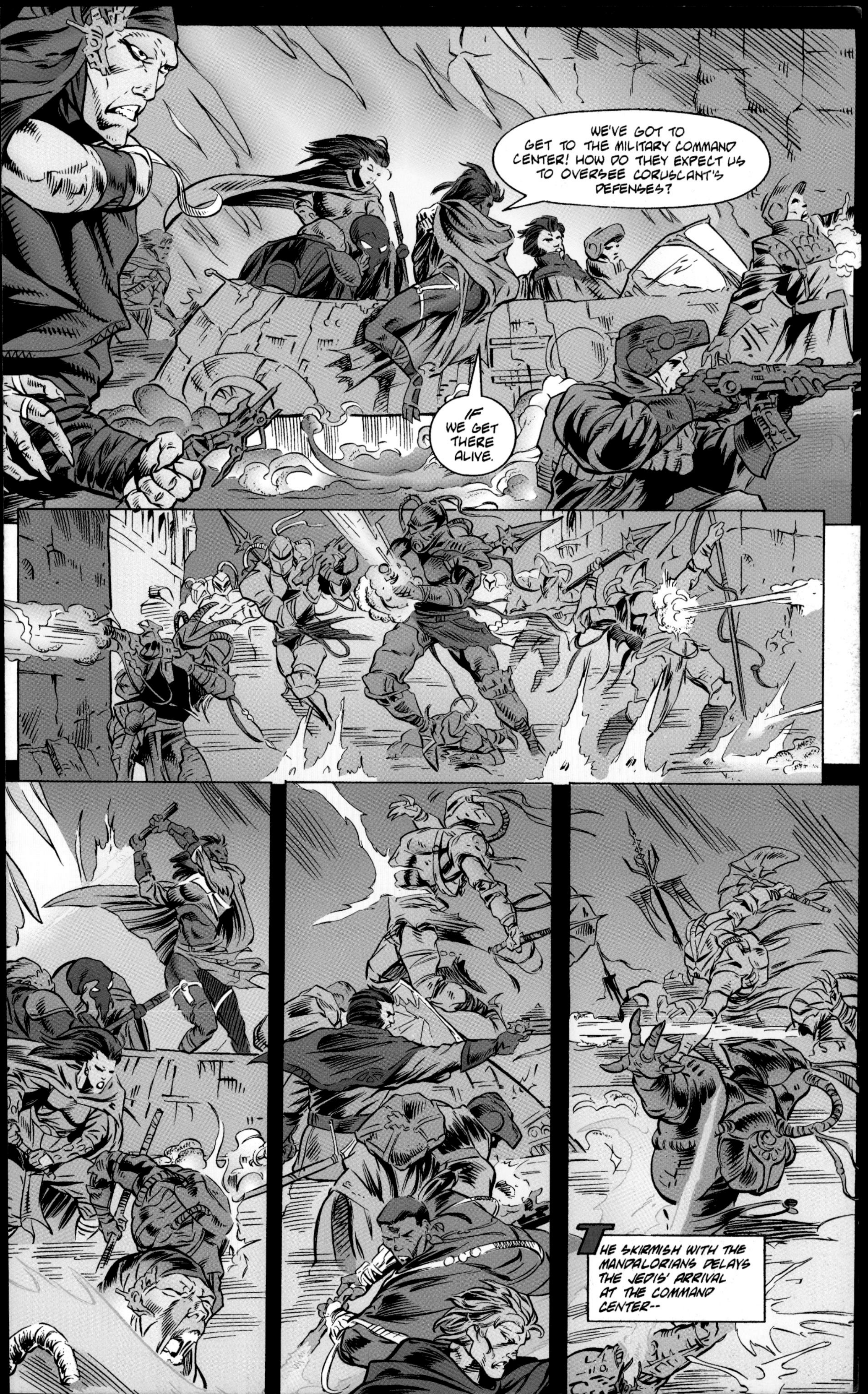
WE'VE GOT TO GET TO THE MILITARY COMMAND CENTER! HOW DO THEY EXPECT US TO OVERSEE CORUSCANT'S DEFENSES?
IF WE GET THERE ALIVE.
THE SKIRMISH WITH THE MANDALORIANS DELAYS THE JEDIS' ARRIVAL AT THE COMMAND CENTER--

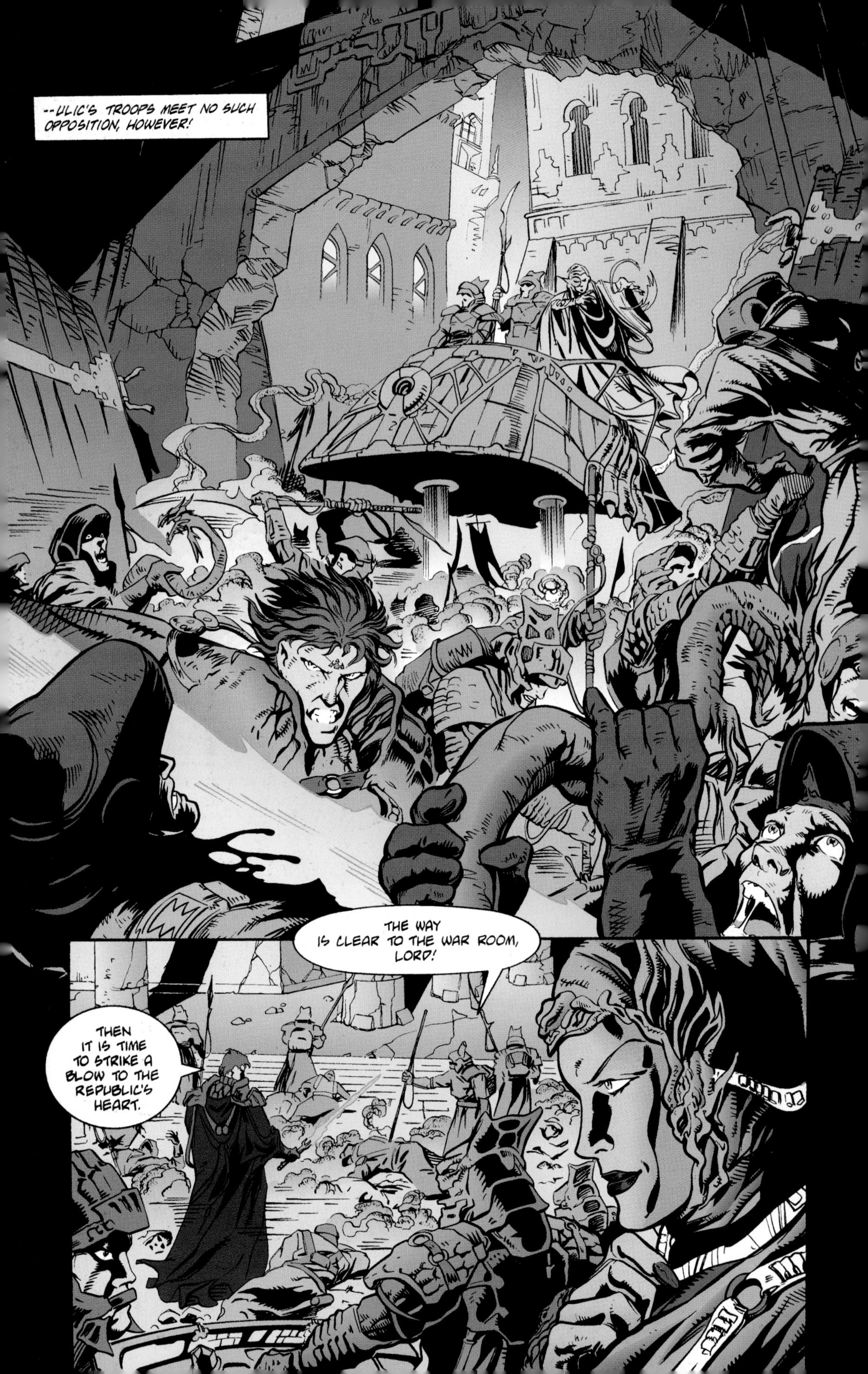
--ULIC'S TROOPS MEET NO SUCH OPPOSITION, HOWEVER!
THE WAY IS CLEAR TO THE WAR ROOM, LORD!
THEN IT IS TIME TO STRIKE A BLOW TO THE REPUBLIC'S HEART.

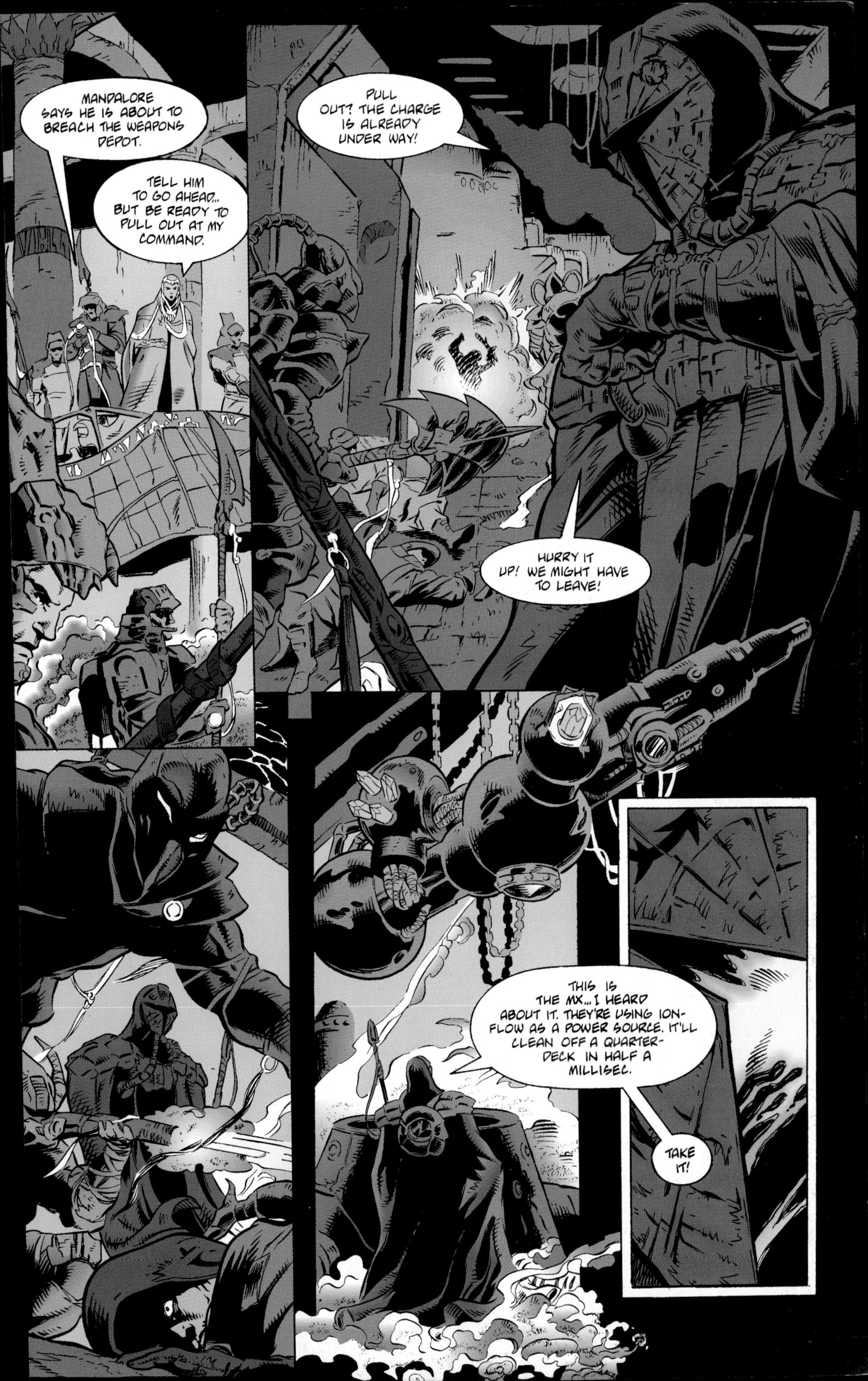
MANDALORE SAYS HE IS ABOUT TO BREACH THE WEAPONS DEPOT.
TELL HIM TO GO AHEAD... BUT BE READY TO PULL OUT AT MY COMMAND.
PULL OUT? THE CHARGE IS ALREADY UNDER WAY!
HURRY IT UP! WE MIGHT HAVE TO LEAVE!
THIS IS THE MX... I HEARD ABOUT IT. THEY'RE USING ION-FLOW AS A POWER SOURCE. IT'LL CLEAN OFF A QUARTER-DECK IN HALF A MILLISEC.
TAKE IT!

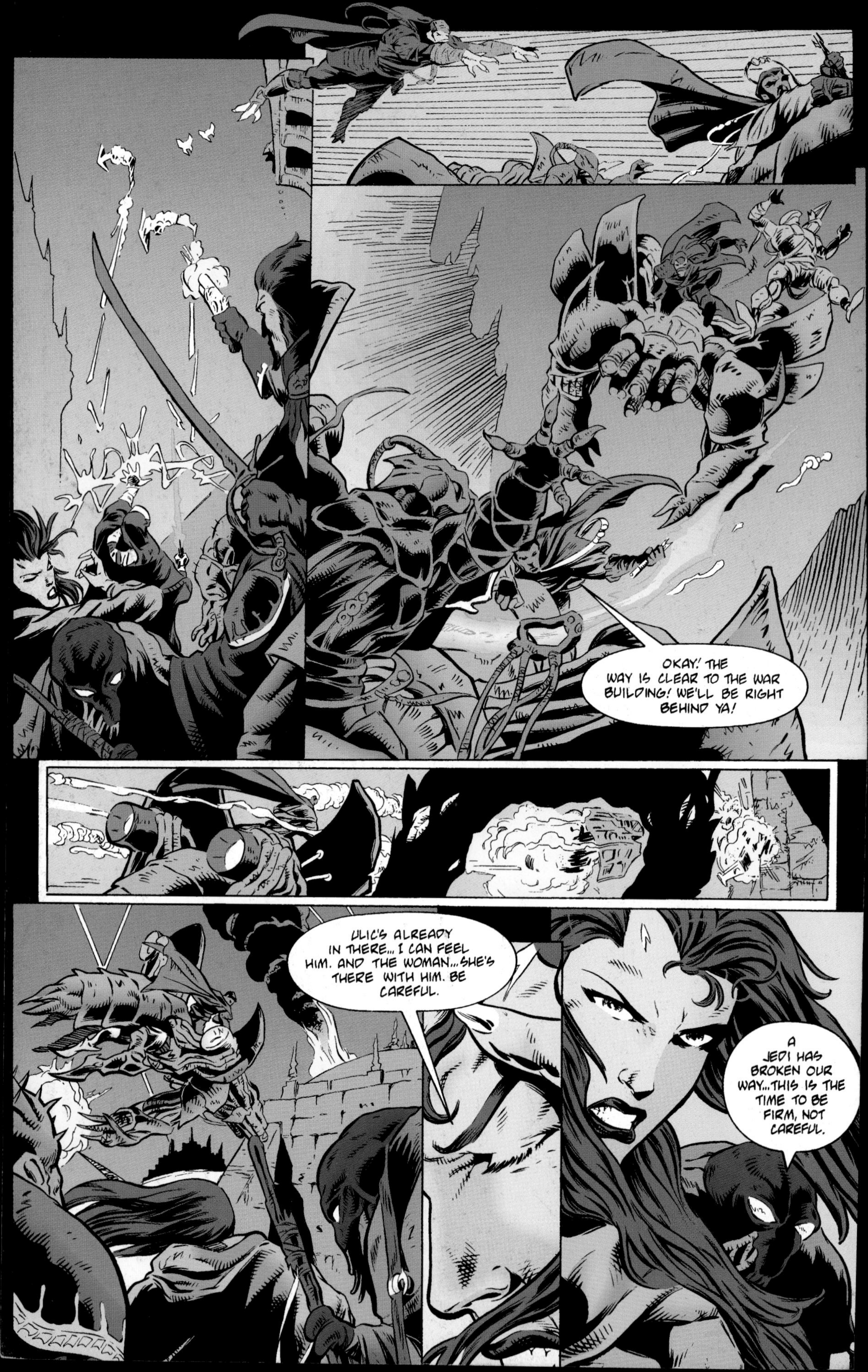
OKAY! THE WAY IS CLEAR TO THE WAR BUILDING! WE'LL BE RIGHT BEHIND YA!
ULIC'S ALREADY IN THERE... I CAN FEEL HIM. AND THE WOMAN... SHE'S THERE WITH HIM. BE CAREFUL.
A JEDI HAS BROKEN OUR WAY... THIS IS THE TIME TO BE FIRM, NOT CAREFUL.

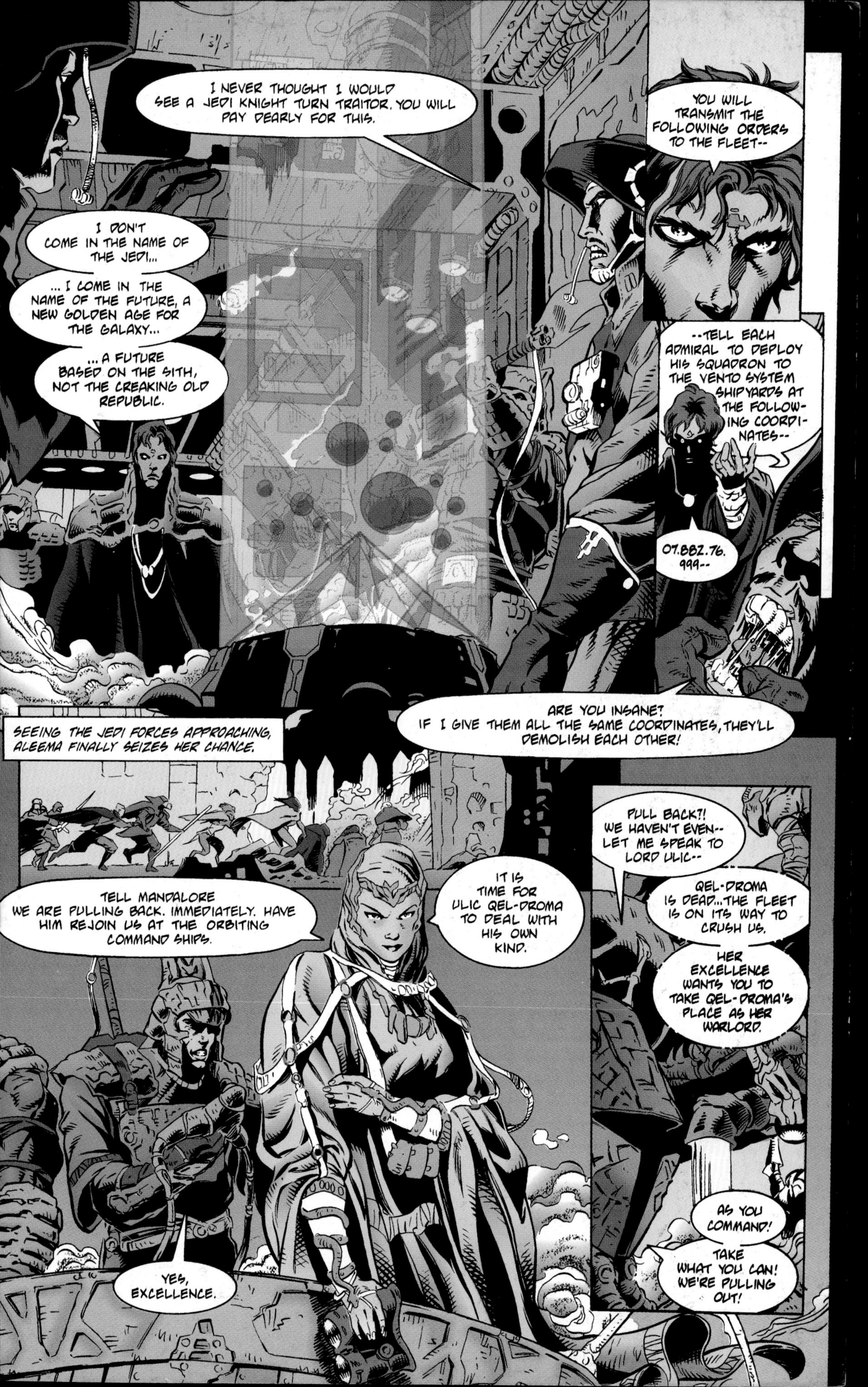
I NEVER THOUGHT I WOULD SEE A JEDI KNIGHT TURN TRAITOR. YOU WILL PAY DEARLY FOR THIS.
I DON'T COME IN THE NAME OF THE JEDI...
... I COME IN THE NAME OF THE FUTURE, A NEW GOLDEN AGE FOR THE GALAXY...
... A FUTURE BASED ON THE SITH, NOT THE CREAKING OLD REPUBLIC.
YOU WILL TRANSMIT THE FOLLOWING ORDERS TO THE FLEET--
--TELL EACH ADMIRAL TO DEPLOY HIS SQUADRON TO THE VENTO SYSTEM SHIPYARDS AT THE FOLLOWING COORDINATES--
07.882.76.999--
ARE YOU INSANE? IF I GIVE THEM ALL THE SAME COORDINATES, THEY'LL DEMOLISH EACH OTHER!
SEEING THE JEDI FORCES APPROACHING, ALEEMA FINALLY SEIZES HER CHANCE.
TELL MANDALORE WE ARE PULLING BACK. IMMEDIATELY. HAVE HIM REJOIN US AT THE ORBITING COMMAND SHIPS.
IT IS TIME FOR ULIC QEL-DROMA TO DEAL WITH HIS OWN KIND.
YES, EXCELLENCE.
PULL BACK?! WE HAVEN'T EVEN-- LET ME SPEAK TO LORD ULIC--
QEL-DROMA IS DEAD...THE FLEET IS ON ITS WAY TO CRUSH US.
HER EXCELLENCE WANTS YOU TO TAKE QEL-DROMA'S PLACE AS HER WARLORD.
AS YOU COMMAND!
TAKE WHAT YOU CAN! WE'RE PULLING OUT!

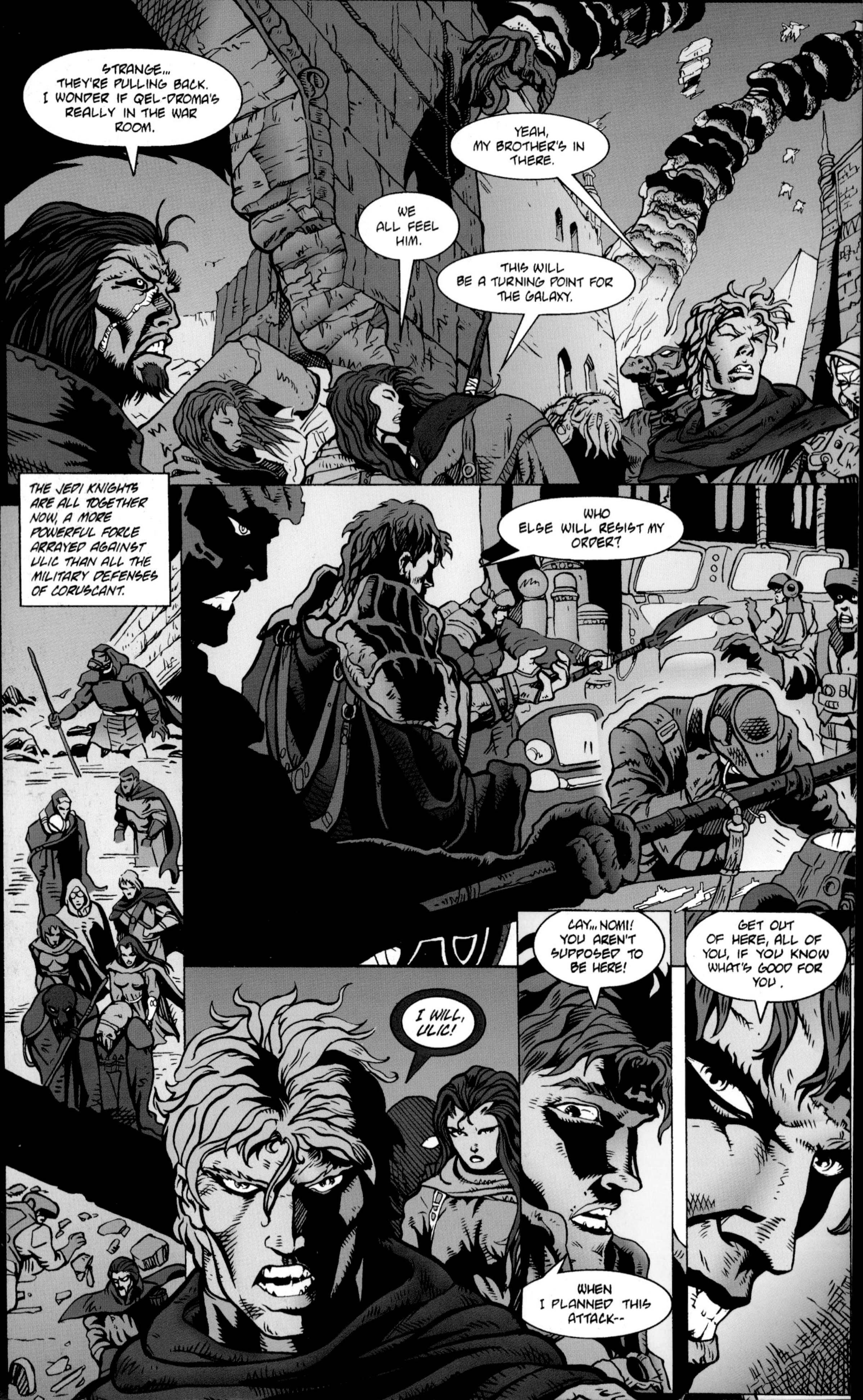
STRANGE... THEY'RE PULLING BACK. I WONDER IF QEL-DROMA'S REALLY IN THE WAR ROOM.
YEAH, MY BROTHER'S IN THERE.
WE ALL FEEL HIM.
THIS WILL BE A TURNING POINT FOR THE GALAXY.
THE JEDI KNIGHTS ARE ALL TOGETHER NOW, A MORE POWERFUL FORCE ARRAYED AGAINST ULIC THAN ALL THE MILITARY DEFENSES OF CORUSCANT.
WHO ELSE WILL RESIST MY ORDER?
I WILL, ULIC!
CAY... NOMI! YOU AREN'T SUPPOSED TO BE HERE!
WHEN I PLANNED THIS ATTACK--
GET OUT OF HERE, ALL OF YOU, IF YOU KNOW WHAT'S GOOD FOR YOU.

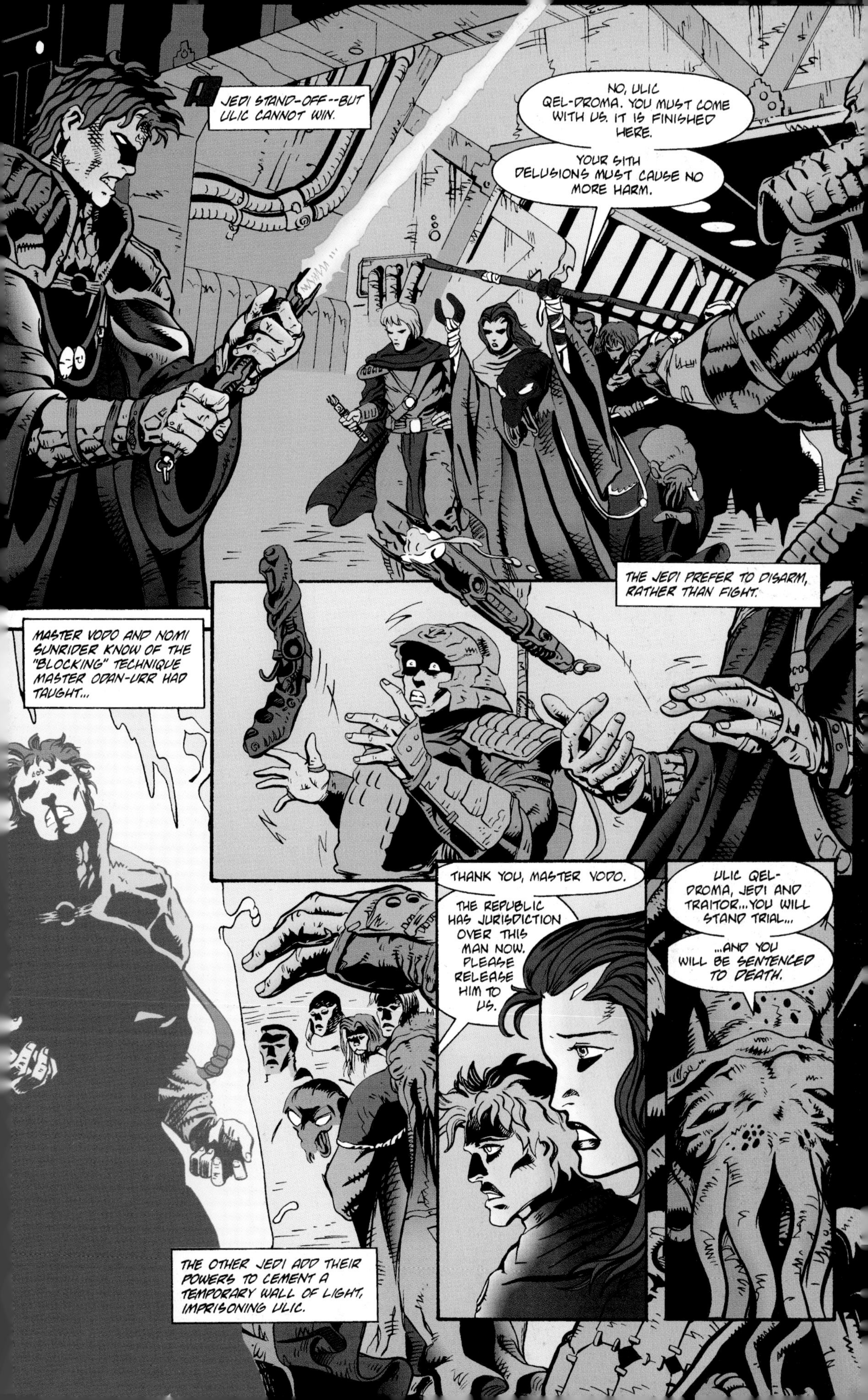

JEDI STAND-OFF--BUT ULIC CANNOT WIN.
NO, ULIC QEL-DROMA. YOU MUST COME WITH US. IT IS FINISHED HERE.
YOUR SITH DELUSIONS MUST CAUSE NO MORE HARM.
THE JEDI PREFER TO DISARM, RATHER THAN FIGHT.
MASTER VODO AND NOMI SUNRIDER KNOW OF THE "BLOCKING" TECHNIQUE MASTER ODAN-URR HAD TAUGHT...
THE OTHER JEDI ADD THEIR POWERS TO CEMENT A TEMPORARY WALL OF LIGHT, IMPRISONING ULIC.
THANK YOU, MASTER VODO.
THE REPUBLIC HAS JURISDICTION OVER THIS MAN NOW. PLEASE RELEASE HIM TO US.
ULIC QEL-DROMA, JEDI AND TRAITOR...YOU WILL STAND TRIAL...
...AND YOU WILL BE SENTENCED TO DEATH.

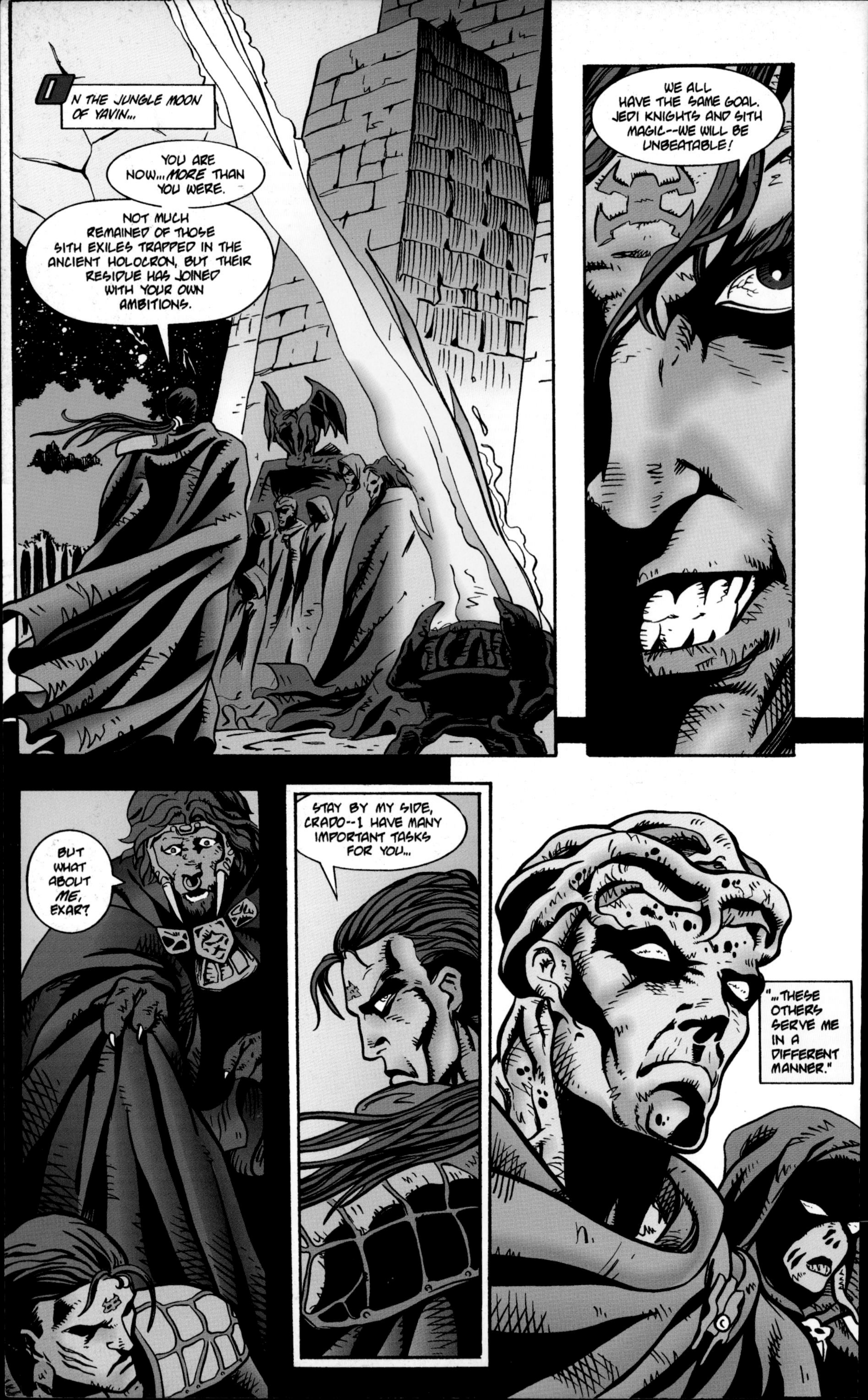
ON THE JUNGLE MOON OF YAVIN...
YOU ARE NOW... MORE THAN YOU WERE.
NOT MUCH REMAINED OF THOSE SITH EXILES TRAPPED IN THE ANCIENT HOLOCRON, BUT THEIR RESIDUE HAS JOINED WITH YOUR OWN AMBITIONS.
WE ALL HAVE THE SAME GOAL. JEDI KNIGHTS AND SITH MAGIC--WE WILL BE UNBEATABLE!
BUT WHAT ABOUT ME, EXAR?
STAY BY MY SIDE, CRADO--I HAVE MANY IMPORTANT TASKS FOR YOU...
"...THESE OTHERS SERVE ME IN A DIFFERENT MANNER."

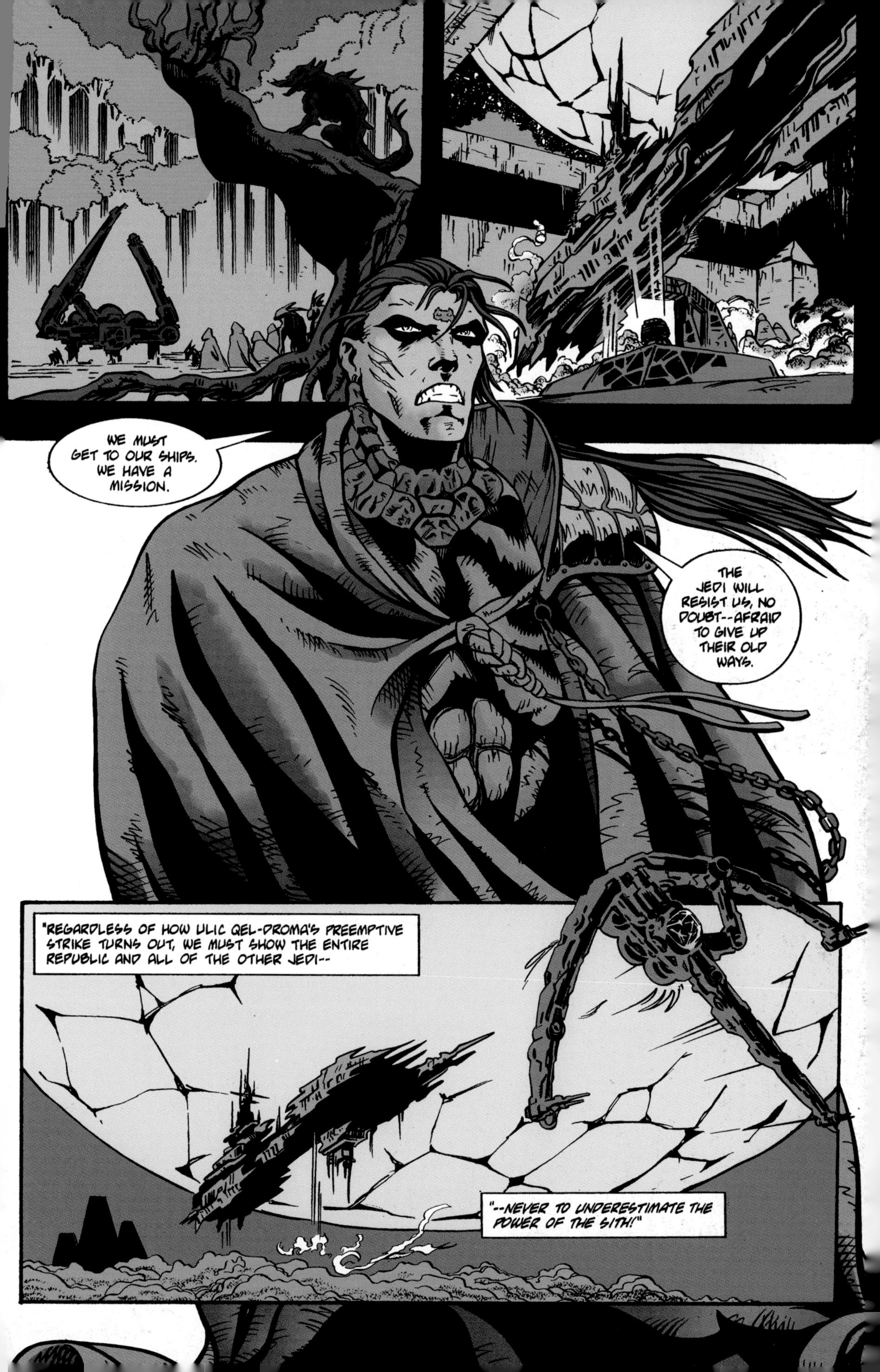
WE MUST GET TO OUR SHIPS. WE HAVE A MISSION.
THE JEDI WILL RESIST US, NO DOUBT--AFRAID TO GIVE UP THEIR OLD WAYS.
"REGARDLESS OF HOW ULIC QEL-DROMA'S PREEMPTIVE STRIKE TURNS OUT, WE MUST SHOW THE ENTIRE REPUBLIC AND ALL OF THE OTHER JEDI--
"--NEVER TO UNDERESTIMATE THE POWER OF THE SITH!"

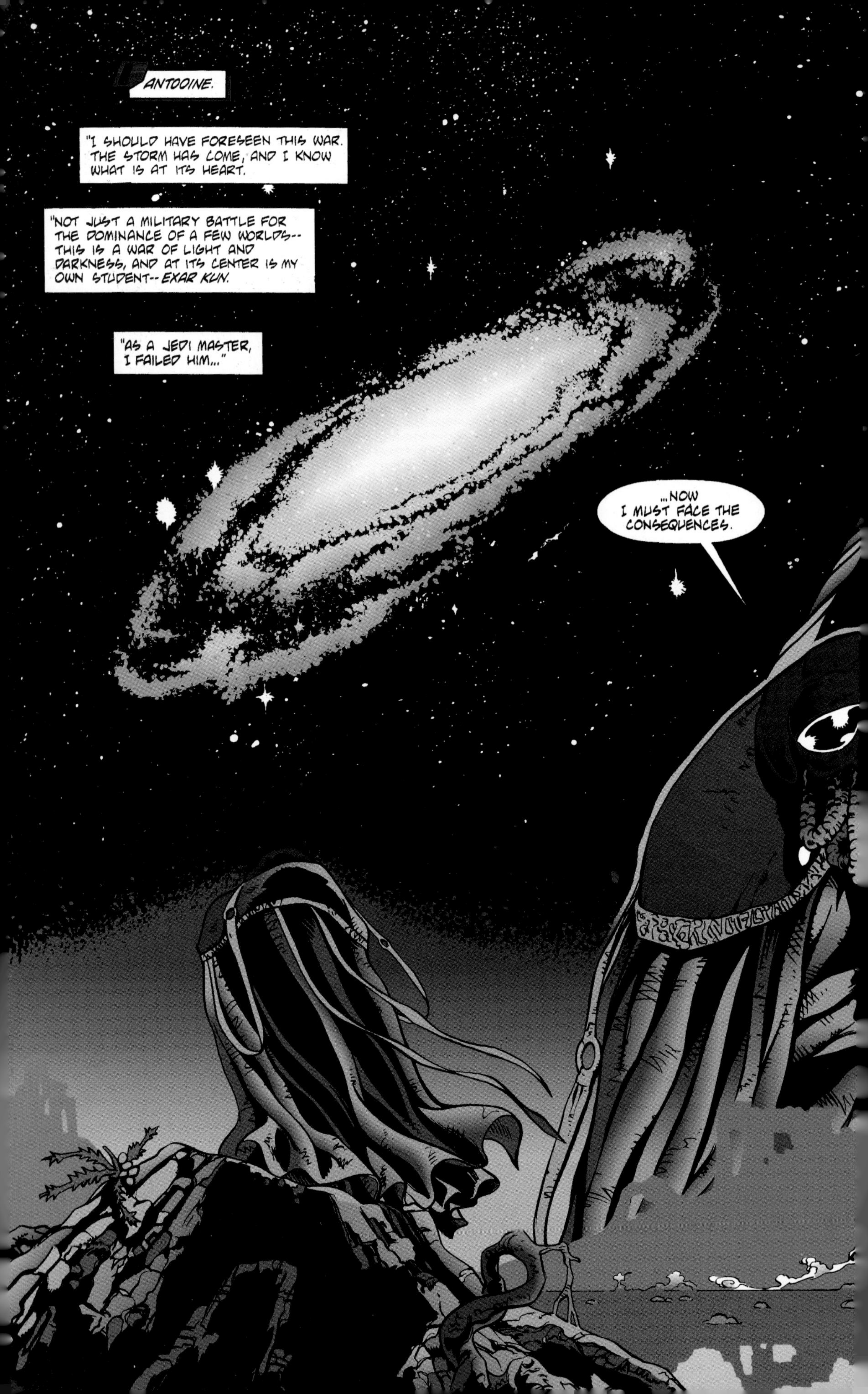
ANTOOINE.
"I SHOULD HAVE FORESEEN THIS WAR. THE STORM HAS COME, AND I KNOW WHAT IS AT ITS HEART.
"NOT JUST A MILITARY BATTLE FOR THE DOMINANCE OF A FEW WORLDS-- THIS IS A WAR OF LIGHT AND DARKNESS, AND AT ITS CENTER IS MY OWN STUDENT-- EXAR KUN.
"AS A JEDI MASTER, I FAILED HIM..."
...NOW I MUST FACE THE CONSEQUENCES.

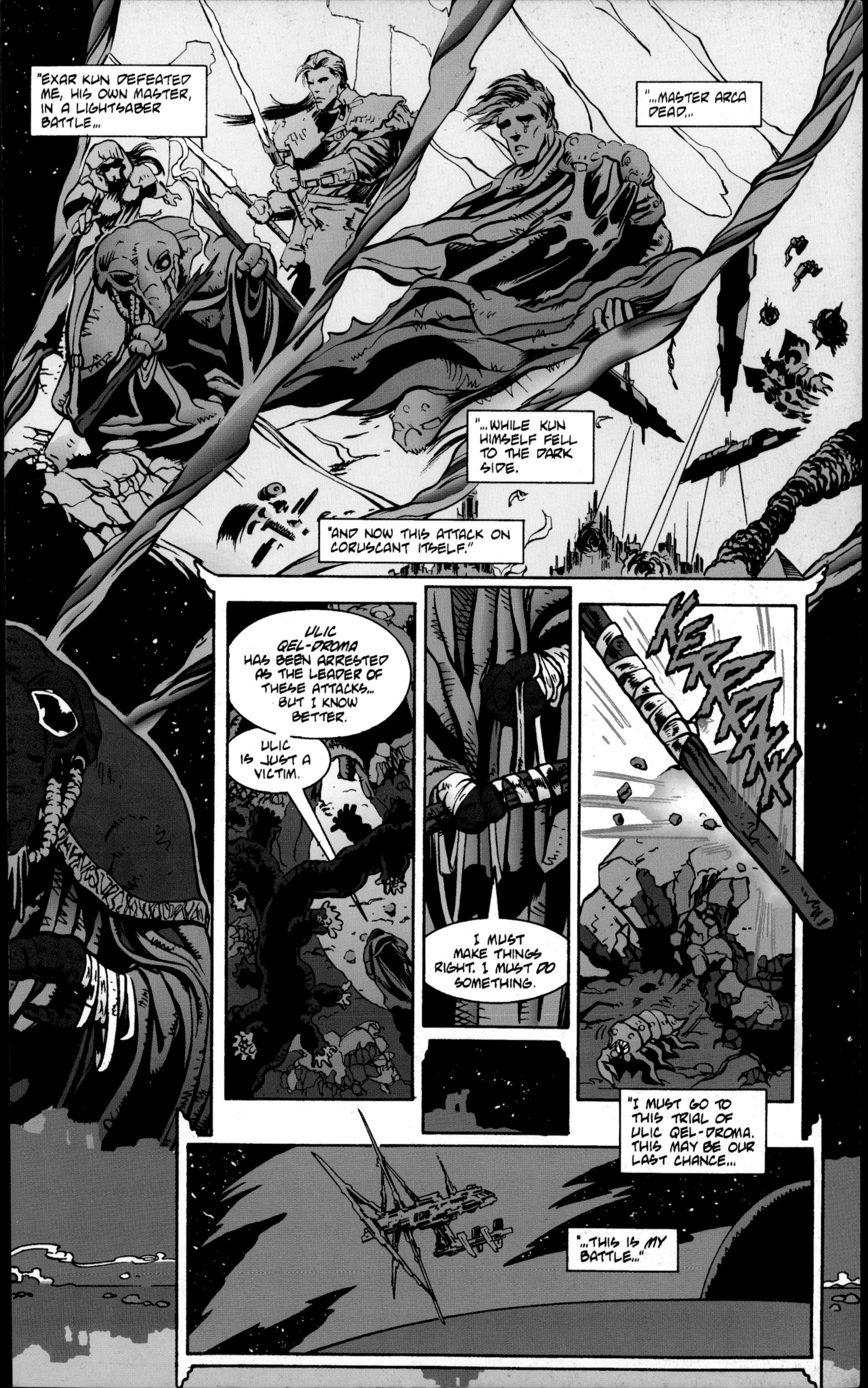
"EXAR KUN DEFEATED ME, HIS OWN MASTER, IN A LIGHTSABER BATTLE...
"...MASTER ARCA DEAD...
"...WHILE KUN HIMSELF FELL TO THE DARK SIDE.
"AND NOW THIS ATTACK ON CORUSCANT ITSELF."
ULIC QEL-DROMA HAS BEEN ARRESTED AS THE LEADER OF THESE ATTACKS... BUT I KNOW BETTER.
ULIC IS JUST A VICTIM.
I MUST MAKE THINGS RIGHT. I MUST DO SOMETHING.
KEKRAK
"I MUST GO TO THIS TRIAL OF ULIC QEL-DROMA. THIS MAY BE OUR LAST CHANCE...
"...THIS IS MY BATTLE..."

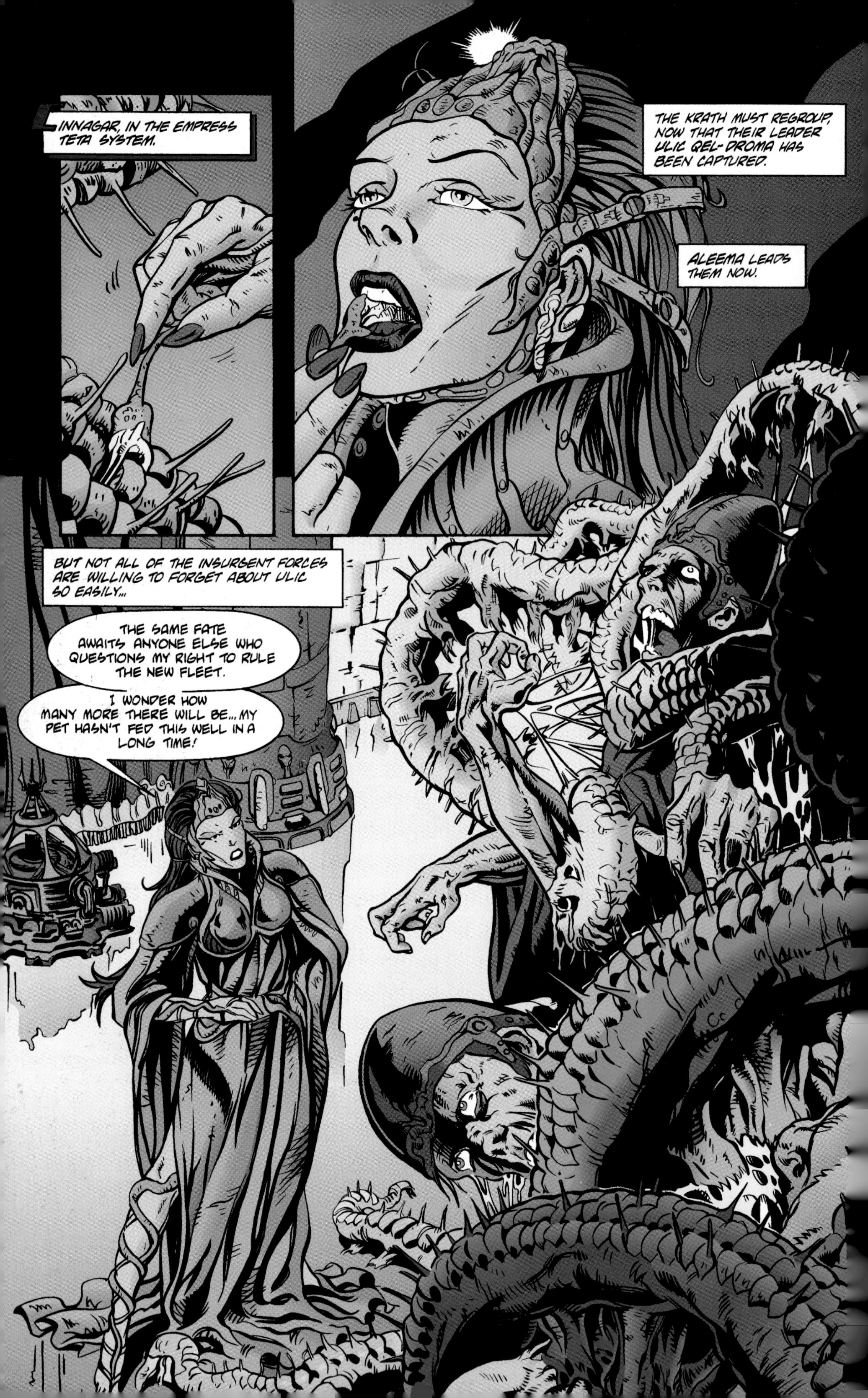

CINNAGAR, IN THE EMPRESS TETA SYSTEM.
THE KRATH MUST REGROUP, NOW THAT THEIR LEADER ULIC QEL-DROMA HAS BEEN CAPTURED.
ALEEMA LEADS THEM NOW.
BUT NOT ALL OF THE INSURGENT FORCES ARE WILLING TO FORGET ABOUT ULIC SO EASILY...
THE SAME FATE AWAITS ANYONE ELSE WHO QUESTIONS MY RIGHT TO RULE THE NEW FLEET.
I WONDER HOW MANY MORE THERE WILL BE... MY PET HASN'T FED THIS WELL IN A LONG TIME!

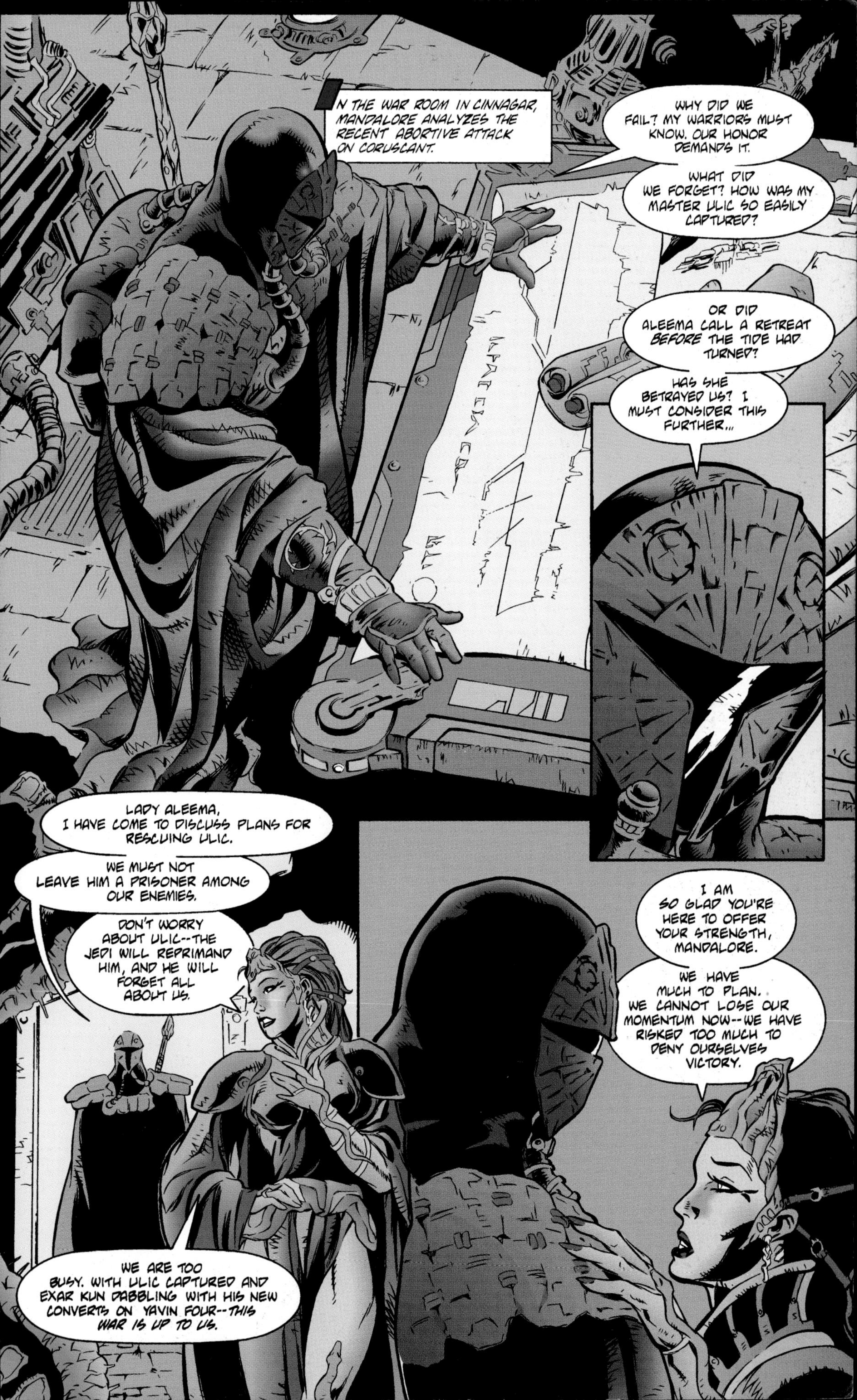
N THE WAR ROOM IN CINNAGAR, MANDALORE ANALYZES THE RECENT ABORTIVE ATTACK ON CORUSCANT.
WHY DID WE FAIL? MY WARRIORS MUST KNOW. OUR HONOR DEMANDS IT.
WHAT DID WE FORGET? HOW WAS MY MASTER ULIC SO EASILY CAPTURED?
OR DID ALEEMA CALL A RETREAT *BEFORE* THE TIDE HAD TURNED?
HAS SHE BETRAYED US? I MUST CONSIDER THIS FURTHER...
LADY ALEEMA, I HAVE COME TO DISCUSS PLANS FOR RESCUING ULIC.
WE MUST NOT LEAVE HIM A PRISONER AMONG OUR ENEMIES.
DON'T WORRY ABOUT ULIC--THE JEDI WILL REPRIMAND HIM, AND HE WILL FORGET ALL ABOUT US.
I AM SO GLAD YOU'RE HERE TO OFFER YOUR STRENGTH, MANDALORE.
WE HAVE MUCH TO PLAN. WE CANNOT LOSE OUR MOMENTUM NOW--WE HAVE RISKED TOO MUCH TO DENY OURSELVES VICTORY.
WE ARE TOO BUSY. WITH ULIC CAPTURED AND EXAR KUN DABBLING WITH HIS NEW CONVERTS ON YAVIN FOUR--*THIS WAR IS UP TO US.*

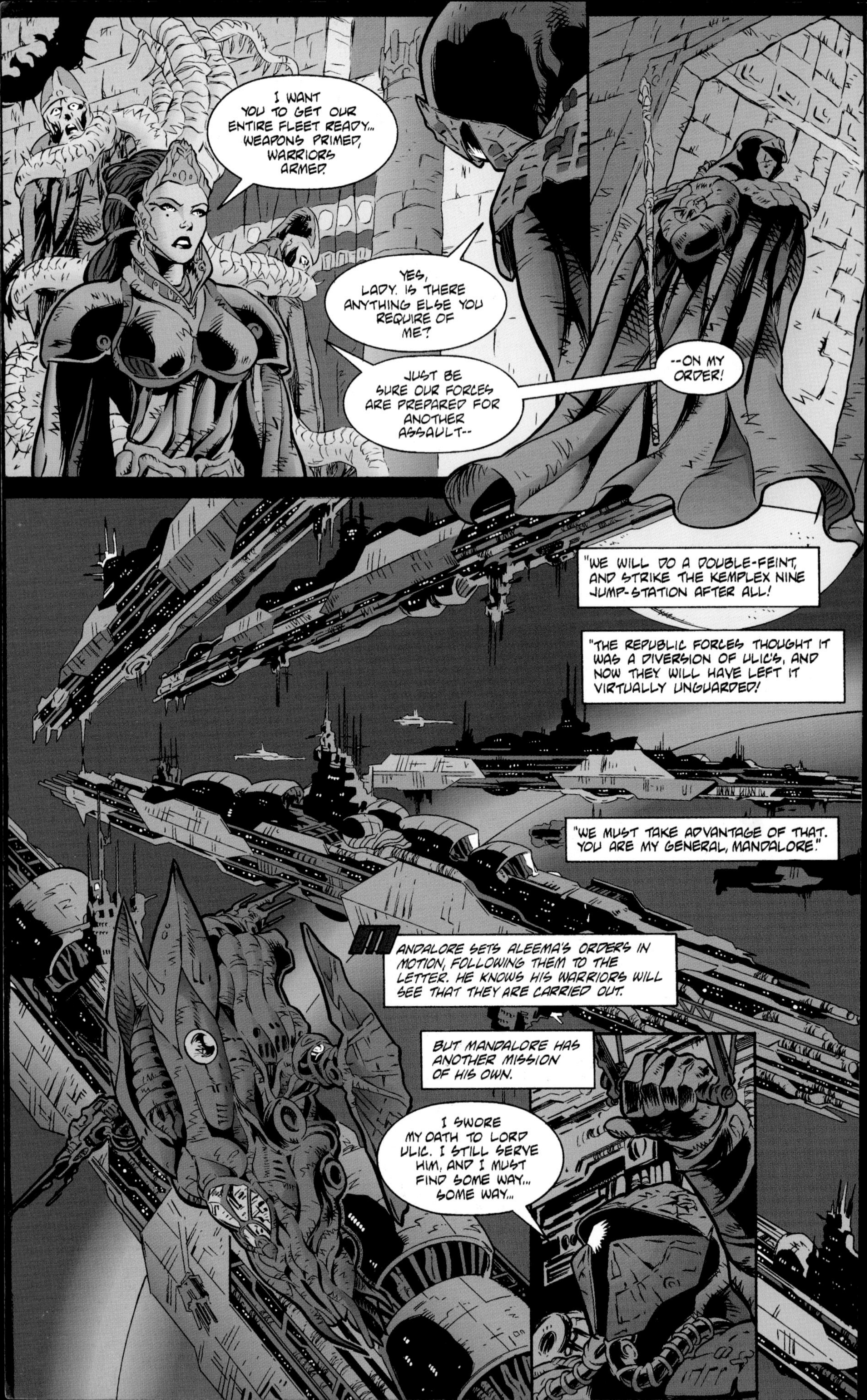
I WANT YOU TO GET OUR ENTIRE FLEET READY... WEAPONS PRIMED, WARRIORS ARMED.
YES, LADY. IS THERE ANYTHING ELSE YOU REQUIRE OF ME?
JUST BE SURE OUR FORCES ARE PREPARED FOR ANOTHER ASSAULT--
--ON MY ORDER!
"WE WILL DO A DOUBLE-FEINT, AND STRIKE THE KEMPLEX NINE JUMP-STATION AFTER ALL!
"THE REPUBLIC FORCES THOUGHT IT WAS A DIVERSION OF ULIC'S, AND NOW THEY WILL HAVE LEFT IT VIRTUALLY UNGUARDED!
"WE MUST TAKE ADVANTAGE OF THAT. YOU ARE MY GENERAL, MANDALORE."
MANDALORE SETS ALEEMA'S ORDERS IN MOTION, FOLLOWING THEM TO THE LETTER. HE KNOWS HIS WARRIORS WILL SEE THAT THEY ARE CARRIED OUT.
BUT MANDALORE HAS ANOTHER MISSION OF HIS OWN.
I SWORE MY OATH TO LORD ULIC. I STILL SERVE HIM, AND I MUST FIND SOME WAY... SOME WAY...

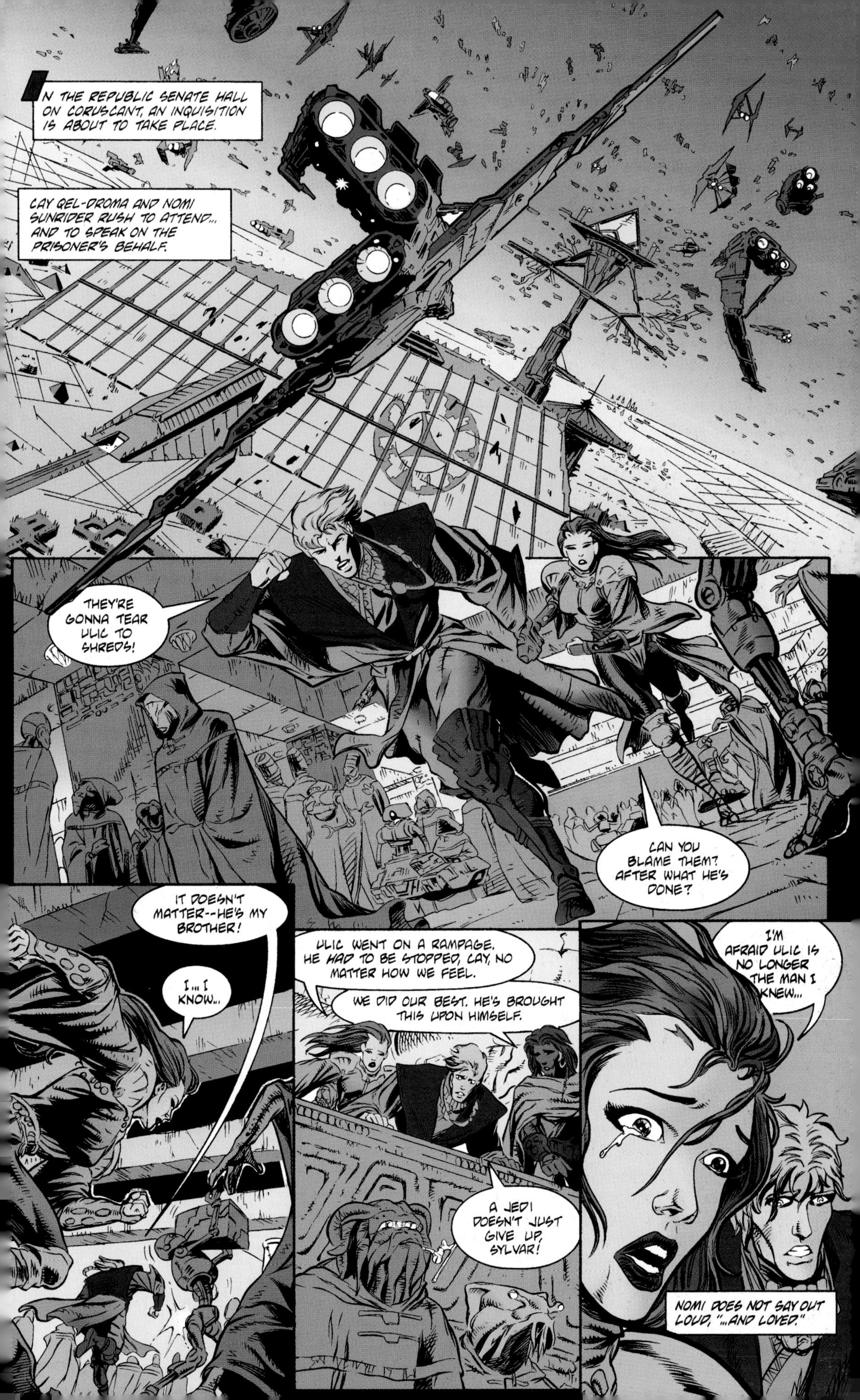
IN THE REPUBLIC SENATE HALL ON CORUSCANT, AN INQUISITION IS ABOUT TO TAKE PLACE.
CAY QEL-DROMA AND NOMI SUNRIDER RUSH TO ATTEND... AND TO SPEAK ON THE PRISONER'S BEHALF.
THEY'RE GONNA TEAR ULIC TO SHREDS!
CAN YOU BLAME THEM? AFTER WHAT HE'S DONE?
IT DOESN'T MATTER--HE'S MY BROTHER!
I... I KNOW...
ULIC WENT ON A RAMPAGE. HE HAD TO BE STOPPED, CAY, NO MATTER HOW WE FEEL.
WE DID OUR BEST. HE'S BROUGHT THIS UPON HIMSELF.
A JEDI DOESN'T JUST GIVE UP, SYLVAR!
I'M AFRAID ULIC IS NO LONGER THE MAN I KNEW...
NOMI DOES NOT SAY OUT LOUD, "...AND LOVED."

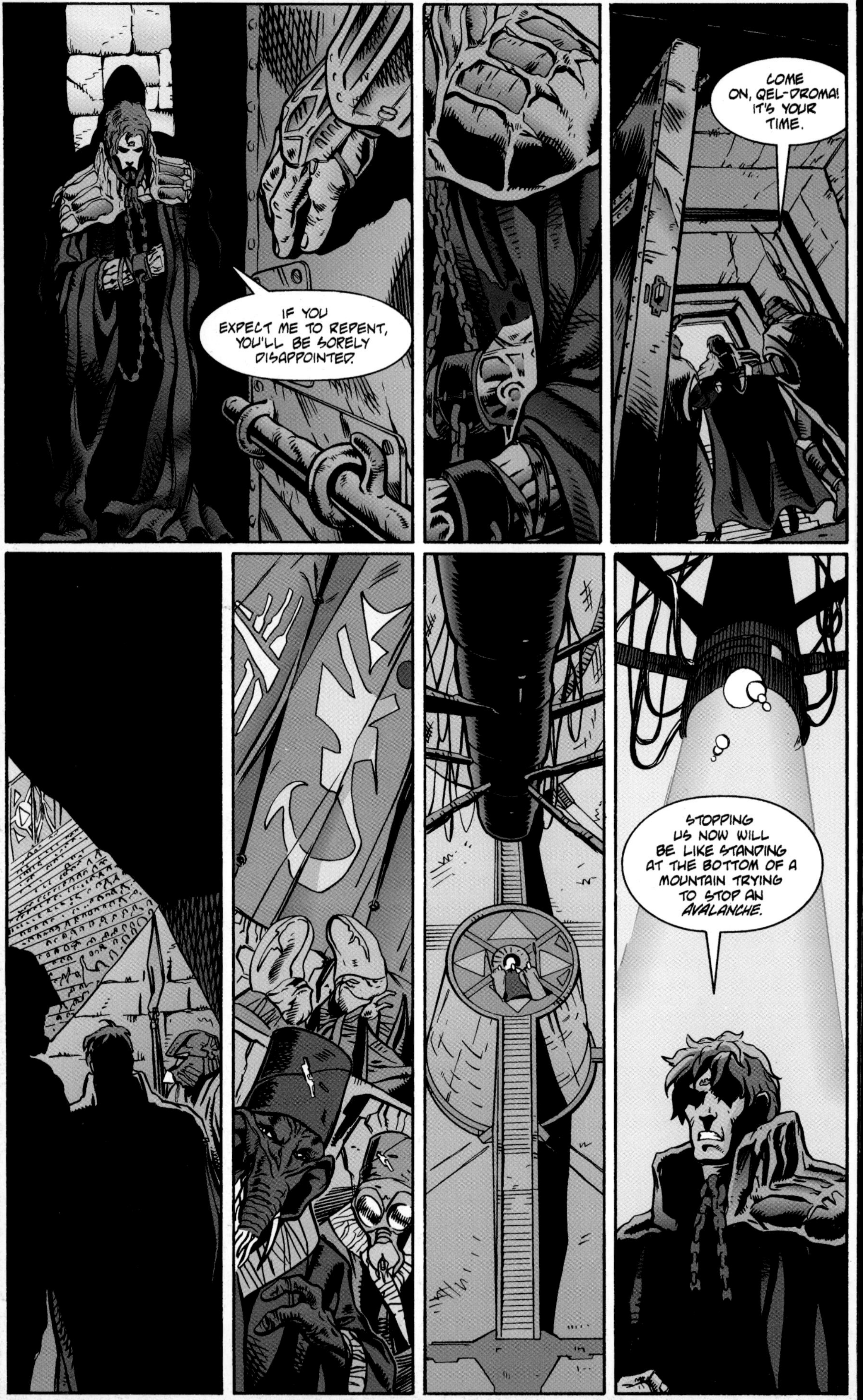
IF YOU EXPECT ME TO REPENT, YOU'LL BE SORELY DISAPPOINTED.
COME ON, QEL-DROMA! IT'S YOUR TIME.
STOPPING US NOW WILL BE LIKE STANDING AT THE BOTTOM OF A MOUNTAIN TRYING TO STOP AN *AVALANCHE*.

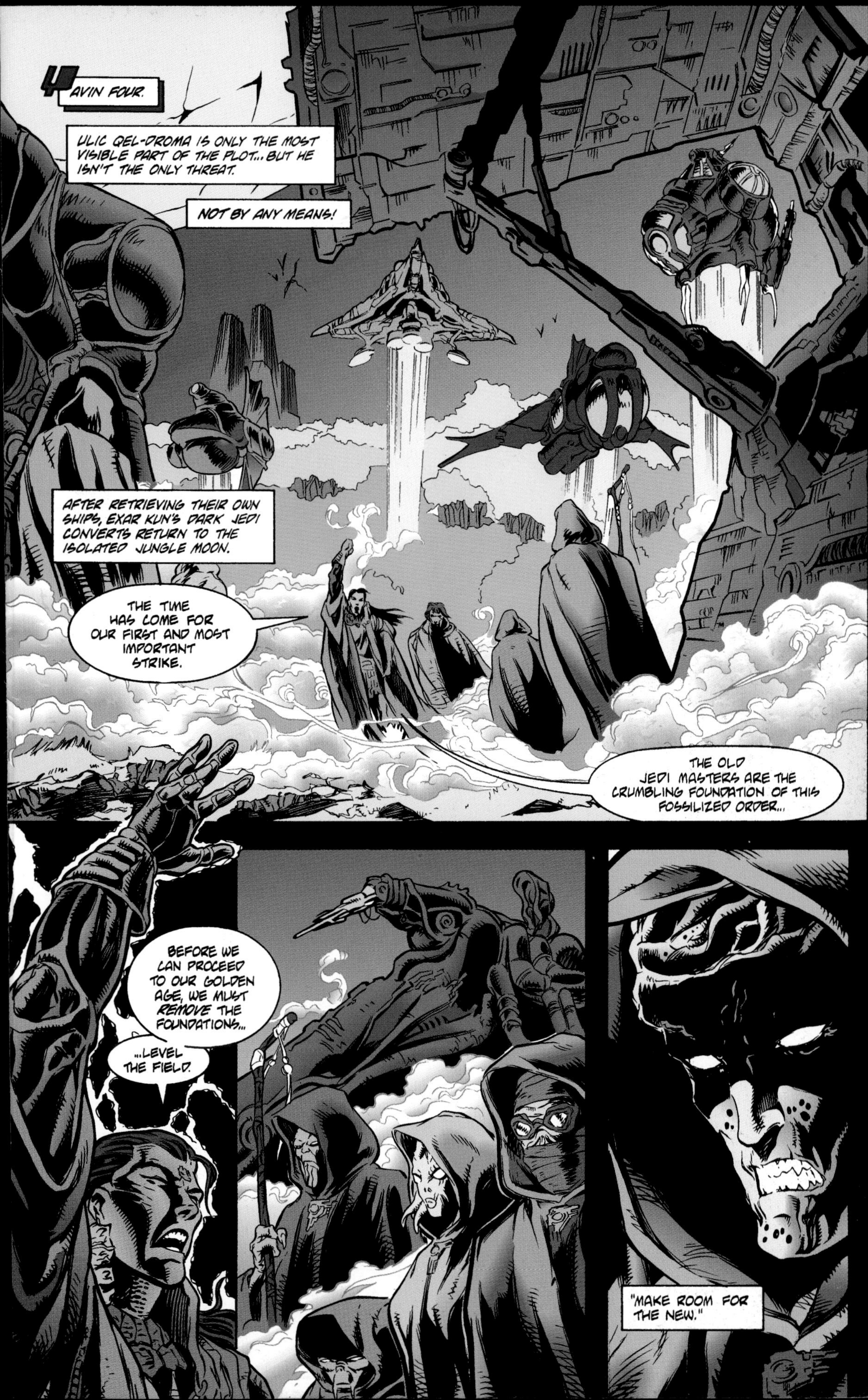
YAVIN FOUR.
ULIC QEL-DROMA IS ONLY THE MOST VISIBLE PART OF THE PLOT... BUT HE ISN'T THE ONLY THREAT.
NOT BY ANY MEANS!
AFTER RETRIEVING THEIR OWN SHIPS, EXAR KUN'S DARK JEDI CONVERTS RETURN TO THE ISOLATED JUNGLE MOON.
THE TIME HAS COME FOR OUR FIRST AND MOST IMPORTANT STRIKE.
THE OLD JEDI MASTERS ARE THE CRUMBLING FOUNDATION OF THIS FOSSILIZED ORDER...
BEFORE WE CAN PROCEED TO OUR GOLDEN AGE, WE MUST REMOVE THE FOUNDATIONS...
...LEVEL THE FIELD.
"MAKE ROOM FOR THE NEW."

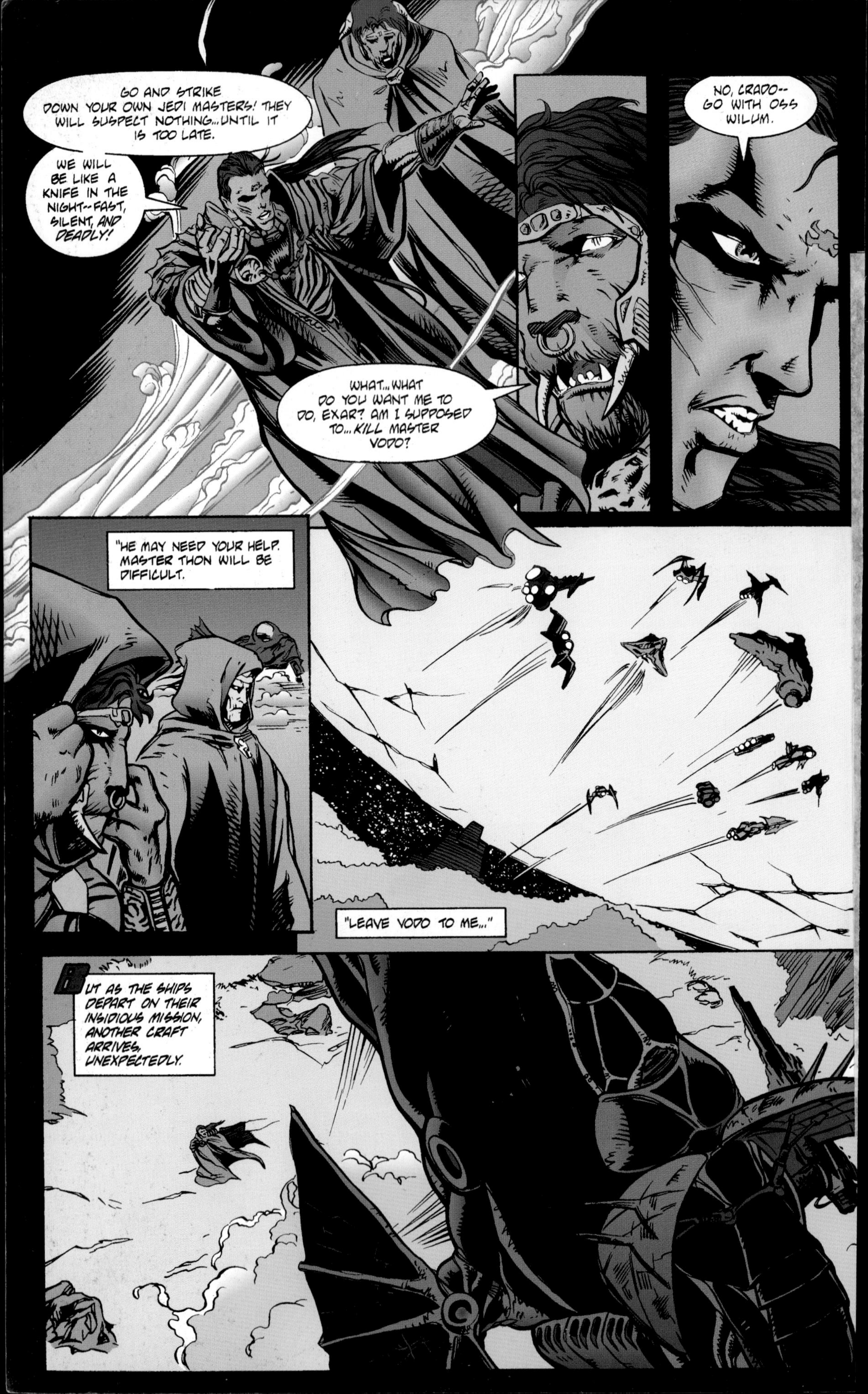
GO AND STRIKE DOWN YOUR OWN JEDI MASTERS! THEY WILL SUSPECT NOTHING... UNTIL IT IS TOO LATE.
WE WILL BE LIKE A KNIFE IN THE NIGHT--FAST, SILENT, AND DEADLY!
NO, CRADO-- GO WITH OSS WILUM.
WHAT... WHAT DO YOU WANT ME TO DO, EXAR? AM I SUPPOSED TO... KILL MASTER VODO?
"HE MAY NEED YOUR HELP. MASTER THON WILL BE DIFFICULT.
"LEAVE VODO TO ME..."
BUT AS THE SHIPS DEPART ON THEIR INSIDIOUS MISSION, ANOTHER CRAFT ARRIVES, UNEXPECTEDLY.

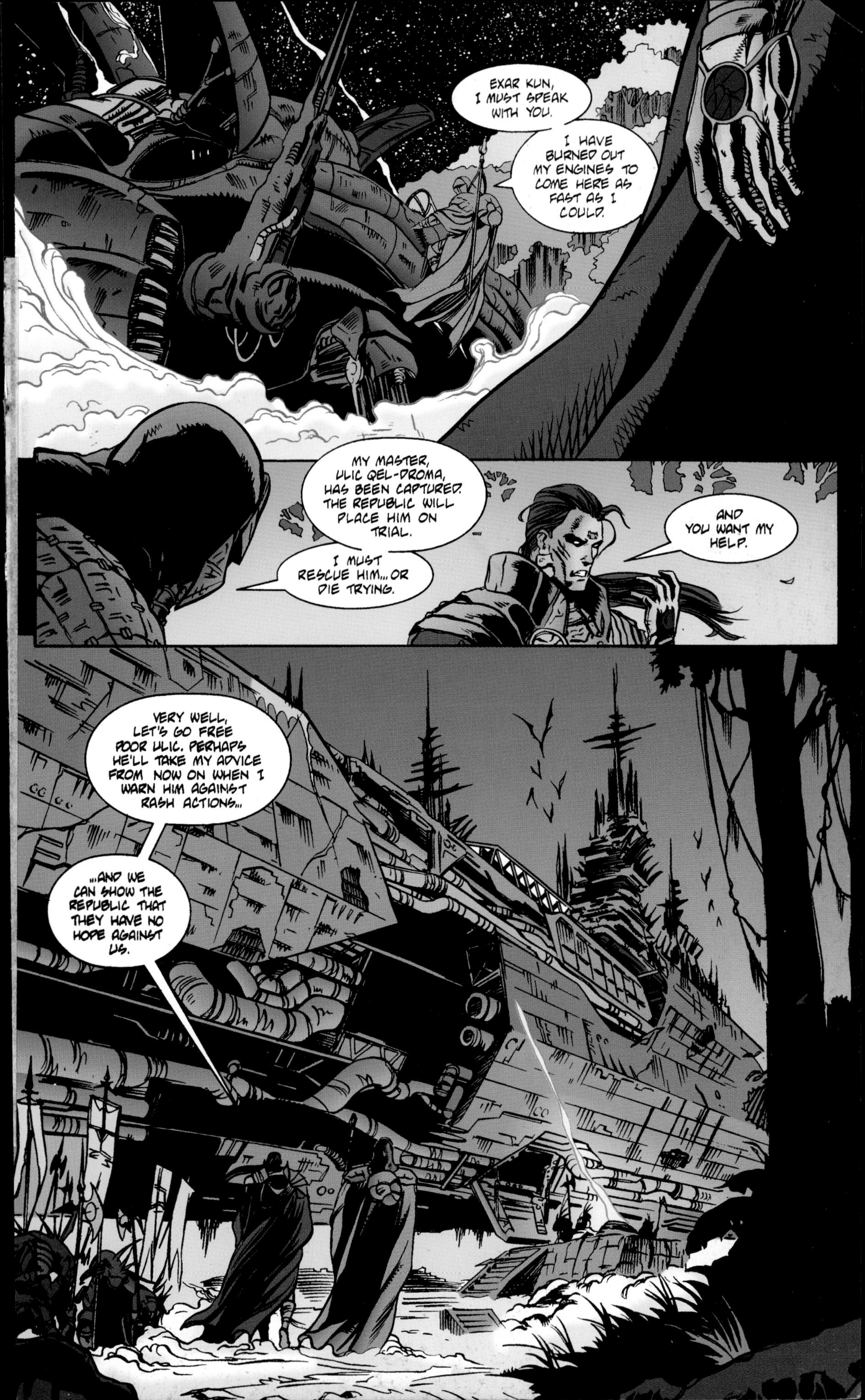
EXAR KUN, I MUST SPEAK WITH YOU.
I HAVE BURNED OUT MY ENGINES TO COME HERE AS FAST AS I COULD.
MY MASTER, ULIC QEL-DROMA, HAS BEEN CAPTURED. THE REPUBLIC WILL PLACE HIM ON TRIAL.
I MUST RESCUE HIM...OR DIE TRYING.
AND YOU WANT MY HELP.
VERY WELL, LET'S GO FREE POOR ULIC. PERHAPS HE'LL TAKE MY ADVICE FROM NOW ON WHEN I WARN HIM AGAINST RASH ACTIONS...
...AND WE CAN SHOW THE REPUBLIC THAT THEY HAVE NO HOPE AGAINST US.

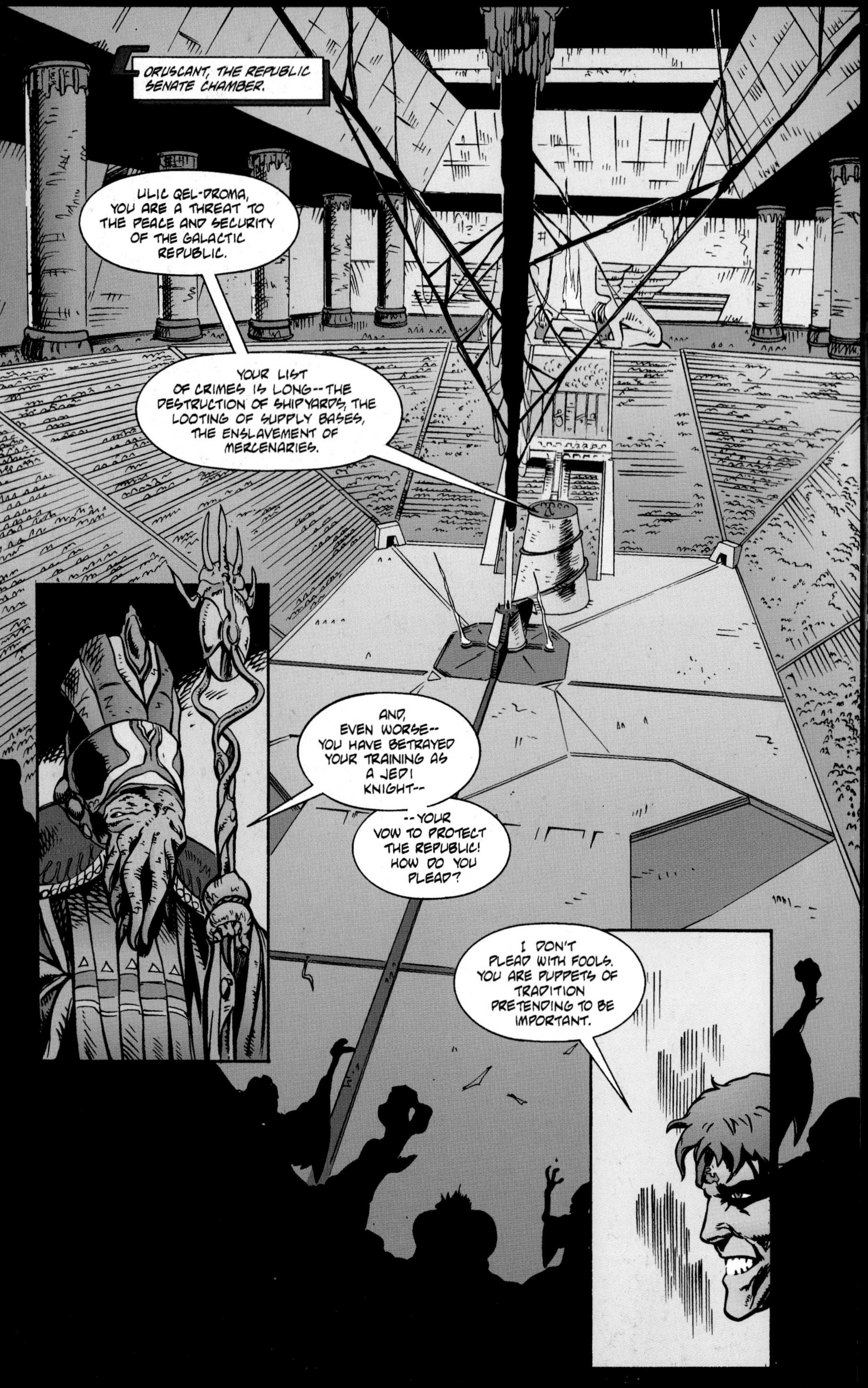
CORUSCANT, THE REPUBLIC SENATE CHAMBER.
ULIC QEL-DROMA, YOU ARE A THREAT TO THE PEACE AND SECURITY OF THE GALACTIC REPUBLIC.
YOUR LIST OF CRIMES IS LONG--THE DESTRUCTION OF SHIPYARDS, THE LOOTING OF SUPPLY BASES, THE ENSLAVEMENT OF MERCENARIES.
AND, EVEN WORSE--YOU HAVE BETRAYED YOUR TRAINING AS A JEDI KNIGHT--
--YOUR VOW TO PROTECT THE REPUBLIC! HOW DO YOU PLEAD?
I DON'T PLEAD WITH FOOLS. YOU ARE PUPPETS OF TRADITION PRETENDING TO BE IMPORTANT.

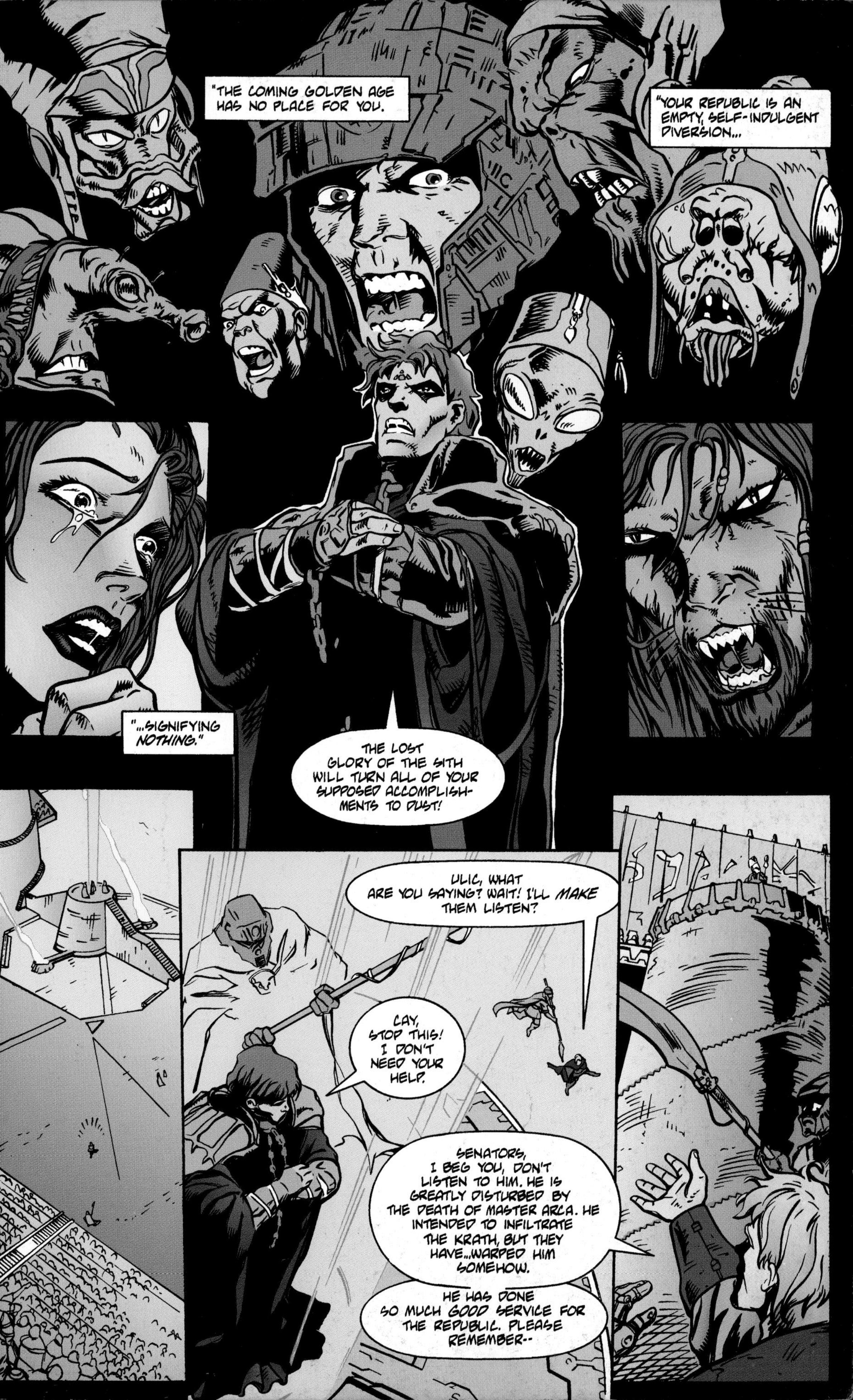
"THE COMING GOLDEN AGE HAS NO PLACE FOR YOU.
"YOUR REPUBLIC IS AN EMPTY, SELF-INDULGENT DIVERSION...
"...SIGNIFYING NOTHING."
THE LOST GLORY OF THE SITH WILL TURN ALL OF YOUR SUPPOSED ACCOMPLISHMENTS TO DUST!
ULIC, WHAT ARE YOU SAYING? WAIT! I'LL MAKE THEM LISTEN?
CAY, STOP THIS! I DON'T NEED YOUR HELP.
SENATORS, I BEG YOU, DON'T LISTEN TO HIM. HE IS GREATLY DISTURBED BY THE DEATH OF MASTER ARCA. HE INTENDED TO INFILTRATE THE KRATH, BUT THEY HAVE...WARPED HIM SOMEHOW.
HE HAS DONE SO MUCH GOOD SERVICE FOR THE REPUBLIC. PLEASE REMEMBER--

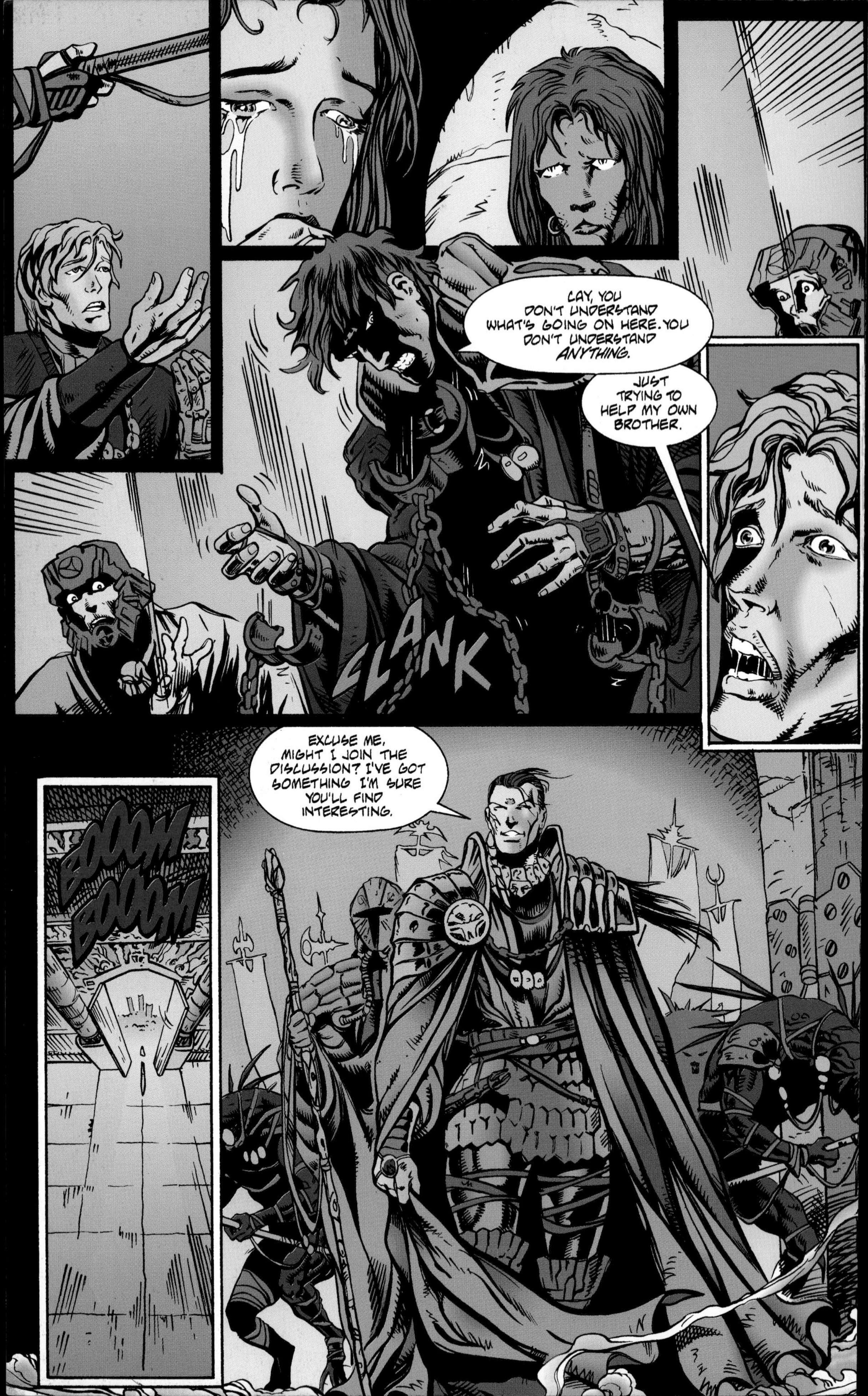
CAY, YOU DON'T UNDERSTAND WHAT'S GOING ON HERE. YOU DON'T UNDERSTAND ANYTHING.
JUST TRYING TO HELP MY OWN BROTHER.
CLANK
EXCUSE ME. MIGHT I JOIN THE DISCUSSION? I'VE GOT SOMETHING I'M SURE YOU'LL FIND INTERESTING.
BOOOM BOOOM

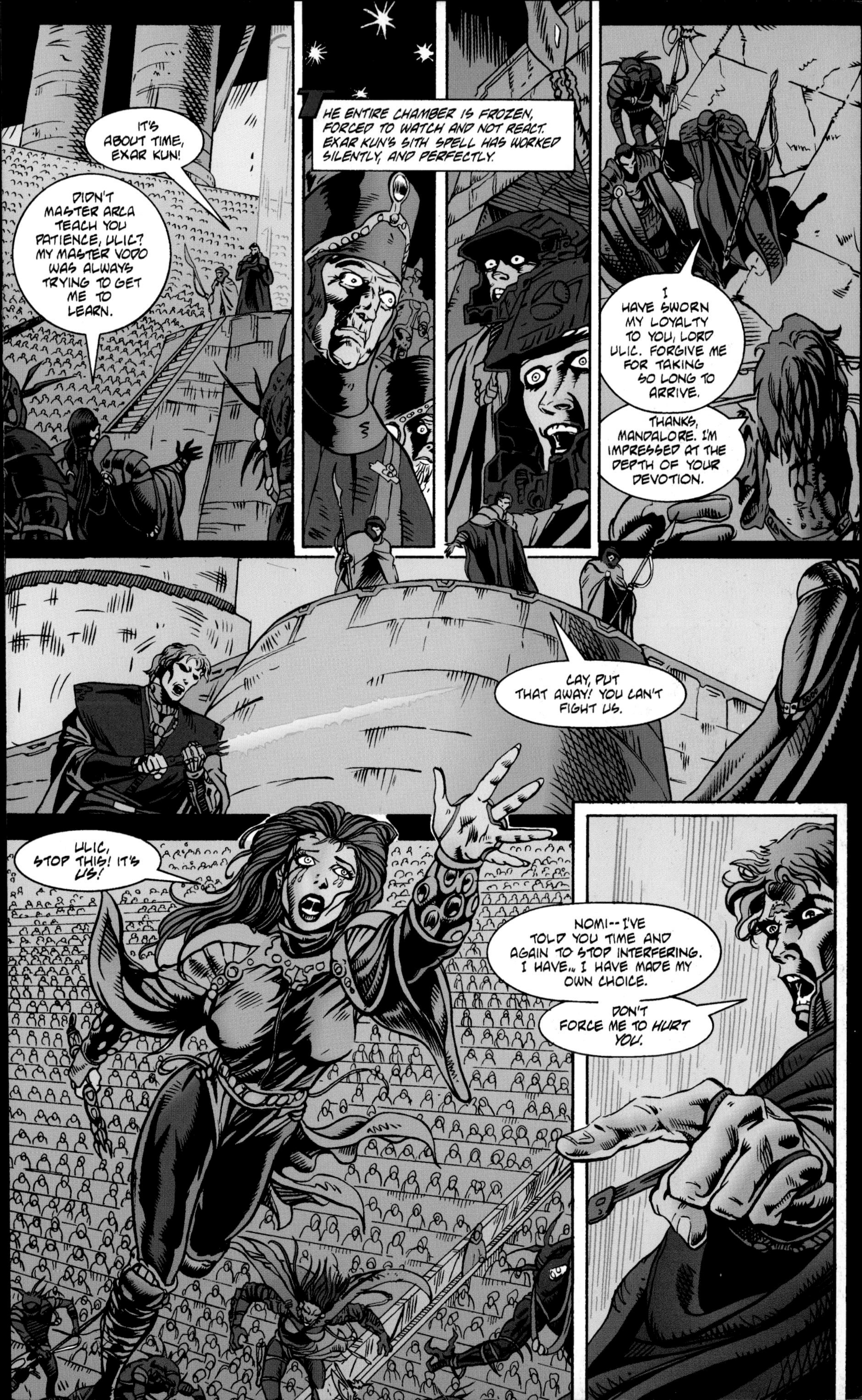
IT'S ABOUT TIME, EXAR KUN!
DIDN'T MASTER ARCA TEACH YOU PATIENCE, ULIC? MY MASTER VODO WAS ALWAYS TRYING TO GET ME TO LEARN.
THE ENTIRE CHAMBER IS FROZEN, FORCED TO WATCH AND NOT REACT. EXAR KUN'S SITH SPELL HAS WORKED SILENTLY, AND PERFECTLY.
I HAVE SWORN MY LOYALTY TO YOU, LORD ULIC. FORGIVE ME FOR TAKING SO LONG TO ARRIVE.
THANKS, MANDALORE. I'M IMPRESSED AT THE DEPTH OF YOUR DEVOTION.
CAY, PUT THAT AWAY! YOU CAN'T FIGHT US.
ULIC, STOP THIS! IT'S US!
NOMI-- I'VE TOLD YOU TIME AND AGAIN TO STOP INTERFERING. I HAVE.. I HAVE MADE MY OWN CHOICE.
DON'T FORCE ME TO HURT YOU.

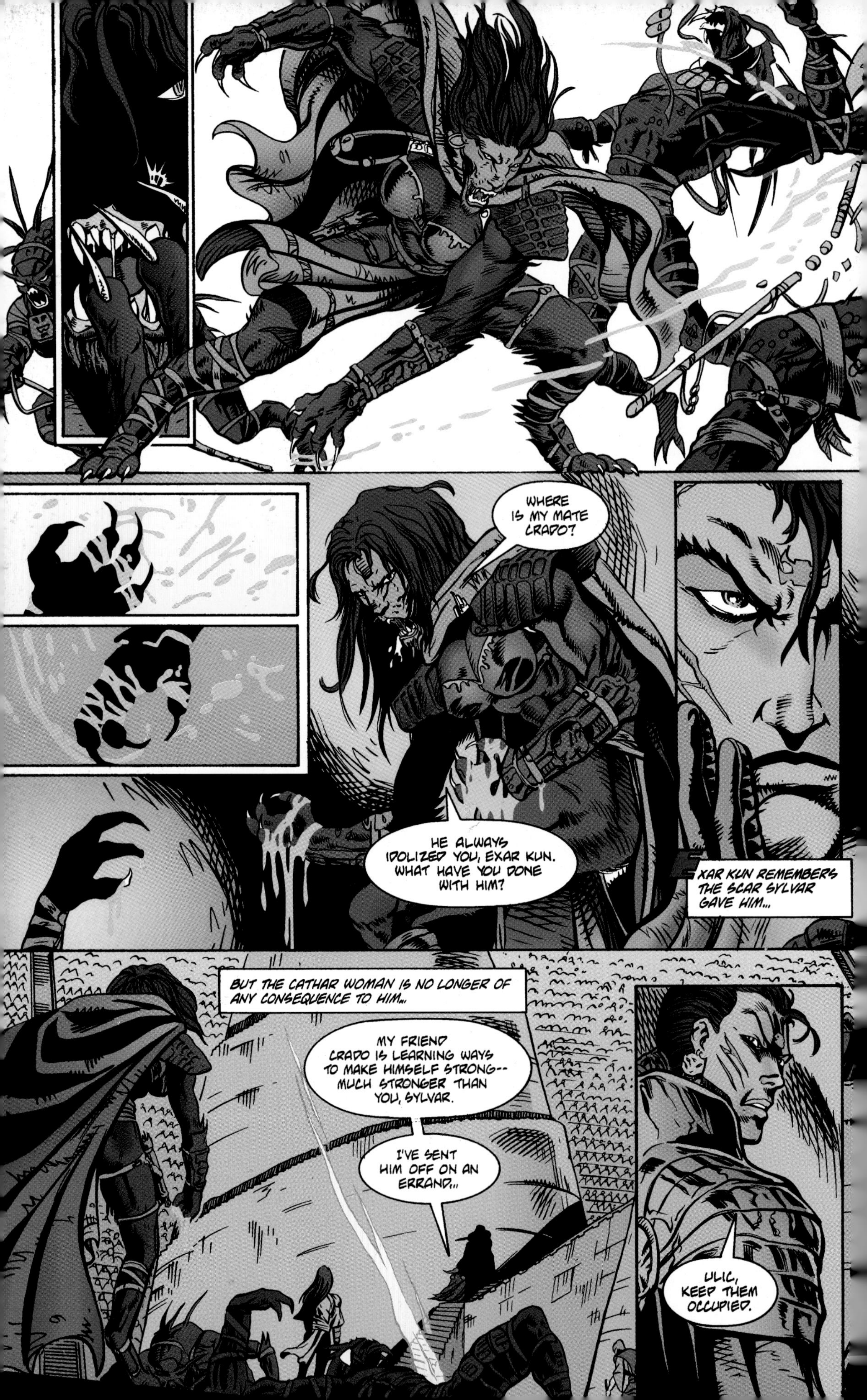
WHERE IS MY MATE CRADO?
HE ALWAYS IDOLIZED YOU, EXAR KUN. WHAT HAVE YOU DONE WITH HIM?
EXAR KUN REMEMBERS THE SCAR SYLVAR GAVE HIM...
BUT THE CATHAR WOMAN IS NO LONGER OF ANY CONSEQUENCE TO HIM...
MY FRIEND CRADO IS LEARNING WAYS TO MAKE HIMSELF STRONG-- MUCH STRONGER THAN YOU, SYLVAR.
I'VE SENT HIM OFF ON AN ERRAND...
ULIC, KEEP THEM OCCUPIED.

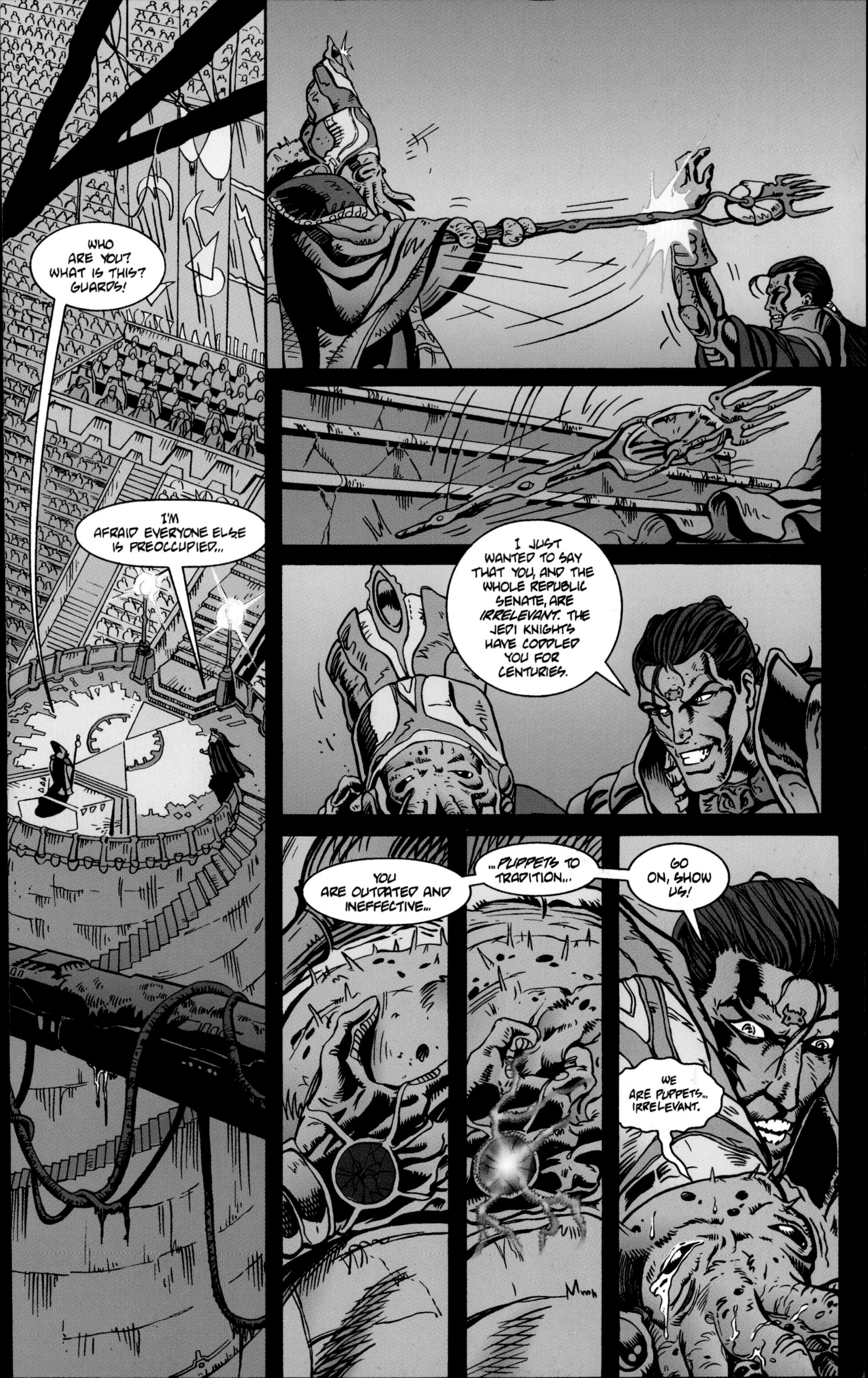
WHO ARE YOU? WHAT IS THIS? GUARDS!
I'M AFRAID EVERYONE ELSE IS PREOCCUPIED...
I JUST WANTED TO SAY THAT YOU, AND THE WHOLE REPUBLIC SENATE, ARE IRRELEVANT. THE JEDI KNIGHTS HAVE CODDLED YOU FOR CENTURIES.
YOU ARE OUTDATED AND INEFFECTIVE...
...PUPPETS TO TRADITION...
GO ON, SHOW US!
WE ARE PUPPETS... IRRELEVANT.

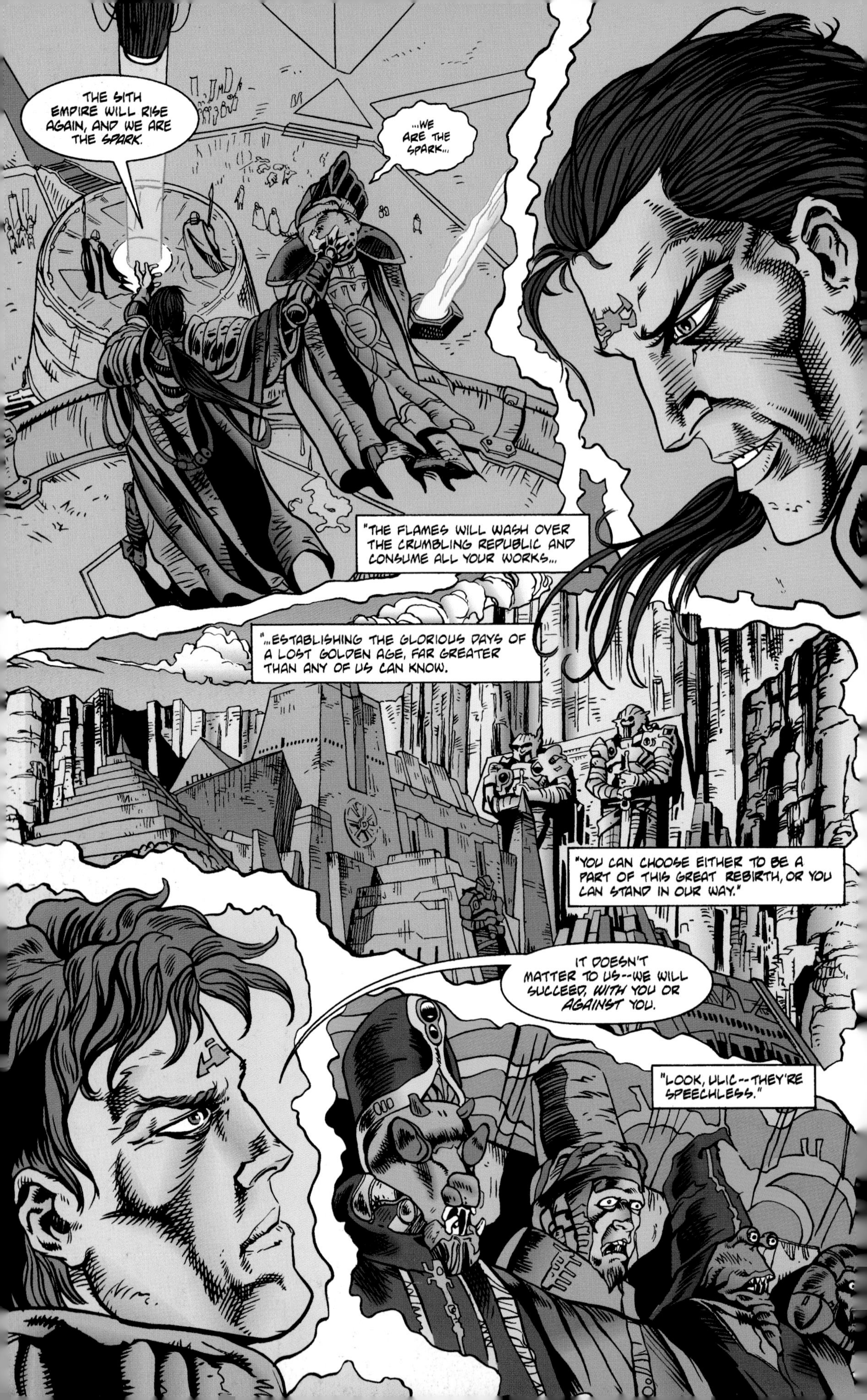
THE SITH EMPIRE WILL RISE AGAIN, AND WE ARE THE SPARK.
...WE ARE THE SPARK...
"THE FLAMES WILL WASH OVER THE CRUMBLING REPUBLIC AND CONSUME ALL YOUR WORKS...
"...ESTABLISHING THE GLORIOUS DAYS OF A LOST GOLDEN AGE, FAR GREATER THAN ANY OF US CAN KNOW.
"YOU CAN CHOOSE EITHER TO BE A PART OF THIS GREAT REBIRTH, OR YOU CAN STAND IN OUR WAY."
IT DOESN'T MATTER TO US--WE WILL SUCCEED, WITH YOU OR AGAINST YOU.
"LOOK, ULIC--THEY'RE SPEECHLESS."

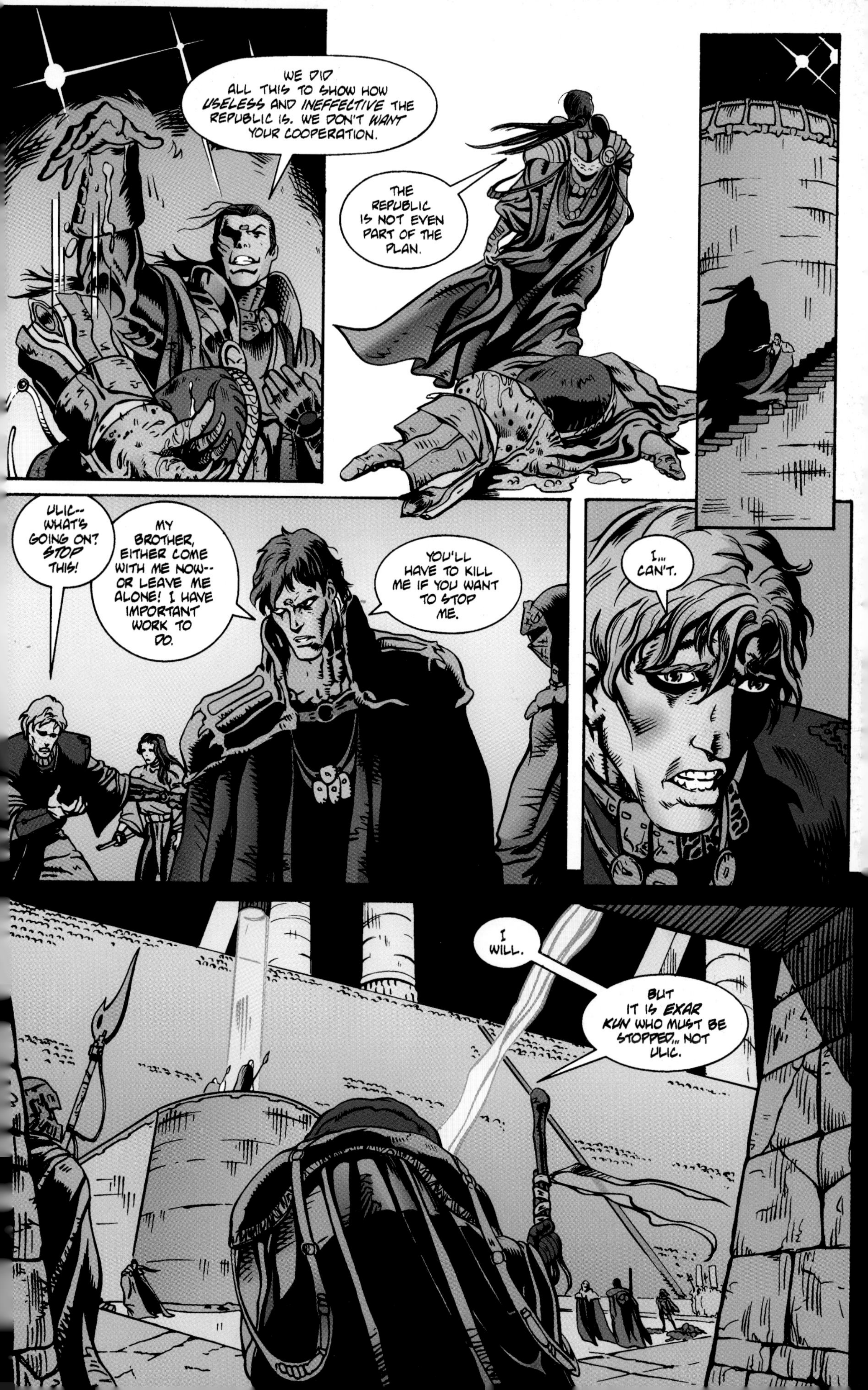
WE DID ALL THIS TO SHOW HOW *USELESS* AND *INEFFECTIVE* THE REPUBLIC IS. WE DON'T *WANT* YOUR COOPERATION.
THE REPUBLIC IS NOT EVEN PART OF THE PLAN.
ULIC-- WHAT'S GOING ON? *STOP* THIS!
MY BROTHER, EITHER COME WITH ME NOW-- OR LEAVE ME ALONE! I HAVE IMPORTANT WORK TO DO.
YOU'LL HAVE TO KILL ME IF YOU WANT TO STOP ME.
I... CAN'T.
I WILL.
BUT IT IS *EXAR KUN* WHO MUST BE STOPPED... NOT ULIC.

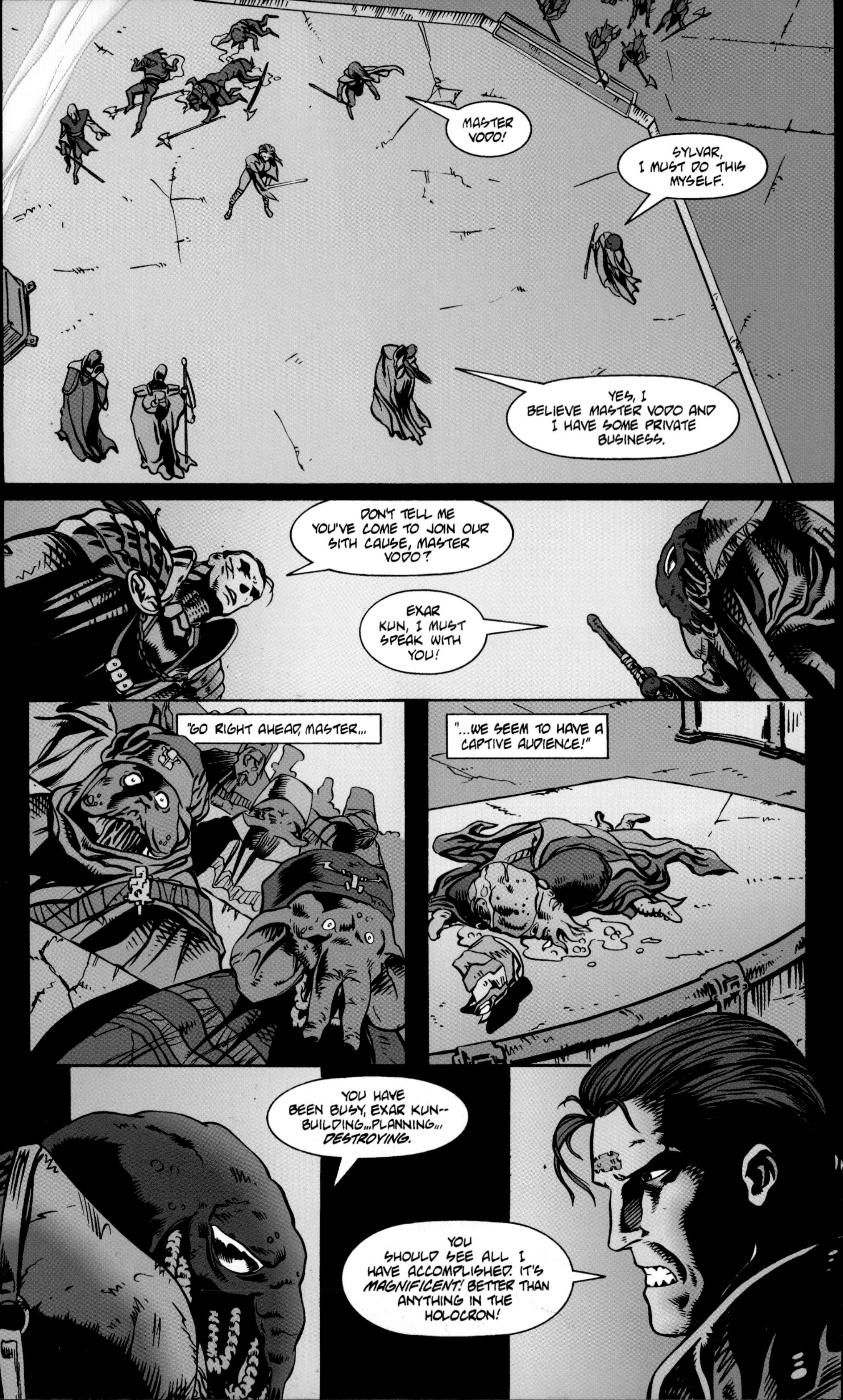
MASTER VODO!
SYLVAR, I MUST DO THIS MYSELF.
YES, I BELIEVE MASTER VODO AND I HAVE SOME PRIVATE BUSINESS.
DON'T TELL ME YOU'VE COME TO JOIN OUR SITH CAUSE, MASTER VODO?
EXAR KUN, I MUST SPEAK WITH YOU!
"GO RIGHT AHEAD, MASTER...
"...WE SEEM TO HAVE A CAPTIVE AUDIENCE!"
YOU HAVE BEEN BUSY, EXAR KUN-- BUILDING...PLANNING... *DESTROYING.*
YOU SHOULD SEE ALL I HAVE ACCOMPLISHED. IT'S *MAGNIFICENT!* BETTER THAN ANYTHING IN THE HOLOCRON!

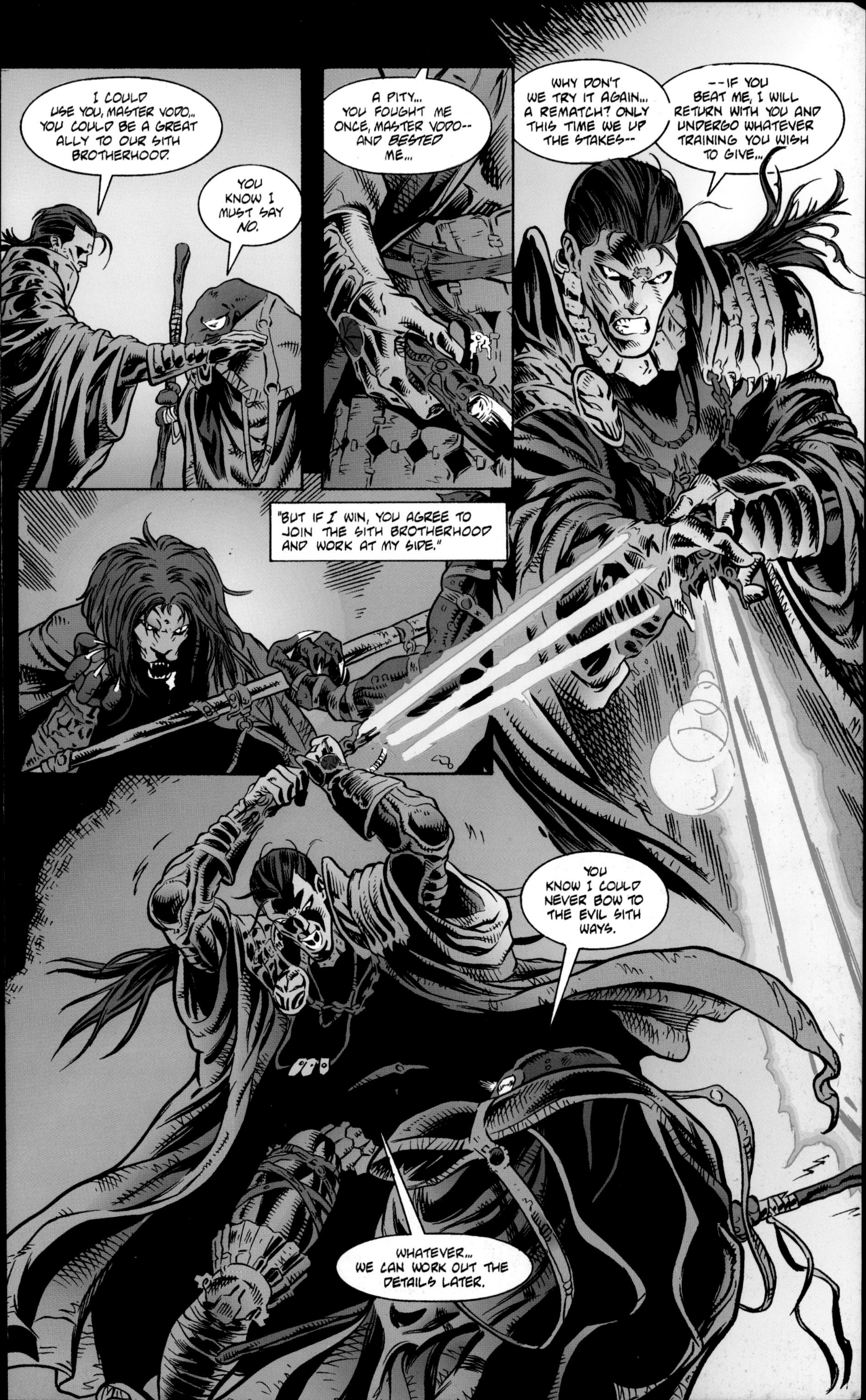
I COULD USE YOU, MASTER VODO... YOU COULD BE A GREAT ALLY TO OUR SITH BROTHERHOOD.
YOU KNOW I MUST SAY NO.
A PITY... YOU FOUGHT ME ONCE, MASTER VODO-- AND *BESTED* ME...
WHY DON'T WE TRY IT AGAIN... A REMATCH? ONLY THIS TIME WE UP THE STAKES--
--IF YOU BEAT ME, I WILL RETURN WITH YOU AND UNDERGO WHATEVER TRAINING YOU WISH TO GIVE...
"BUT IF I WIN, YOU AGREE TO JOIN THE SITH BROTHERHOOD AND WORK AT MY SIDE."
YOU KNOW I COULD NEVER BOW TO THE EVIL SITH WAYS.
WHATEVER... WE CAN WORK OUT THE DETAILS LATER.

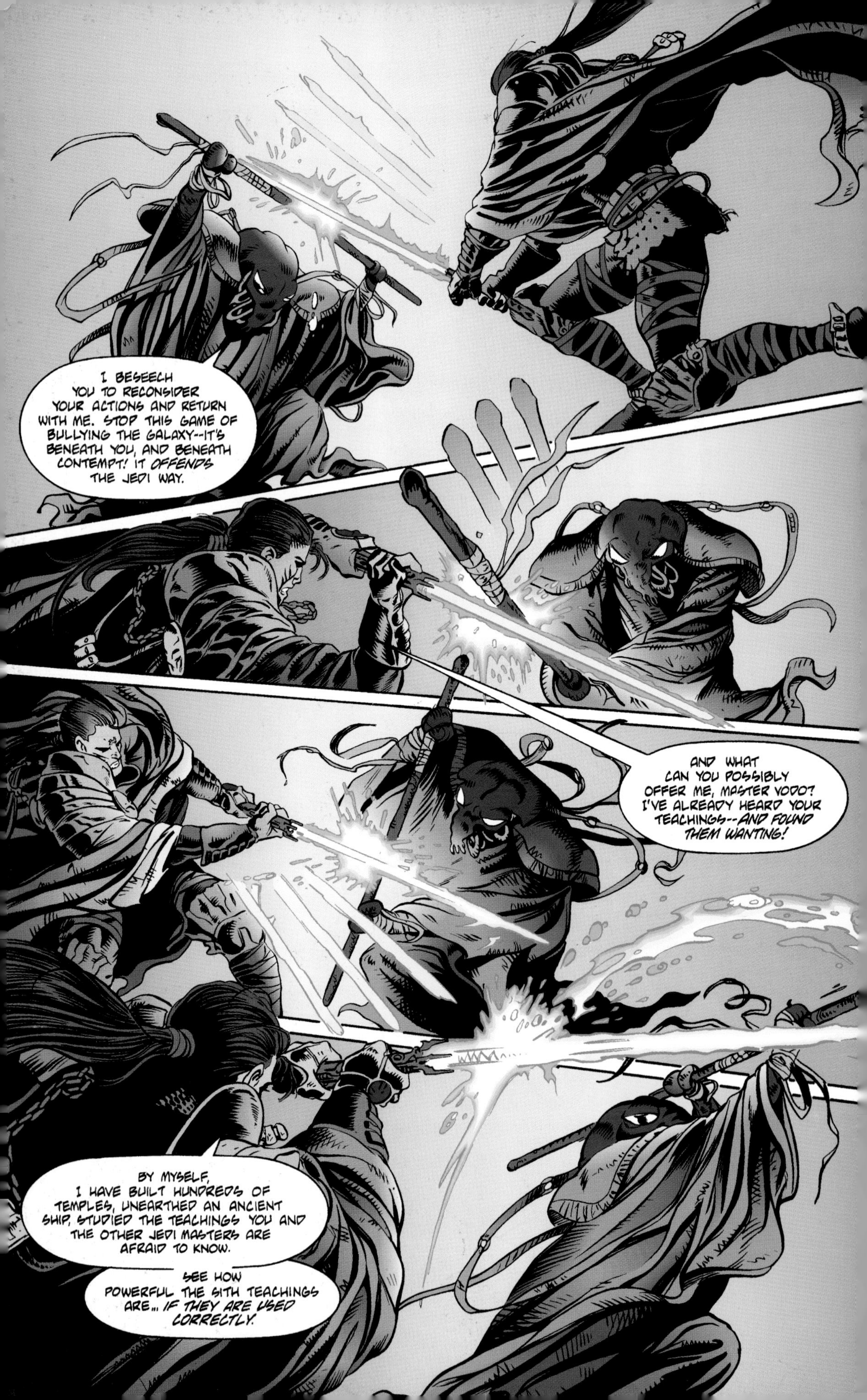
I BESEECH YOU TO RECONSIDER YOUR ACTIONS AND RETURN WITH ME. STOP THIS GAME OF BULLYING THE GALAXY--IT'S BENEATH YOU, AND BENEATH CONTEMPT! IT *OFFENDS* THE JEDI WAY.
AND WHAT CAN YOU POSSIBLY OFFER ME, MASTER VODO? I'VE ALREADY HEARD YOUR TEACHINGS--*AND FOUND THEM WANTING!*
BY MYSELF, I HAVE BUILT HUNDREDS OF TEMPLES, UNEARTHED AN ANCIENT SHIP, STUDIED THE TEACHINGS YOU AND THE OTHER JEDI MASTERS ARE AFRAID TO KNOW.
SEE HOW POWERFUL THE SITH TEACHINGS ARE... *IF THEY ARE USED CORRECTLY.*

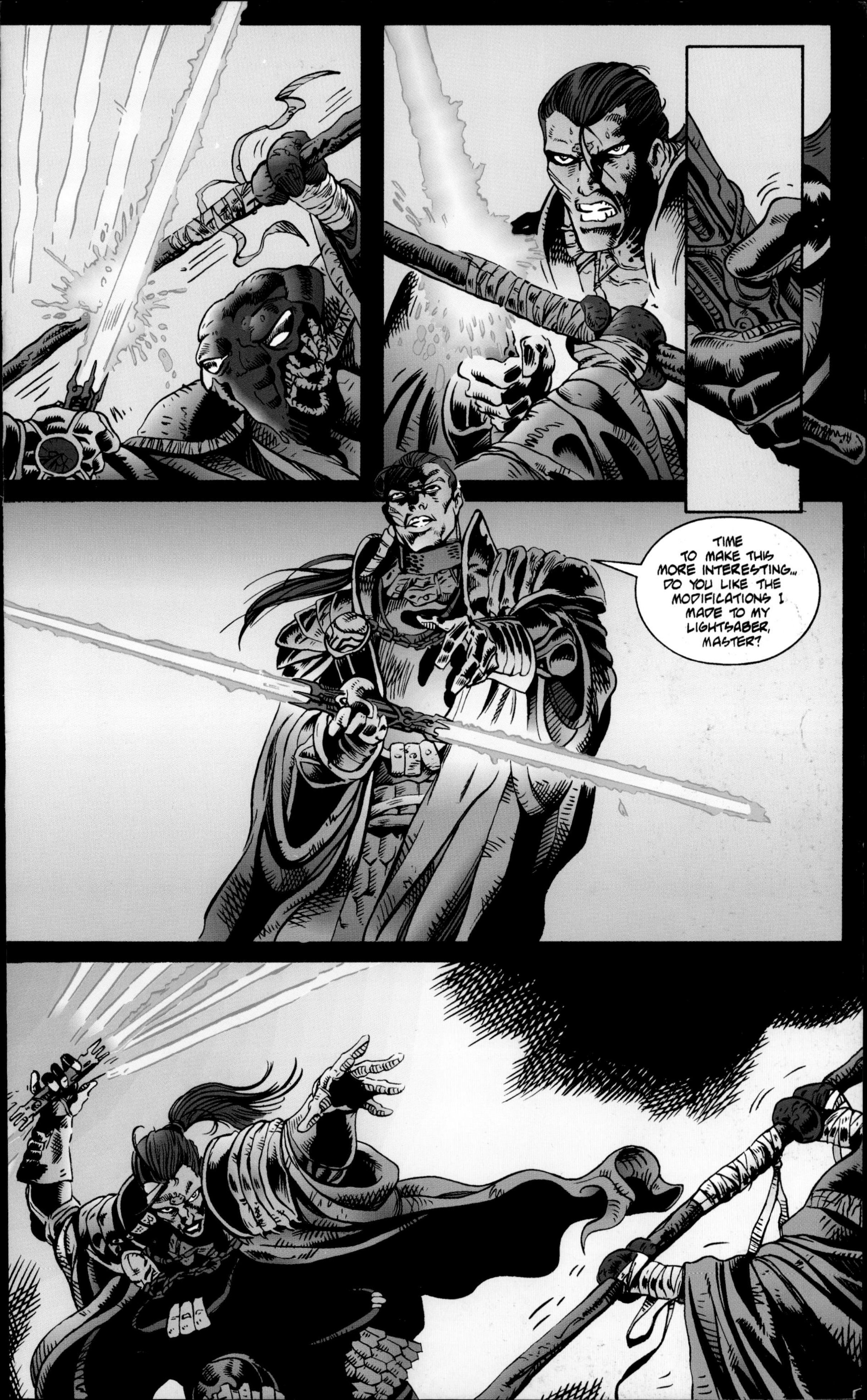
TIME TO MAKE THIS MORE INTERESTING... DO YOU LIKE THE MODIFICATIONS I MADE TO MY LIGHTSABER, MASTER?

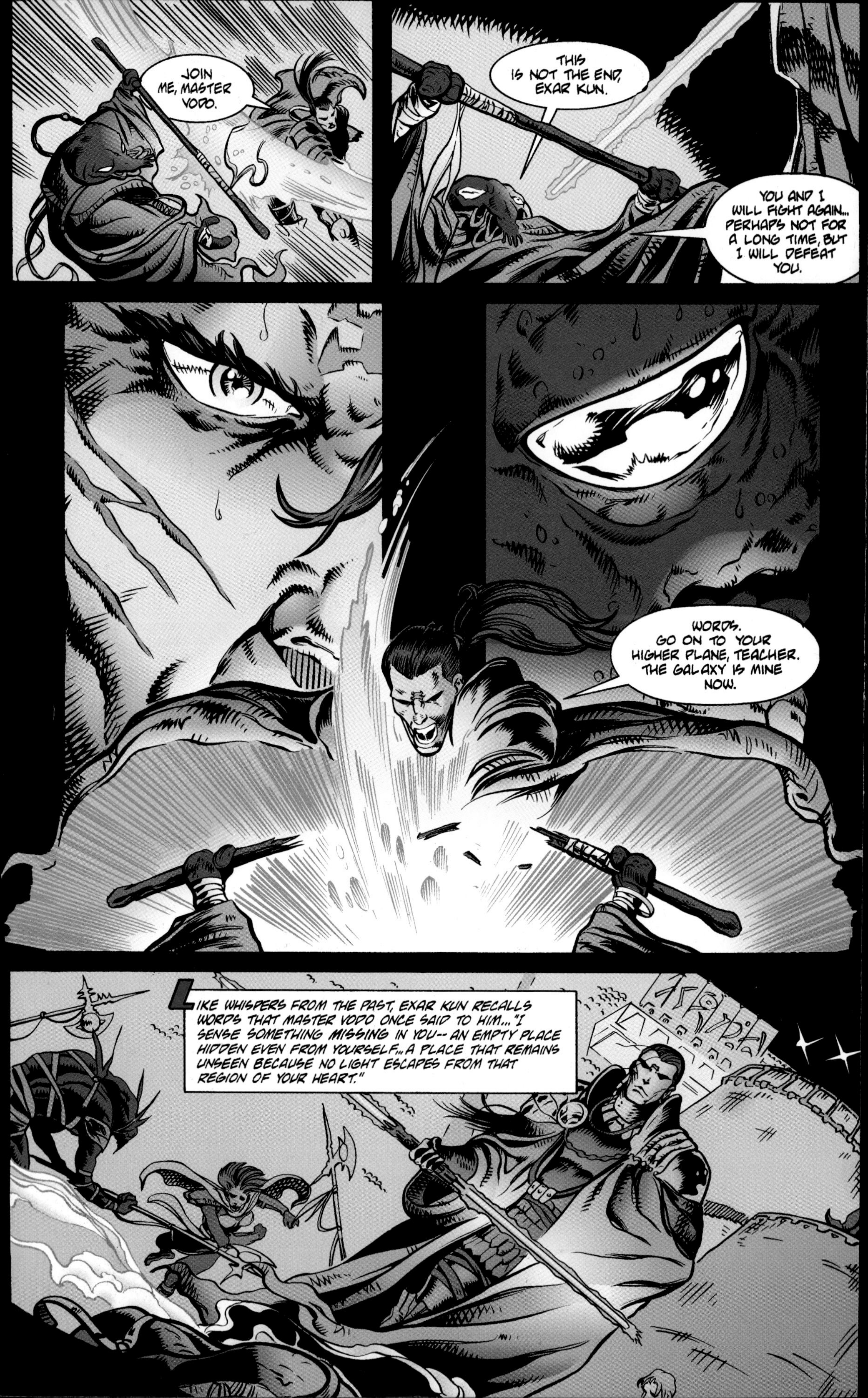
JOIN ME, MASTER VODO.
THIS IS NOT THE END, EXAR KUN.
YOU AND I WILL FIGHT AGAIN... PERHAPS NOT FOR A LONG TIME, BUT I WILL DEFEAT YOU.
WORDS. GO ON TO YOUR HIGHER PLANE, TEACHER. THE GALAXY IS MINE NOW.
LIKE WHISPERS FROM THE PAST, EXAR KUN RECALLS WORDS THAT MASTER VODO ONCE SAID TO HIM... "I SENSE SOMETHING MISSING IN YOU-- AN EMPTY PLACE HIDDEN EVEN FROM YOURSELF... A PLACE THAT REMAINS UNSEEN BECAUSE NO LIGHT ESCAPES FROM THAT REGION OF YOUR HEART."

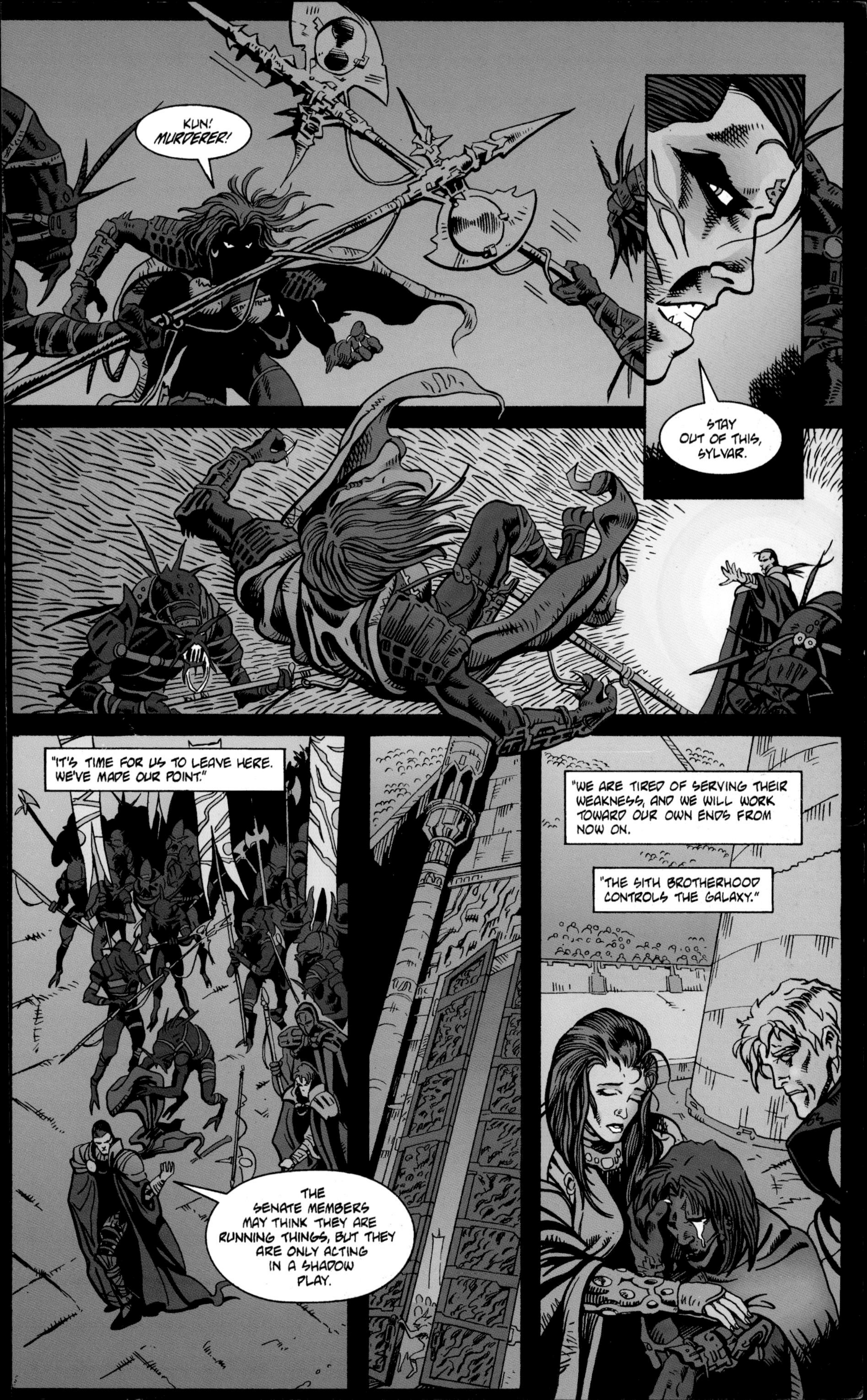
KUN! MURDERER!
STAY OUT OF THIS, SYLVAR.
"IT'S TIME FOR US TO LEAVE HERE. WE'VE MADE OUR POINT."
THE SENATE MEMBERS MAY THINK THEY ARE RUNNING THINGS, BUT THEY ARE ONLY ACTING IN A SHADOW PLAY.
"WE ARE TIRED OF SERVING THEIR WEAKNESS, AND WE WILL WORK TOWARD OUR OWN ENDS FROM NOW ON.
"THE SITH BROTHERHOOD CONTROLS THE GALAXY."

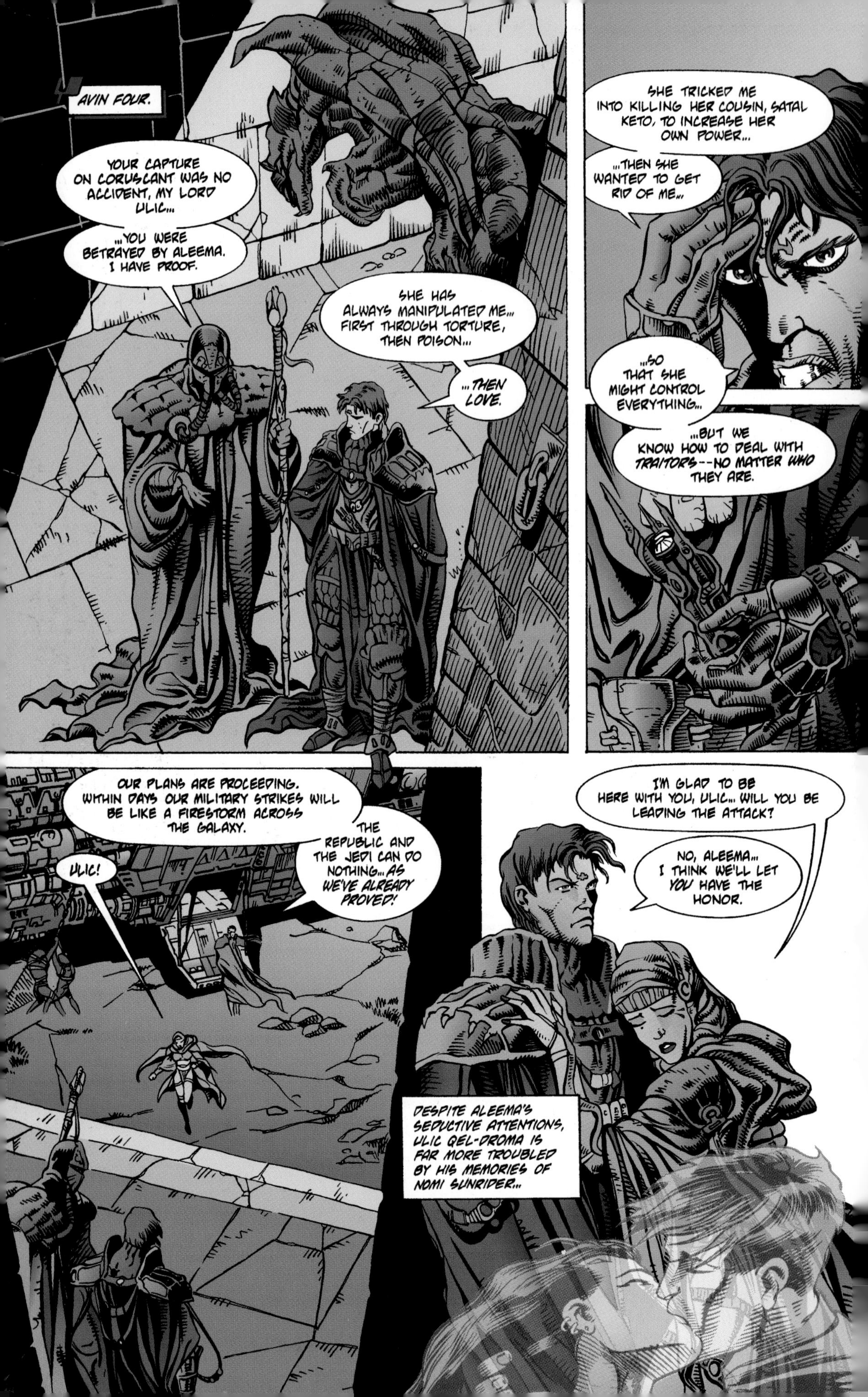
AVIN FOUR.
YOUR CAPTURE ON CORUSCANT WAS NO ACCIDENT, MY LORD ULIC...
...YOU WERE BETRAYED BY ALEEMA. I HAVE PROOF.
SHE HAS ALWAYS MANIPULATED ME... FIRST THROUGH TORTURE, THEN POISON...
...THEN LOVE.
SHE TRICKED ME INTO KILLING HER COUSIN, SATAL KETO, TO INCREASE HER OWN POWER...
...THEN SHE WANTED TO GET RID OF ME...
...SO THAT SHE MIGHT CONTROL EVERYTHING...
...BUT WE KNOW HOW TO DEAL WITH TRAITORS--NO MATTER WHO THEY ARE.
OUR PLANS ARE PROCEEDING. WITHIN DAYS OUR MILITARY STRIKES WILL BE LIKE A FIRESTORM ACROSS THE GALAXY.
THE REPUBLIC AND THE JEDI CAN DO NOTHING... AS WE'VE ALREADY PROVED!
ULIC!
I'M GLAD TO BE HERE WITH YOU, ULIC... WILL YOU BE LEADING THE ATTACK?
NO, ALEEMA... I THINK WE'LL LET YOU HAVE THE HONOR.
DESPITE ALEEMA'S SEDUCTIVE ATTENTIONS, ULIC QEL-DROMA IS FAR MORE TROUBLED BY HIS MEMORIES OF NOMI SUNRIDER...

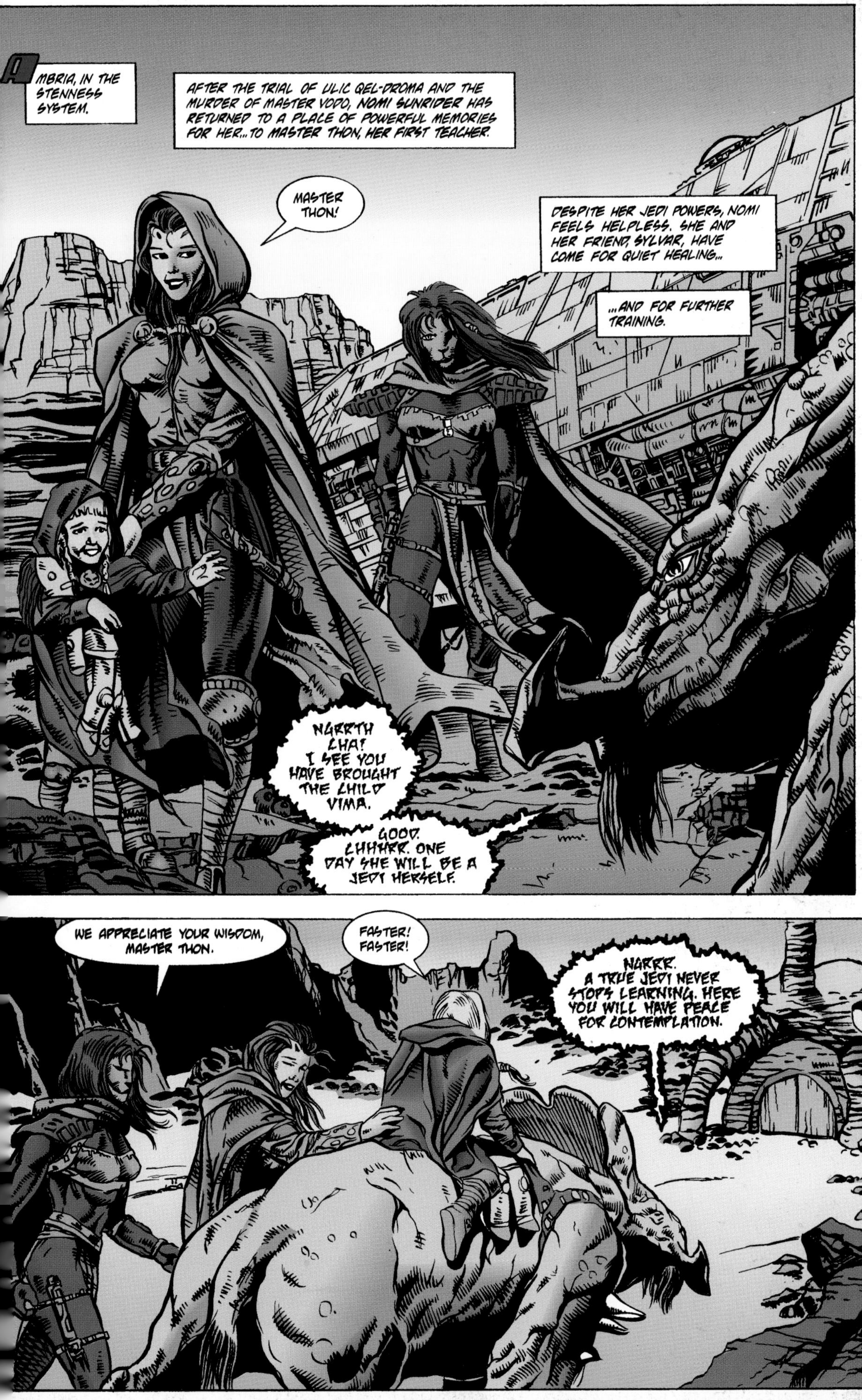
AMBRIA, IN THE STENNESS SYSTEM.
AFTER THE TRIAL OF ULIC QEL-DROMA AND THE MURDER OF MASTER VODO, NOMI SUNRIDER HAS RETURNED TO A PLACE OF POWERFUL MEMORIES FOR HER...TO MASTER THON, HER FIRST TEACHER.
MASTER THON!
DESPITE HER JEDI POWERS, NOMI FEELS HELPLESS. SHE AND HER FRIEND, SYLVAR, HAVE COME FOR QUIET HEALING...
...AND FOR FURTHER TRAINING.
NGRRTH CHA! I SEE YOU HAVE BROUGHT THE CHILD VIMA.
GOOD. CHHHRR. ONE DAY SHE WILL BE A JEDI HERSELF.
WE APPRECIATE YOUR WISDOM, MASTER THON.
FASTER! FASTER!
NARRR. A TRUE JEDI NEVER STOPS LEARNING. HERE YOU WILL HAVE PEACE FOR CONTEMPLATION.

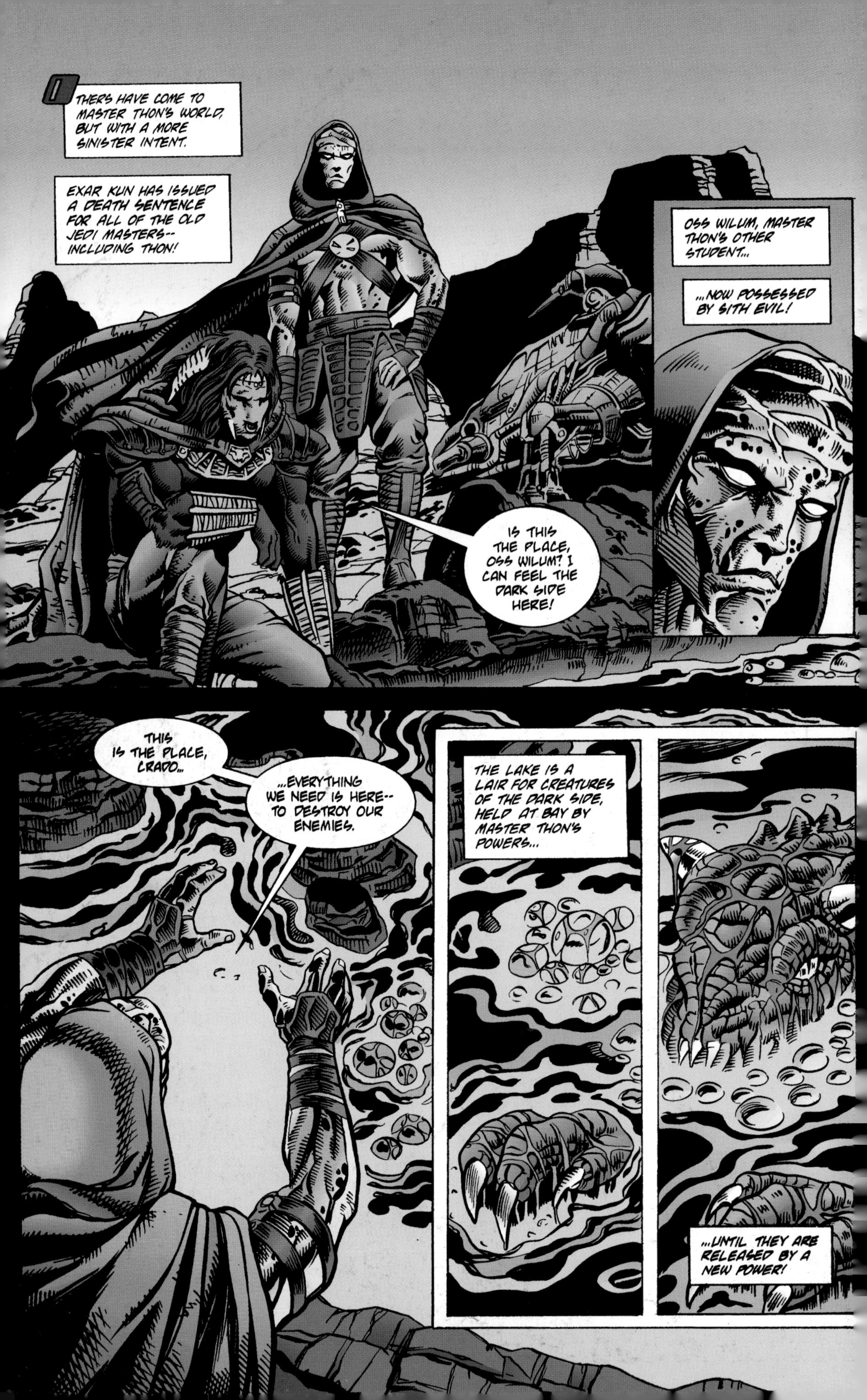
OTHERS HAVE COME TO MASTER THON'S WORLD, BUT WITH A MORE SINISTER INTENT.
EXAR KUN HAS ISSUED A DEATH SENTENCE FOR ALL OF THE OLD JEDI MASTERS-- INCLUDING THON!
OSS WILUM, MASTER THON'S OTHER STUDENT...
...NOW POSSESSED BY SITH EVIL!
IS THIS THE PLACE, OSS WILUM? I CAN FEEL THE DARK SIDE HERE!
THIS IS THE PLACE, CRADO...
...EVERYTHING WE NEED IS HERE-- TO DESTROY OUR ENEMIES.
THE LAKE IS A LAIR FOR CREATURES OF THE DARK SIDE, HELD AT BAY BY MASTER THON'S POWERS...
...UNTIL THEY ARE RELEASED BY A NEW POWER!

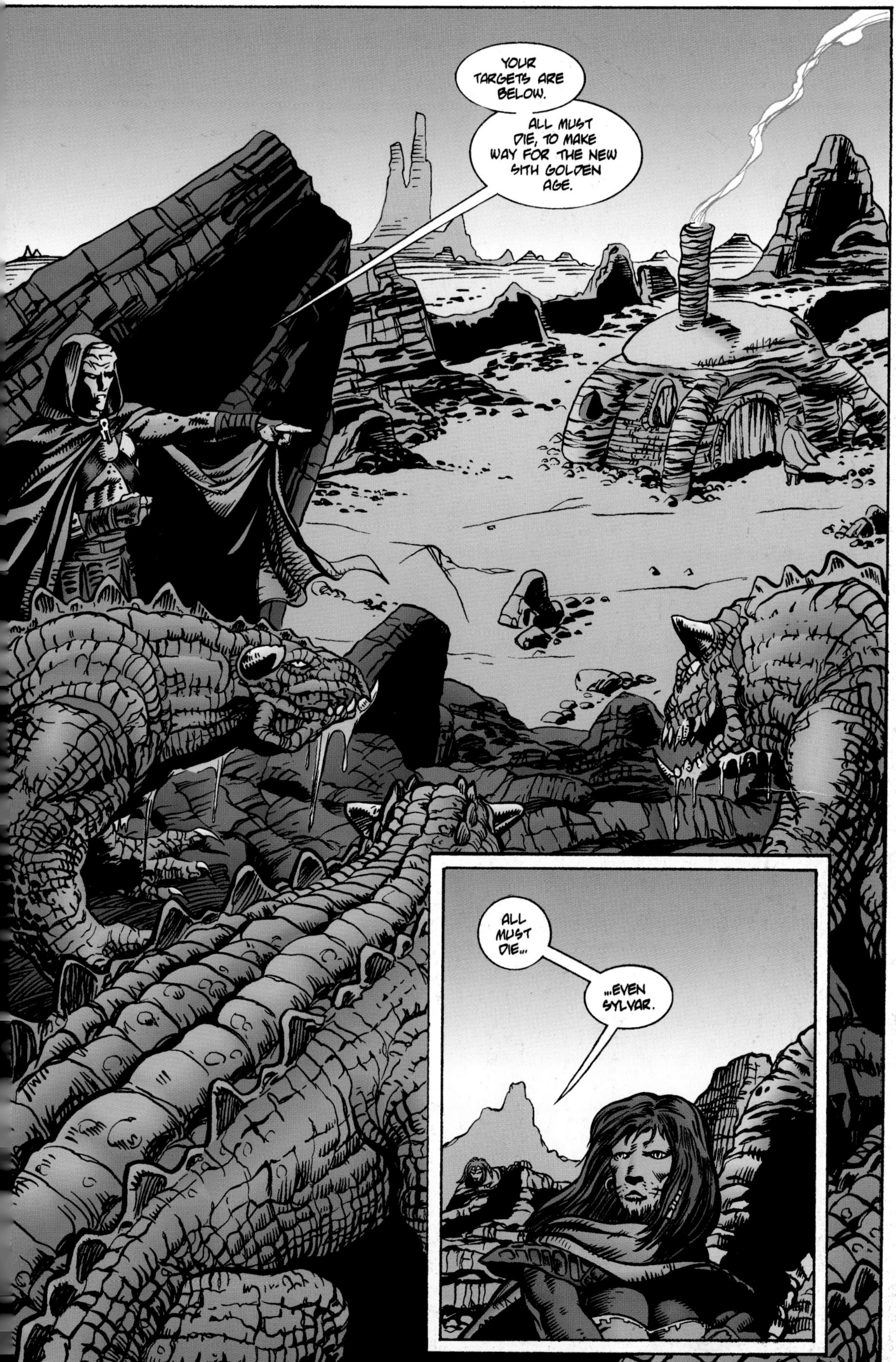
YOUR TARGETS ARE BELOW.
ALL MUST DIE, TO MAKE WAY FOR THE NEW SITH GOLDEN AGE.
ALL MUST DIE...
...EVEN SYLVAR.

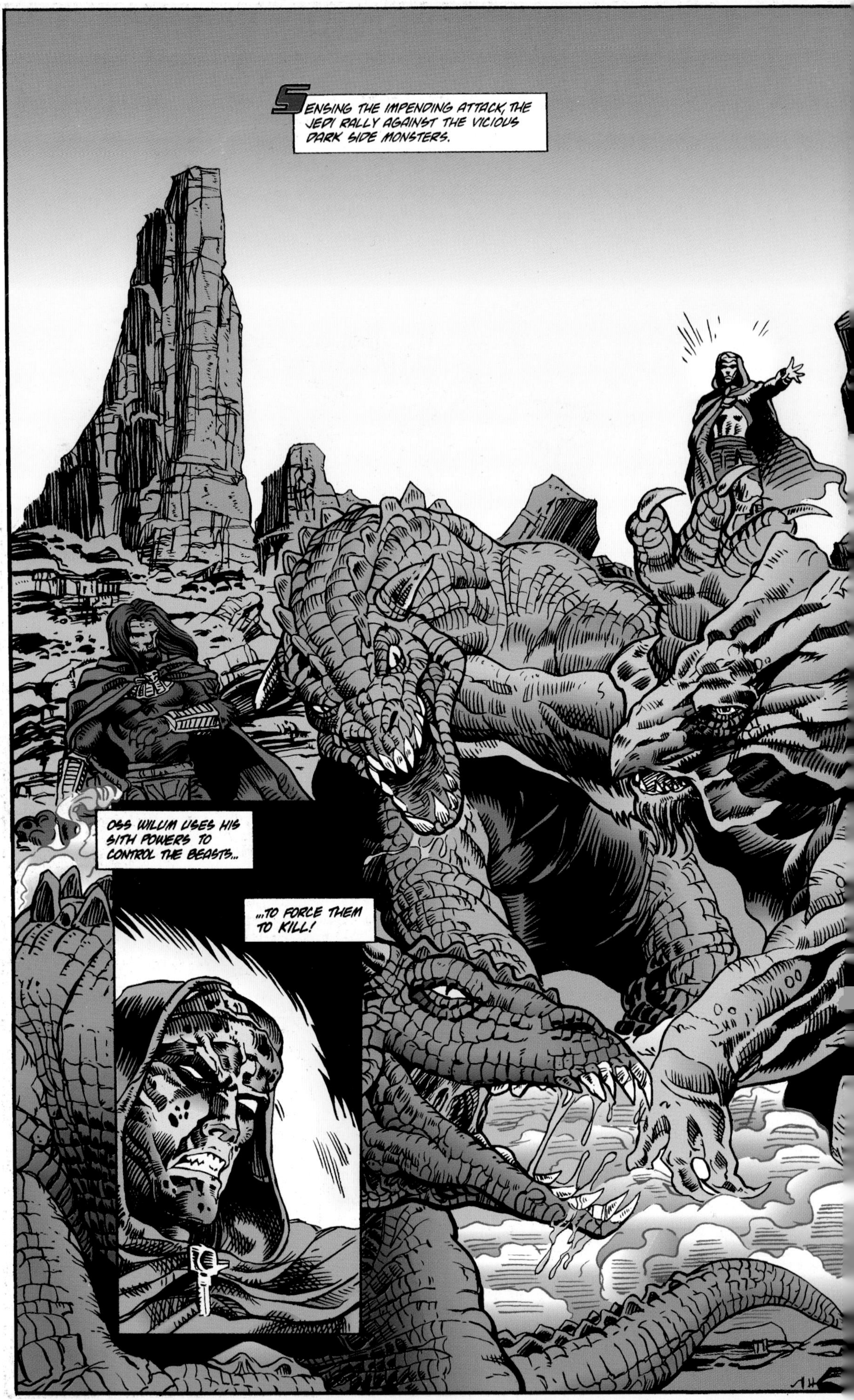
SENSING THE IMPENDING ATTACK, THE JEDI RALLY AGAINST THE VICIOUS DARK SIDE MONSTERS.
OSS WILUM USES HIS SITH POWERS TO CONTROL THE BEASTS...
...TO FORCE THEM TO KILL!

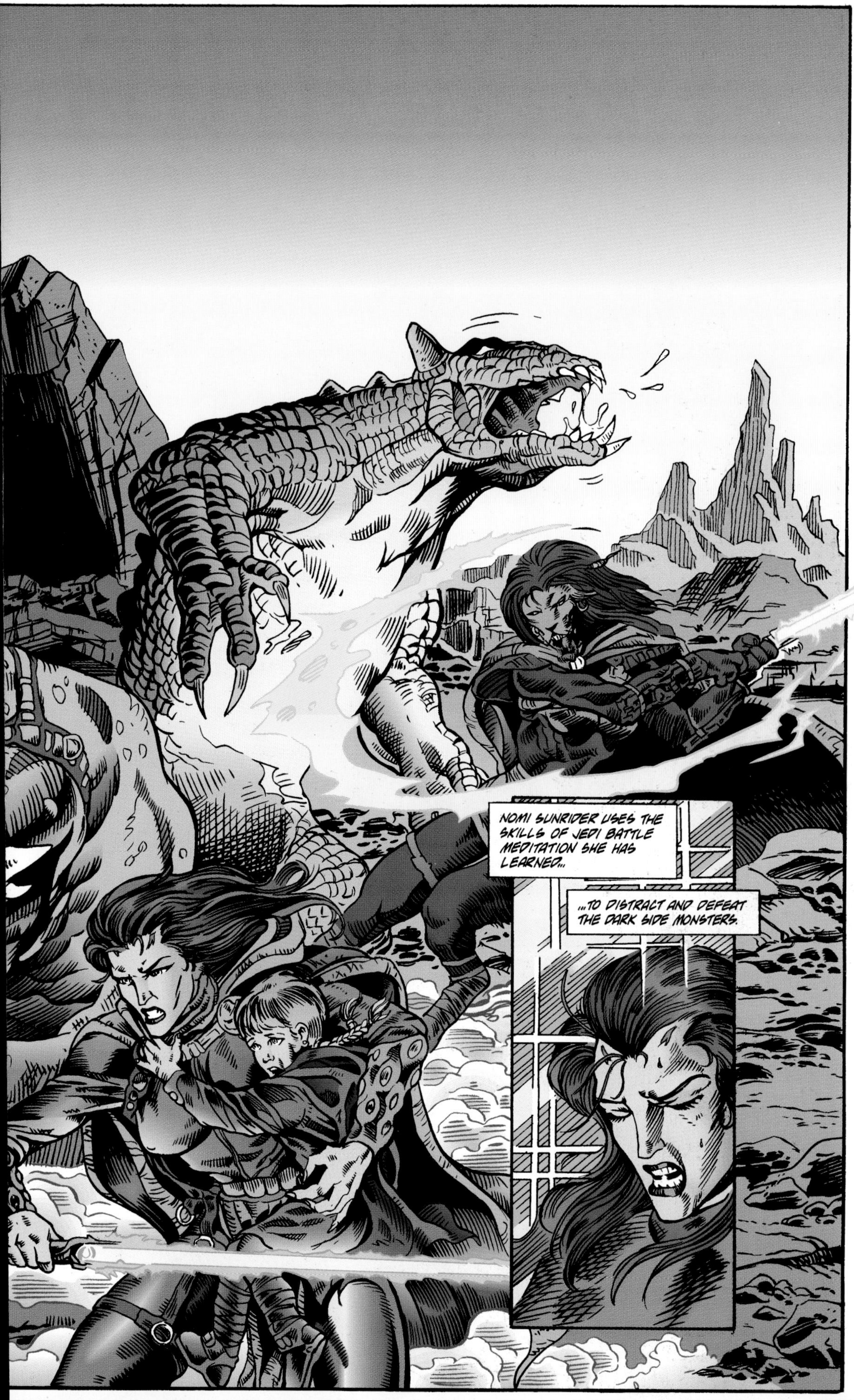
NOMI SUNRIDER USES THE SKILLS OF JEDI BATTLE MEDITATION SHE HAS LEARNED...
...TO DISTRACT AND DEFEAT THE DARK SIDE MONSTERS.

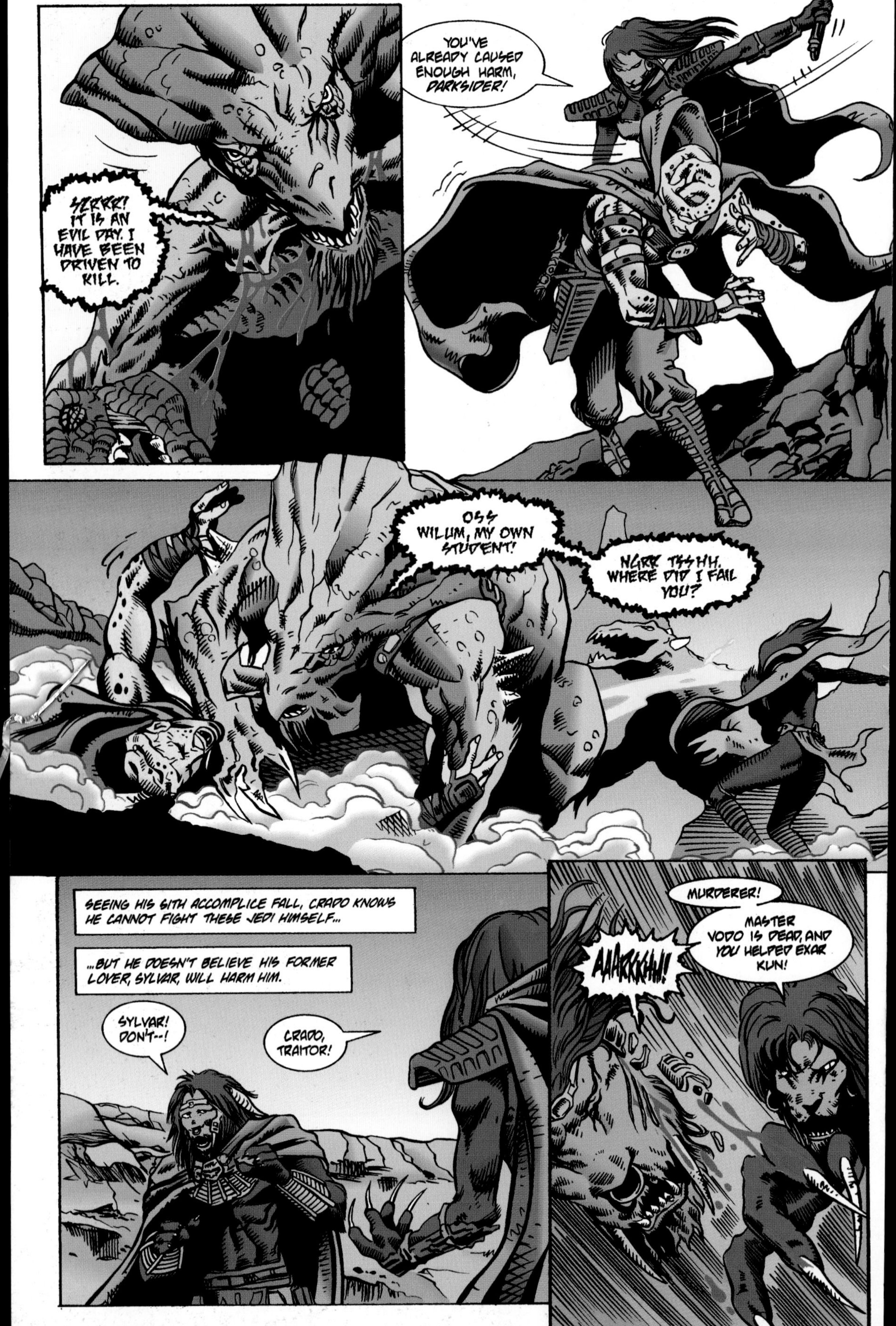
SZRRR! IT IS AN EVIL DAY. I HAVE BEEN DRIVEN TO KILL.
YOU'VE ALREADY CAUSED ENOUGH HARM, DARKSIDER!
OSS WILUM, MY OWN STUDENT!
NGRR TSSHH. WHERE DID I FAIL YOU?
SEEING HIS SITH ACCOMPLICE FALL, CRADO KNOWS HE CANNOT FIGHT THESE JEDI HIMSELF...
...BUT HE DOESN'T BELIEVE HIS FORMER LOVER, SYLVAR, WILL HARM HIM.
SYLVAR! DON'T--!
CRADO, TRAITOR!
MURDERER!
AAARKKHH!
MASTER VODO IS DEAD, AND YOU HELPED EXAR KUN!

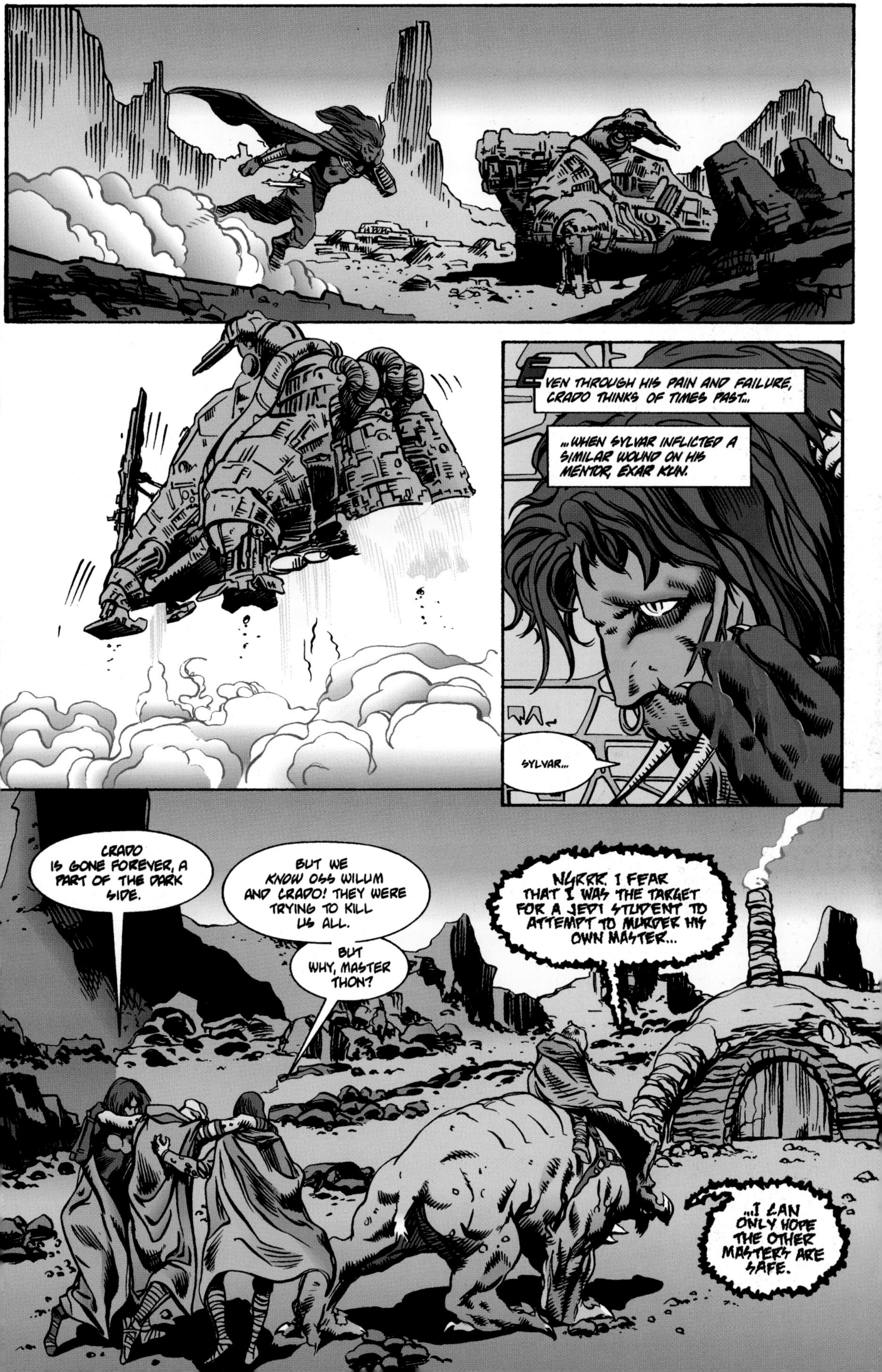
EVEN THROUGH HIS PAIN AND FAILURE, CRADO THINKS OF TIMES PAST...
...WHEN SYLVAR INFLICTED A SIMILAR WOUND ON HIS MENTOR, EXAR KUN.
SYLVAR...
CRADO IS GONE FOREVER, A PART OF THE DARK SIDE.
BUT WE KNOW OSS WILUM AND CRADO! THEY WERE TRYING TO KILL US ALL.
BUT WHY, MASTER THON?
NGRRR. I FEAR THAT I WAS THE TARGET FOR A JEDI STUDENT TO ATTEMPT TO MURDER HIS OWN MASTER...
...I CAN ONLY HOPE THE OTHER MASTERS ARE SAFE.

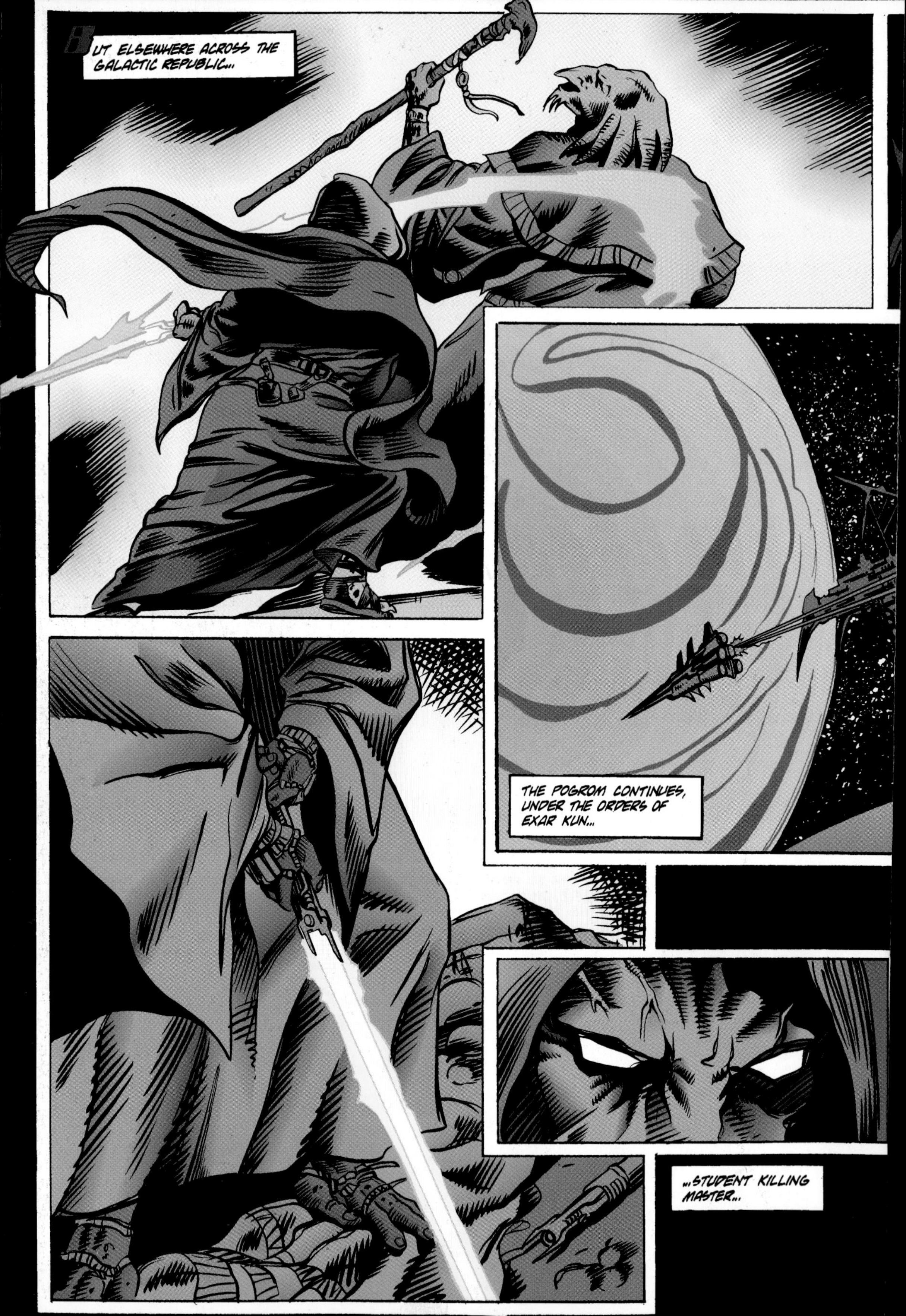
UT ELSEWHERE ACROSS THE GALACTIC REPUBLIC...
THE POGROM CONTINUES, UNDER THE ORDERS OF EXAR KUN...
...STUDENT KILLING MASTER...

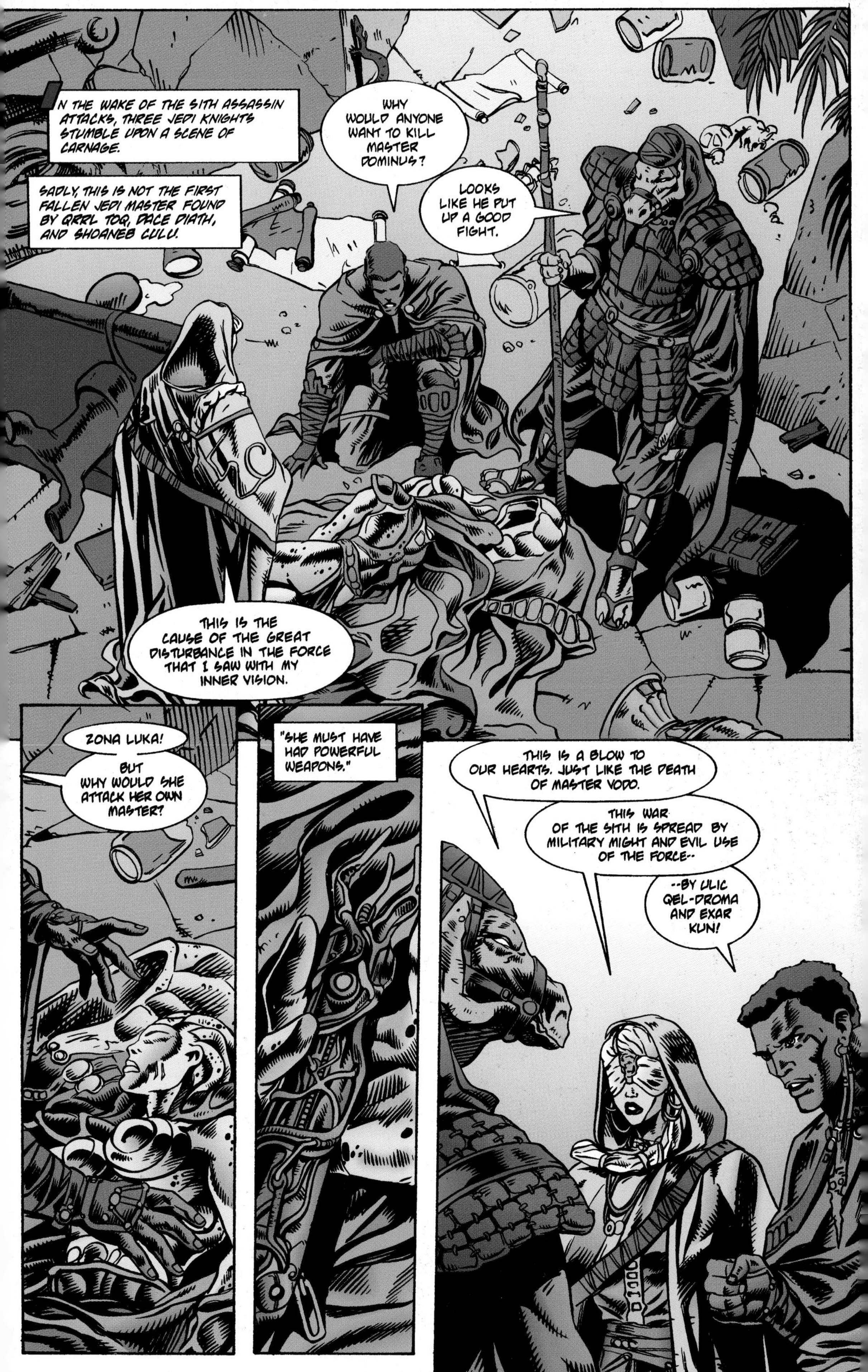
IN THE WAKE OF THE SITH ASSASSIN ATTACKS, THREE JEDI KNIGHTS STUMBLE UPON A SCENE OF CARNAGE.
SADLY, THIS IS NOT THE FIRST FALLEN JEDI MASTER FOUND BY QRRL TOQ, DACE DIATH, AND SHOANEB CULU.
WHY WOULD ANYONE WANT TO KILL MASTER DOMINUS?
LOOKS LIKE HE PUT UP A GOOD FIGHT.
THIS IS THE CAUSE OF THE GREAT DISTURBANCE IN THE FORCE THAT I SAW WITH MY INNER VISION.
ZONA LUKA!
BUT WHY WOULD SHE ATTACK HER OWN MASTER?
"SHE MUST HAVE HAD POWERFUL WEAPONS."
THIS IS A BLOW TO OUR HEARTS. JUST LIKE THE DEATH OF MASTER VODO.
THIS WAR OF THE SITH IS SPREAD BY MILITARY MIGHT AND EVIL USE OF THE FORCE--
--BY ULIC QEL-DROMA AND EXAR KUN!

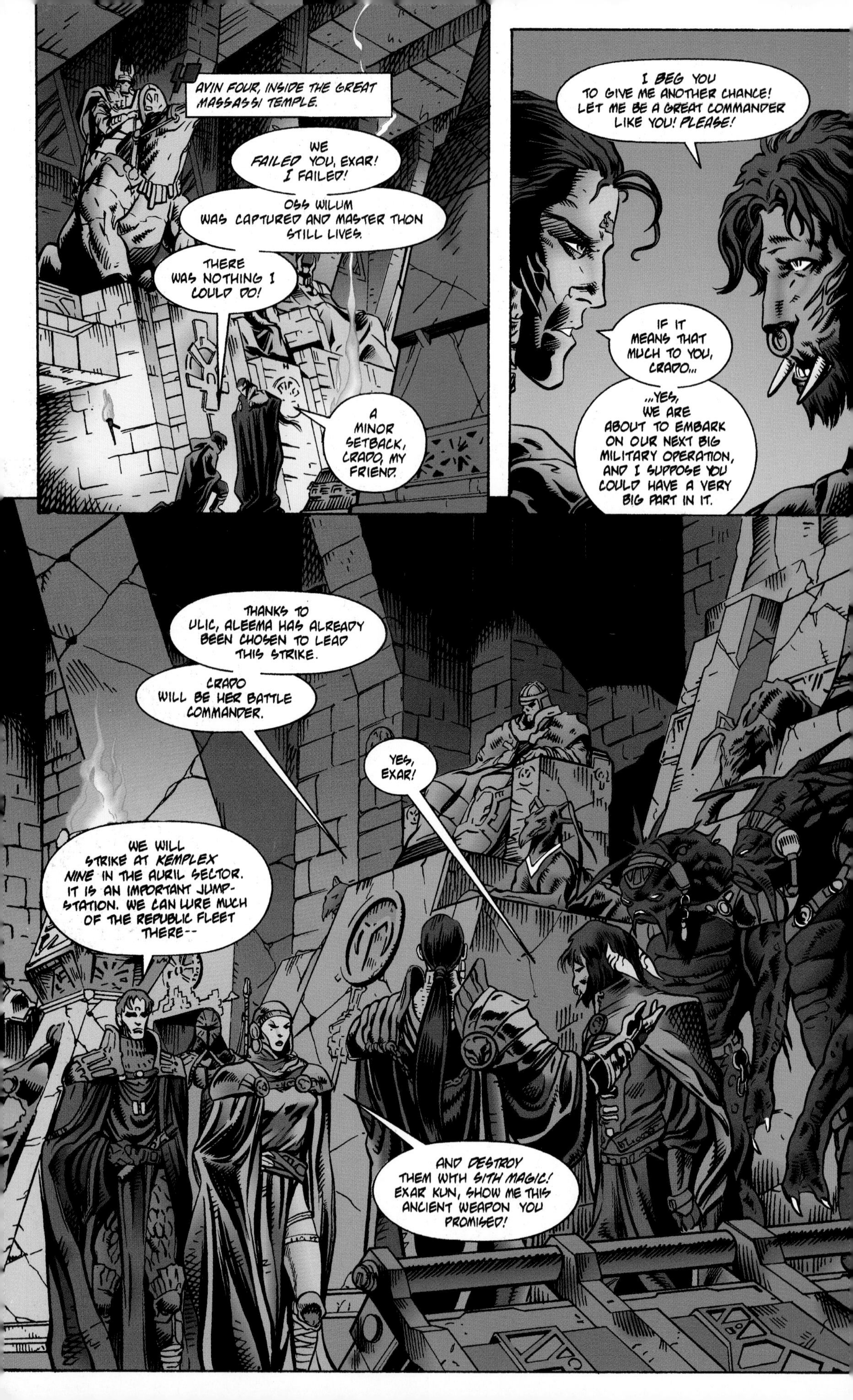
AVIN FOUR, INSIDE THE GREAT MASSASSI TEMPLE.
WE FAILED YOU, EXAR! I FAILED!
OSS WILUM WAS CAPTURED AND MASTER THON STILL LIVES.
THERE WAS NOTHING I COULD DO!
A MINOR SETBACK, CRADO, MY FRIEND.
I BEG YOU TO GIVE ME ANOTHER CHANCE! LET ME BE A GREAT COMMANDER LIKE YOU! PLEASE!
IF IT MEANS THAT MUCH TO YOU, CRADO...
...YES, WE ARE ABOUT TO EMBARK ON OUR NEXT BIG MILITARY OPERATION, AND I SUPPOSE YOU COULD HAVE A VERY BIG PART IN IT.
THANKS TO ULIC, ALEEMA HAS ALREADY BEEN CHOSEN TO LEAD THIS STRIKE.
CRADO WILL BE HER BATTLE COMMANDER.
YES, EXAR!
WE WILL STRIKE AT KEMPLEX NINE IN THE AURIL SECTOR. IT IS AN IMPORTANT JUMP-STATION. WE CAN LURE MUCH OF THE REPUBLIC FLEET THERE--
AND DESTROY THEM WITH SITH MAGIC! EXAR KUN, SHOW ME THIS ANCIENT WEAPON YOU PROMISED!

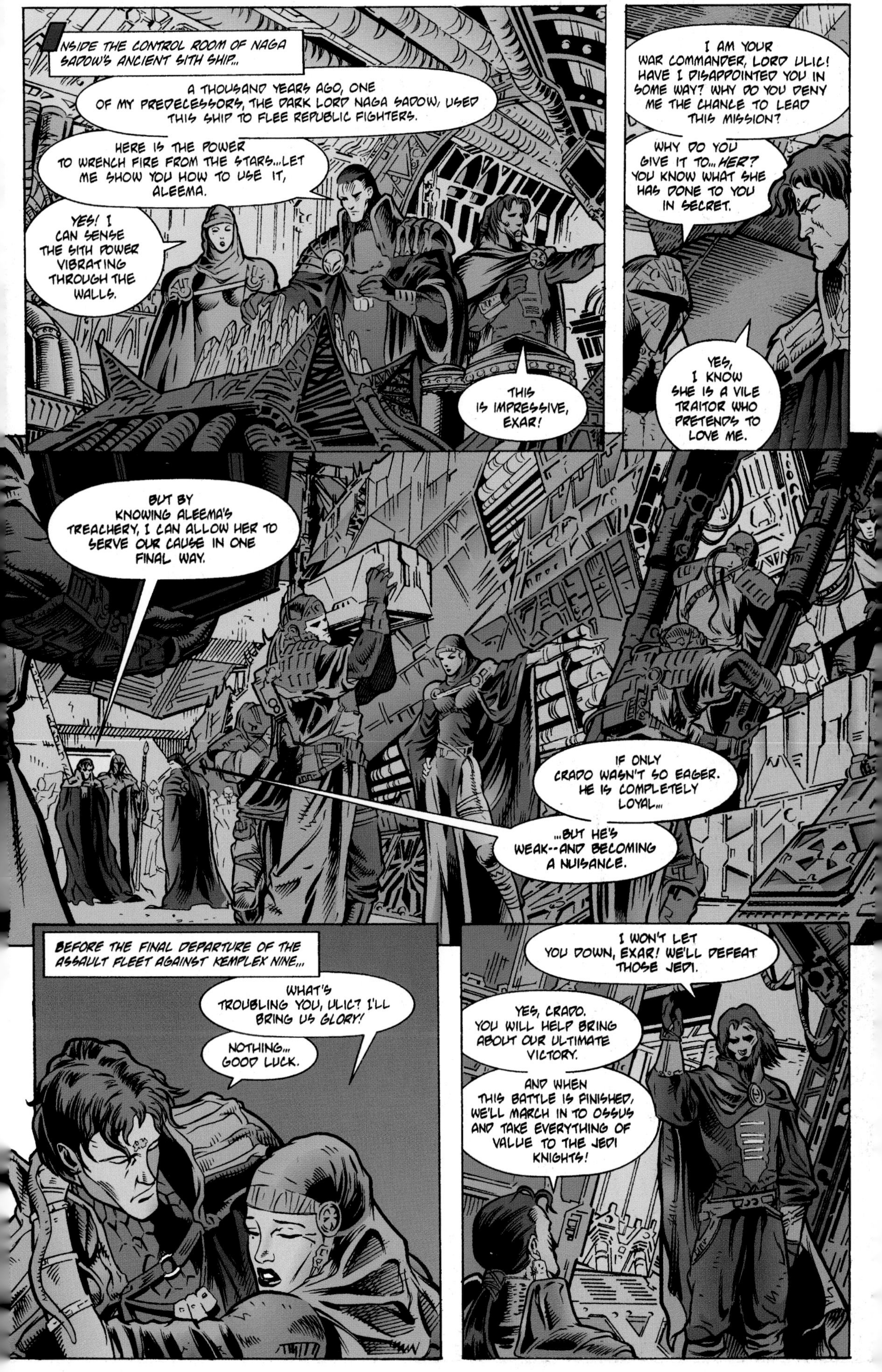
INSIDE THE CONTROL ROOM OF NAGA SADOW'S ANCIENT SITH SHIP...
A THOUSAND YEARS AGO, ONE OF MY PREDECESSORS, THE DARK LORD NAGA SADOW, USED THIS SHIP TO FLEE REPUBLIC FIGHTERS.
HERE IS THE POWER TO WRENCH FIRE FROM THE STARS...LET ME SHOW YOU HOW TO USE IT, ALEEMA.
YES! I CAN SENSE THE SITH POWER VIBRATING THROUGH THE WALLS.
THIS IS IMPRESSIVE, EXAR!
I AM YOUR WAR COMMANDER, LORD ULIC! HAVE I DISAPPOINTED YOU IN SOME WAY? WHY DO YOU DENY ME THE CHANCE TO LEAD THIS MISSION?
WHY DO YOU GIVE IT TO... HER? YOU KNOW WHAT SHE HAS DONE TO YOU IN SECRET.
YES, I KNOW SHE IS A VILE TRAITOR WHO PRETENDS TO LOVE ME.
BUT BY KNOWING ALEEMA'S TREACHERY, I CAN ALLOW HER TO SERVE OUR CAUSE IN ONE FINAL WAY.
IF ONLY CRADO WASN'T SO EAGER. HE IS COMPLETELY LOYAL...
...BUT HE'S WEAK--AND BECOMING A NUISANCE.
BEFORE THE FINAL DEPARTURE OF THE ASSAULT FLEET AGAINST KEMPLEX NINE...
WHAT'S TROUBLING YOU, ULIC? I'LL BRING US GLORY!
NOTHING... GOOD LUCK.
I WON'T LET YOU DOWN, EXAR! WE'LL DEFEAT THOSE JEDI.
YES, CRADO. YOU WILL HELP BRING ABOUT OUR ULTIMATE VICTORY.
AND WHEN THIS BATTLE IS FINISHED, WE'LL MARCH IN TO OSSUS AND TAKE EVERYTHING OF VALUE TO THE JEDI KNIGHTS!

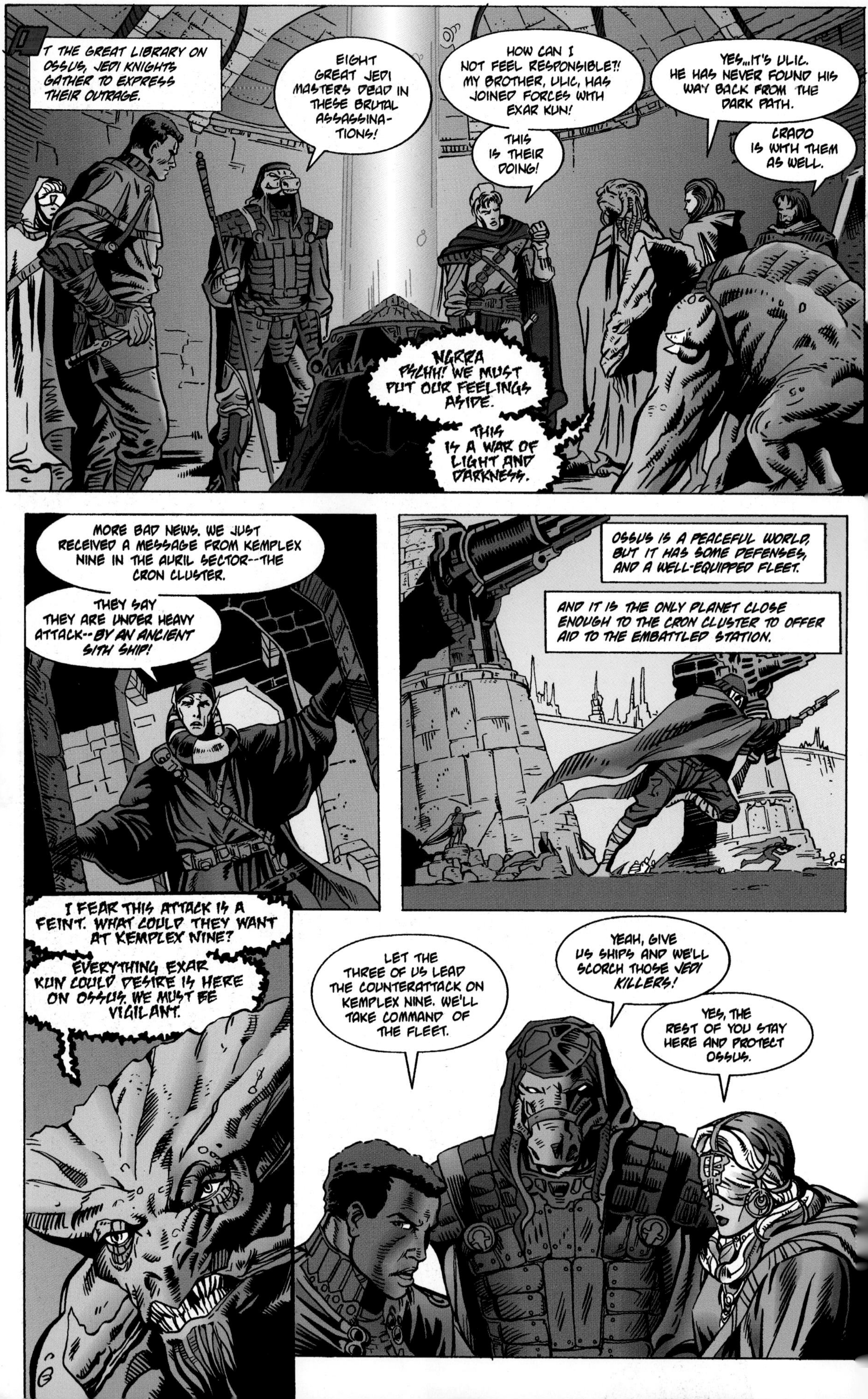
AT THE GREAT LIBRARY ON OSSUS, JEDI KNIGHTS GATHER TO EXPRESS THEIR OUTRAGE.
EIGHT GREAT JEDI MASTERS DEAD IN THESE BRUTAL ASSASSINATIONS!
HOW CAN I NOT FEEL RESPONSIBLE?! MY BROTHER, ULIC, HAS JOINED FORCES WITH EXAR KUN!
THIS IS THEIR DOING!
YES...IT'S ULIC. HE HAS NEVER FOUND HIS WAY BACK FROM THE DARK PATH.
CRADO IS WITH THEM AS WELL.
NGRRA PSCHH! WE MUST PUT OUR FEELINGS ASIDE.
THIS IS A WAR OF LIGHT AND DARKNESS.
MORE BAD NEWS. WE JUST RECEIVED A MESSAGE FROM KEMPLEX NINE IN THE AURIL SECTOR--THE CRON CLUSTER.
THEY SAY THEY ARE UNDER HEAVY ATTACK--BY AN ANCIENT SITH SHIP!
OSSUS IS A PEACEFUL WORLD, BUT IT HAS SOME DEFENSES, AND A WELL-EQUIPPED FLEET.
AND IT IS THE ONLY PLANET CLOSE ENOUGH TO THE CRON CLUSTER TO OFFER AID TO THE EMBATTLED STATION.
I FEAR THIS ATTACK IS A FEINT. WHAT COULD THEY WANT AT KEMPLEX NINE?
EVERYTHING EXAR KUN COULD DESIRE IS HERE ON OSSUS. WE MUST BE VIGILANT.
LET THE THREE OF US LEAD THE COUNTERATTACK ON KEMPLEX NINE. WE'LL TAKE COMMAND OF THE FLEET.
YEAH, GIVE US SHIPS AND WE'LL SCORCH THOSE JEDI KILLERS!
YES, THE REST OF YOU STAY HERE AND PROTECT OSSUS.

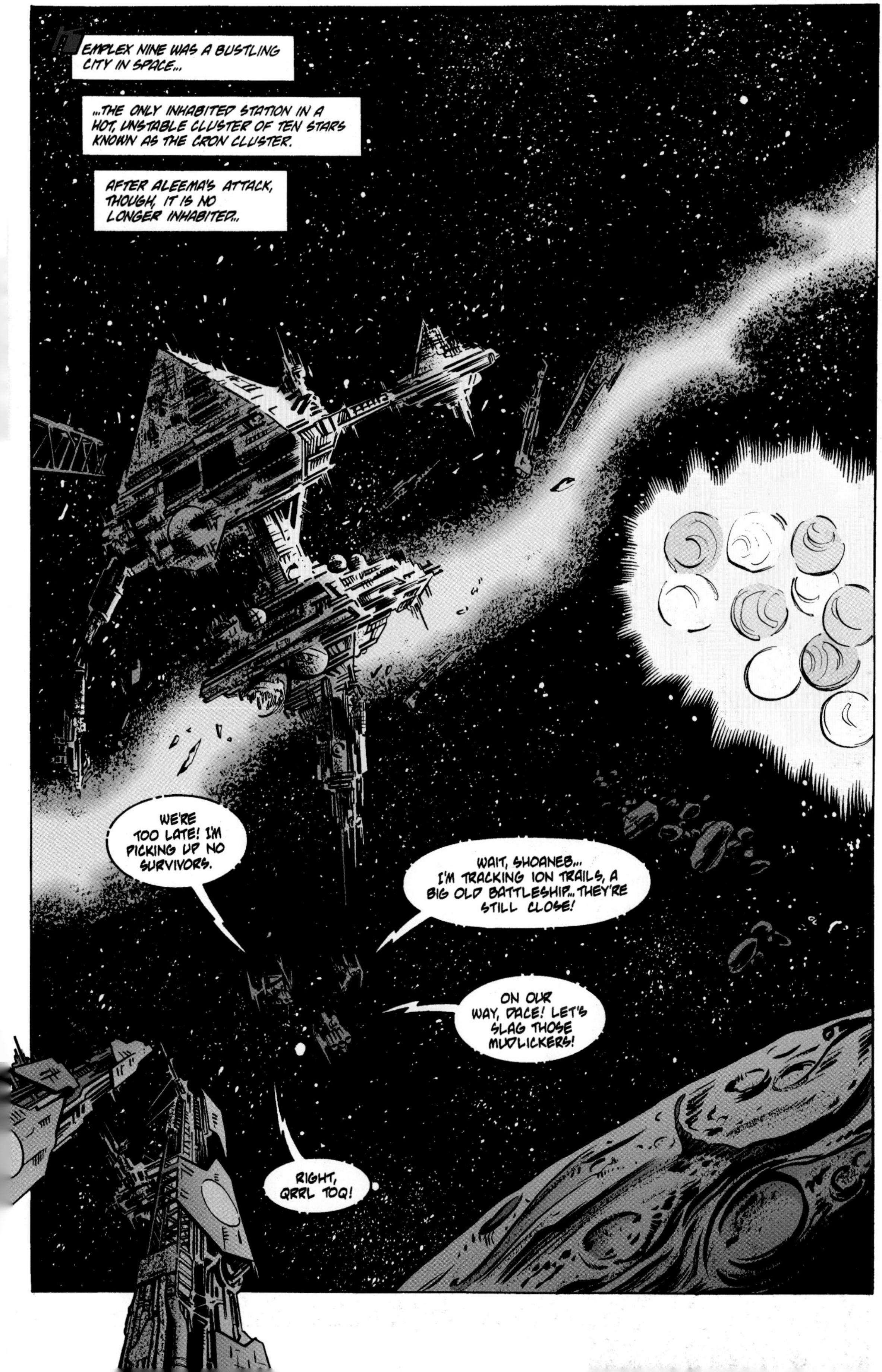
EMPLEX NINE WAS A BUSTLING CITY IN SPACE...
...THE ONLY INHABITED STATION IN A HOT, UNSTABLE CLUSTER OF TEN STARS KNOWN AS THE CRON CLUSTER.
AFTER ALEEMA'S ATTACK, THOUGH, IT IS NO LONGER INHABITED...
WE'RE TOO LATE! I'M PICKING UP NO SURVIVORS.
WAIT, SHOANEB... I'M TRACKING ION TRAILS, A BIG OLD BATTLESHIP... THEY'RE STILL CLOSE!
ON OUR WAY, DACE! LET'S SLAG THOSE MUDLICKERS!
RIGHT, QRRL TOQ!

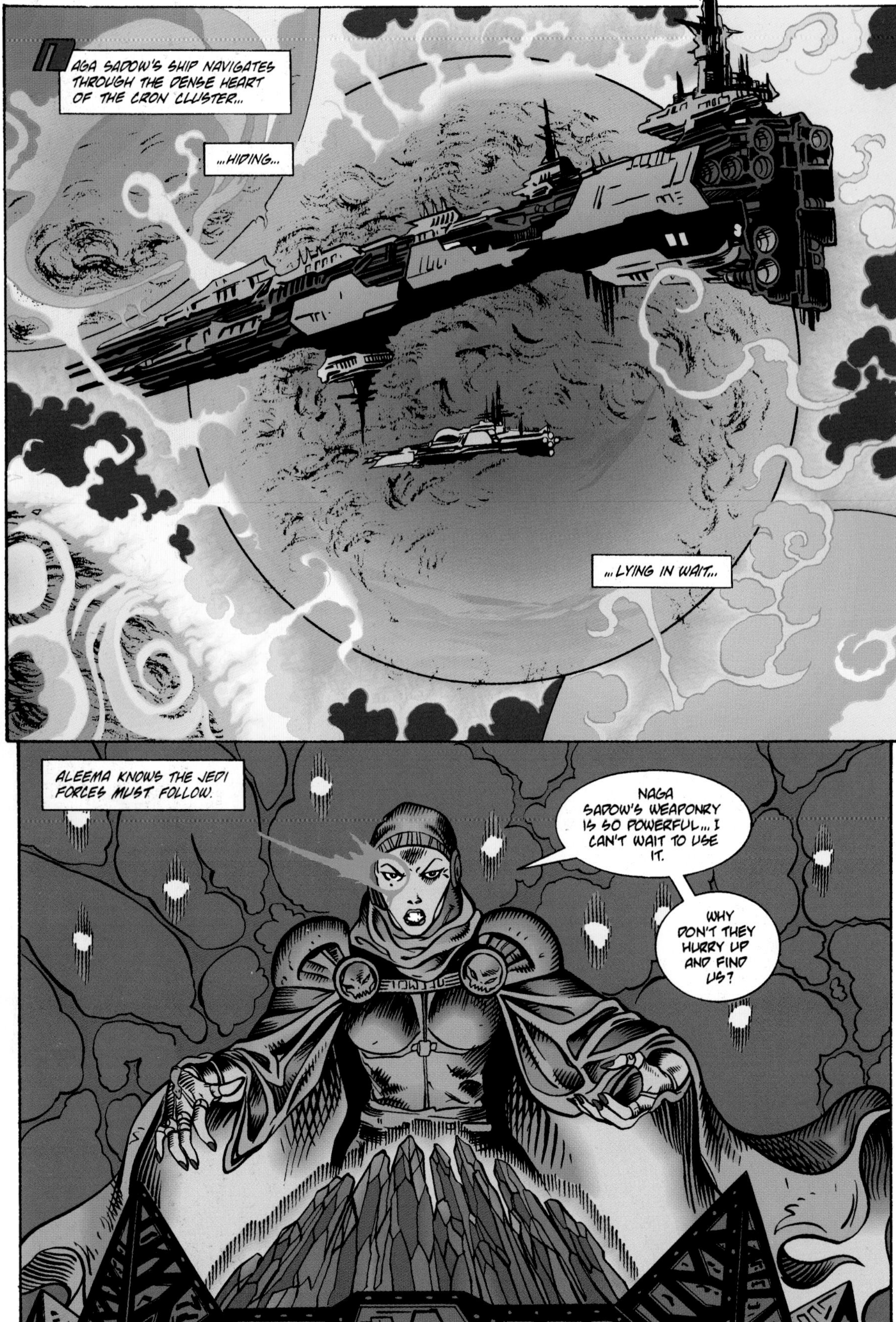
NAGA SADOW'S SHIP NAVIGATES THROUGH THE DENSE HEART OF THE CRON CLUSTER...
...HIDING...
...LYING IN WAIT...
ALEEMA KNOWS THE JEDI FORCES MUST FOLLOW.
NAGA SADOW'S WEAPONRY IS SO POWERFUL... I CAN'T WAIT TO USE IT.
WHY DON'T THEY HURRY UP AND FIND US?

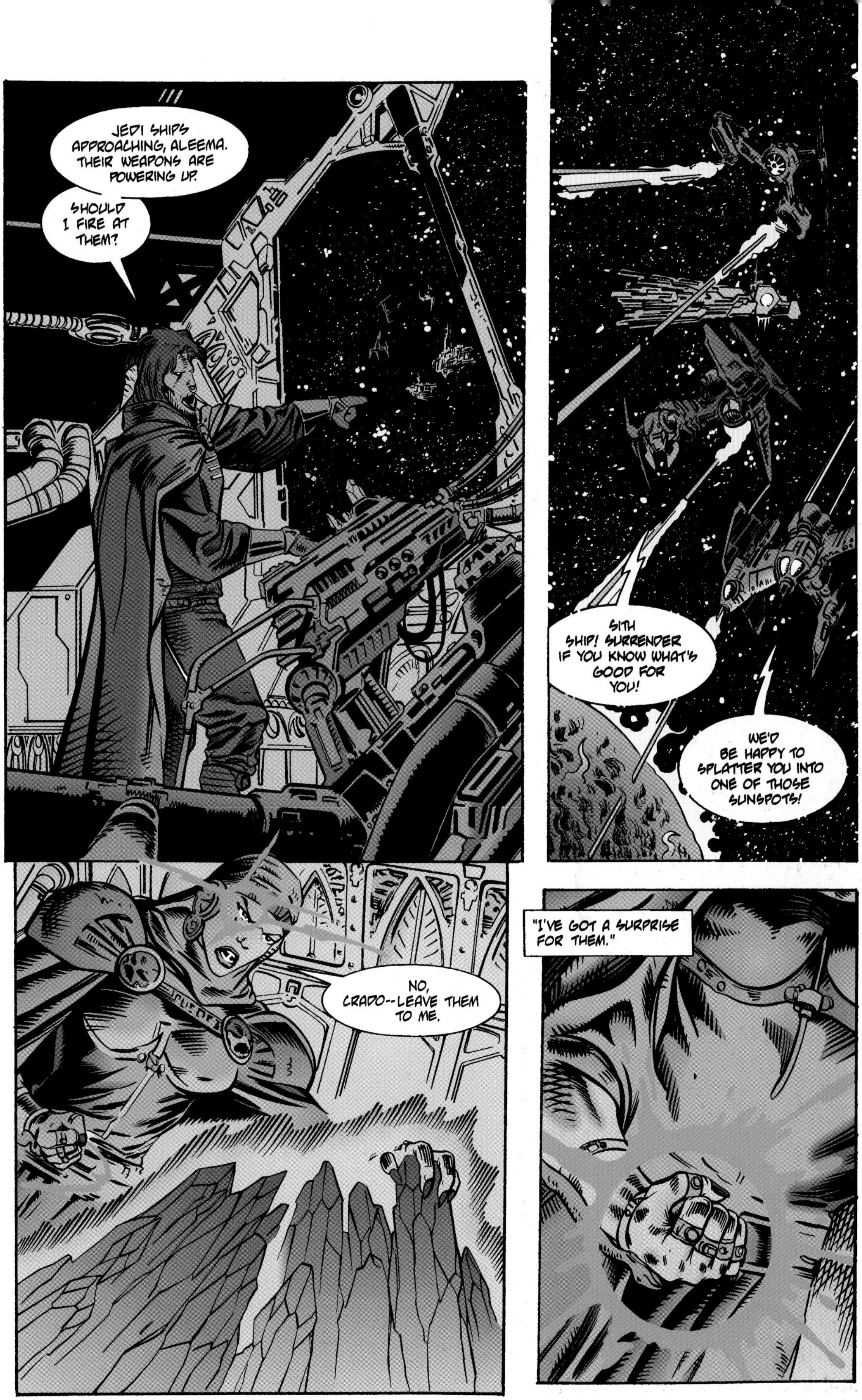
JEDI SHIPS APPROACHING, ALEEMA. THEIR WEAPONS ARE POWERING UP.
SHOULD I FIRE AT THEM?
SITH SHIP! SURRENDER IF YOU KNOW WHAT'S GOOD FOR YOU!
WE'D BE HAPPY TO SPLATTER YOU INTO ONE OF THOSE SUNSPOTS!
NO, CRADO--LEAVE THEM TO ME.
"I'VE GOT A SURPRISE FOR THEM."

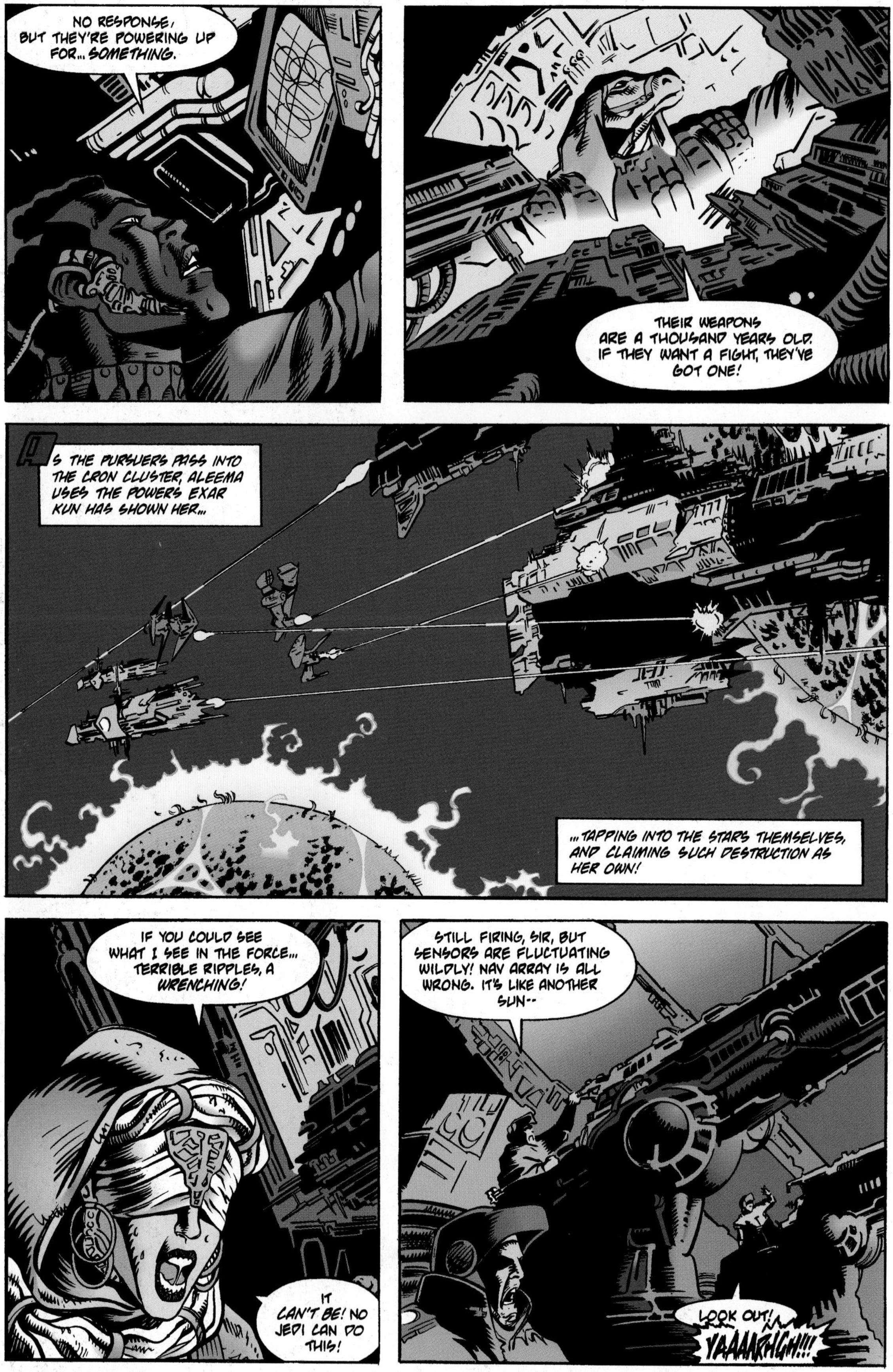
NO RESPONSE, BUT THEY'RE POWERING UP FOR... SOMETHING.
THEIR WEAPONS ARE A THOUSAND YEARS OLD. IF THEY WANT A FIGHT, THEY'VE GOT ONE!
AS THE PURSUERS PASS INTO THE CRON CLUSTER, ALEEMA USES THE POWERS EXAR KUN HAS SHOWN HER...
...TAPPING INTO THE STARS THEMSELVES, AND CLAIMING SUCH DESTRUCTION AS HER OWN!
IF YOU COULD SEE WHAT I SEE IN THE FORCE... TERRIBLE RIPPLES, A WRENCHING!
IT CAN'T BE! NO JEDI CAN DO THIS!
STILL FIRING, SIR, BUT SENSORS ARE FLUCTUATING WILDLY! NAV ARRAY IS ALL WRONG. IT'S LIKE ANOTHER SUN--
LOOK OUT!
YAAAARHGH!!!

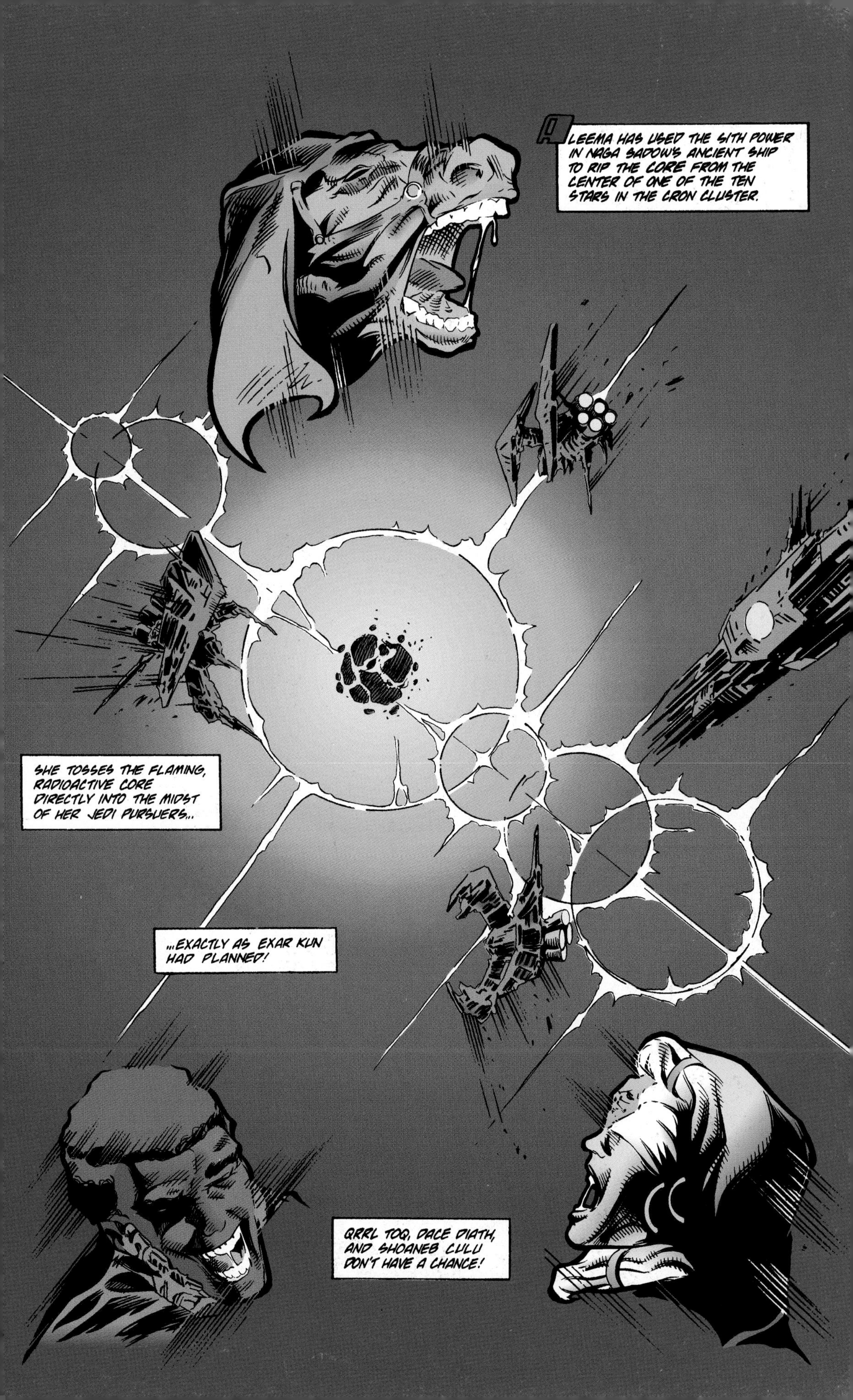
ALEEMA HAS USED THE SITH POWER IN NAGA SADOW'S ANCIENT SHIP TO RIP THE CORE FROM THE CENTER OF ONE OF THE TEN STARS IN THE CRON CLUSTER.
SHE TOSSES THE FLAMING, RADIOACTIVE CORE DIRECTLY INTO THE MIDST OF HER JEDI PURSUERS...
...EXACTLY AS EXAR KUN HAD PLANNED!
QRRL TOQ, DACE DIATH, AND SHOANEB CULU DON'T HAVE A CHANCE!

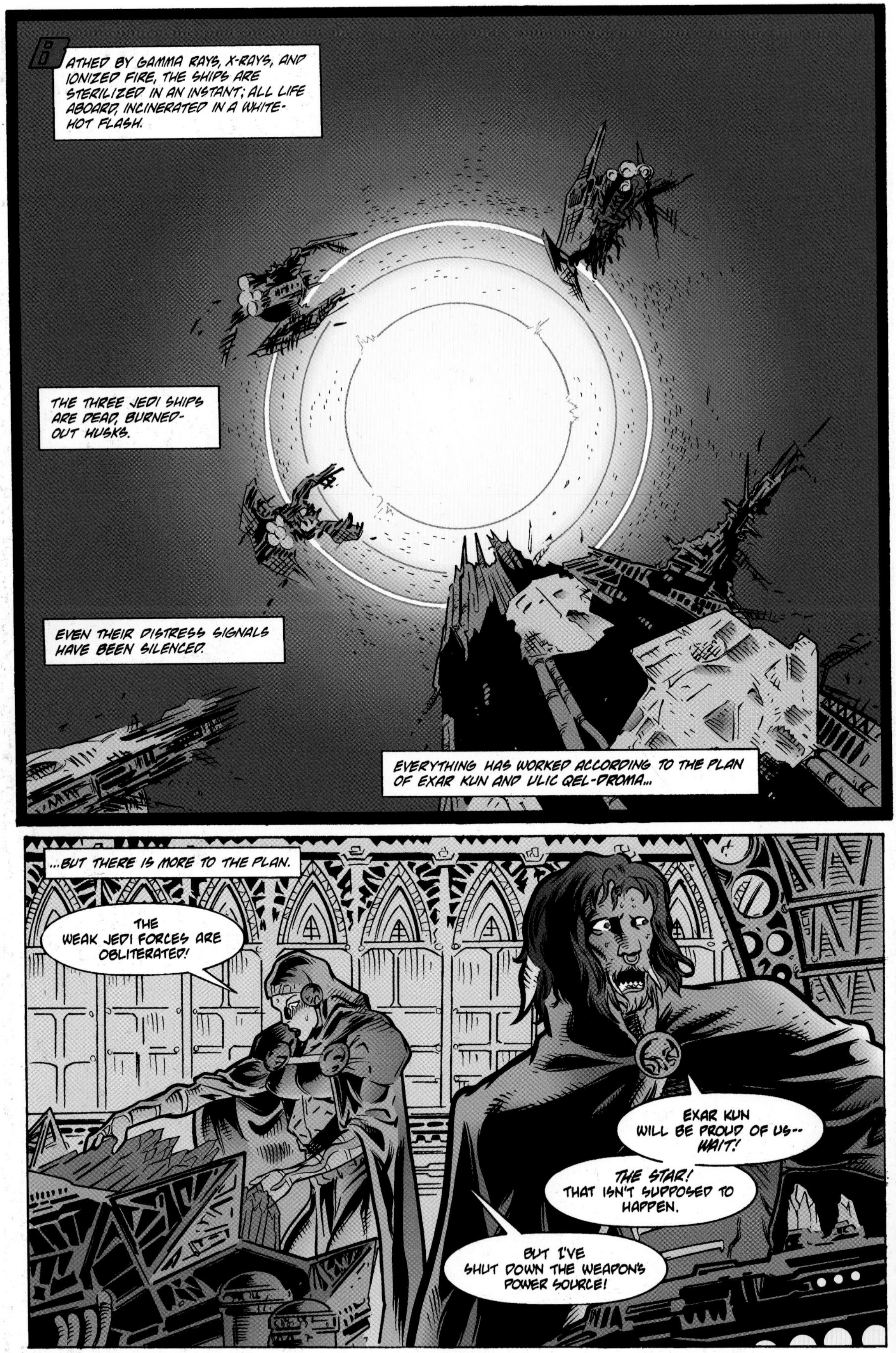
BATHED BY GAMMA RAYS, X-RAYS, AND IONIZED FIRE, THE SHIPS ARE STERILIZED IN AN INSTANT; ALL LIFE ABOARD, INCINERATED IN A WHITE-HOT FLASH.
THE THREE JEDI SHIPS ARE DEAD, BURNED-OUT HUSKS.
EVEN THEIR DISTRESS SIGNALS HAVE BEEN SILENCED.
EVERYTHING HAS WORKED ACCORDING TO THE PLAN OF EXAR KUN AND ULIC QEL-DROMA...
...BUT THERE IS MORE TO THE PLAN.
THE WEAK JEDI FORCES ARE OBLITERATED!
EXAR KUN WILL BE PROUD OF US-- WAIT!
THE STAR! THAT ISN'T SUPPOSED TO HAPPEN.
BUT I'VE SHUT DOWN THE WEAPON'S POWER SOURCE!

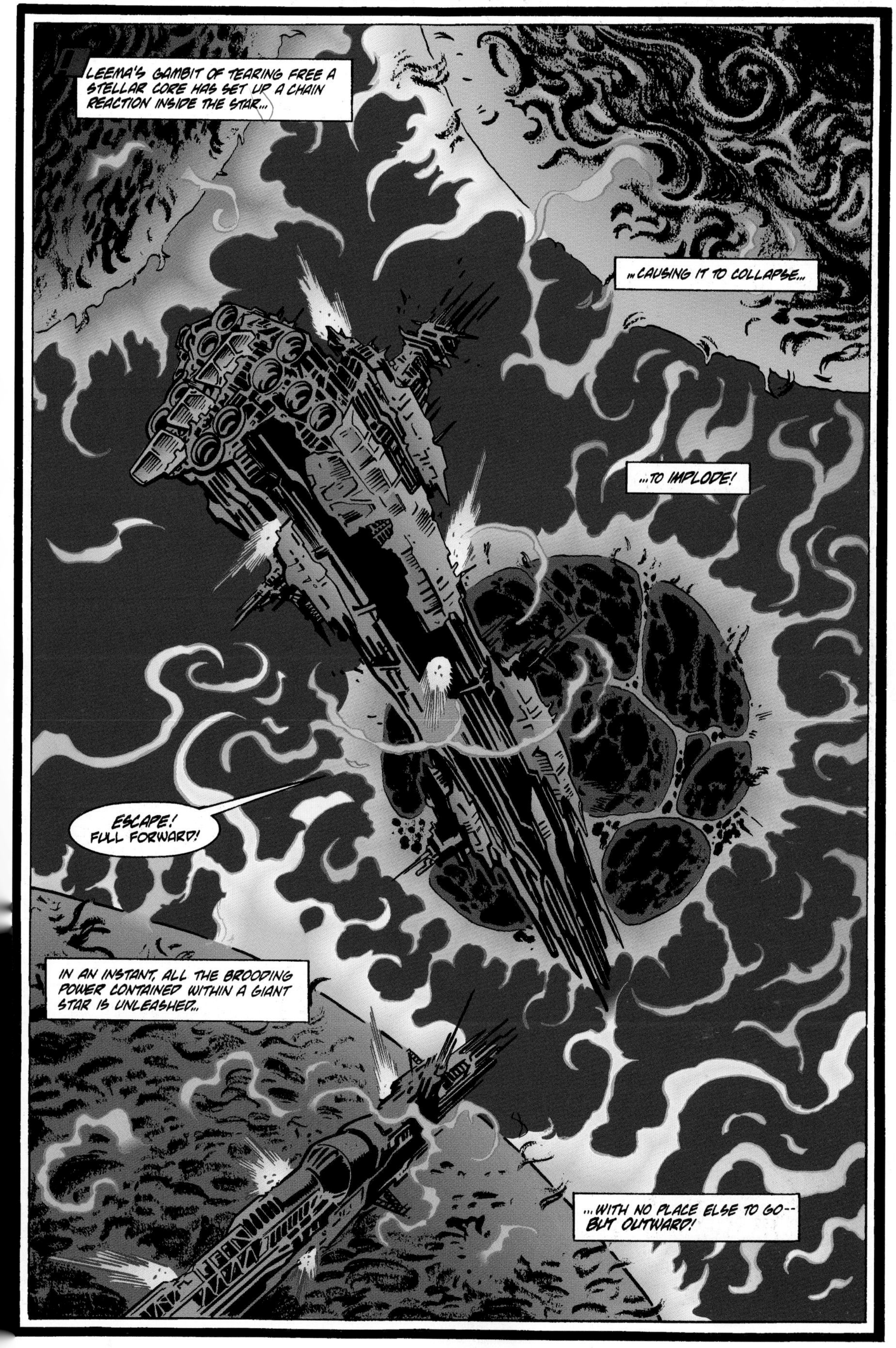
LEEMA'S GAMBIT OF TEARING FREE A STELLAR CORE HAS SET UP A CHAIN REACTION INSIDE THE STAR...
...CAUSING IT TO COLLAPSE...
...TO IMPLODE!
ESCAPE! FULL FORWARD!
IN AN INSTANT, ALL THE BROODING POWER CONTAINED WITHIN A GIANT STAR IS UNLEASHED...
...WITH NO PLACE ELSE TO GO-- BUT OUTWARD!

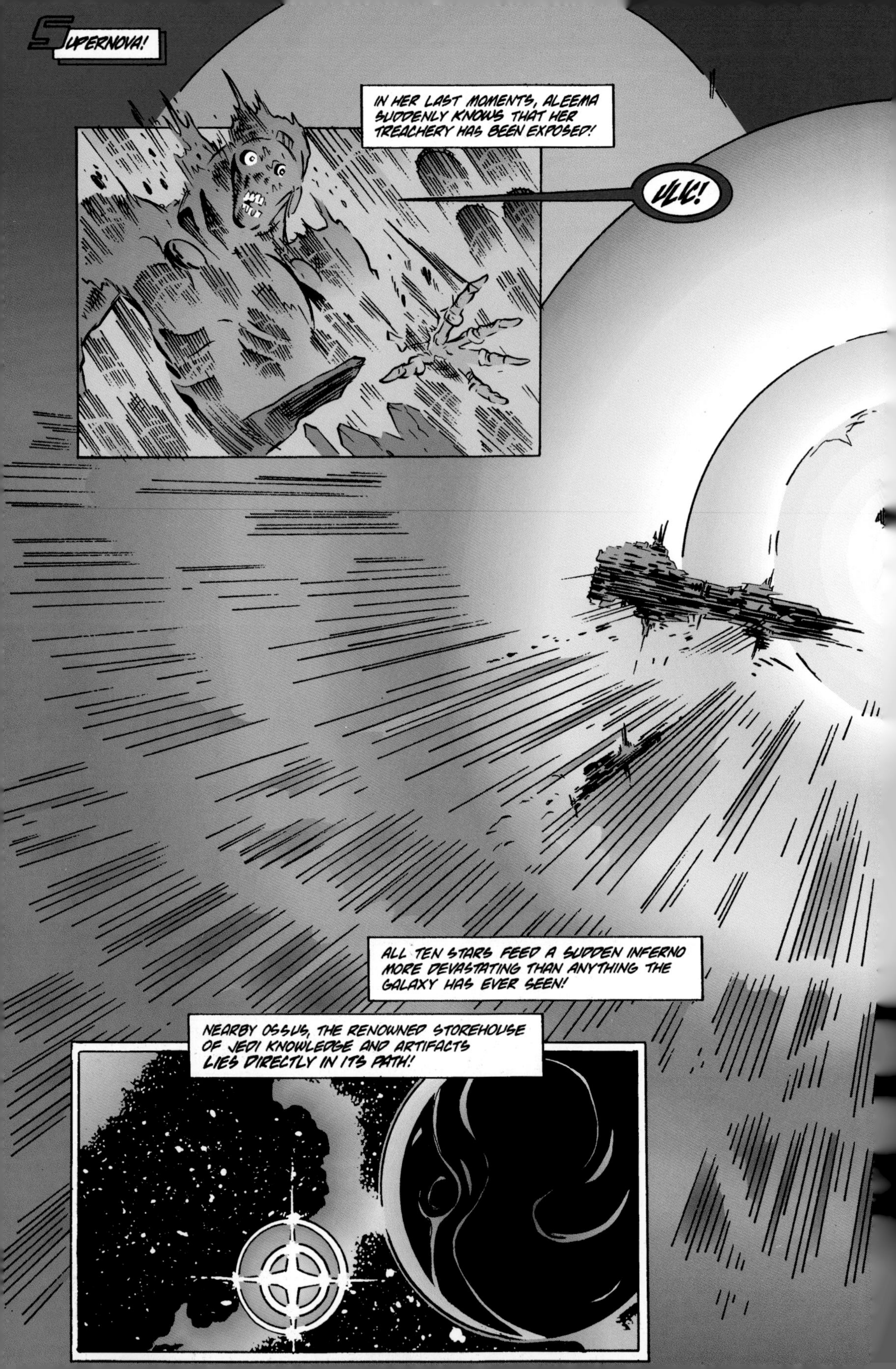
SUPERNOVA!
IN HER LAST MOMENTS, ALEEMA SUDDENLY KNOWS THAT HER TREACHERY HAS BEEN EXPOSED!
ULIC!
ALL TEN STARS FEED A SUDDEN INFERNO MORE DEVASTATING THAN ANYTHING THE GALAXY HAS EVER SEEN!
NEARBY OSSUS, THE RENOWNED STOREHOUSE OF JEDI KNOWLEDGE AND ARTIFACTS LIES DIRECTLY IN ITS PATH!

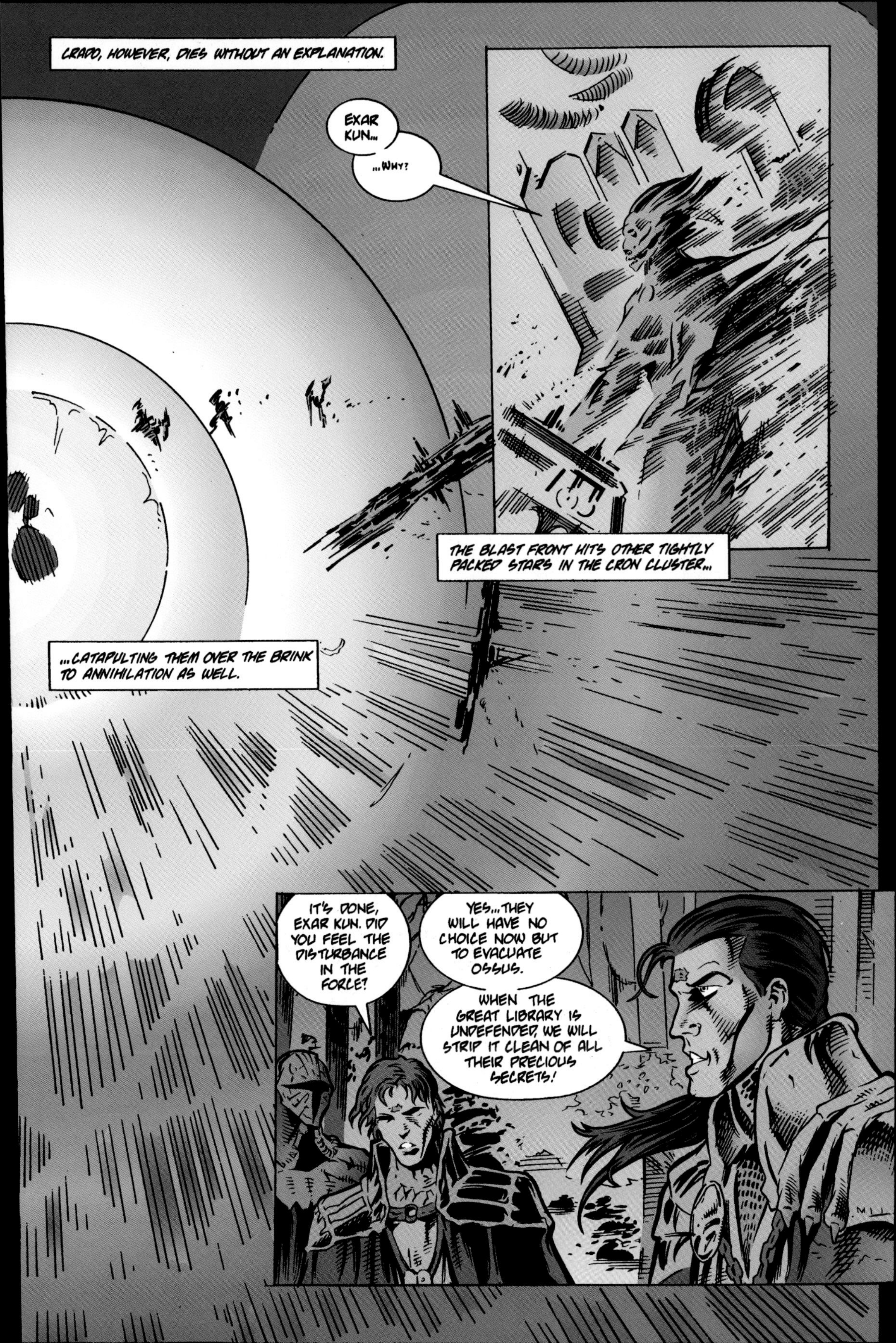
CRADO, HOWEVER, DIES WITHOUT AN EXPLANATION.
EXAR KUN...
...WHY?
THE BLAST FRONT HITS OTHER TIGHTLY PACKED STARS IN THE CRON CLUSTER...
...CATAPULTING THEM OVER THE BRINK TO ANNIHILATION AS WELL.
IT'S DONE, EXAR KUN. DID YOU FEEL THE DISTURBANCE IN THE FORCE?
YES... THEY WILL HAVE NO CHOICE NOW BUT TO EVACUATE OSSUS.
WHEN THE GREAT LIBRARY IS UNDEFENDED, WE WILL STRIP IT CLEAN OF ALL THEIR PRECIOUS SECRETS!

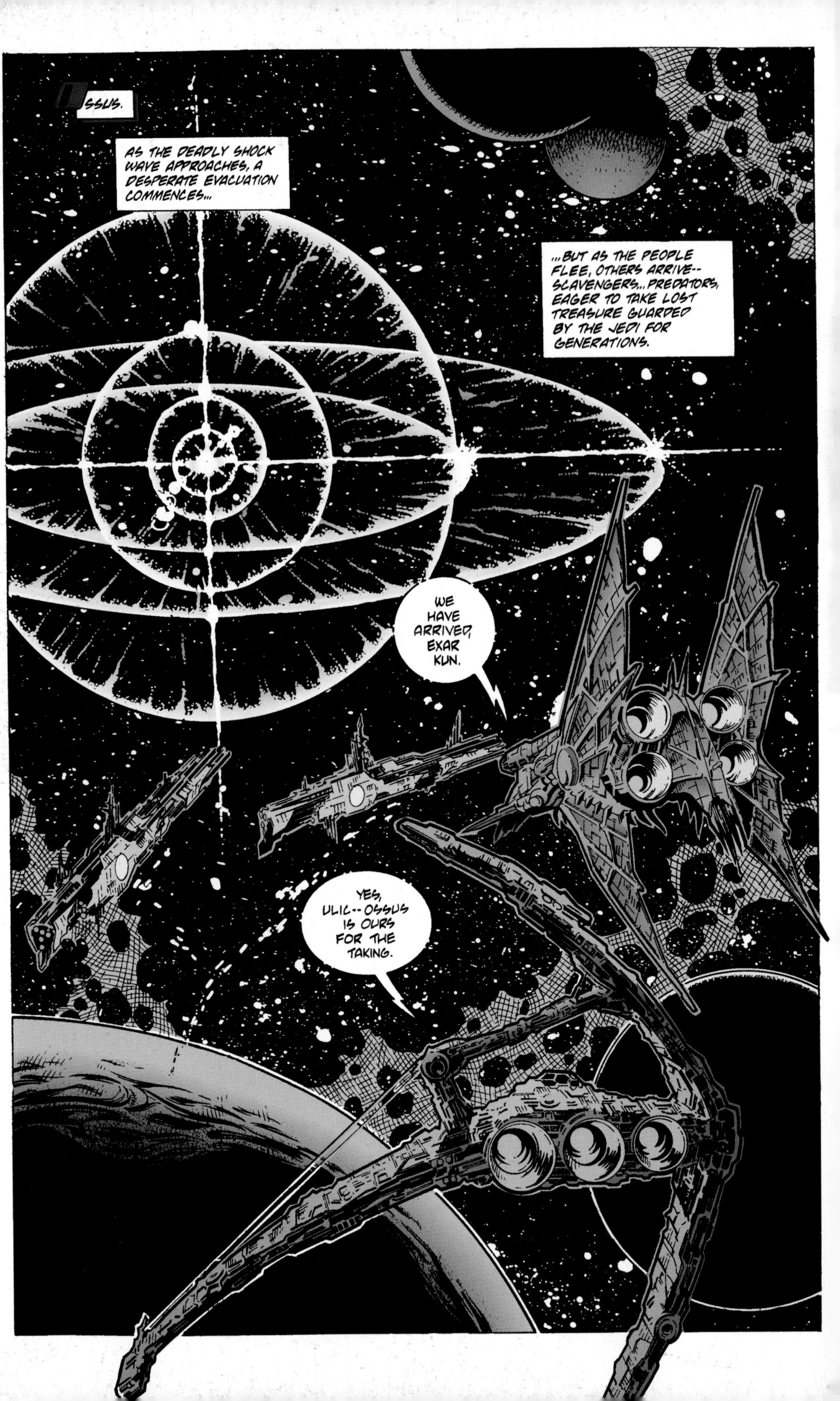
OSSUS.
AS THE DEADLY SHOCK WAVE APPROACHES, A DESPERATE EVACUATION COMMENCES...
...BUT AS THE PEOPLE FLEE, OTHERS ARRIVE--SCAVENGERS... PREDATORS, EAGER TO TAKE LOST TREASURE GUARDED BY THE JEDI FOR GENERATIONS.
WE HAVE ARRIVED, EXAR KUN.
YES, ULIC--OSSUS IS OURS FOR THE TAKING.

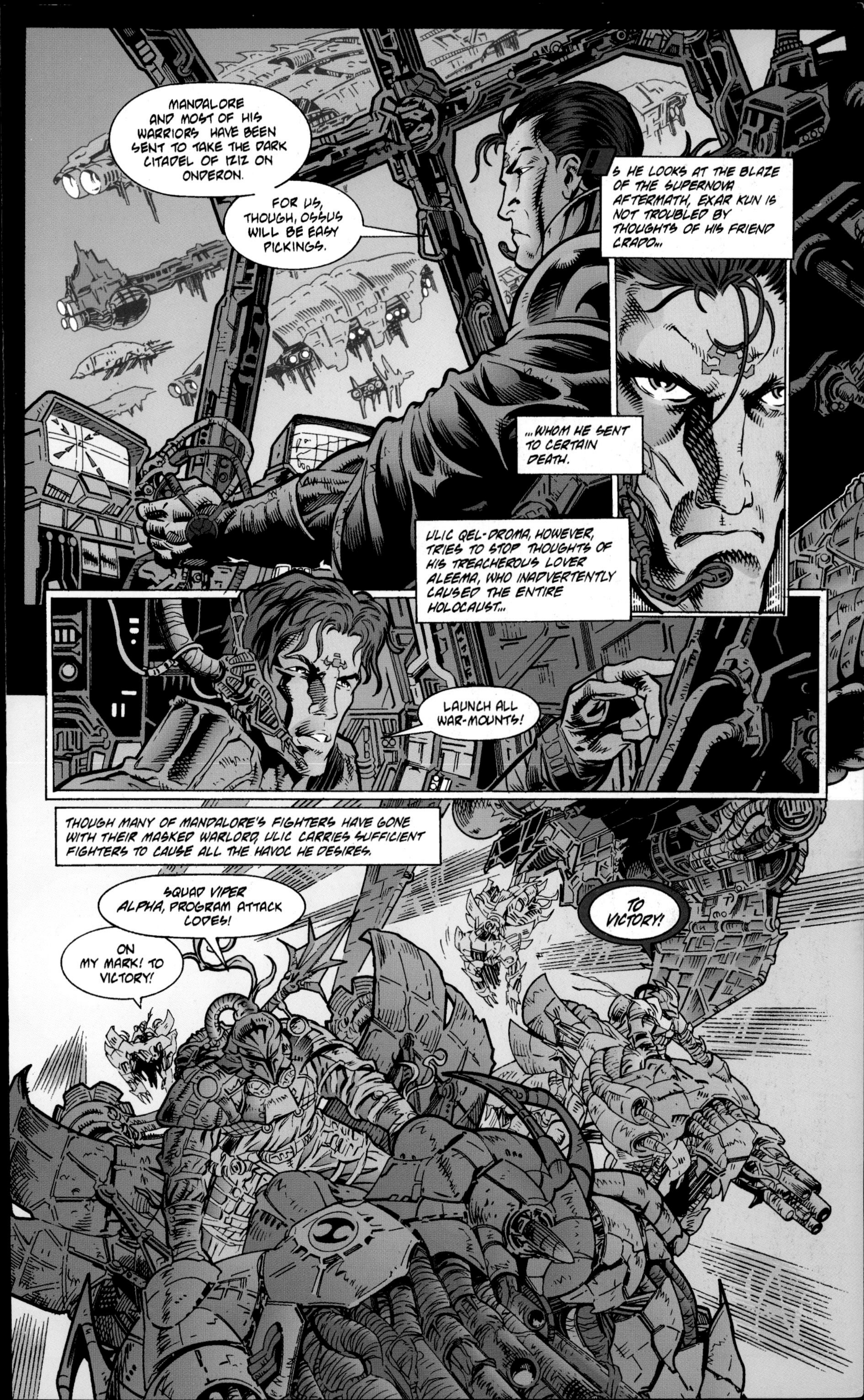
MANDALORE AND MOST OF HIS WARRIORS HAVE BEEN SENT TO TAKE THE DARK CITADEL OF IZIZ ON ONDERON.
FOR US, THOUGH, OSSUS WILL BE EASY PICKINGS.
S HE LOOKS AT THE BLAZE OF THE SUPERNOVA AFTERMATH, EXAR KUN IS NOT TROUBLED BY THOUGHTS OF HIS FRIEND CRADO...
...WHOM HE SENT TO CERTAIN DEATH.
ULIC QEL-DROMA, HOWEVER, TRIES TO STOP THOUGHTS OF HIS TREACHEROUS LOVER ALEEMA, WHO INADVERTENTLY CAUSED THE ENTIRE HOLOCAUST...
LAUNCH ALL WAR-MOUNTS!
THOUGH MANY OF MANDALORE'S FIGHTERS HAVE GONE WITH THEIR MASKED WARLORD, ULIC CARRIES SUFFICIENT FIGHTERS TO CAUSE ALL THE HAVOC HE DESIRES.
SQUAD VIPER ALPHA, PROGRAM ATTACK CODES!
ON MY MARK! TO VICTORY!
TO VICTORY!

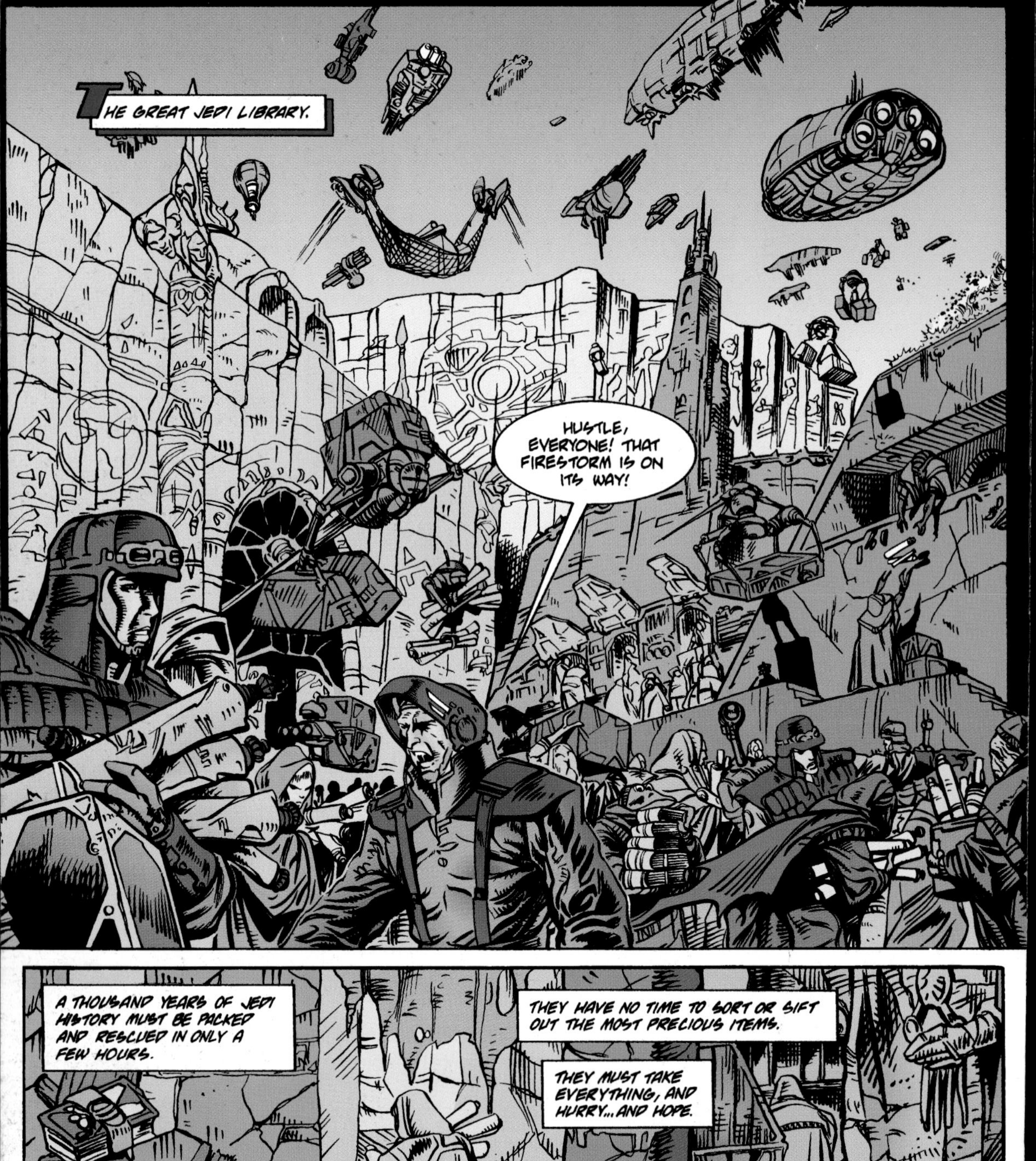
THE GREAT JEDI LIBRARY.
HUSTLE, EVERYONE! THAT FIRESTORM IS ON ITS WAY!

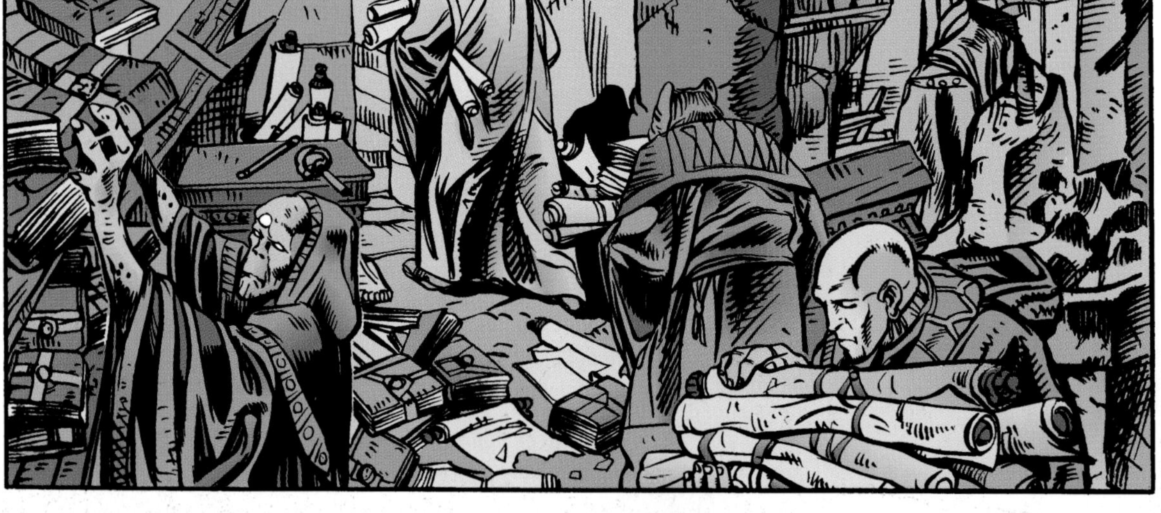
A THOUSAND YEARS OF JEDI HISTORY MUST BE PACKED AND RESCUED IN ONLY A FEW HOURS.
THEY HAVE NO TIME TO SORT OR SIFT OUT THE MOST PRECIOUS ITEMS.
THEY MUST TAKE EVERYTHING, AND HURRY... AND HOPE.

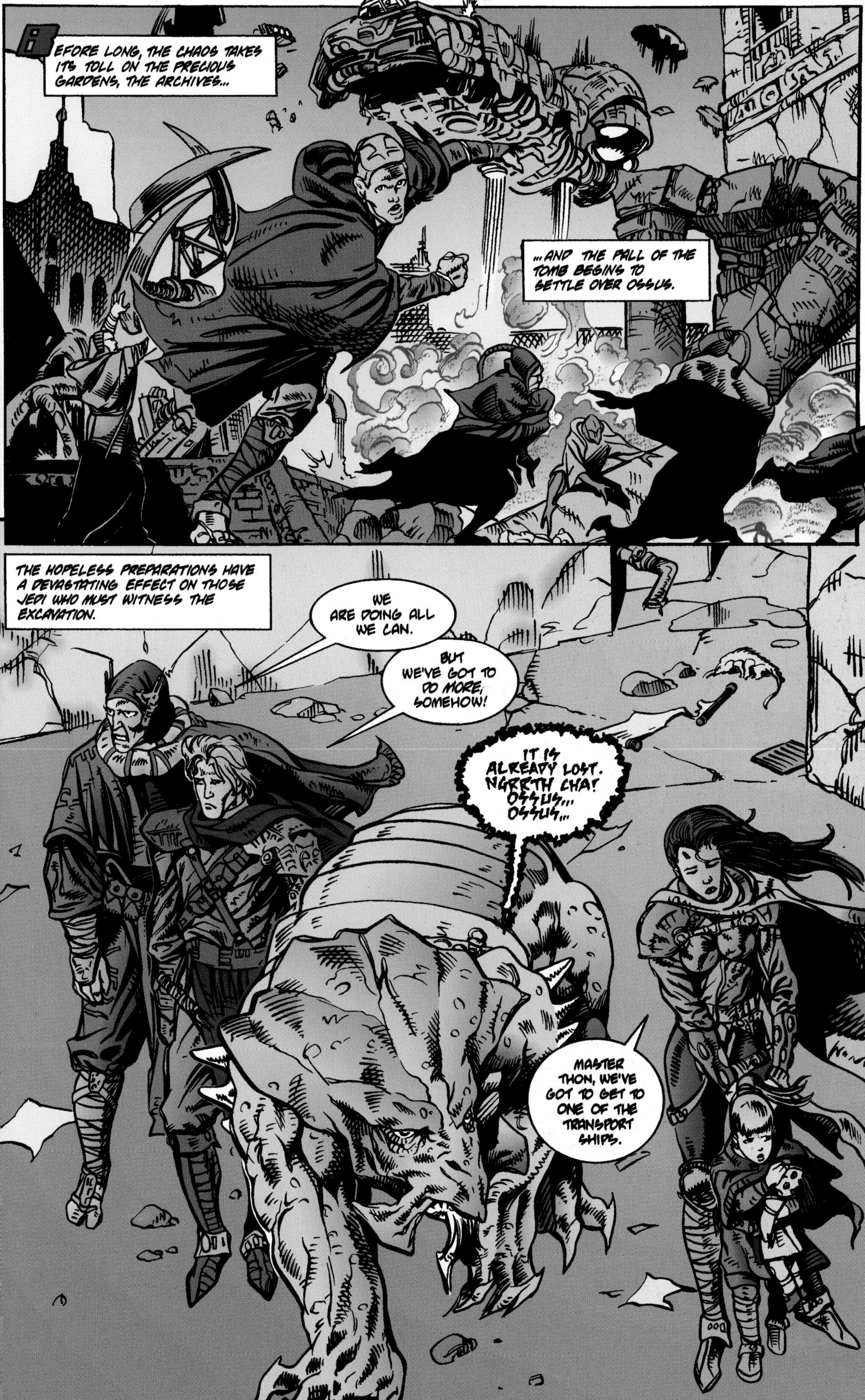
BEFORE LONG, THE CHAOS TAKES ITS TOLL ON THE PRECIOUS GARDENS, THE ARCHIVES...
...AND THE PALL OF THE TOMB BEGINS TO SETTLE OVER OSSUS.
THE HOPELESS PREPARATIONS HAVE A DEVASTATING EFFECT ON THOSE JEDI WHO MUST WITNESS THE EXCAVATION.
WE ARE DOING ALL WE CAN.
BUT WE'VE GOT TO DO MORE, SOMEHOW!
IT IS ALREADY LOST. NGRRTH CHA! OSSUS... OSSUS...
MASTER THON, WE'VE GOT TO GET TO ONE OF THE TRANSPORT SHIPS.

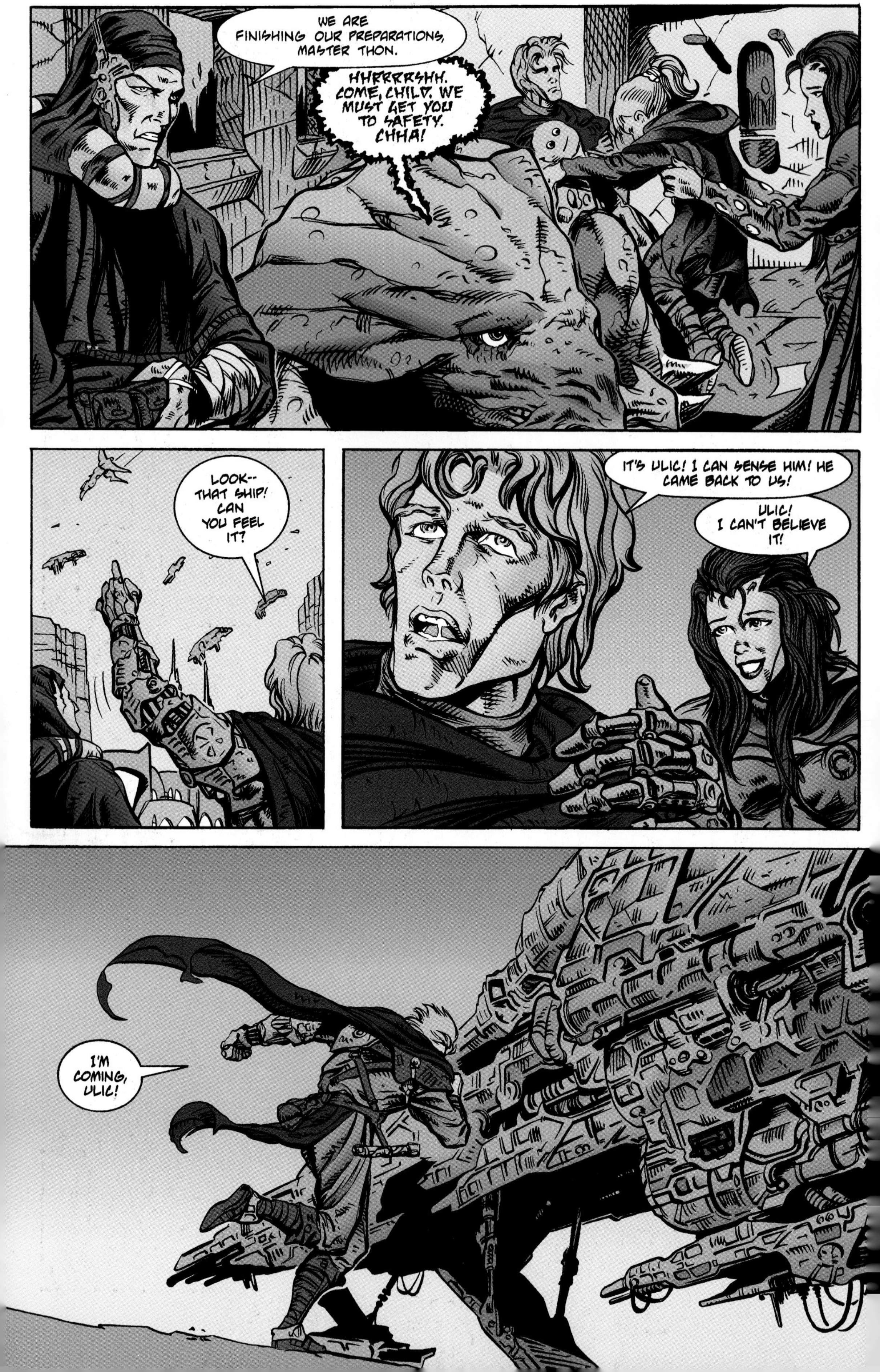
WE ARE FINISHING OUR PREPARATIONS, MASTER THON.
HHRRRRSHH. COME, CHILD. WE MUST GET YOU TO SAFETY. CHHA!
LOOK-- THAT SHIP! CAN YOU FEEL IT?
IT'S ULIC! I CAN SENSE HIM! HE CAME BACK TO US!
ULIC! I CAN'T BELIEVE IT!
I'M COMING, ULIC!

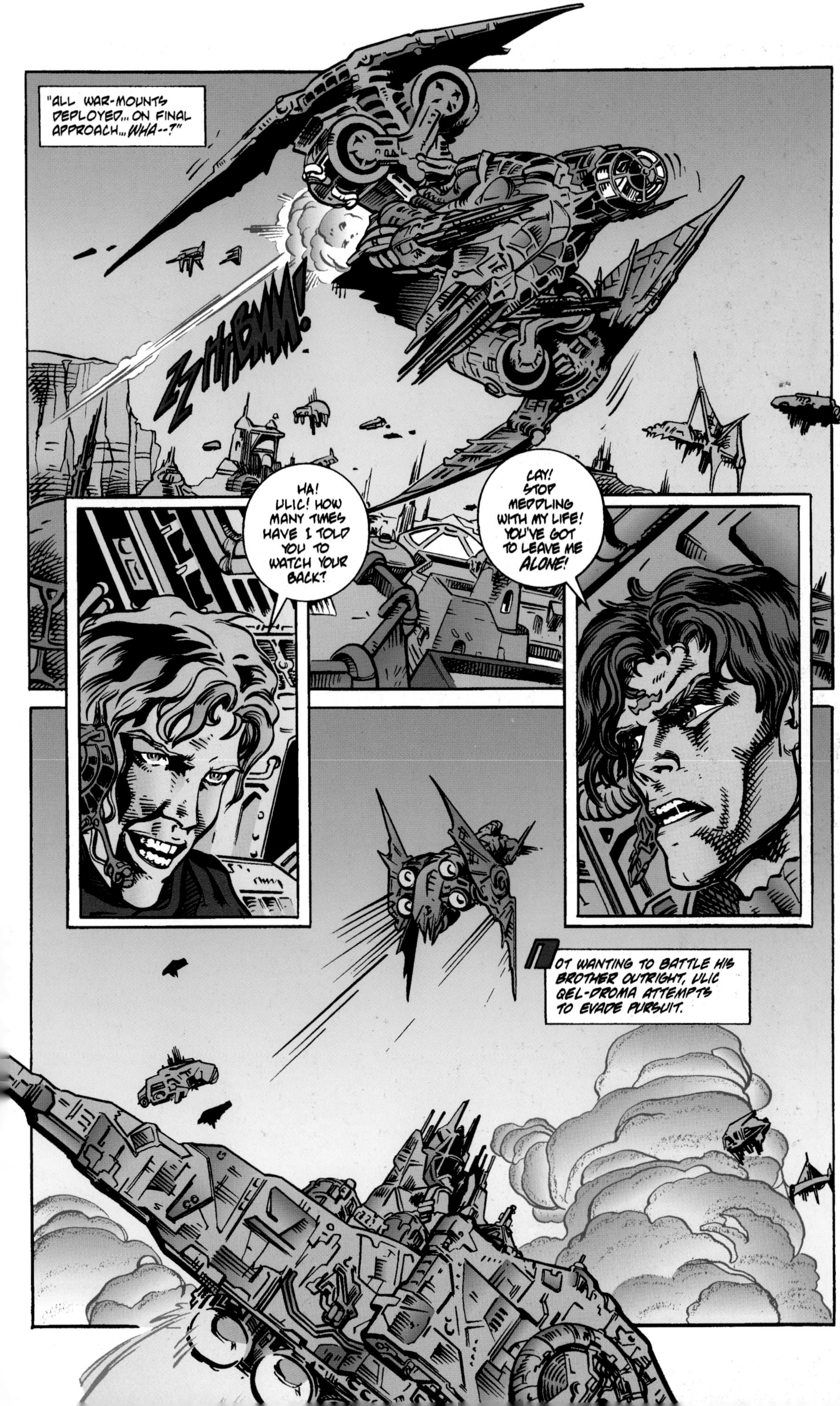
"ALL WAR-MOUNTS DEPLOYED... ON FINAL APPROACH... WHA--?"
ZZHHABMM!
HA! ULIC! HOW MANY TIMES HAVE I TOLD YOU TO WATCH YOUR BACK?
CAY! STOP MEDDLING WITH MY LIFE! YOU'VE GOT TO LEAVE ME ALONE!
NOT WANTING TO BATTLE HIS BROTHER OUTRIGHT, ULIC QEL-DROMA ATTEMPTS TO EVADE PURSUIT.

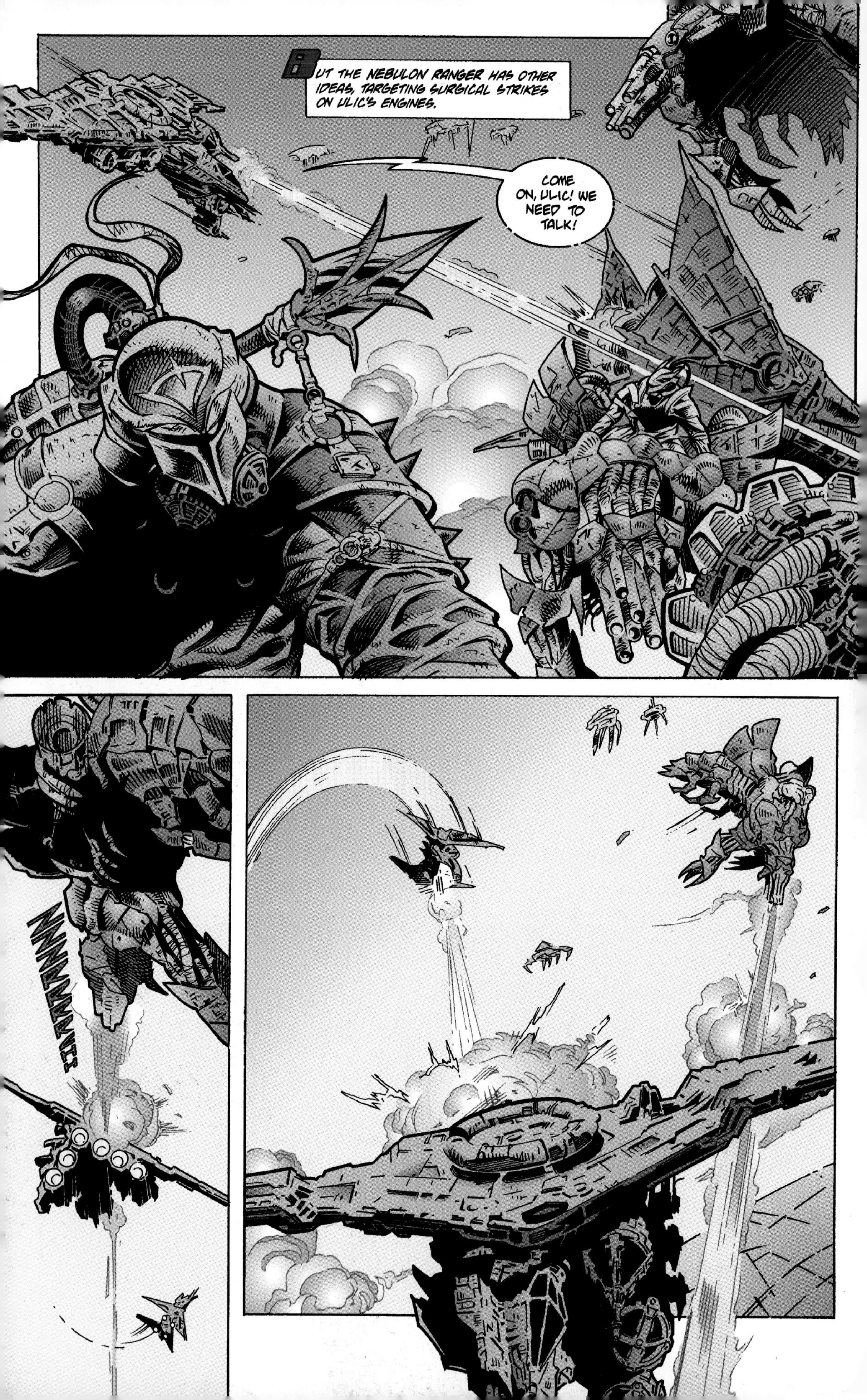
BUT THE NEBULON RANGER HAS OTHER IDEAS, TARGETING SURGICAL STRIKES ON ULIC'S ENGINES.
COME ON, ULIC! WE NEED TO TALK!

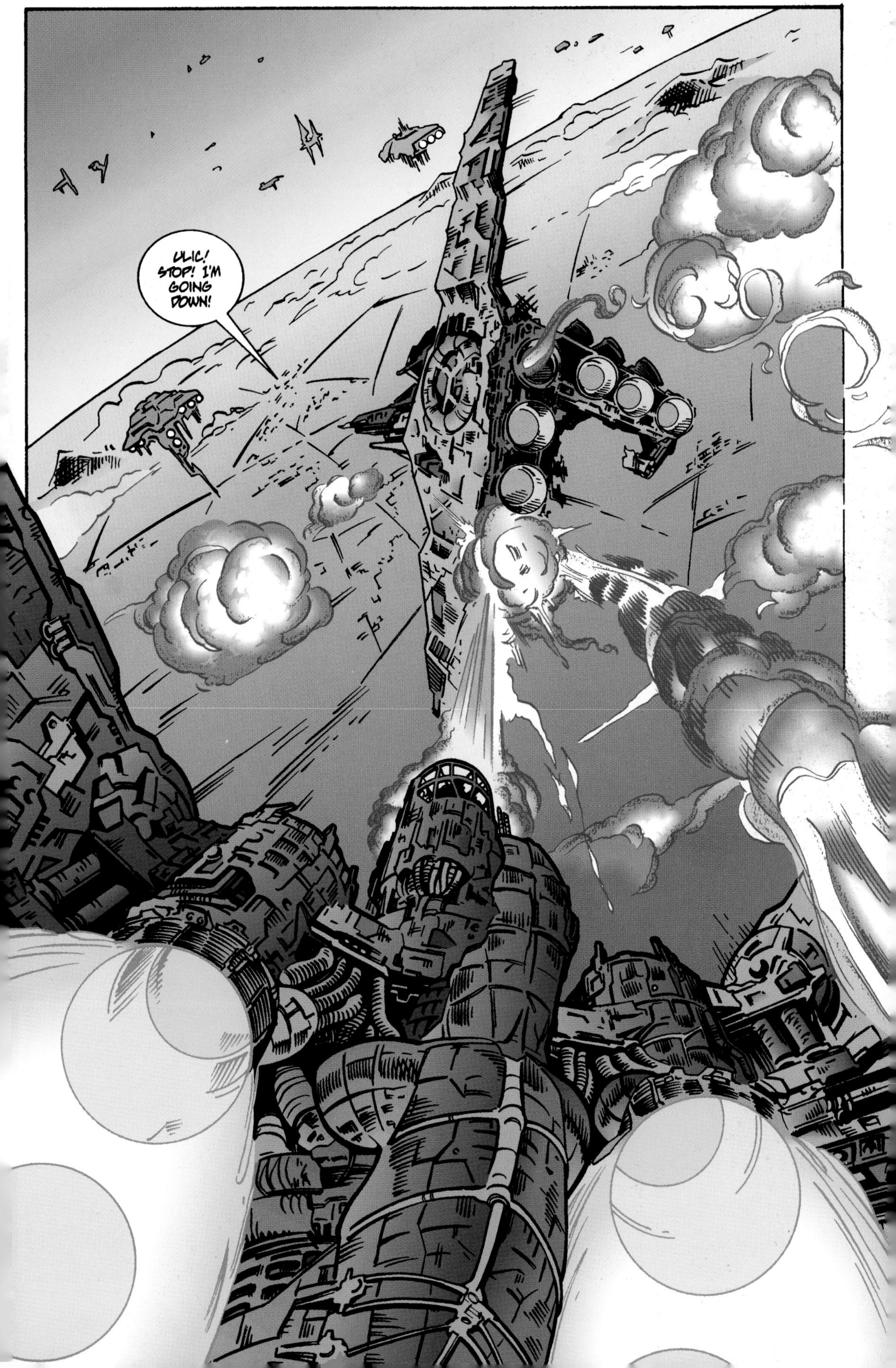
ULIC! STOP! I'M GOING DOWN!

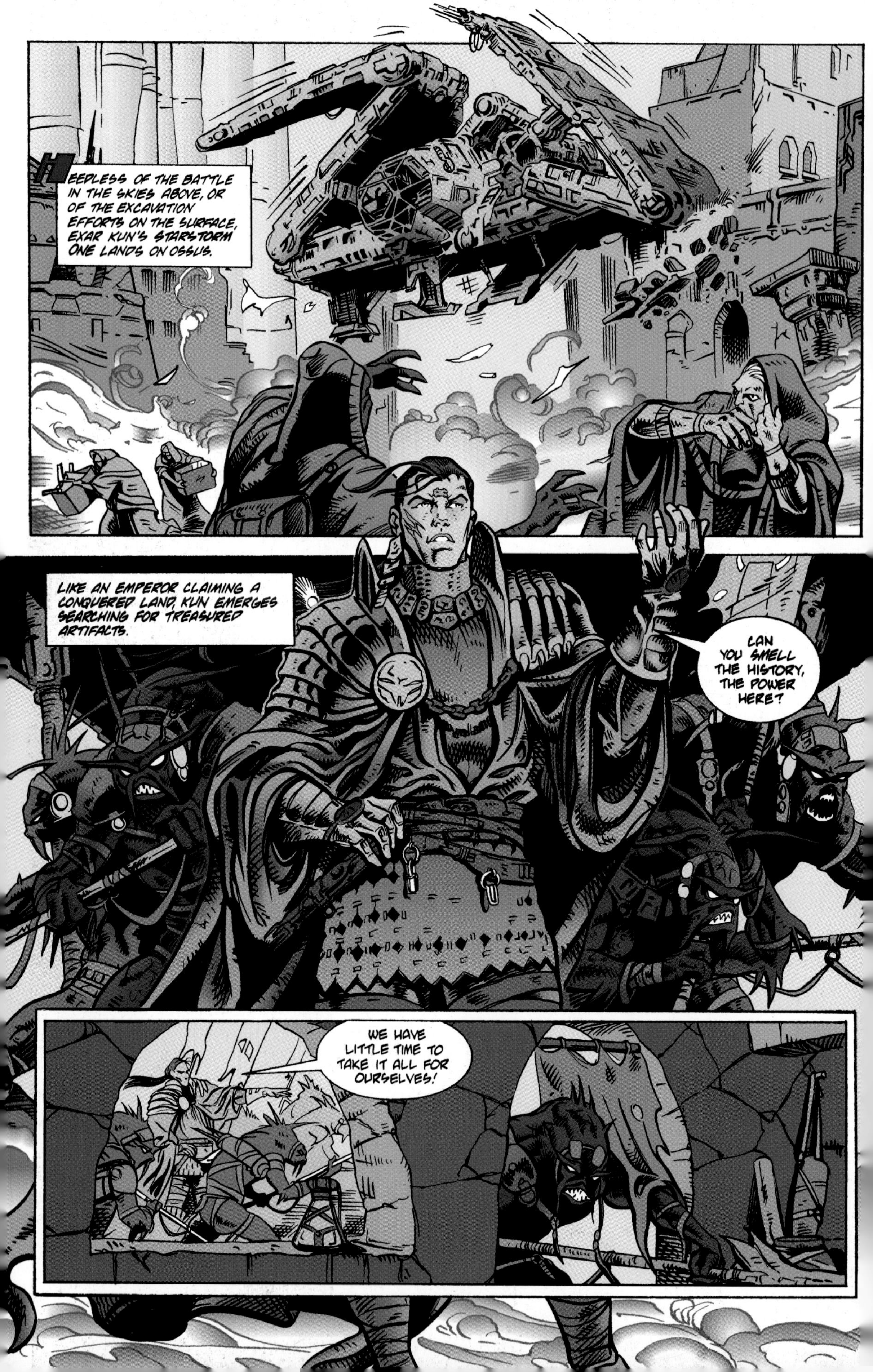
HEEDLESS OF THE BATTLE IN THE SKIES ABOVE, OR OF THE EXCAVATION EFFORTS ON THE SURFACE, EXAR KUN'S STARSTORM ONE LANDS ON OSSUS.
LIKE AN EMPEROR CLAIMING A CONQUERED LAND, KUN EMERGES SEARCHING FOR TREASURED ARTIFACTS.
CAN YOU SMELL THE HISTORY, THE POWER HERE?
WE HAVE LITTLE TIME TO TAKE IT ALL FOR OURSELVES!

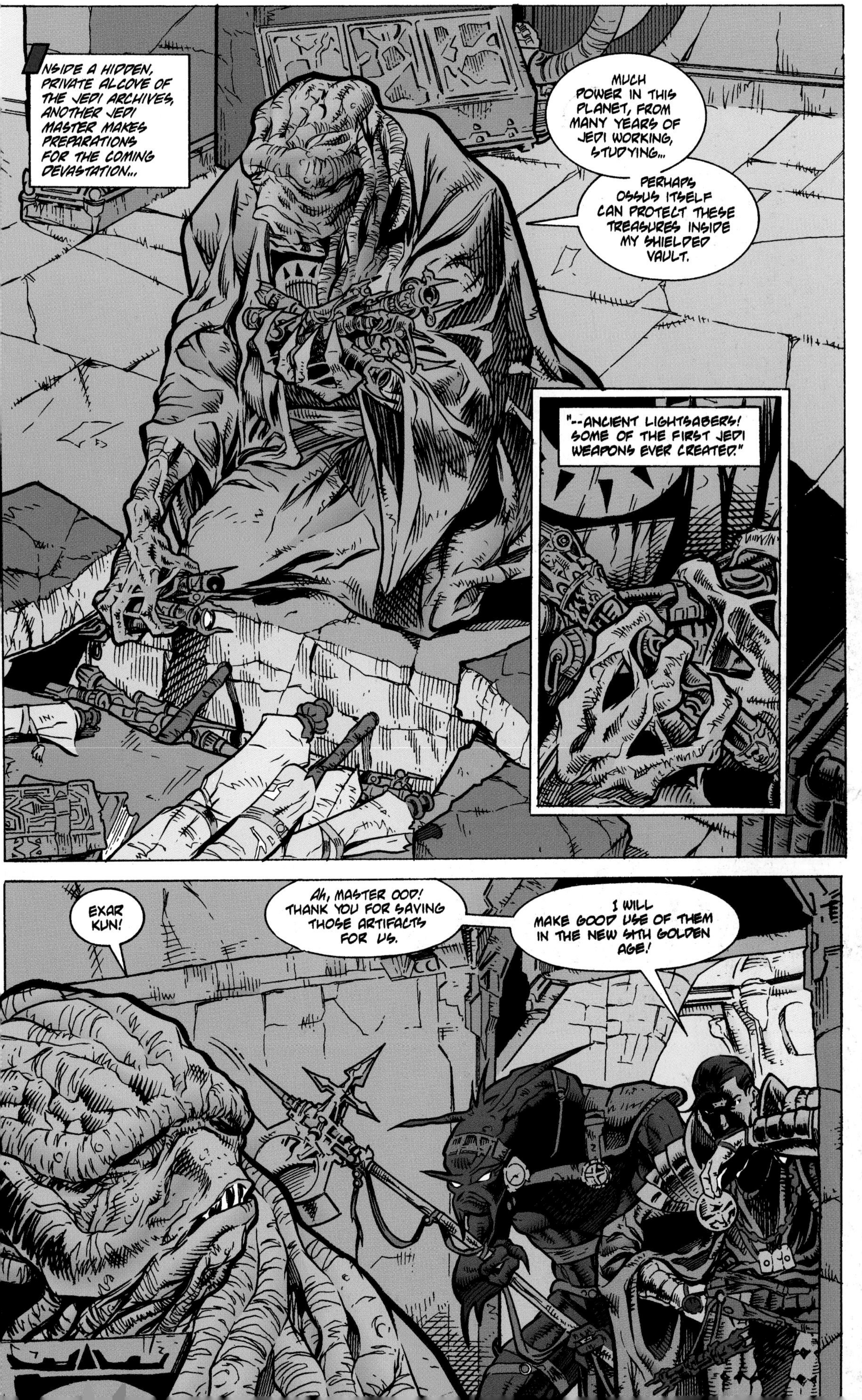
INSIDE A HIDDEN, PRIVATE ALCOVE OF THE JEDI ARCHIVES, ANOTHER JEDI MASTER MAKES PREPARATIONS FOR THE COMING DEVASTATION...
MUCH POWER IN THIS PLANET, FROM MANY YEARS OF JEDI WORKING, STUDYING...
PERHAPS OSSUS ITSELF CAN PROTECT THESE TREASURES INSIDE MY SHIELDED VAULT.
"--ANCIENT LIGHTSABERS! SOME OF THE FIRST JEDI WEAPONS EVER CREATED."
EXAR KUN!
AH, MASTER OOD! THANK YOU FOR SAVING THOSE ARTIFACTS FOR US.
I WILL MAKE GOOD USE OF THEM IN THE NEW SITH GOLDEN AGE!

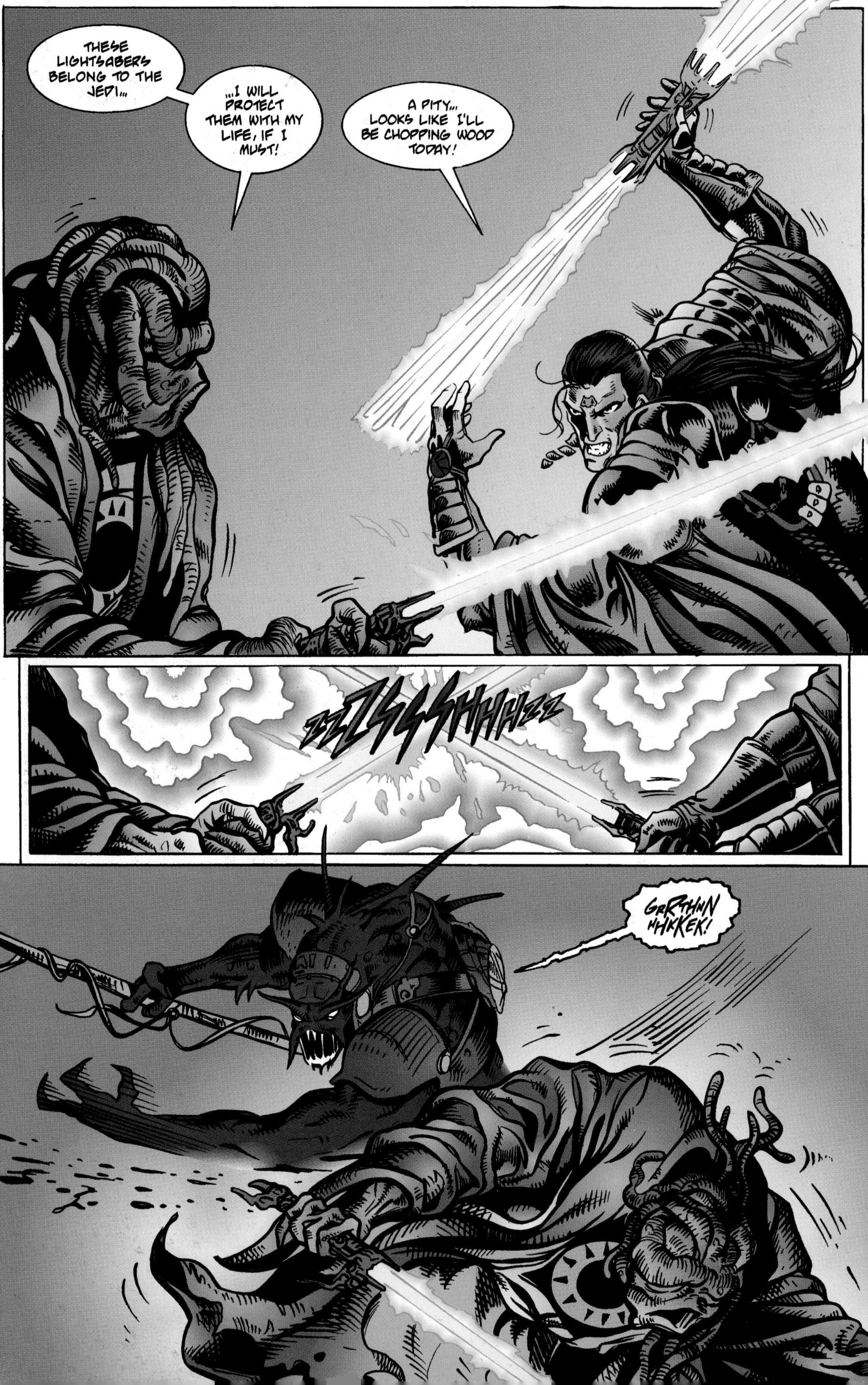
THESE LIGHTSABERS BELONG TO THE JEDI...
...I WILL PROTECT THEM WITH MY LIFE, IF I MUST!
A PITY... LOOKS LIKE I'LL BE CHOPPING WOOD TODAY!
ZZZSSSHHHZZZ
GRRTHNN HHKKEK!

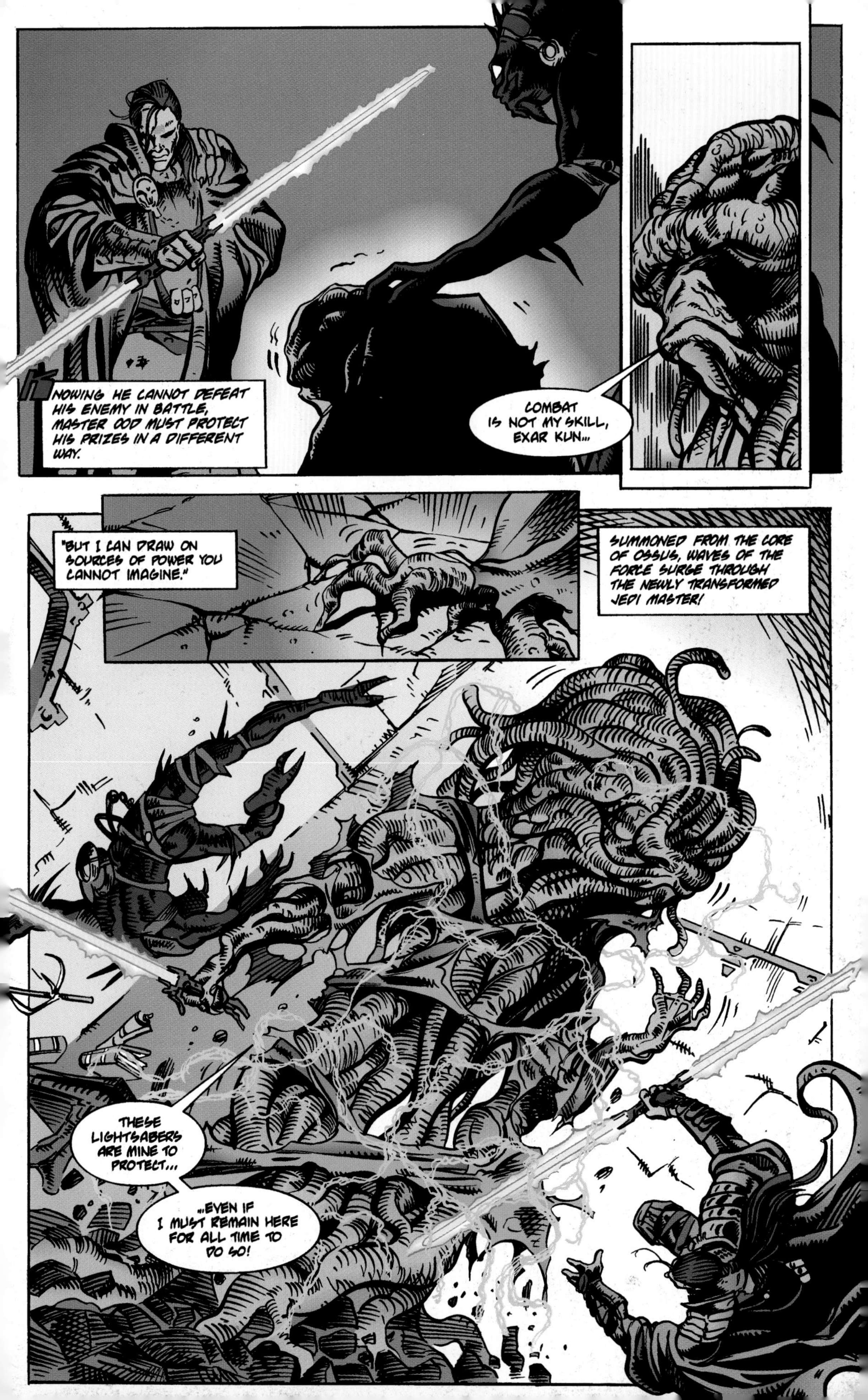
KNOWING HE CANNOT DEFEAT HIS ENEMY IN BATTLE, MASTER ODD MUST PROTECT HIS PRIZES IN A DIFFERENT WAY.
COMBAT IS NOT MY SKILL, EXAR KUN...
"BUT I CAN DRAW ON SOURCES OF POWER YOU CANNOT IMAGINE."
SUMMONED FROM THE CORE OF OSSUS, WAVES OF THE FORCE SURGE THROUGH THE NEWLY TRANSFORMED JEDI MASTER!
THESE LIGHTSABERS ARE MINE TO PROTECT...
...EVEN IF I MUST REMAIN HERE FOR ALL TIME TO DO SO!

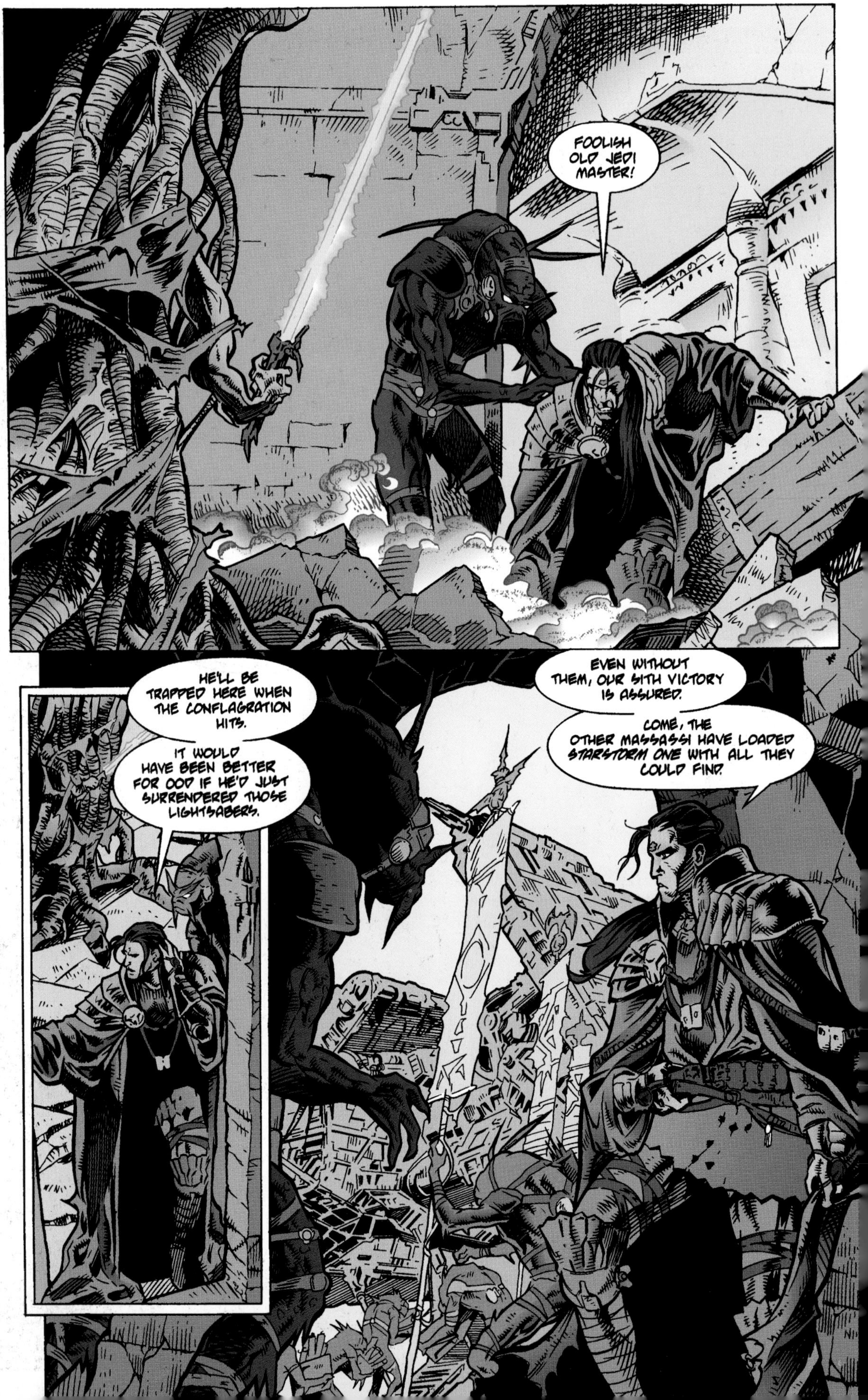
FOOLISH OLD JEDI MASTER!
HE'LL BE TRAPPED HERE WHEN THE CONFLAGRATION HITS.
IT WOULD HAVE BEEN BETTER FOR ODD IF HE'D JUST SURRENDERED THOSE LIGHTSABERS.
EVEN WITHOUT THEM, OUR SITH VICTORY IS ASSURED.
COME, THE OTHER MASSASSI HAVE LOADED STARSTORM ONE WITH ALL THEY COULD FIND.

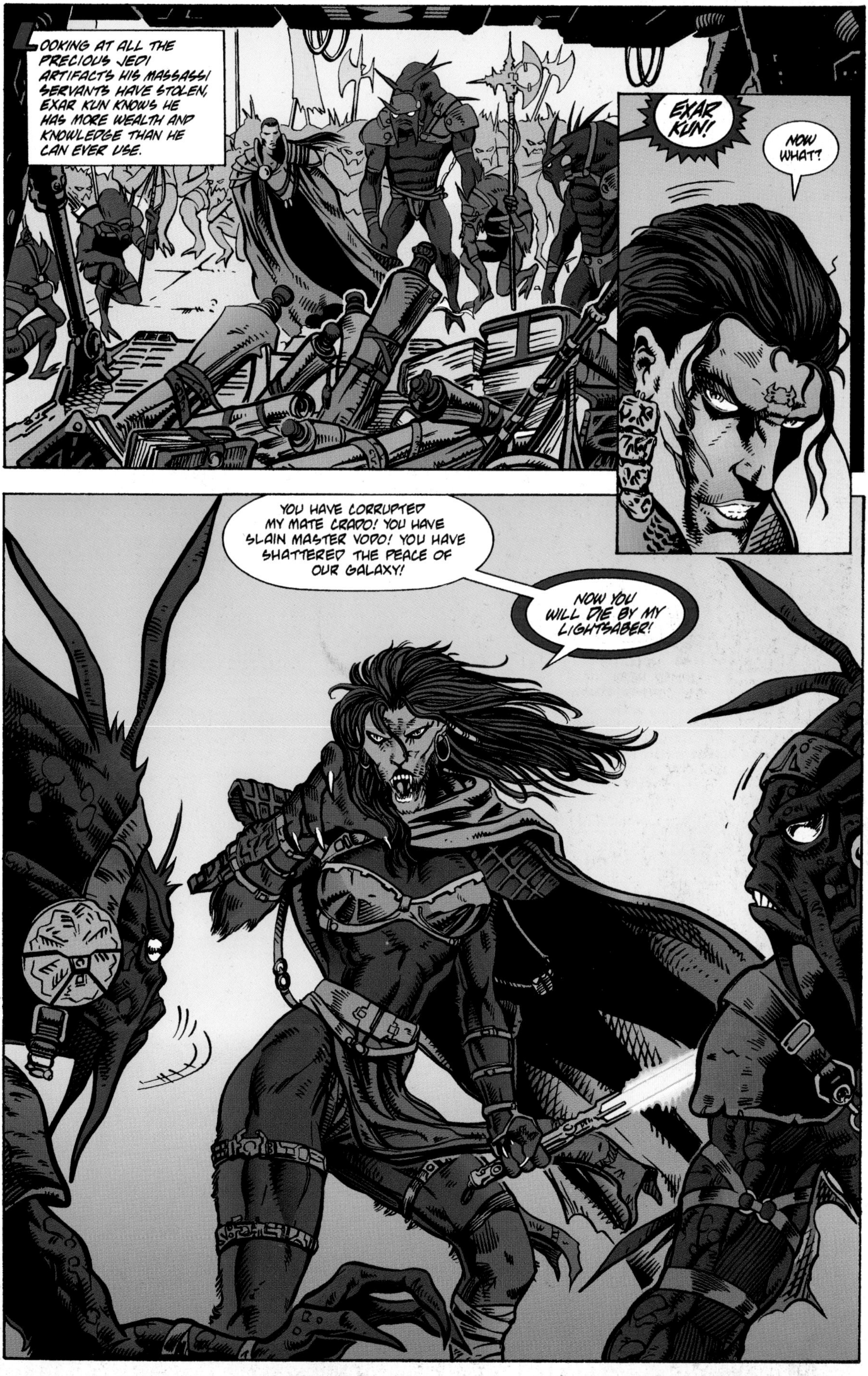
LOOKING AT ALL THE PRECIOUS JEDI ARTIFACTS HIS MASSASSI SERVANTS HAVE STOLEN, EXAR KUN KNOWS HE HAS MORE WEALTH AND KNOWLEDGE THAN HE CAN EVER USE.
EXAR KUN!
NOW WHAT?
YOU HAVE CORRUPTED MY MATE CRADO! YOU HAVE SLAIN MASTER VODO! YOU HAVE SHATTERED THE PEACE OF OUR GALAXY!
NOW YOU WILL DIE BY MY LIGHTSABER!

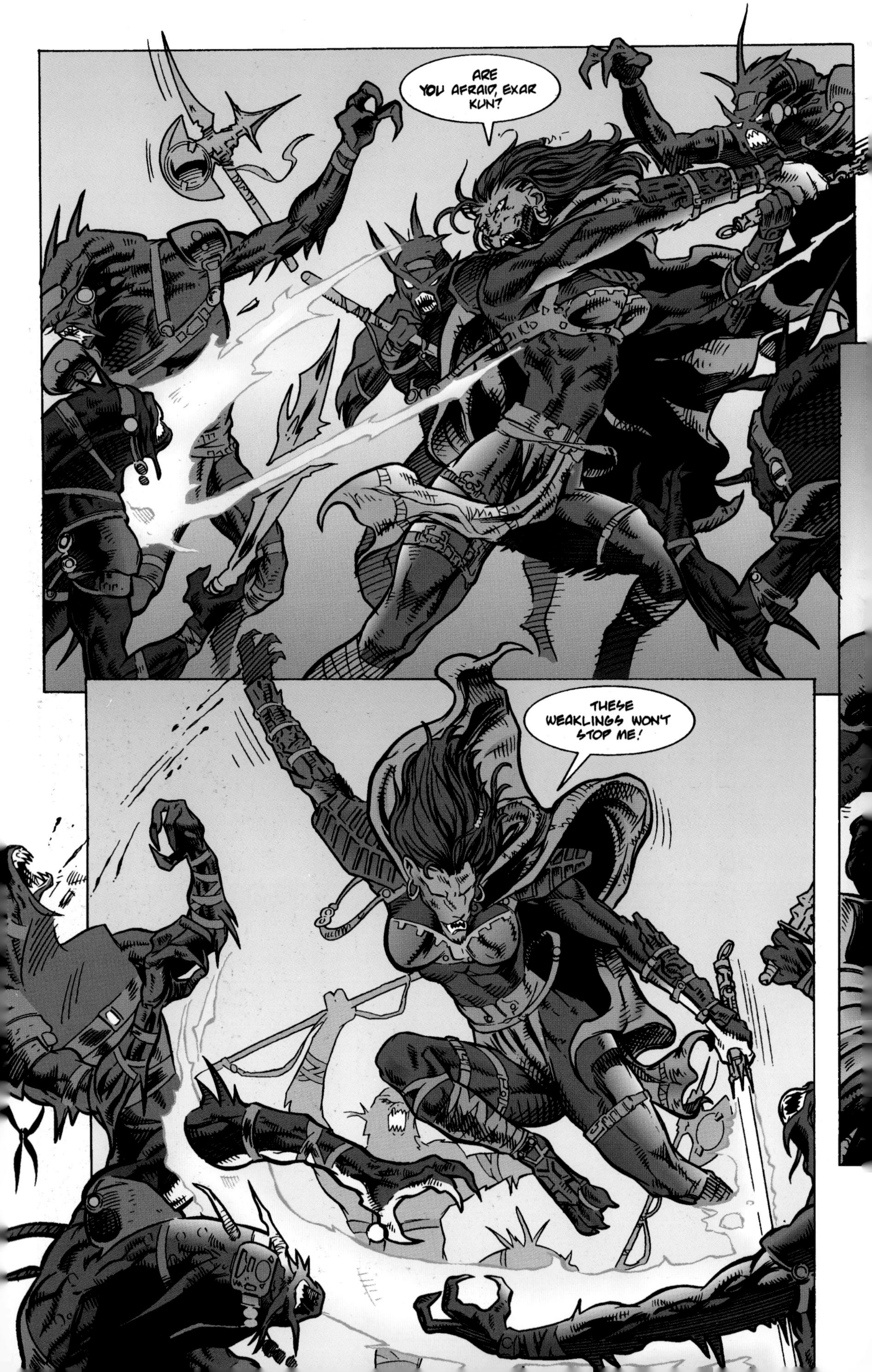
ARE YOU AFRAID, EXAR KUN?
THESE WEAKLINGS WON'T STOP ME!

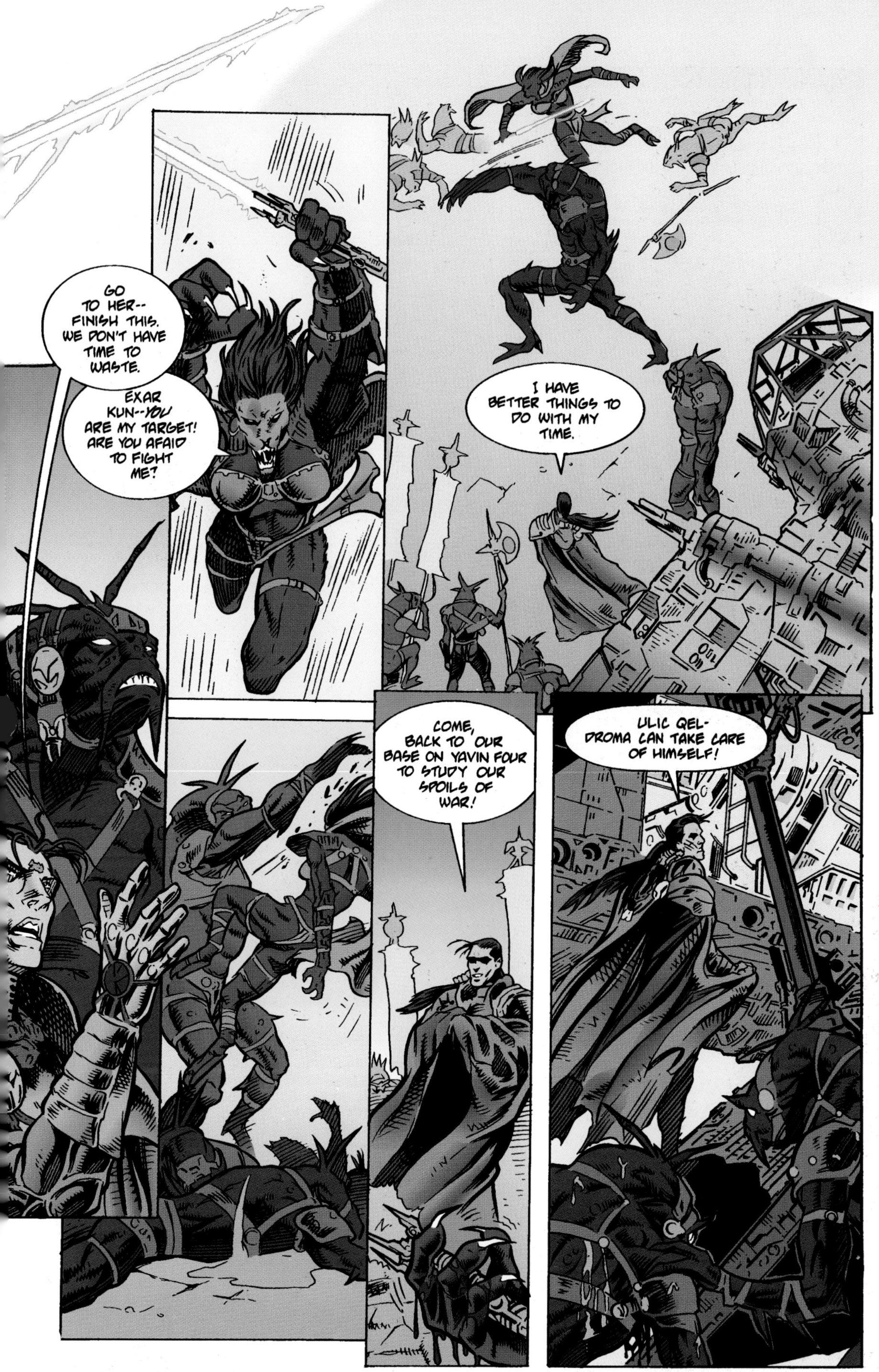
GO TO HER-- FINISH THIS. WE DON'T HAVE TIME TO WASTE.
EXAR KUN--YOU ARE MY TARGET! ARE YOU AFAID TO FIGHT ME?
I HAVE BETTER THINGS TO DO WITH MY TIME.
COME, BACK TO OUR BASE ON YAVIN FOUR TO STUDY OUR SPOILS OF WAR!
ULIC QEL-DROMA CAN TAKE CARE OF HIMSELF!

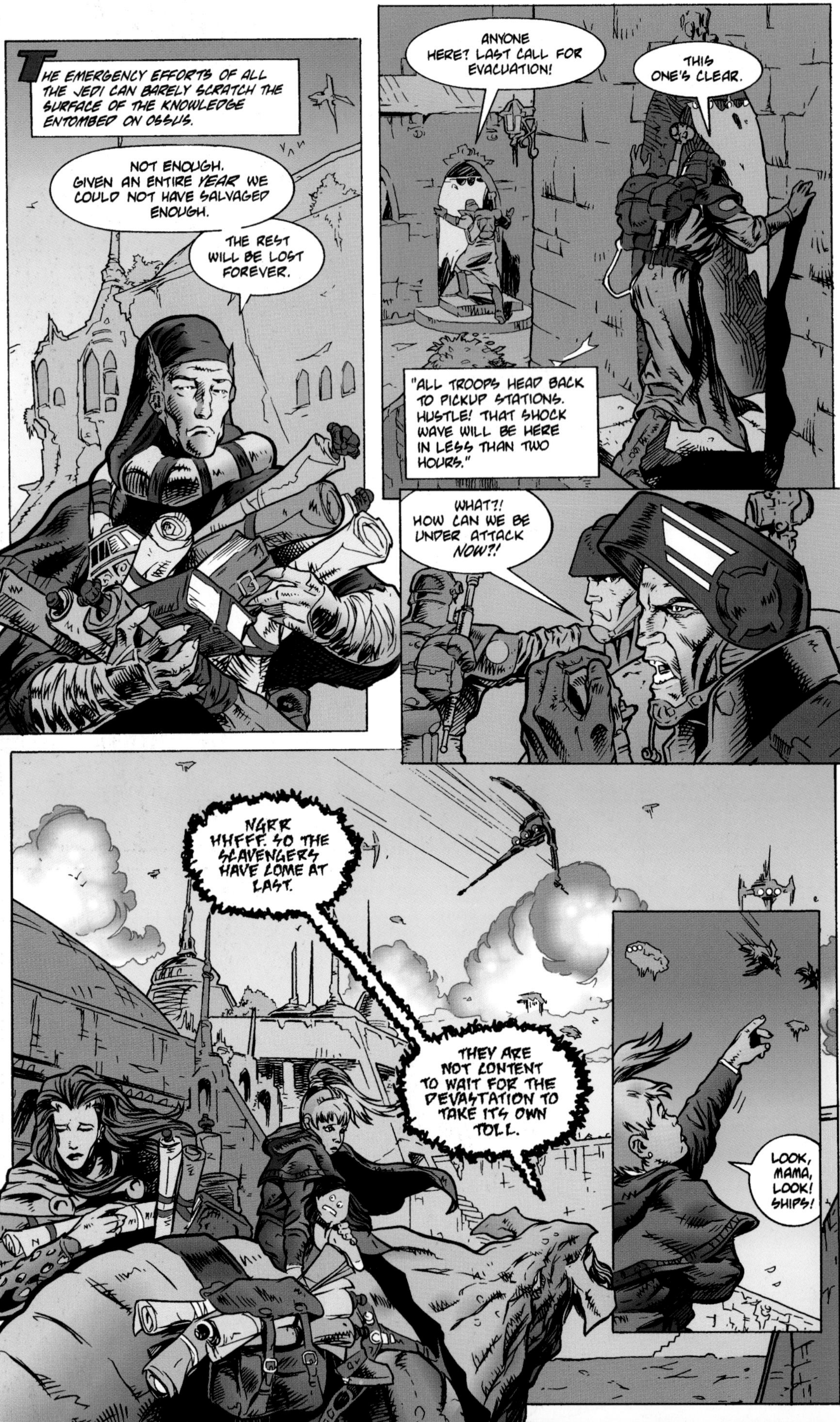
THE EMERGENCY EFFORTS OF ALL THE JEDI CAN BARELY SCRATCH THE SURFACE OF THE KNOWLEDGE ENTOMBED ON OSSUS.
NOT ENOUGH. GIVEN AN ENTIRE YEAR WE COULD NOT HAVE SALVAGED ENOUGH.
THE REST WILL BE LOST FOREVER.
ANYONE HERE? LAST CALL FOR EVACUATION!
THIS ONE'S CLEAR.
"ALL TROOPS HEAD BACK TO PICKUP STATIONS. HUSTLE! THAT SHOCK WAVE WILL BE HERE IN LESS THAN TWO HOURS."
WHAT?! HOW CAN WE BE UNDER ATTACK NOW?!
NGRR HHFFF. SO THE SCAVENGERS HAVE COME AT LAST.
THEY ARE NOT CONTENT TO WAIT FOR THE DEVASTATION TO TAKE ITS OWN TOLL.
LOOK, MAMA, LOOK! SHIPS!

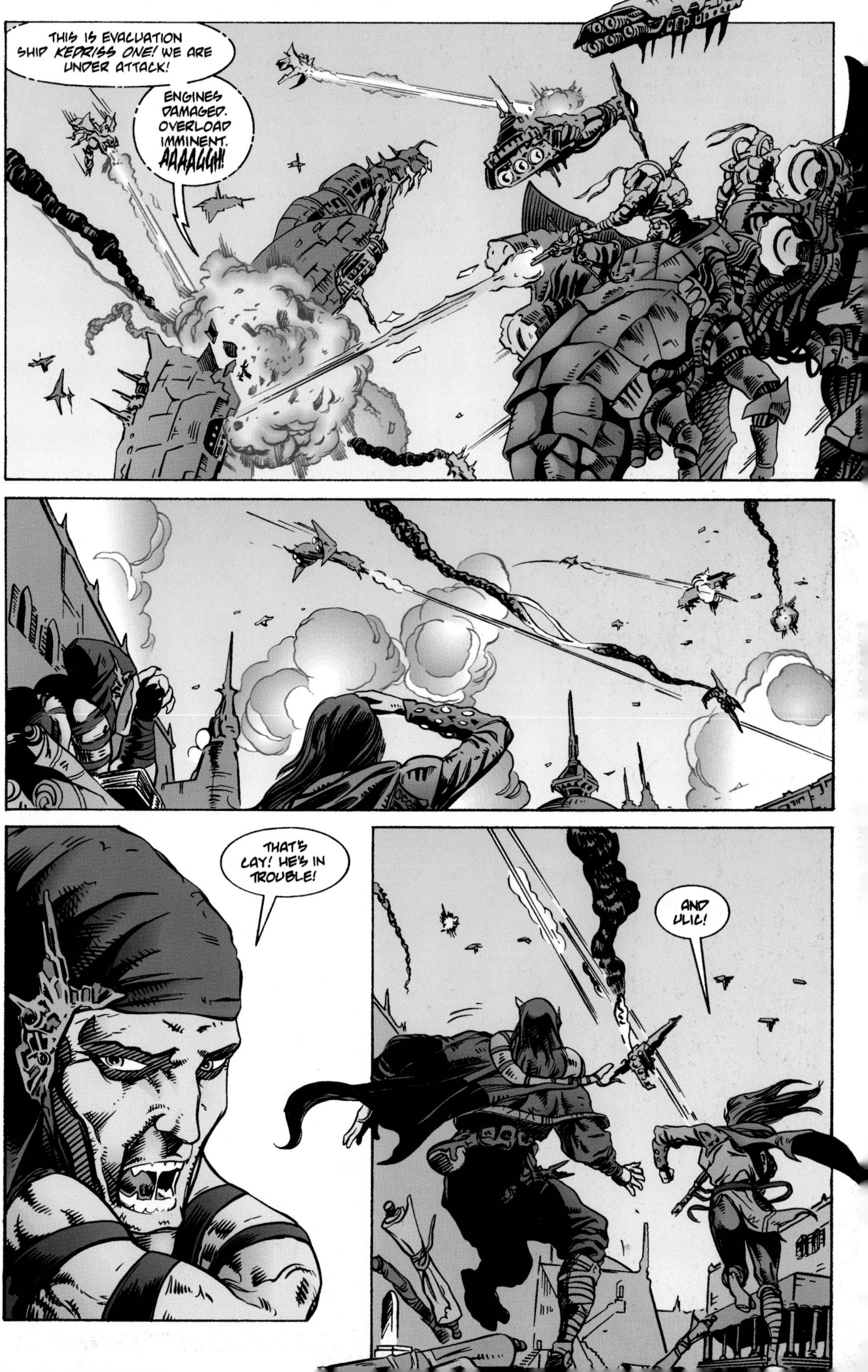
THIS IS EVACUATION SHIP *KEDRISS ONE!* WE ARE UNDER ATTACK!
ENGINES DAMAGED. OVERLOAD IMMINENT. **AAAAGGH!**
THAT'S CAY! HE'S IN TROUBLE!
AND ULIC!

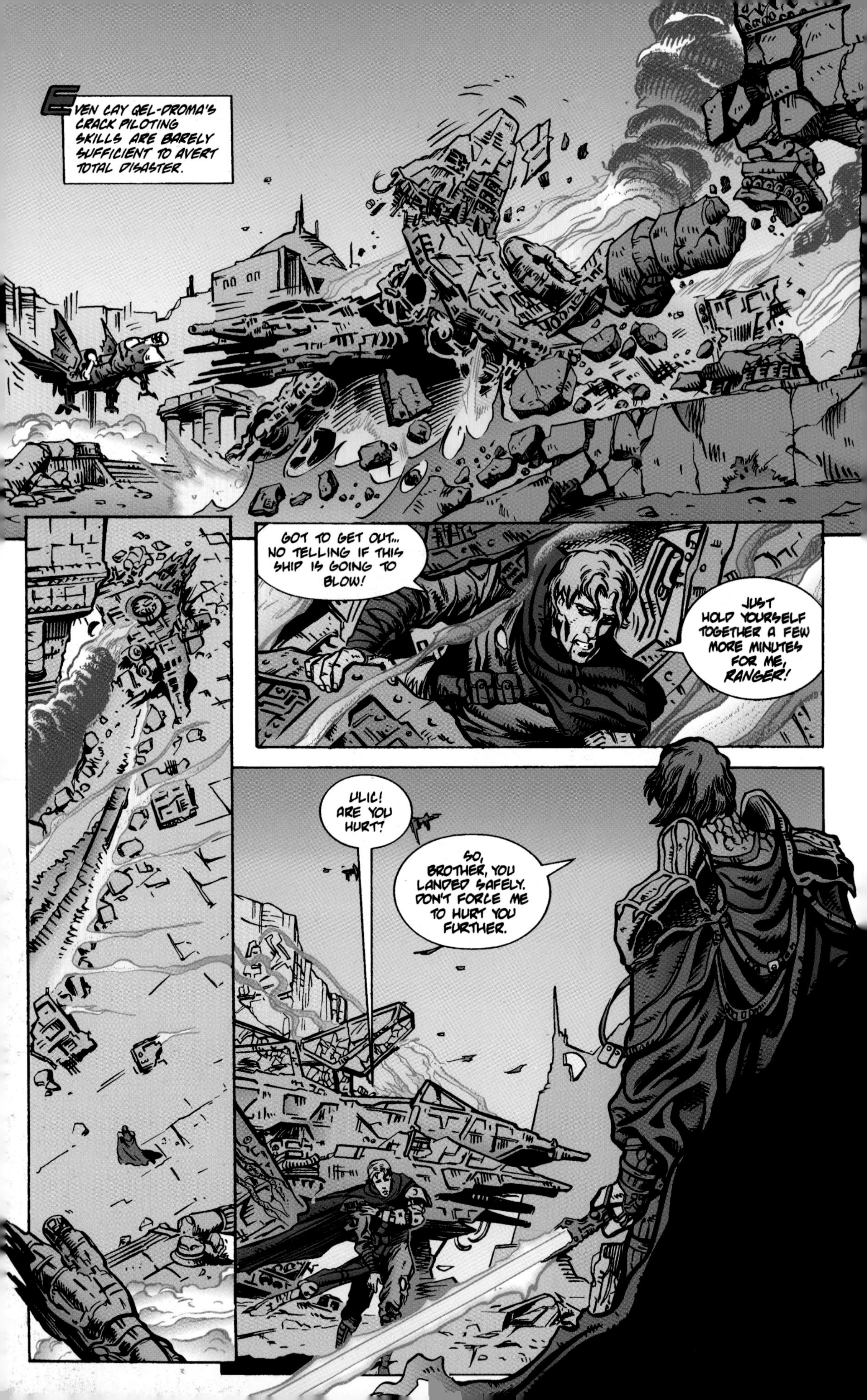
EVEN CAY QEL-DROMA'S CRACK PILOTING SKILLS ARE BARELY SUFFICIENT TO AVERT TOTAL DISASTER.
GOT TO GET OUT... NO TELLING IF THIS SHIP IS GOING TO BLOW!
JUST HOLD YOURSELF TOGETHER A FEW MORE MINUTES FOR ME, RANGER!
ULIC! ARE YOU HURT?
SO, BROTHER, YOU LANDED SAFELY. DON'T FORCE ME TO HURT YOU FURTHER.

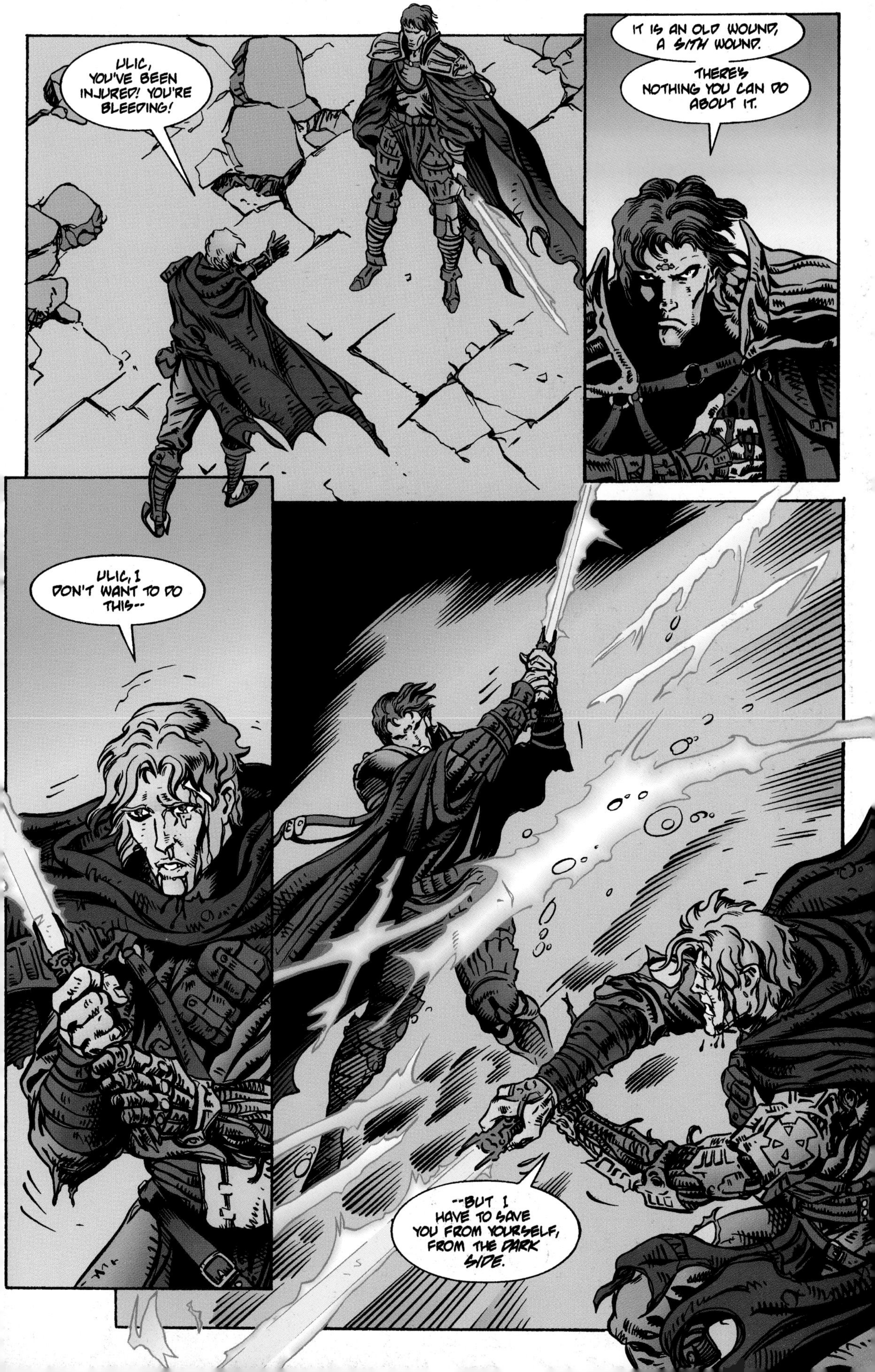
ULIC, YOU'VE BEEN INJURED! YOU'RE BLEEDING!
IT IS AN OLD WOUND, A SITH WOUND.
THERE'S NOTHING YOU CAN DO ABOUT IT.
ULIC, I DON'T WANT TO DO THIS--
--BUT I HAVE TO SAVE YOU FROM YOURSELF, FROM THE DARK SIDE.

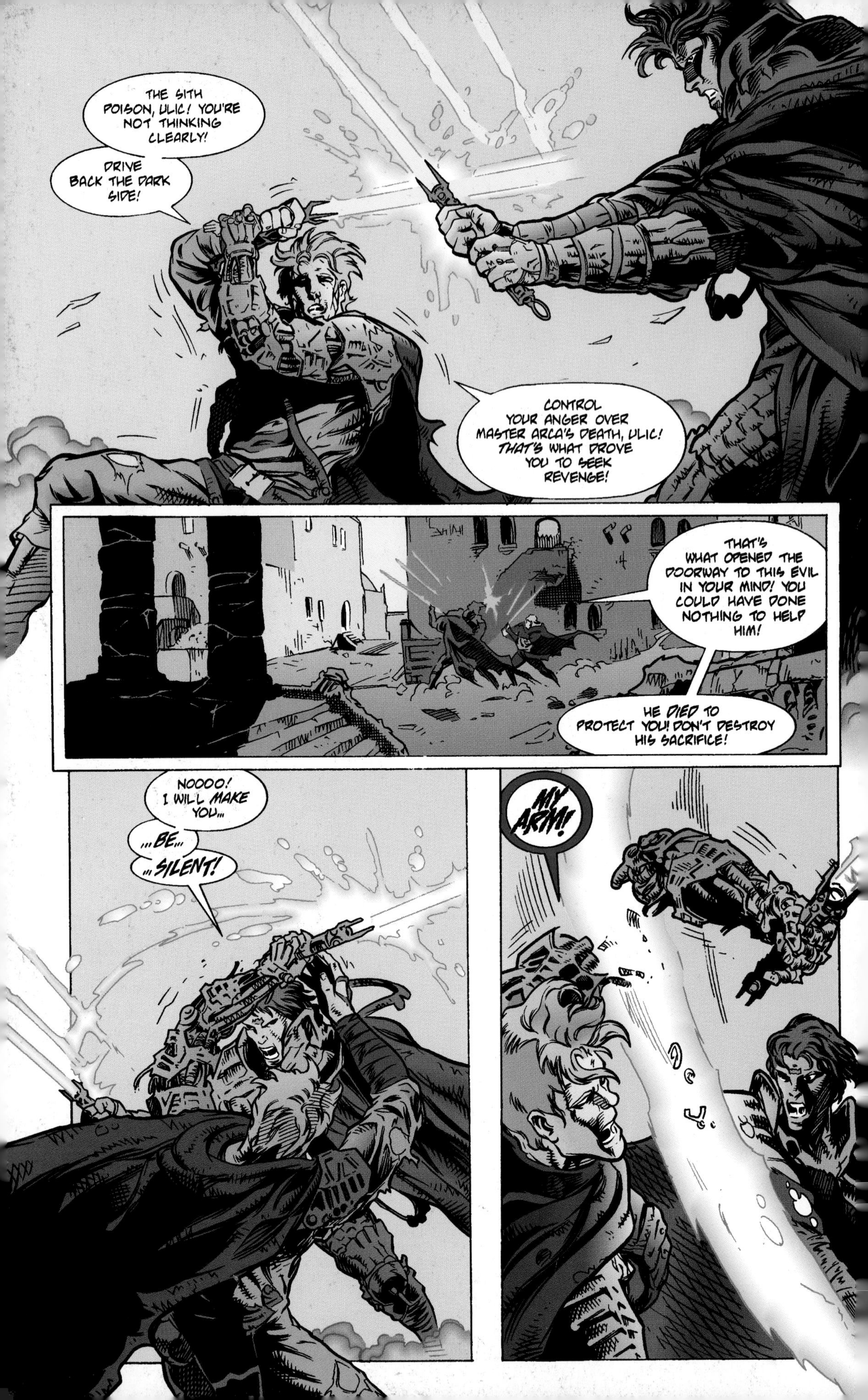
THE SITH POISON, ULIC! YOU'RE NOT THINKING CLEARLY!
DRIVE BACK THE DARK SIDE!
CONTROL YOUR ANGER OVER MASTER ARCA'S DEATH, ULIC! *THAT'S* WHAT DROVE YOU TO SEEK REVENGE!
THAT'S WHAT OPENED THE DOORWAY TO THIS EVIL IN YOUR MIND! YOU COULD HAVE DONE NOTHING TO HELP HIM!
HE *DIED* TO PROTECT YOU! DON'T DESTROY HIS SACRIFICE!
NOOOO! I WILL *MAKE* YOU...
...BE...
...SILENT!
MY ARM!

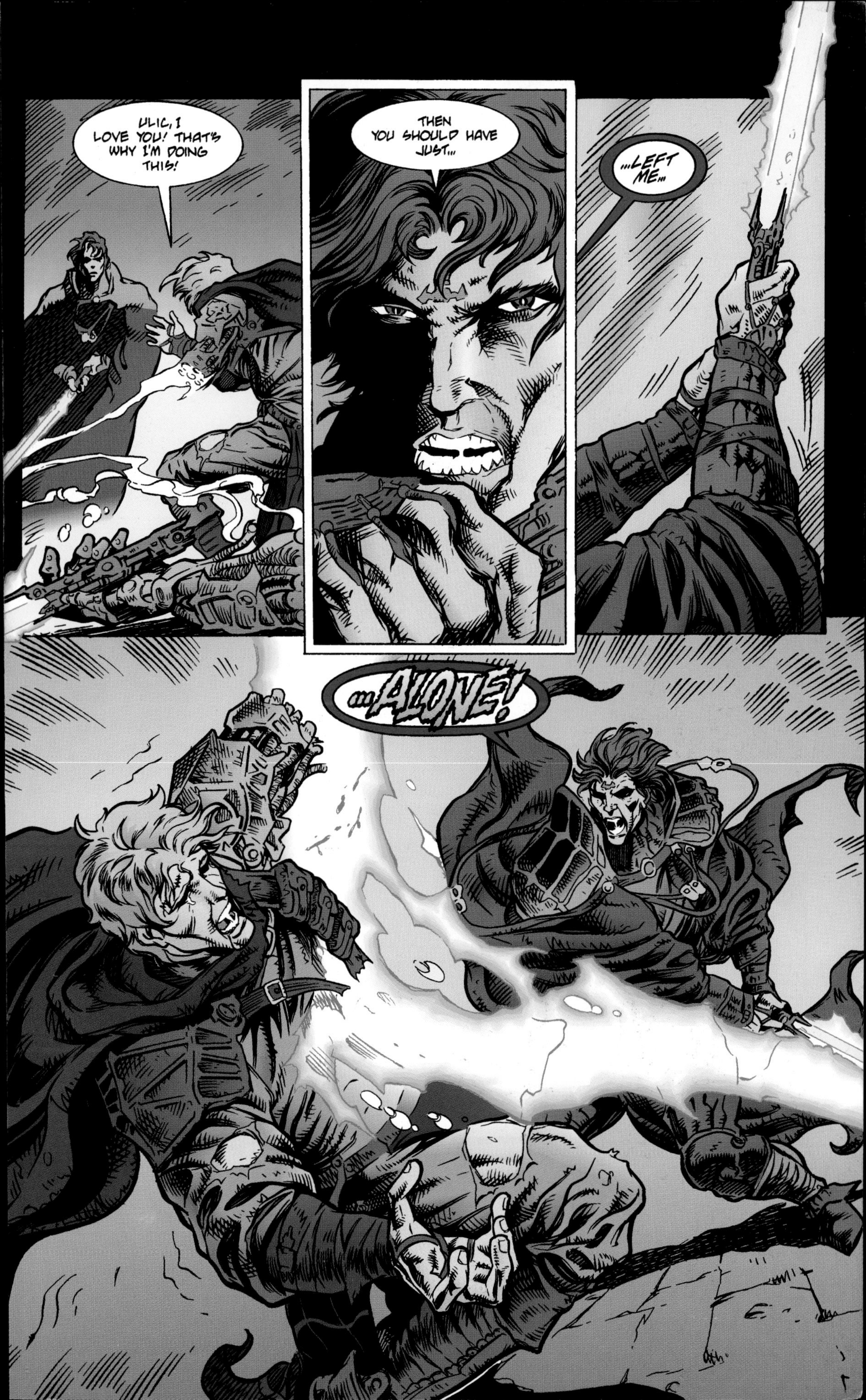
ULIC, I LOVE YOU! THAT'S WHY I'M DOING THIS!
THEN YOU SHOULD HAVE JUST...
...LEFT ME...
...ALONE!

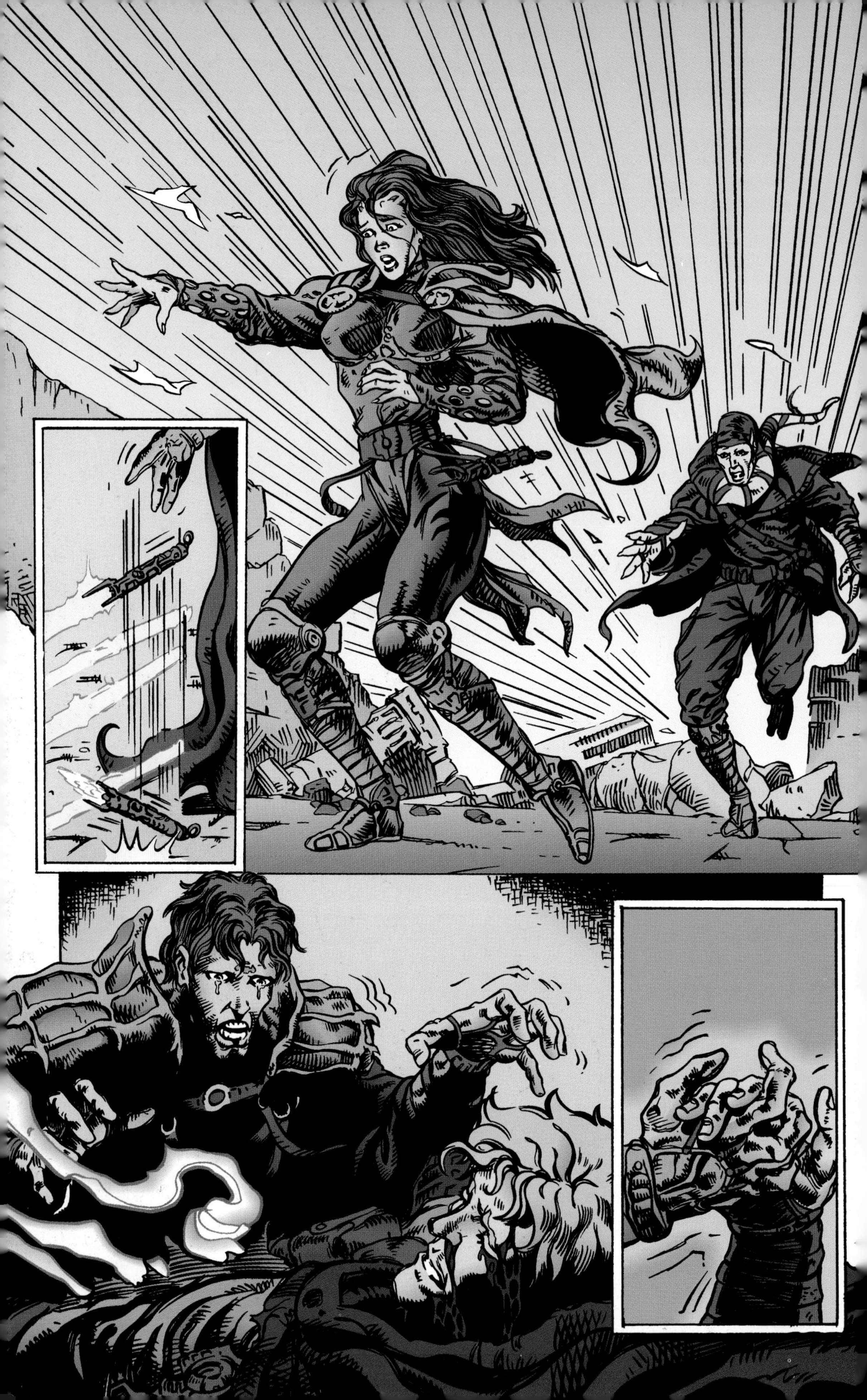

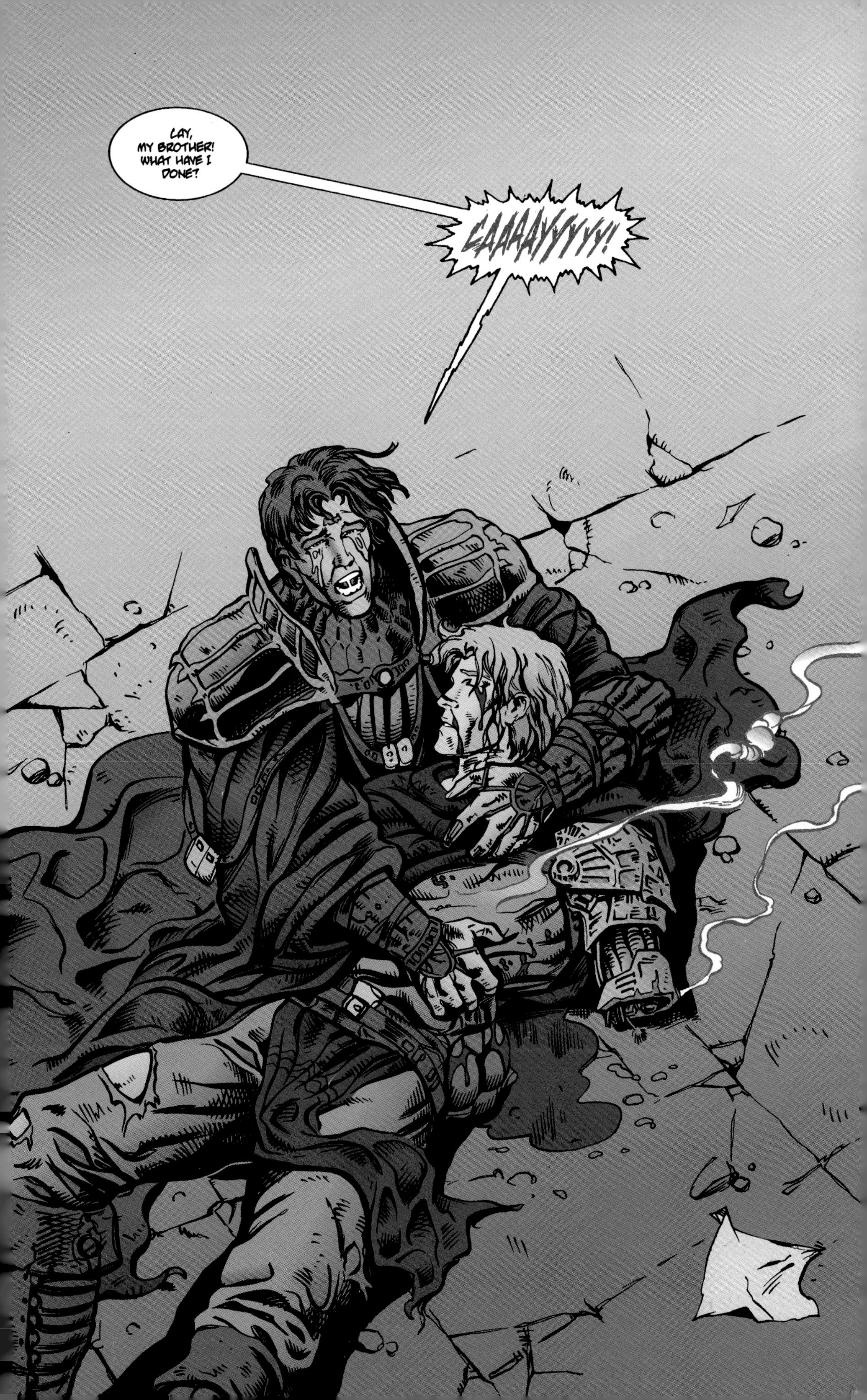
CAAAAYYYYY!
CAY,
MY BROTHER!
WHAT HAVE I
DONE?

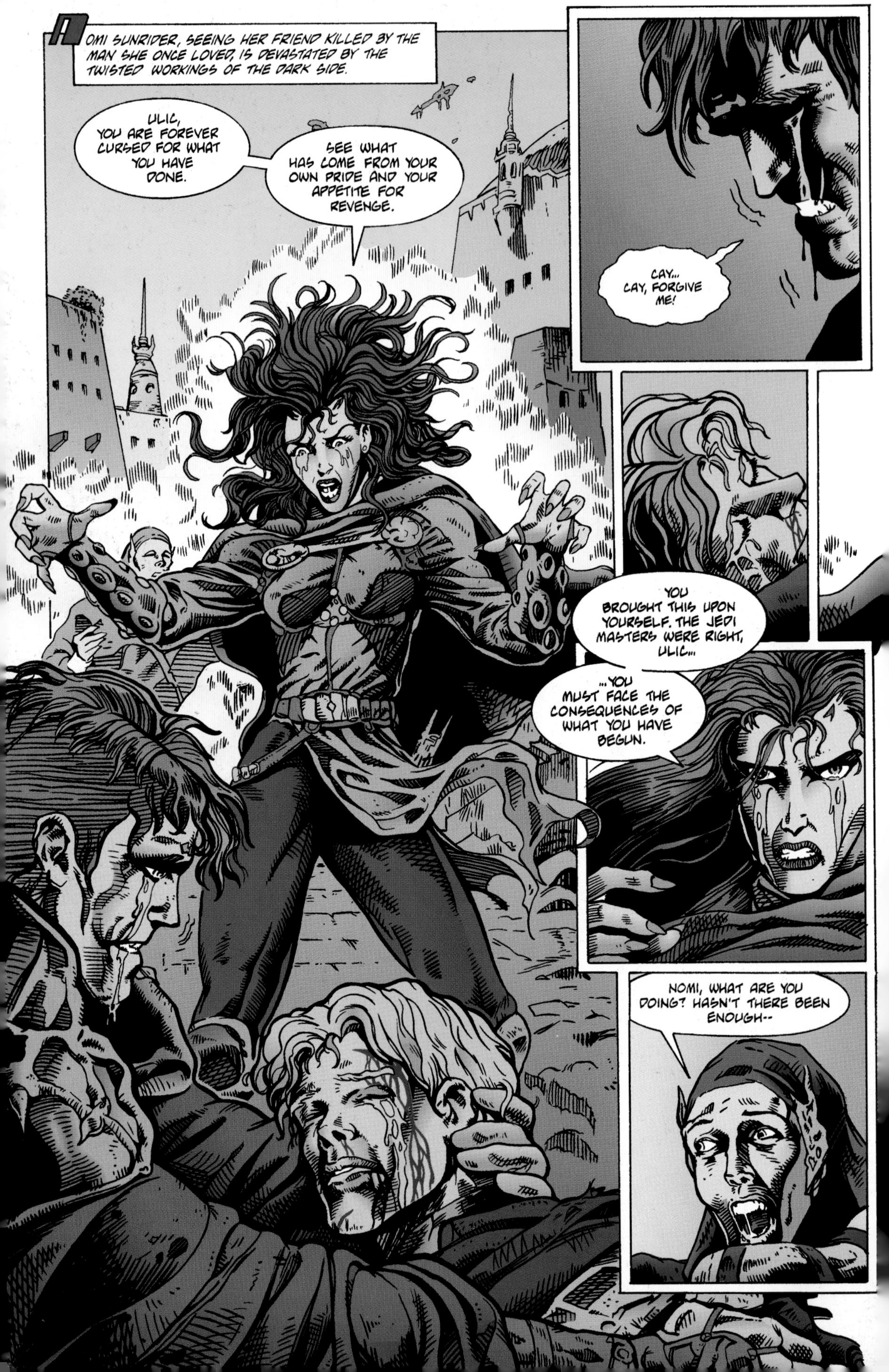
NOMI SUNRIDER, SEEING HER FRIEND KILLED BY THE MAN SHE ONCE LOVED, IS DEVASTATED BY THE TWISTED WORKINGS OF THE DARK SIDE.
ULIC, YOU ARE FOREVER CURSED FOR WHAT YOU HAVE DONE.
SEE WHAT HAS COME FROM YOUR OWN PRIDE AND YOUR APPETITE FOR REVENGE.
CAY... CAY, FORGIVE ME!
YOU BROUGHT THIS UPON YOURSELF. THE JEDI MASTERS WERE RIGHT, ULIC...
...YOU MUST FACE THE CONSEQUENCES OF WHAT YOU HAVE BEGUN.
NOMI, WHAT ARE YOU DOING? HASN'T THERE BEEN ENOUGH--

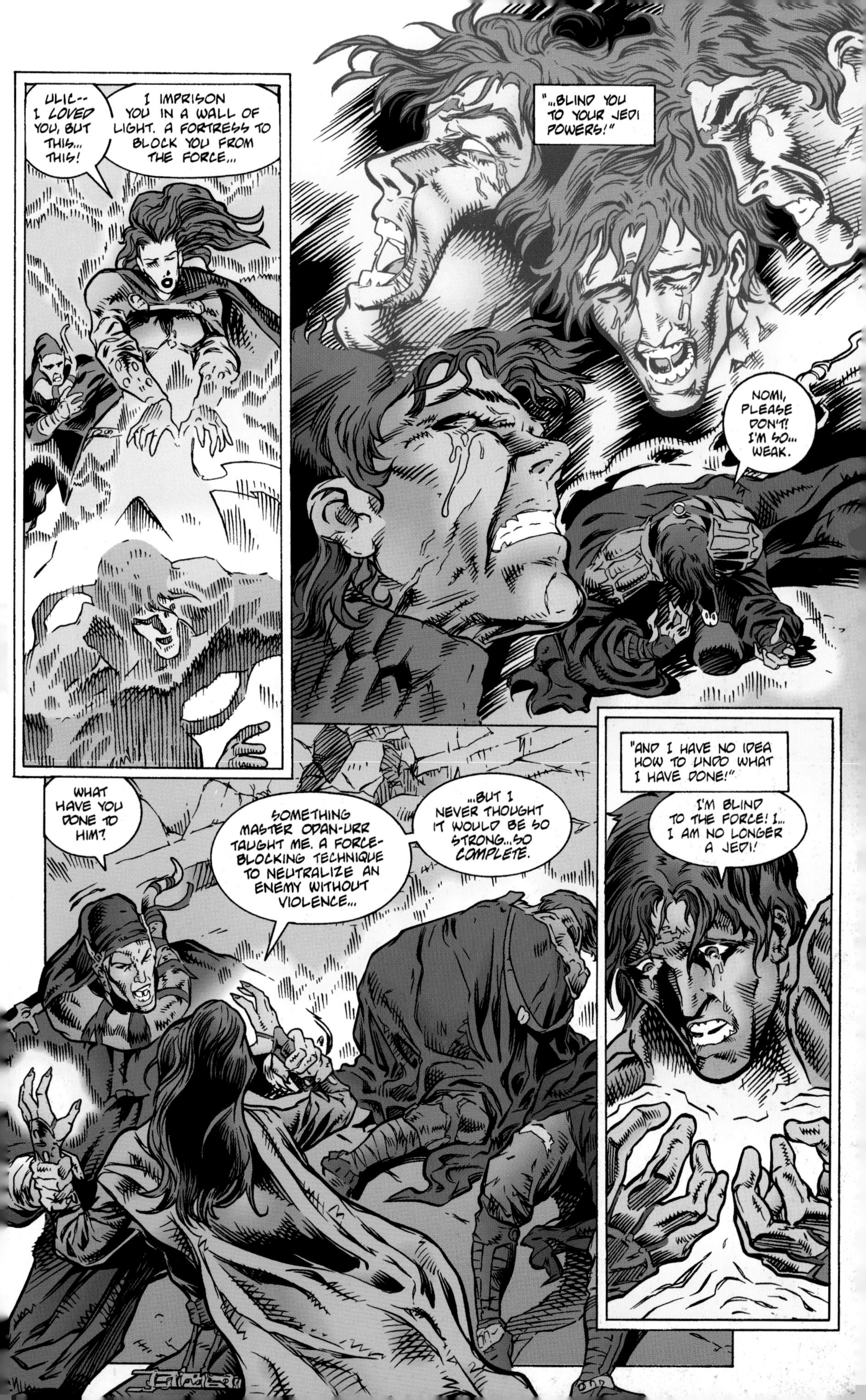
ULIC-- I LOVED YOU, BUT THIS... THIS!
I IMPRISON YOU IN A WALL OF LIGHT. A FORTRESS TO BLOCK YOU FROM THE FORCE...
"...BLIND YOU TO YOUR JEDI POWERS!"
NOMI, PLEASE DON'T! I'M SO... WEAK.
WHAT HAVE YOU DONE TO HIM?
SOMETHING MASTER ODAN-URR TAUGHT ME. A FORCE-BLOCKING TECHNIQUE TO NEUTRALIZE AN ENEMY WITHOUT VIOLENCE...
...BUT I NEVER THOUGHT IT WOULD BE SO STRONG...SO COMPLETE.
"AND I HAVE NO IDEA HOW TO UNDO WHAT I HAVE DONE!"
I'M BLIND TO THE FORCE! I... I AM NO LONGER A JEDI!

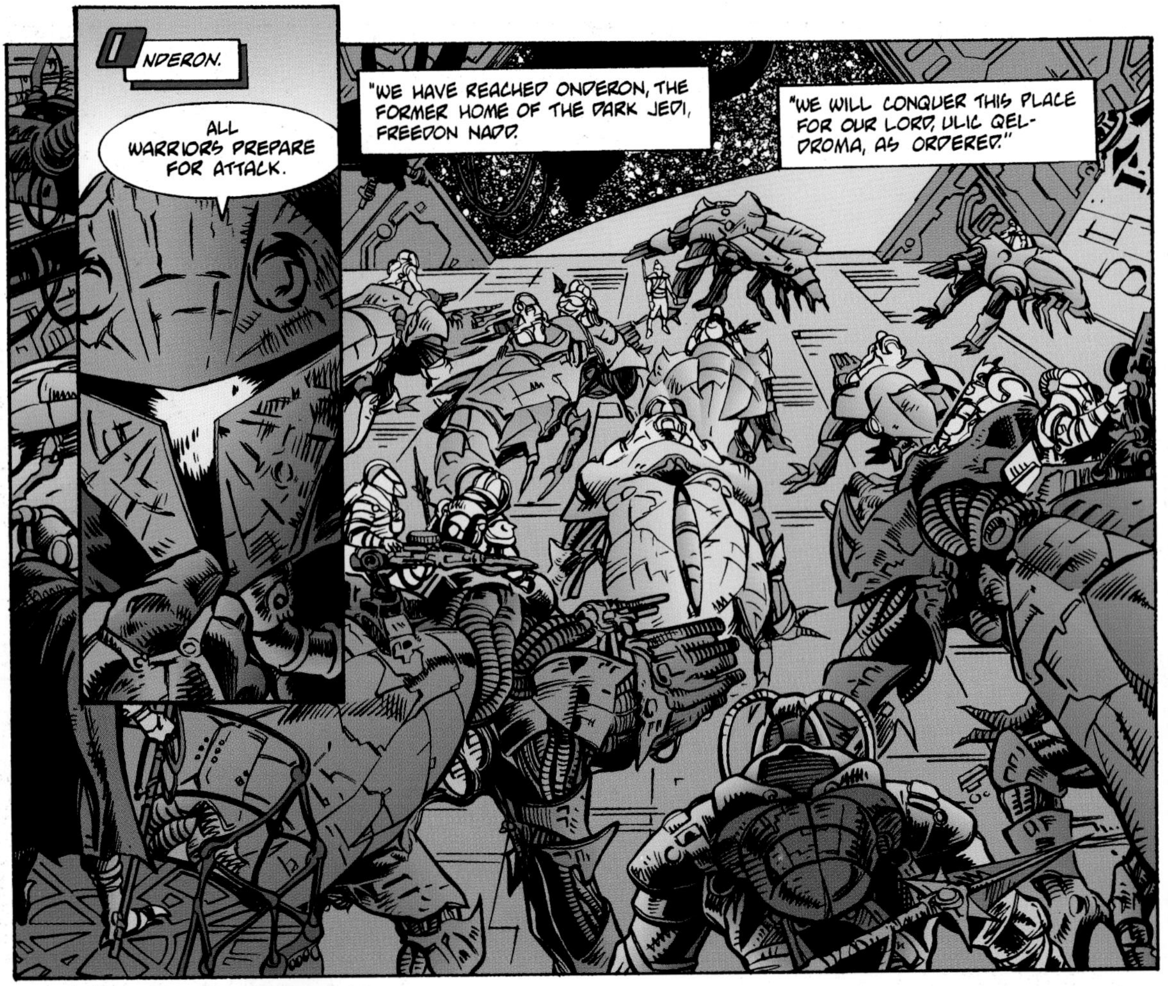
ONDERON.
ALL WARRIORS PREPARE FOR ATTACK.
"WE HAVE REACHED ONDERON, THE FORMER HOME OF THE DARK JEDI, FREEDON NADD.
"WE WILL CONQUER THIS PLACE FOR OUR LORD, ULIC QEL-DROMA, AS ORDERED."

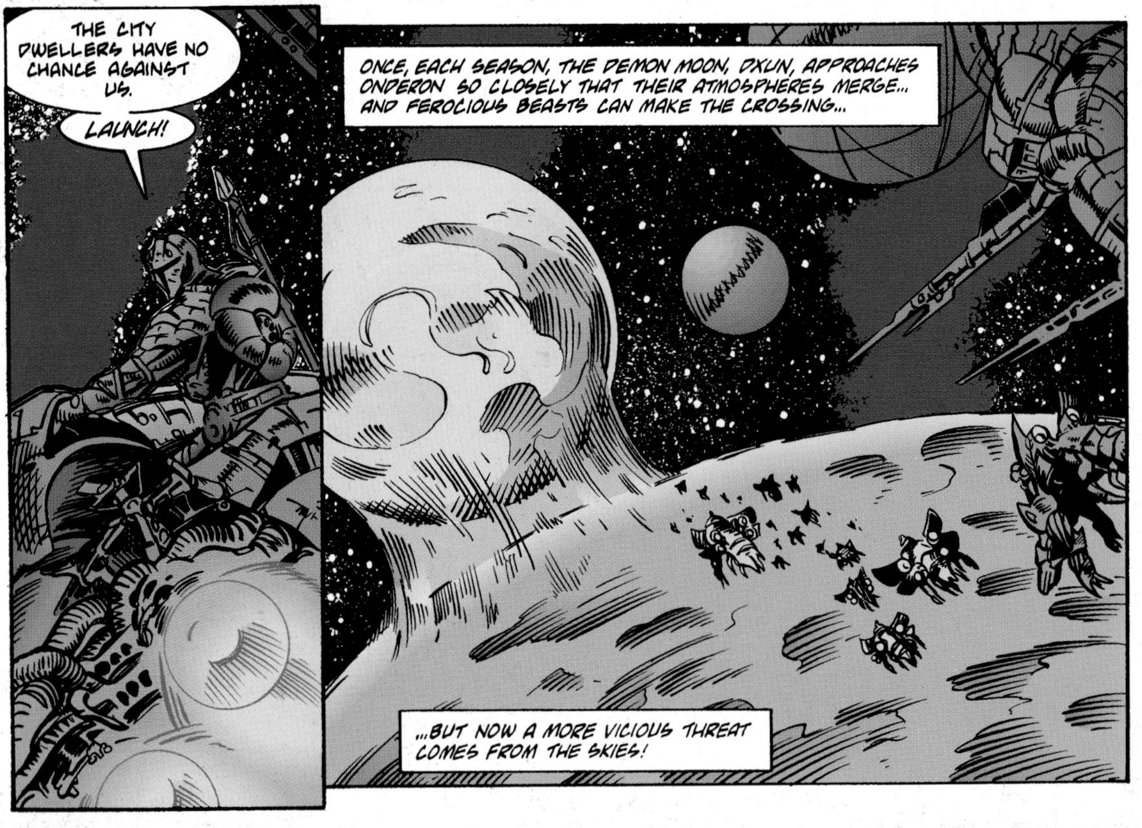
THE CITY DWELLERS HAVE NO CHANCE AGAINST US.
LAUNCH!
ONCE, EACH SEASON, THE DEMON MOON, DXUN, APPROACHES ONDERON SO CLOSELY THAT THEIR ATMOSPHERES MERGE... AND FEROCIOUS BEASTS CAN MAKE THE CROSSING...
...BUT NOW A MORE VICIOUS THREAT COMES FROM THE SKIES!

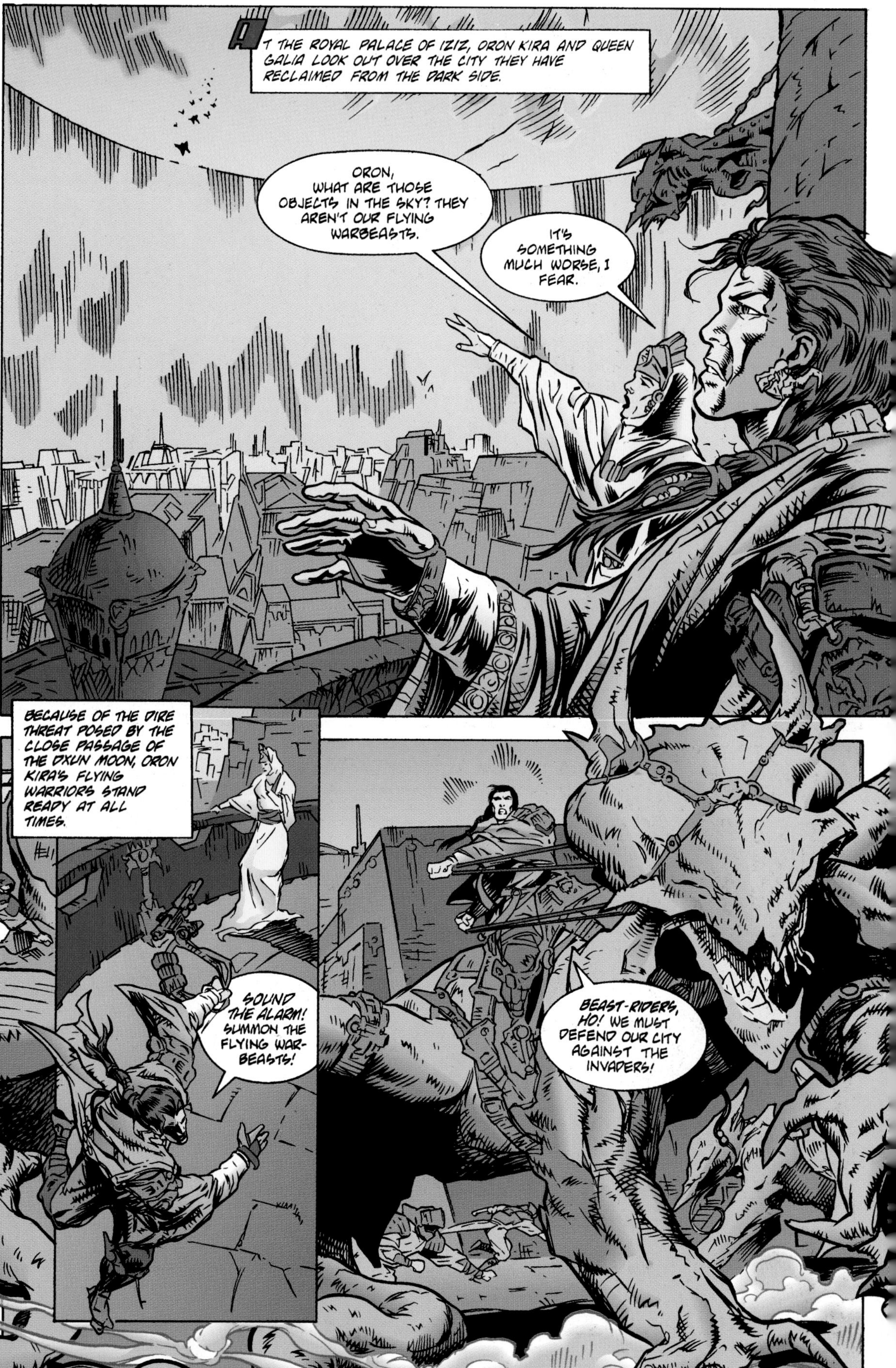
AT THE ROYAL PALACE OF IZIZ, ORON KIRA AND QUEEN GALIA LOOK OUT OVER THE CITY THEY HAVE RECLAIMED FROM THE DARK SIDE.
ORON, WHAT ARE THOSE OBJECTS IN THE SKY? THEY AREN'T OUR FLYING WARBEASTS.
IT'S SOMETHING MUCH WORSE, I FEAR.
BECAUSE OF THE DIRE THREAT POSED BY THE CLOSE PASSAGE OF THE DXUN MOON, ORON KIRA'S FLYING WARRIORS STAND READY AT ALL TIMES.
SOUND THE ALARM! SUMMON THE FLYING WAR-BEASTS!
BEAST-RIDERS, HO! WE MUST DEFEND OUR CITY AGAINST THE INVADERS!

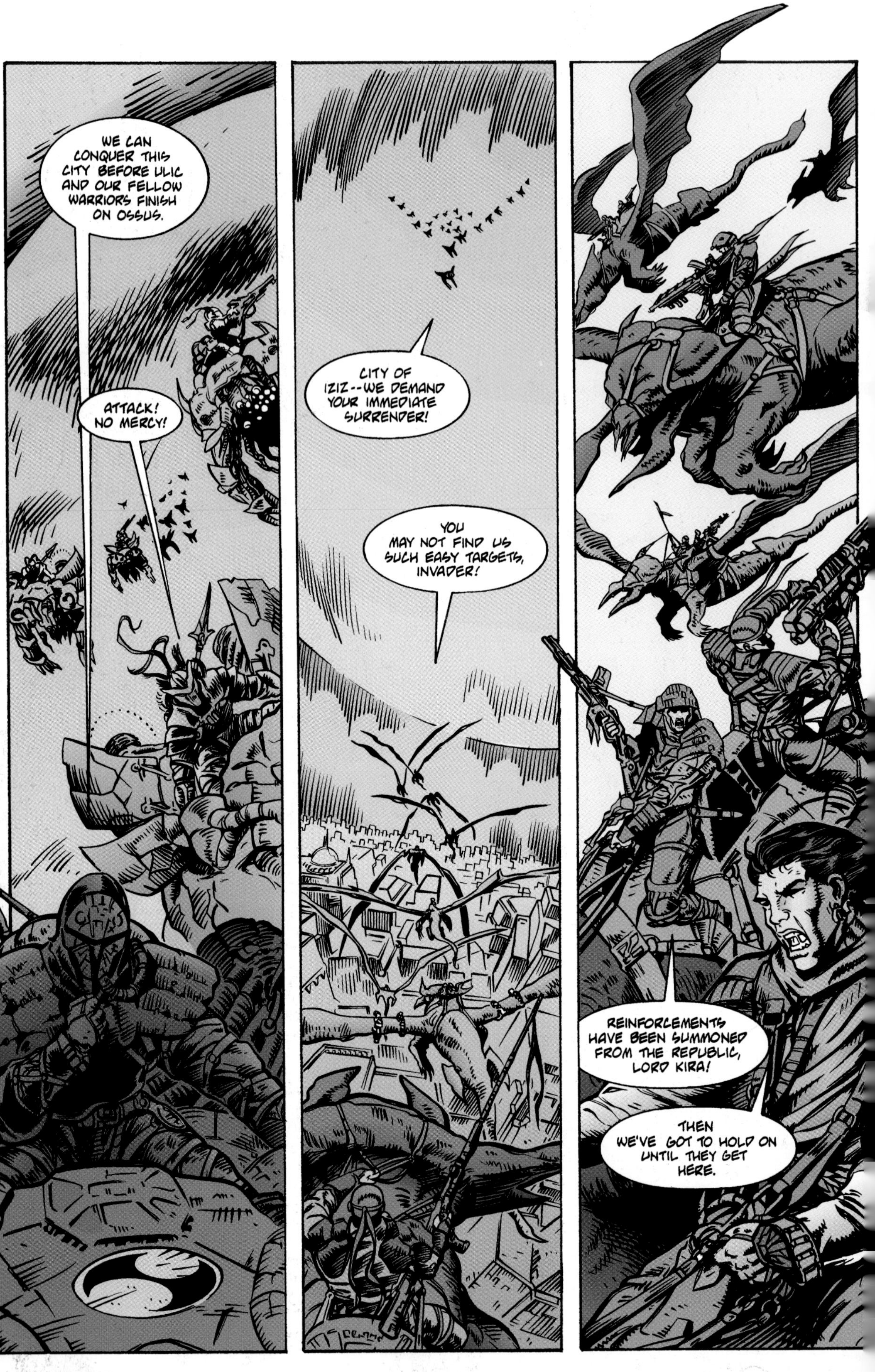
WE CAN CONQUER THIS CITY BEFORE ULIC AND OUR FELLOW WARRIORS FINISH ON OSSUS.
ATTACK! NO MERCY!
CITY OF IZIZ--WE DEMAND YOUR IMMEDIATE SURRENDER!
YOU MAY NOT FIND US SUCH EASY TARGETS, INVADER!
REINFORCEMENTS HAVE BEEN SUMMONED FROM THE REPUBLIC, LORD KIRA!
THEN WE'VE GOT TO HOLD ON UNTIL THEY GET HERE.

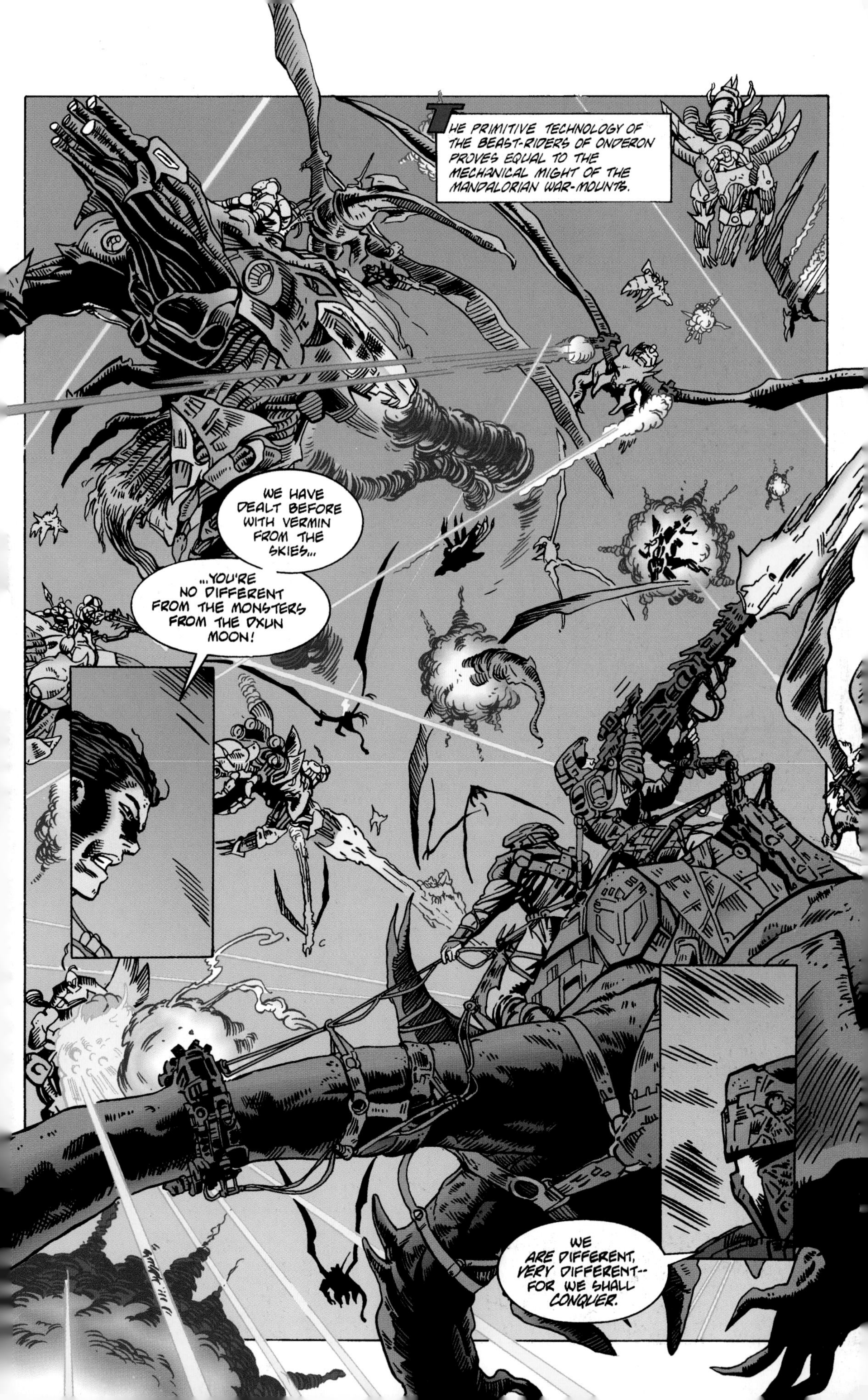
THE PRIMITIVE TECHNOLOGY OF THE BEAST-RIDERS OF ONDERON PROVES EQUAL TO THE MECHANICAL MIGHT OF THE MANDALORIAN WAR-MOUNTS.
WE HAVE DEALT BEFORE WITH VERMIN FROM THE SKIES...
...YOU'RE NO DIFFERENT FROM THE MONSTERS FROM THE DXUN MOON!
WE ARE DIFFERENT, VERY DIFFERENT-- FOR WE SHALL CONQUER.

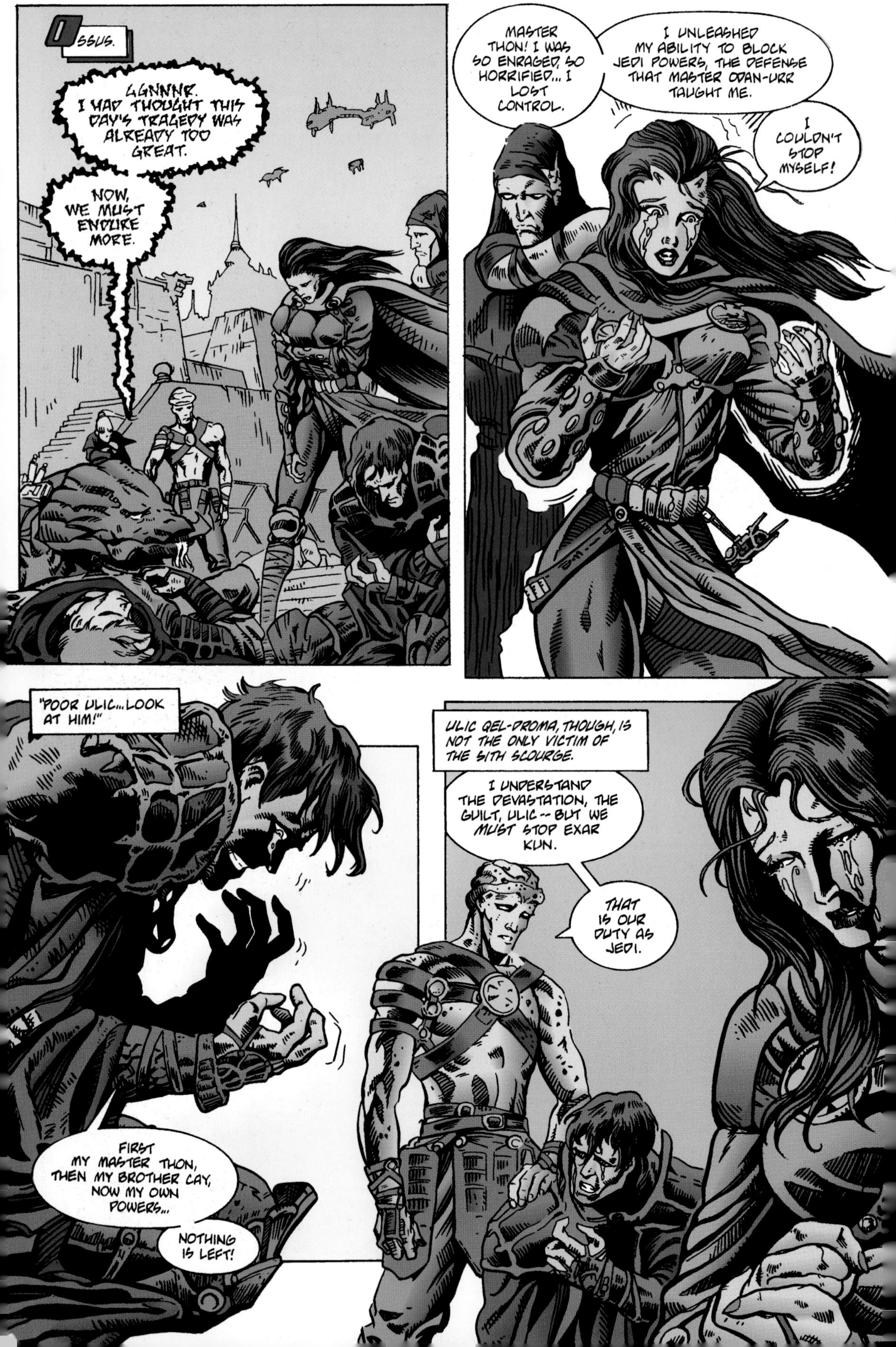
OSSUS.
LGNNNR. I HAD THOUGHT THIS DAY'S TRAGEDY WAS ALREADY TOO GREAT.
NOW, WE MUST ENDURE MORE.
MASTER THON! I WAS SO ENRAGED, SO HORRIFIED... I LOST CONTROL.
I UNLEASHED MY ABILITY TO BLOCK JEDI POWERS, THE DEFENSE THAT MASTER ODAN-URR TAUGHT ME.
I COULDN'T STOP MYSELF!
"POOR ULIC... LOOK AT HIM!"
FIRST MY MASTER THON, THEN MY BROTHER CAY, NOW MY OWN POWERS...
NOTHING IS LEFT!
ULIC QEL-DROMA, THOUGH, IS NOT THE ONLY VICTIM OF THE SITH SCOURGE.
I UNDERSTAND THE DEVASTATION, THE GUILT, ULIC -- BUT WE MUST STOP EXAR KUN.
THAT IS OUR DUTY AS JEDI.

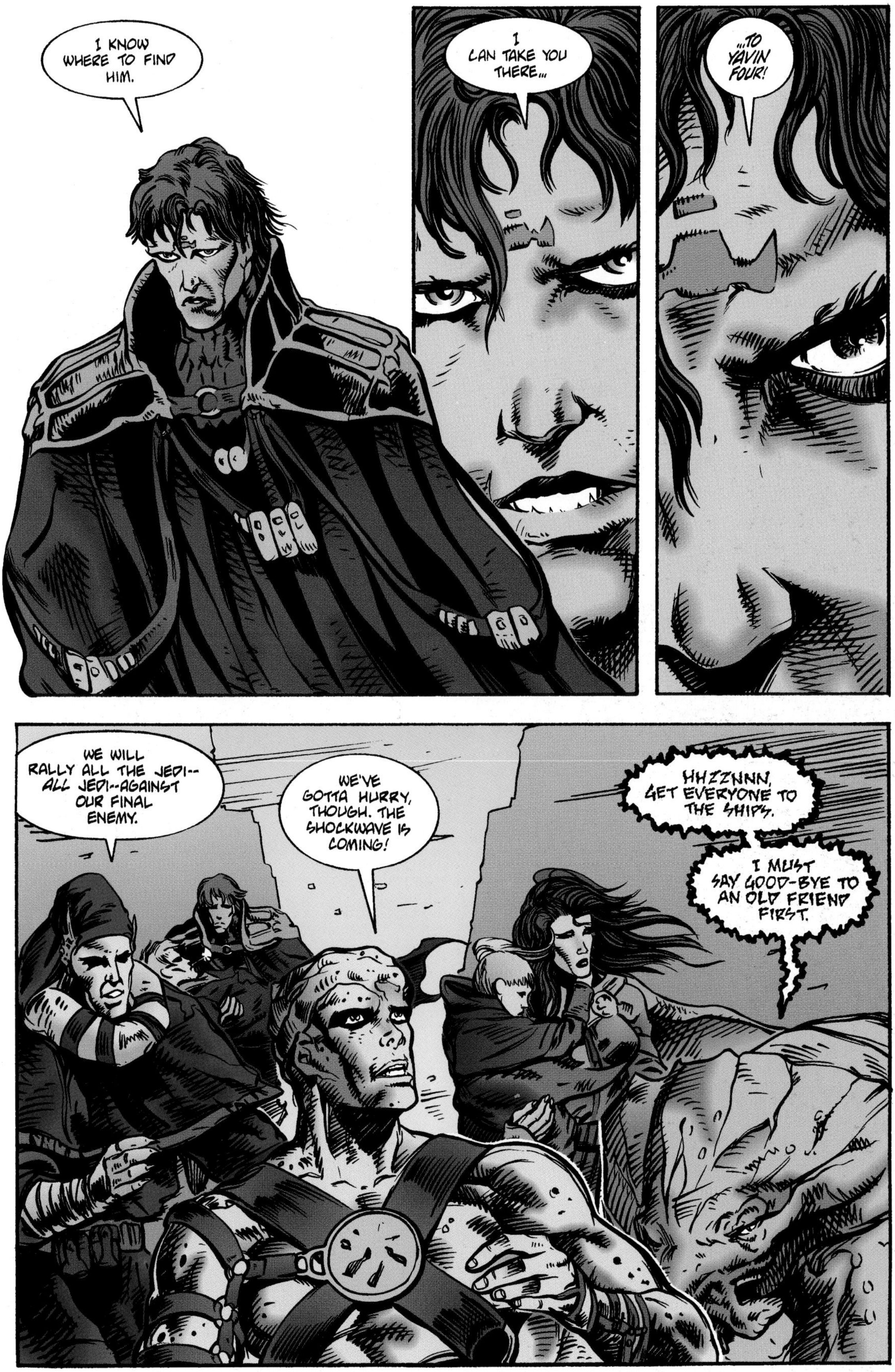
I KNOW WHERE TO FIND HIM.
I CAN TAKE YOU THERE...
...TO YAVIN FOUR!
WE WILL RALLY ALL THE JEDI--ALL JEDI--AGAINST OUR FINAL ENEMY.
WE'VE GOTTA HURRY, THOUGH. THE SHOCKWAVE IS COMING!
HHZZNNN, GET EVERYONE TO THE SHIPS.
I MUST SAY GOOD-BYE TO AN OLD FRIEND FIRST.

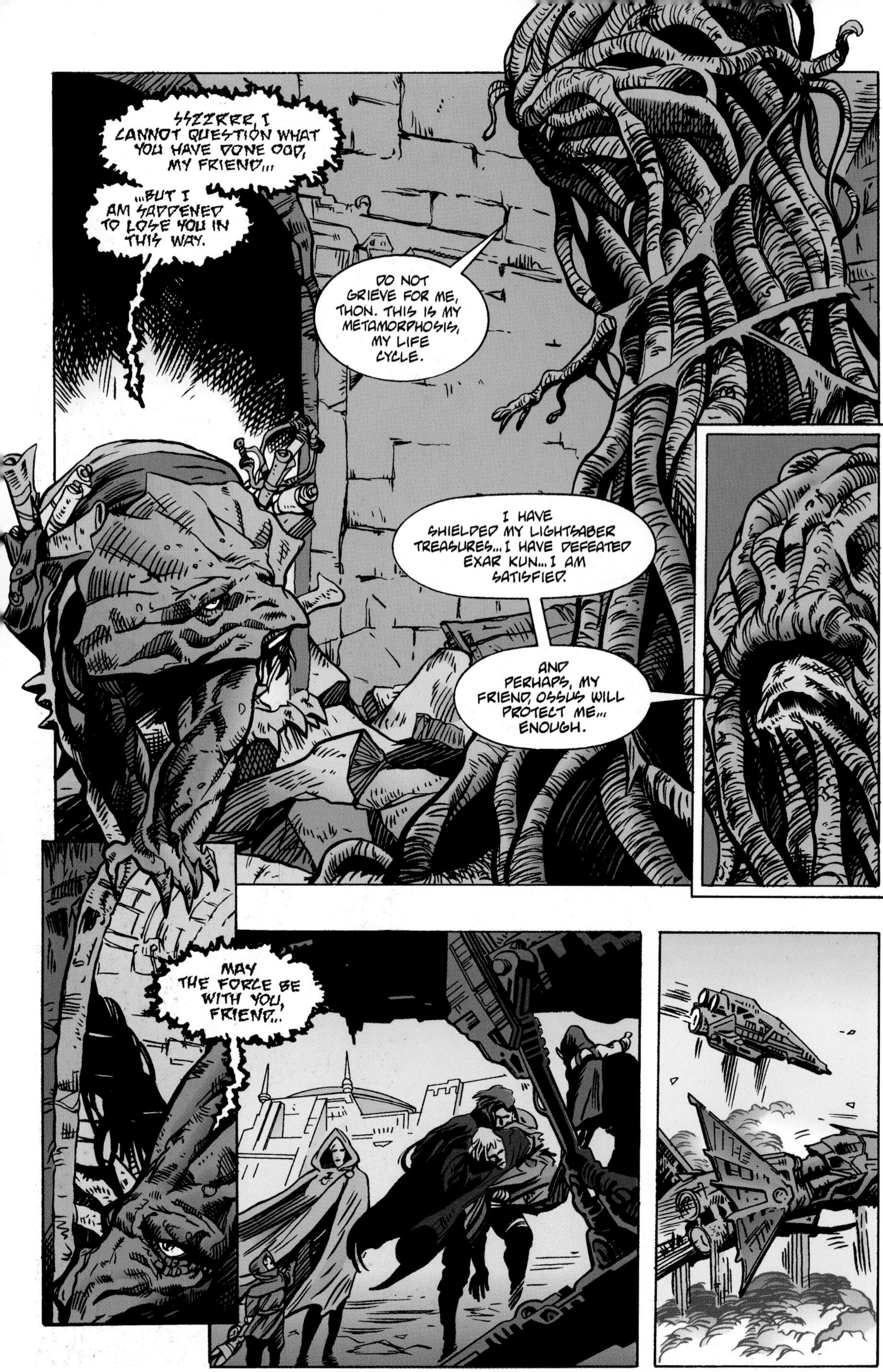
SSZZRRR, I CANNOT QUESTION WHAT YOU HAVE DONE OOD, MY FRIEND...
...BUT I AM SADDENED TO LOSE YOU IN THIS WAY.
DO NOT GRIEVE FOR ME, THON. THIS IS MY METAMORPHOSIS, MY LIFE CYCLE.
I HAVE SHIELDED MY LIGHTSABER TREASURES... I HAVE DEFEATED EXAR KUN... I AM SATISFIED.
AND PERHAPS, MY FRIEND, OSSUS WILL PROTECT ME... ENOUGH.
MAY THE FORCE BE WITH YOU, FRIEND..

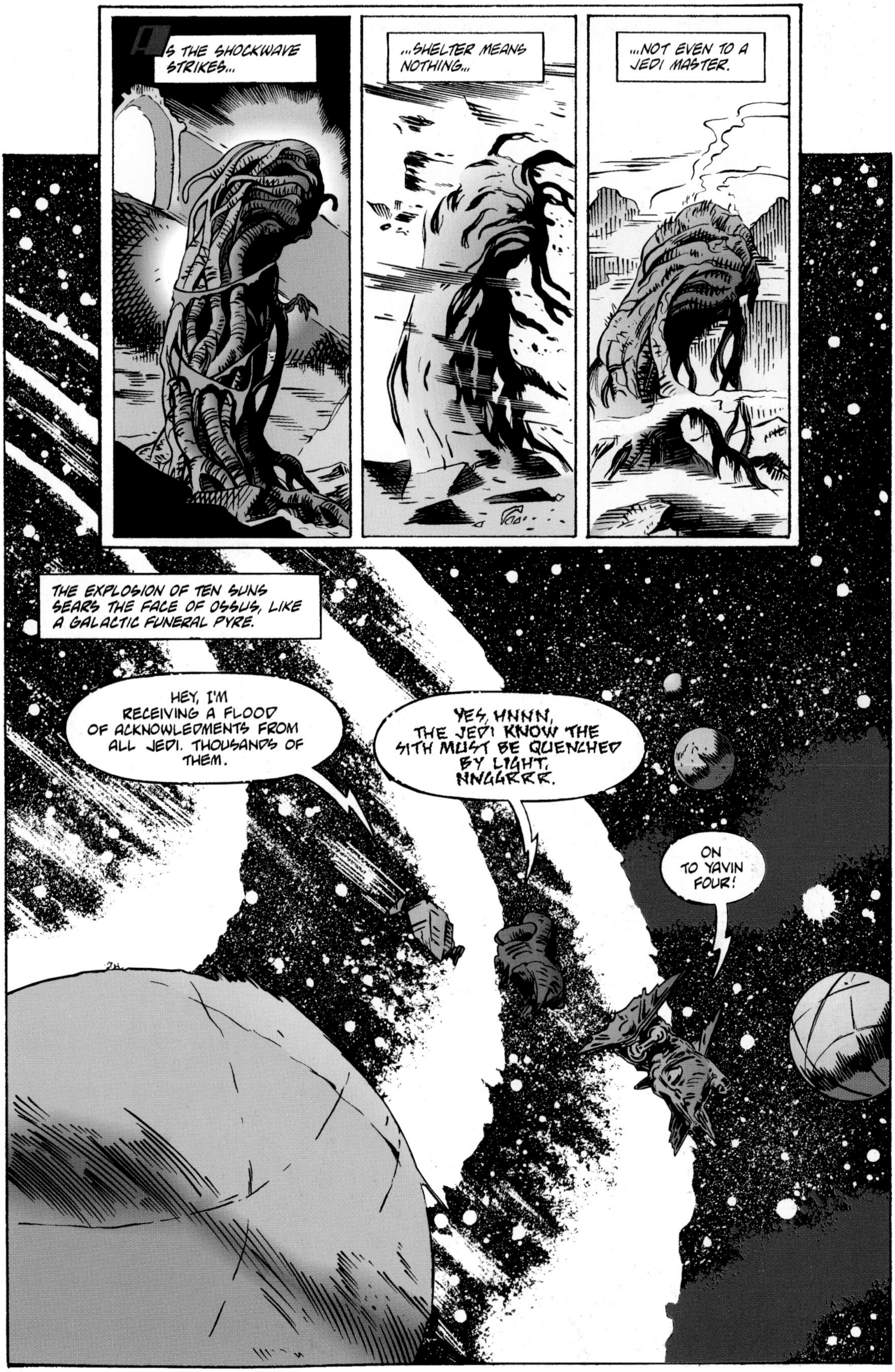

S THE SHOCKWAVE STRIKES...
...SHELTER MEANS NOTHING...
...NOT EVEN TO A JEDI MASTER.
THE EXPLOSION OF TEN SUNS SEARS THE FACE OF OSSUS, LIKE A GALACTIC FUNERAL PYRE.
HEY, I'M RECEIVING A FLOOD OF ACKNOWLEDMENTS FROM ALL JEDI. THOUSANDS OF THEM.
YES, HNNN, THE JEDI KNOW THE SITH MUST BE QUENCHED BY LIGHT. NNGGRRR.
ON TO YAVIN FOUR!

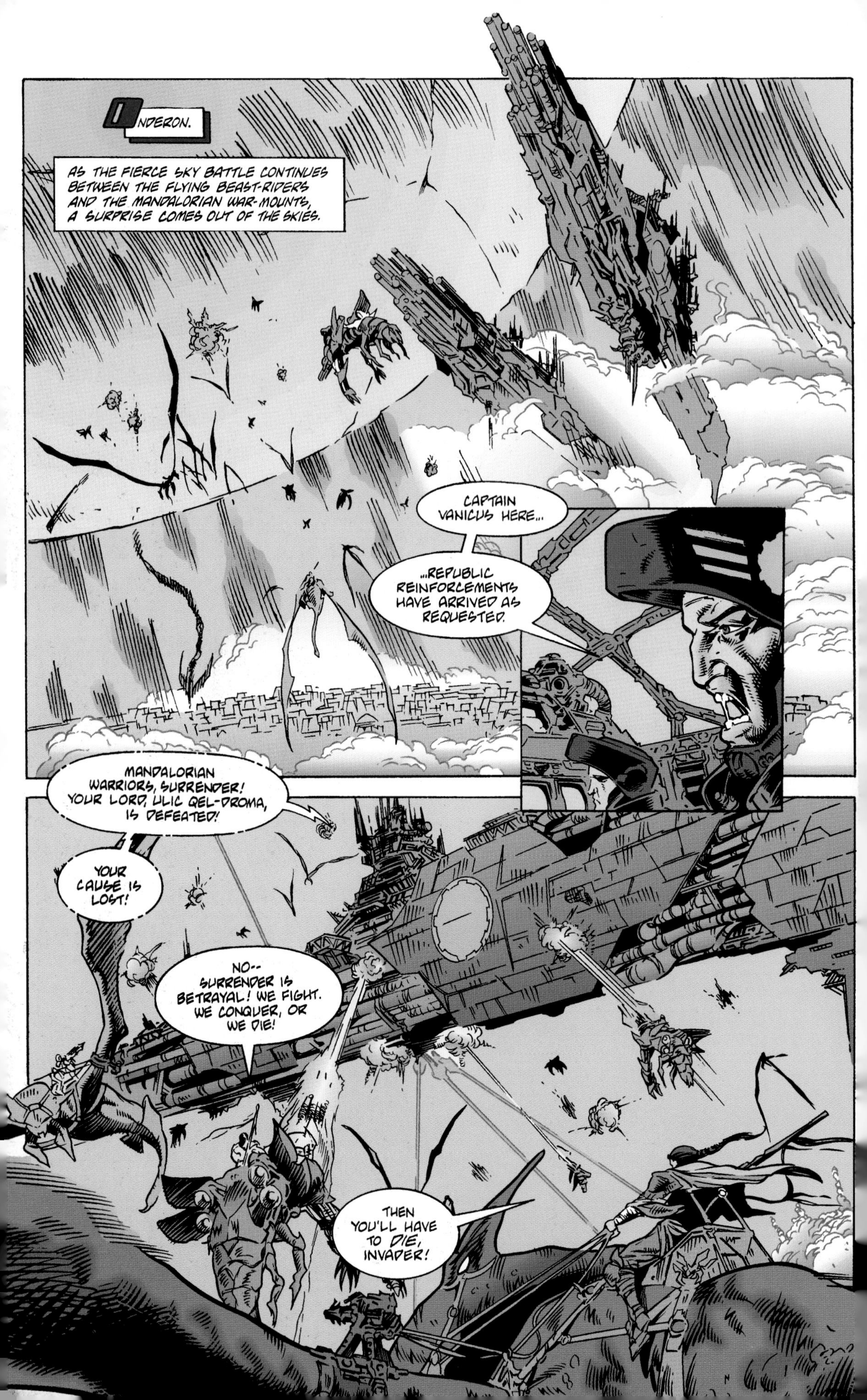
ONDERON.
AS THE FIERCE SKY BATTLE CONTINUES BETWEEN THE FLYING BEAST-RIDERS AND THE MANDALORIAN WAR-MOUNTS, A SURPRISE COMES OUT OF THE SKIES.
CAPTAIN VANICUS HERE...
...REPUBLIC REINFORCEMENTS HAVE ARRIVED AS REQUESTED.
MANDALORIAN WARRIORS, SURRENDER! YOUR LORD, ULIC QEL-DROMA, IS DEFEATED!
YOUR CAUSE IS LOST!
NO-- SURRENDER IS BETRAYAL! WE FIGHT. WE CONQUER, OR WE DIE!
THEN YOU'LL HAVE TO DIE, INVADER!

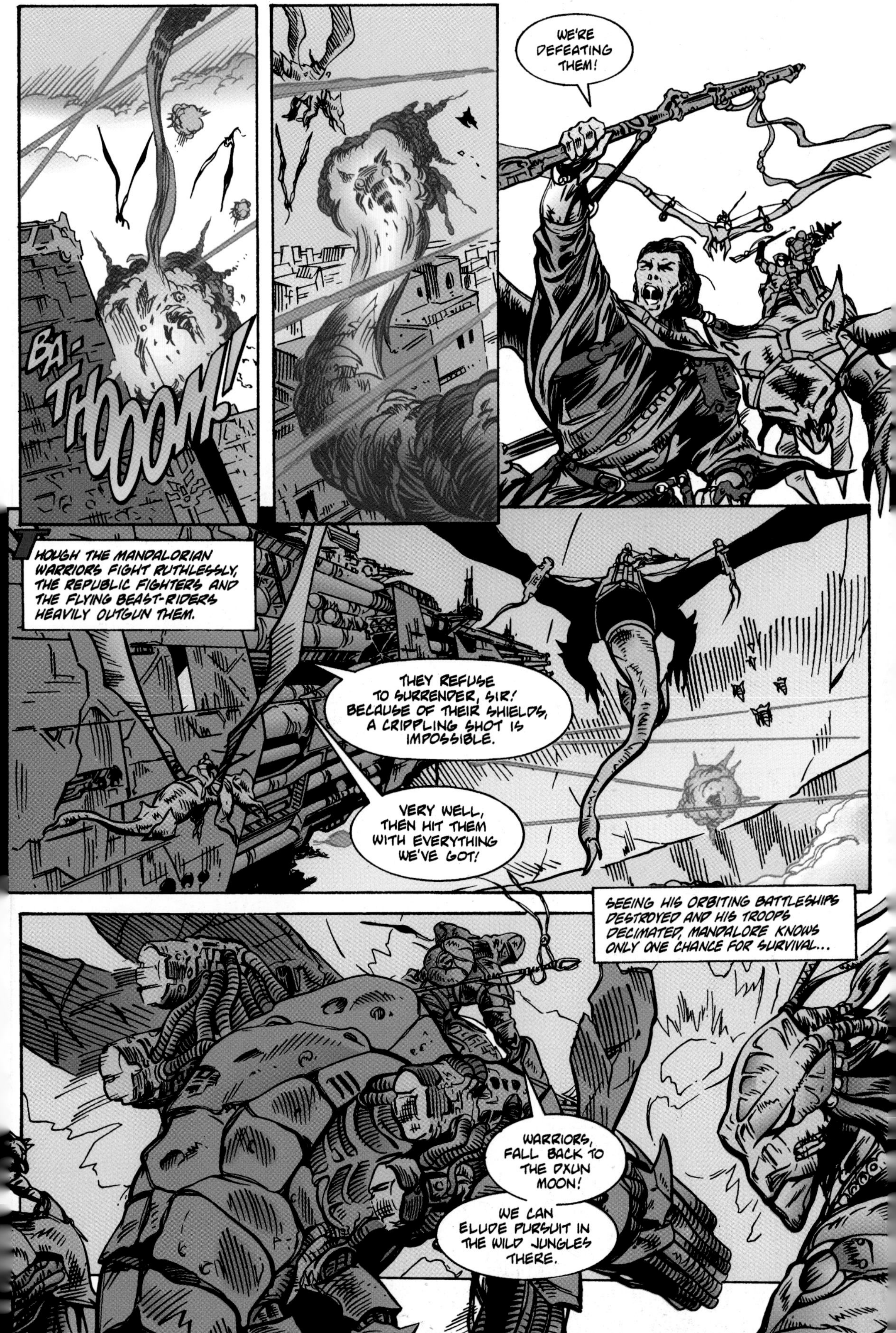
BA-THOOOM!
WE'RE DEFEATING THEM!
THOUGH THE MANDALORIAN WARRIORS FIGHT RUTHLESSLY, THE REPUBLIC FIGHTERS AND THE FLYING BEAST-RIDERS HEAVILY OUTGUN THEM.
THEY REFUSE TO SURRENDER, SIR! BECAUSE OF THEIR SHIELDS, A CRIPPLING SHOT IS IMPOSSIBLE.
VERY WELL, THEN HIT THEM WITH EVERYTHING WE'VE GOT!
SEEING HIS ORBITING BATTLESHIPS DESTROYED AND HIS TROOPS DECIMATED, MANDALORE KNOWS ONLY ONE CHANCE FOR SURVIVAL...
WARRIORS, FALL BACK TO THE DXUN MOON!
WE CAN ELUDE PURSUIT IN THE WILD JUNGLES THERE.

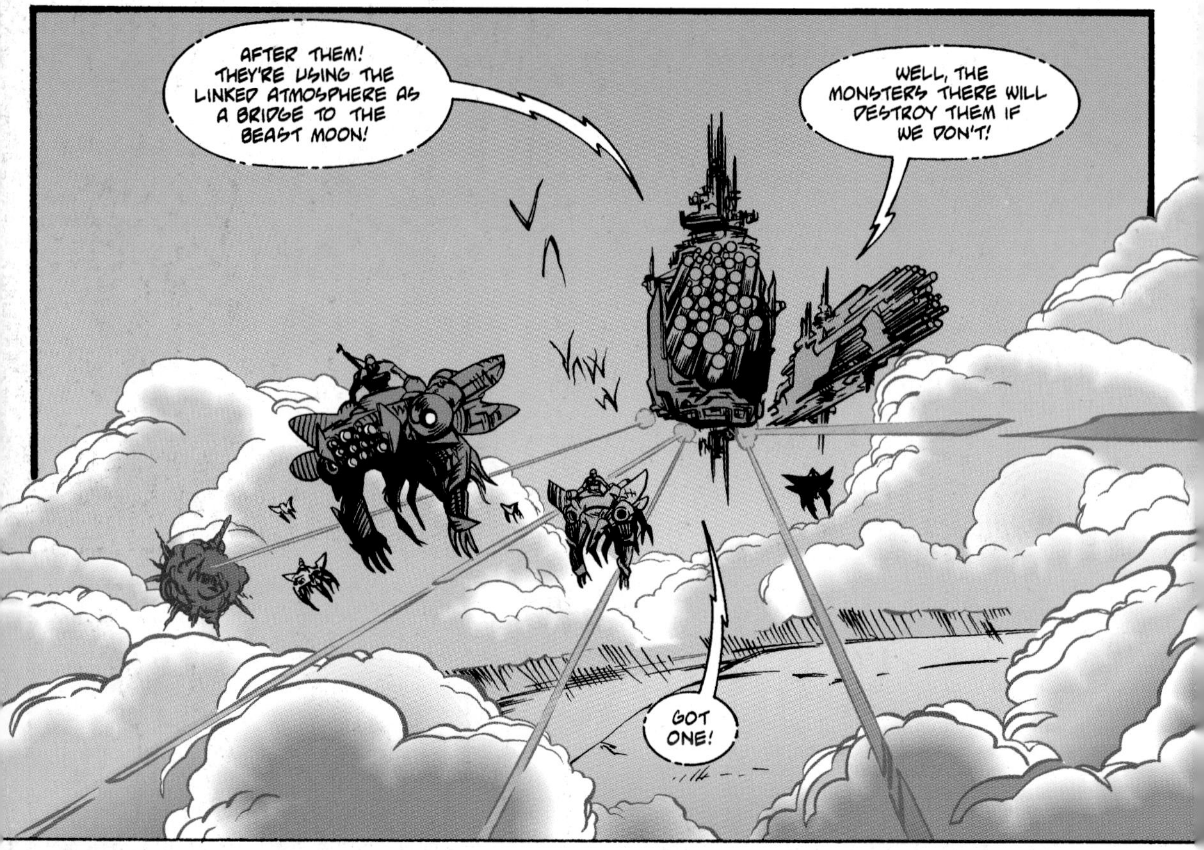
AFTER THEM! THEY'RE USING THE LINKED ATMOSPHERE AS A BRIDGE TO THE BEAST MOON!
WELL, THE MONSTERS THERE WILL DESTROY THEM IF WE DON'T!
GOT ONE!

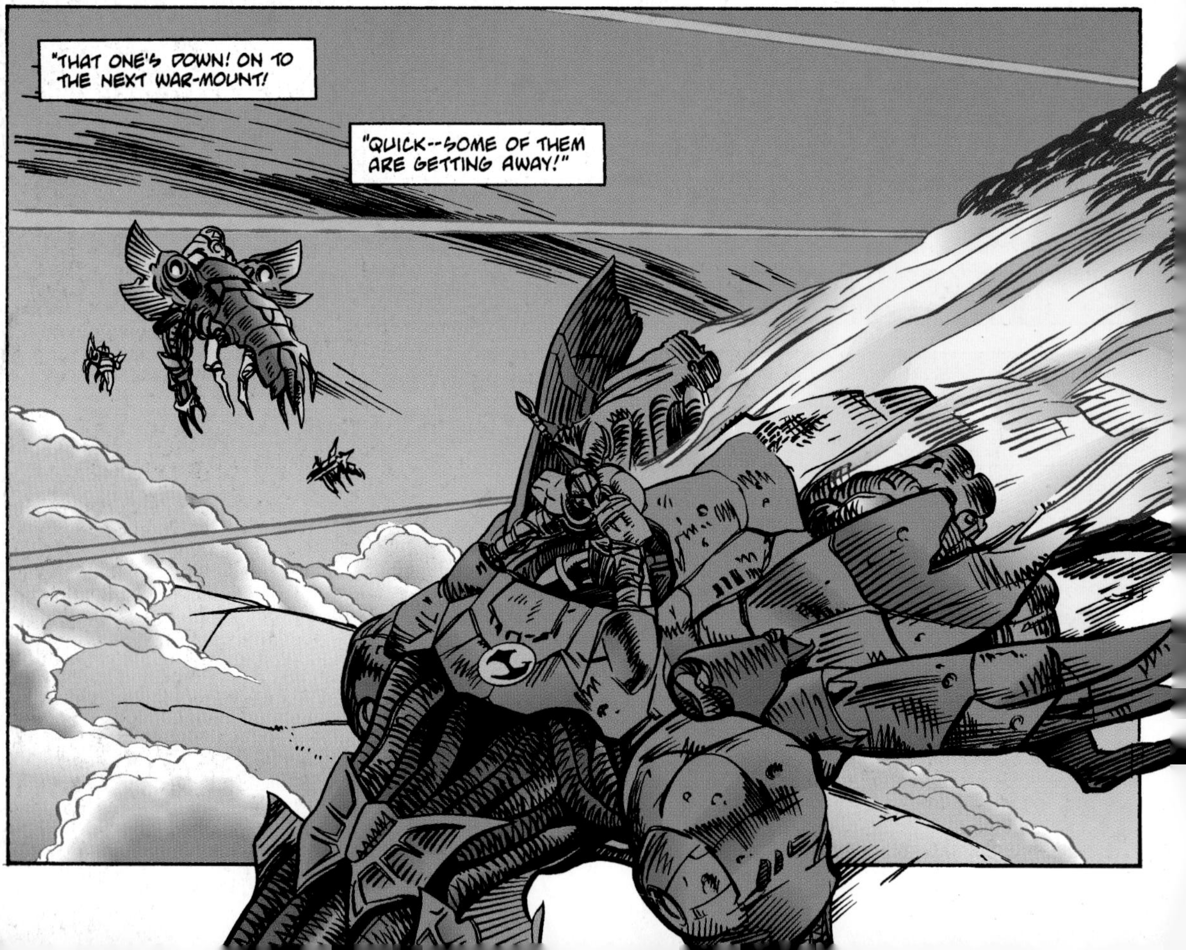
"THAT ONE'S DOWN! ON TO THE NEXT WAR-MOUNT!
"QUICK--SOME OF THEM ARE GETTING AWAY!"

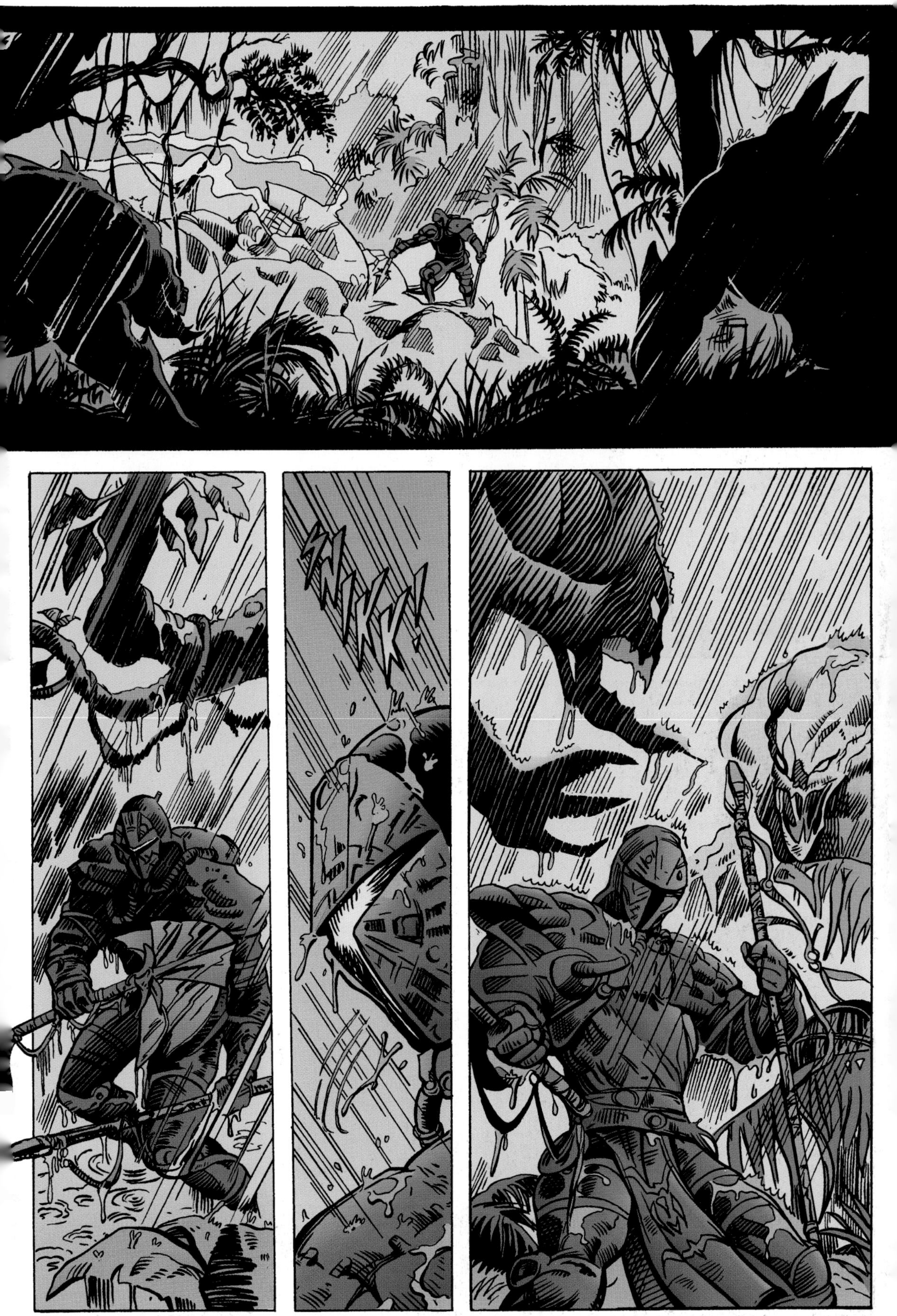
SNIKK!

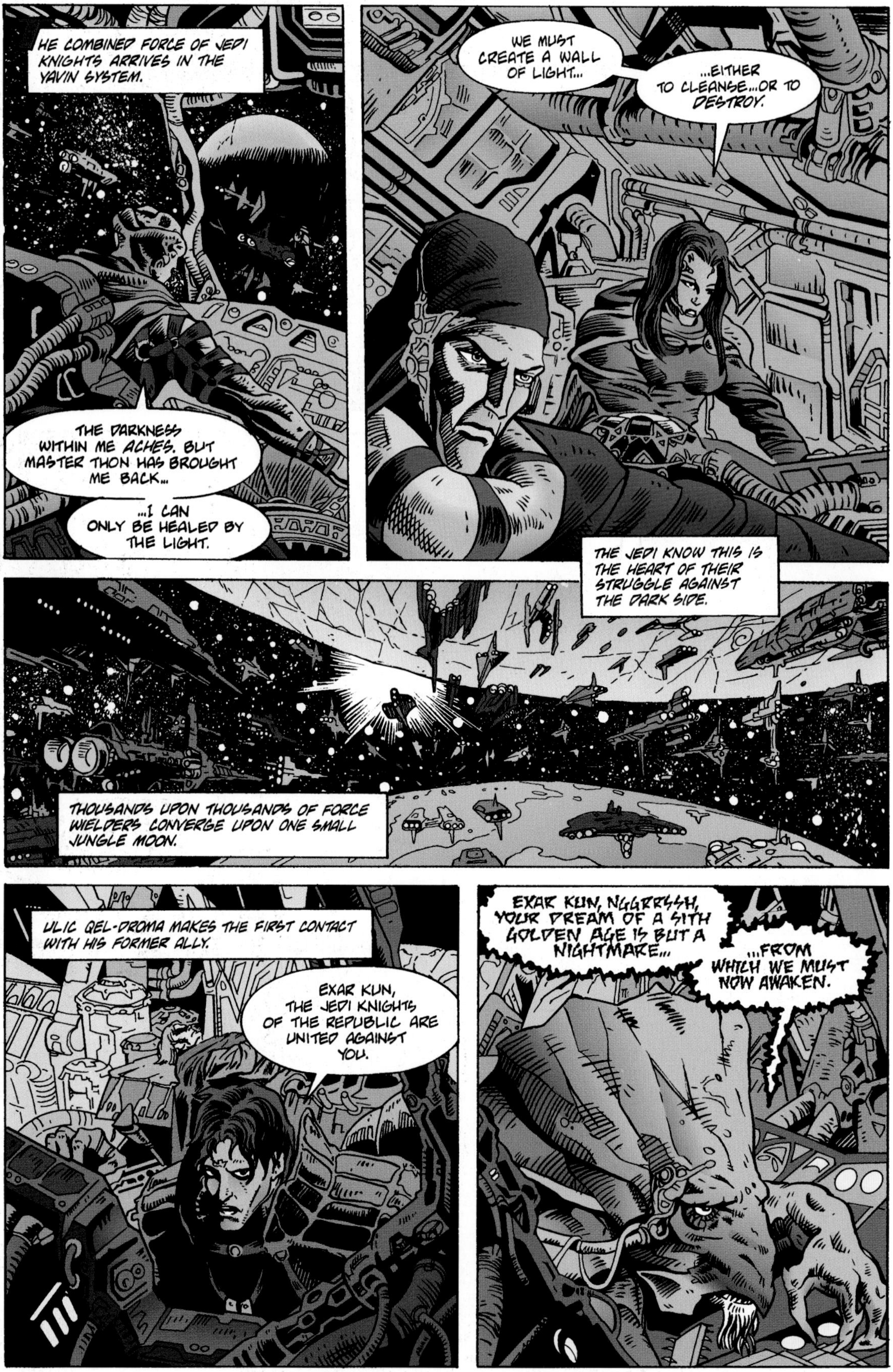
HE COMBINED FORCE OF JEDI KNIGHTS ARRIVES IN THE YAVIN SYSTEM.
THE DARKNESS WITHIN ME ACHES. BUT MASTER THON HAS BROUGHT ME BACK...
...I CAN ONLY BE HEALED BY THE LIGHT.
WE MUST CREATE A WALL OF LIGHT...
...EITHER TO CLEANSE...OR TO DESTROY.
THE JEDI KNOW THIS IS THE HEART OF THEIR STRUGGLE AGAINST THE DARK SIDE.
THOUSANDS UPON THOUSANDS OF FORCE WIELDERS CONVERGE UPON ONE SMALL JUNGLE MOON.
ULIC QEL-DROMA MAKES THE FIRST CONTACT WITH HIS FORMER ALLY.
EXAR KUN, THE JEDI KNIGHTS OF THE REPUBLIC ARE UNITED AGAINST YOU.
EXAR KUN, NGGRRSSH, YOUR DREAM OF A SITH GOLDEN AGE IS BUT A NIGHTMARE...
...FROM WHICH WE MUST NOW AWAKEN.

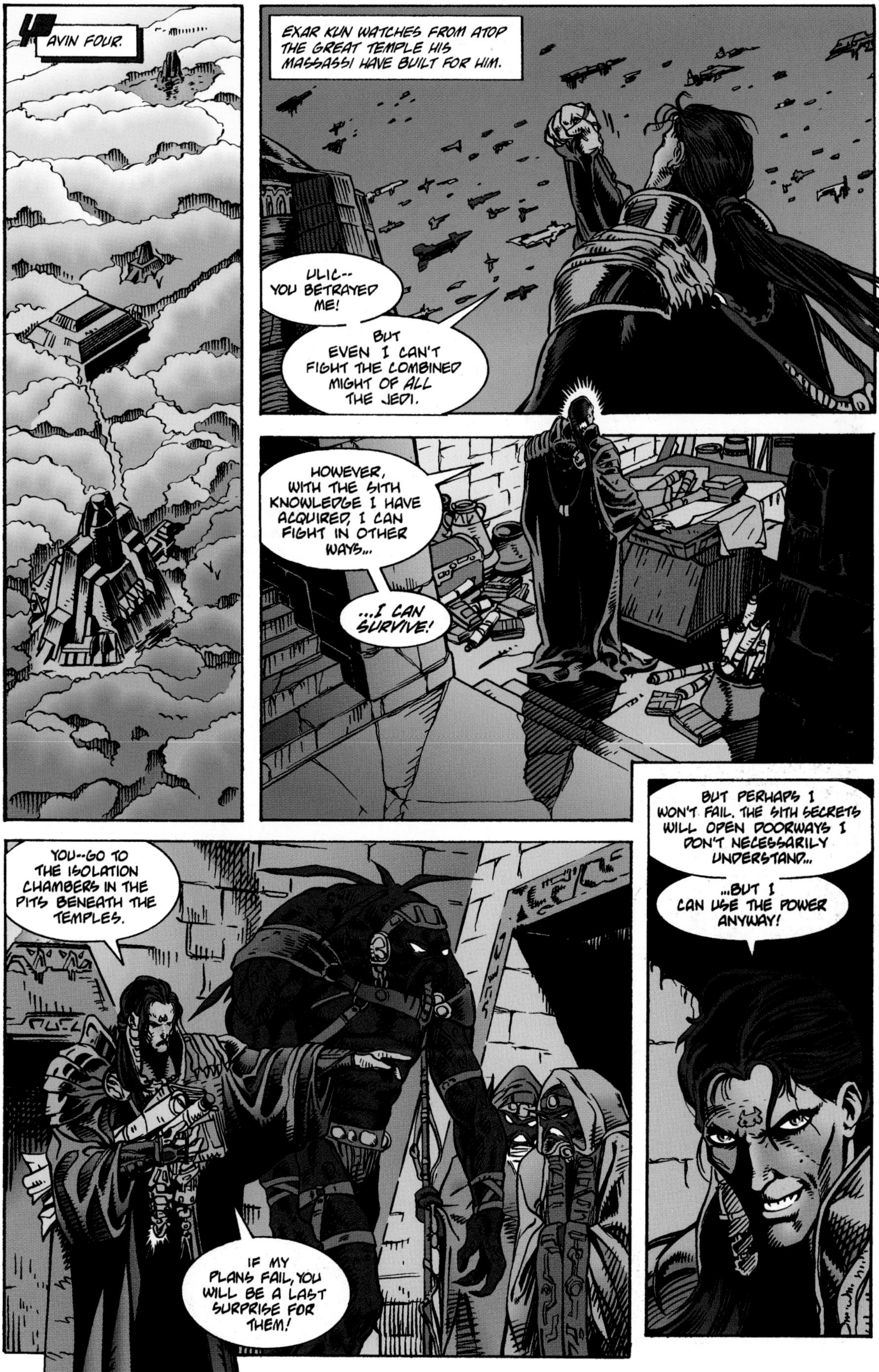
YAVIN FOUR.
EXAR KUN WATCHES FROM ATOP THE GREAT TEMPLE HIS MASSASSI HAVE BUILT FOR HIM.
ULIC-- YOU BETRAYED ME!
BUT EVEN I CAN'T FIGHT THE COMBINED MIGHT OF ALL THE JEDI.
HOWEVER, WITH THE SITH KNOWLEDGE I HAVE ACQUIRED, I CAN FIGHT IN OTHER WAYS...
...I CAN SURVIVE!
BUT PERHAPS I WON'T FAIL. THE SITH SECRETS WILL OPEN DOORWAYS I DON'T NECESSARILY UNDERSTAND...
...BUT I CAN USE THE POWER ANYWAY!
YOU--GO TO THE ISOLATION CHAMBERS IN THE PITS BENEATH THE TEMPLES.
IF MY PLANS FAIL, YOU WILL BE A LAST SURPRISE FOR THEM!

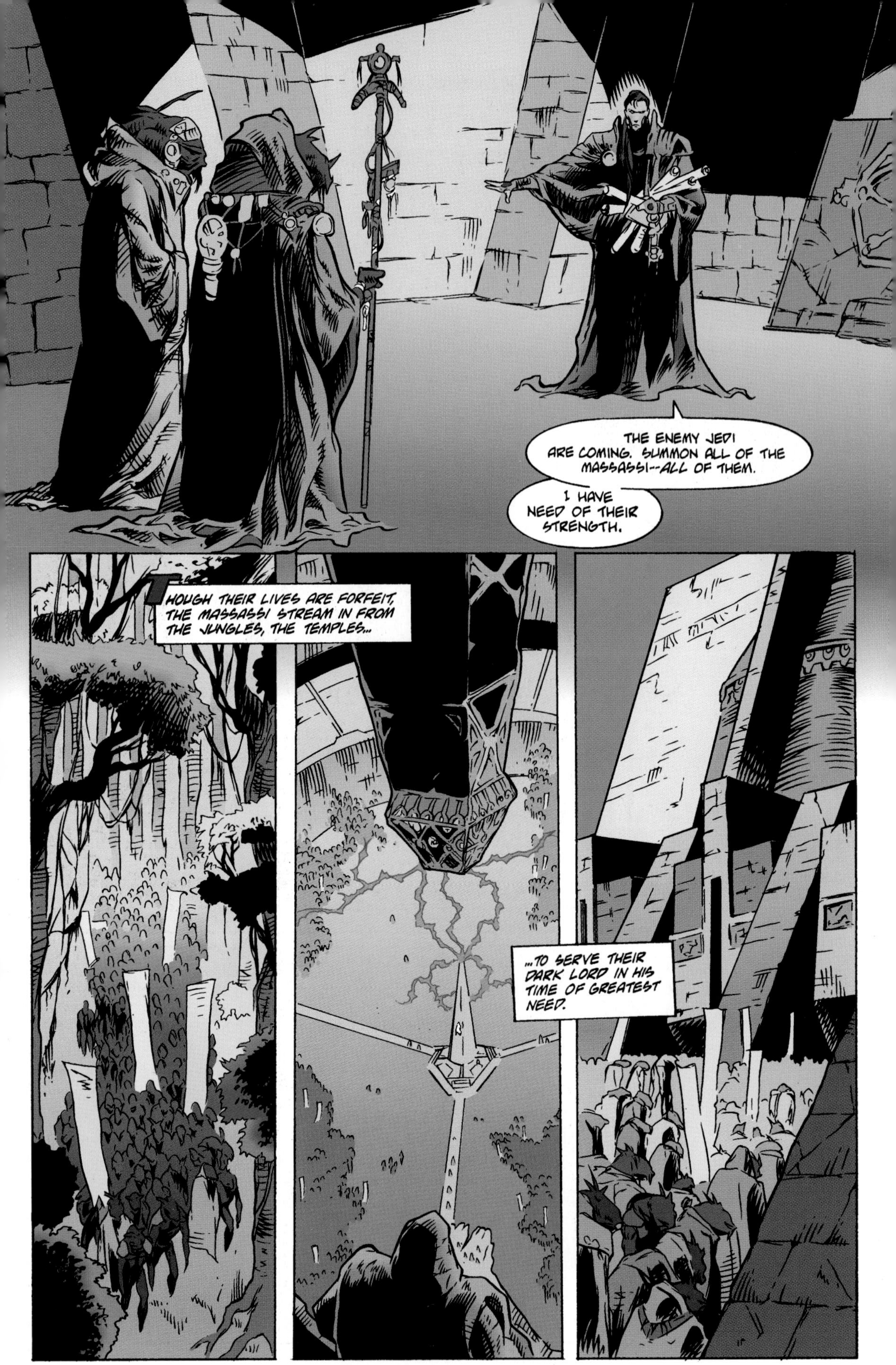
THE ENEMY JEDI ARE COMING. SUMMON ALL OF THE MASSASSI--ALL OF THEM.
I HAVE NEED OF THEIR STRENGTH.
THOUGH THEIR LIVES ARE FORFEIT, THE MASSASSI STREAM IN FROM THE JUNGLES, THE TEMPLES...
...TO SERVE THEIR DARK LORD IN HIS TIME OF GREATEST NEED.

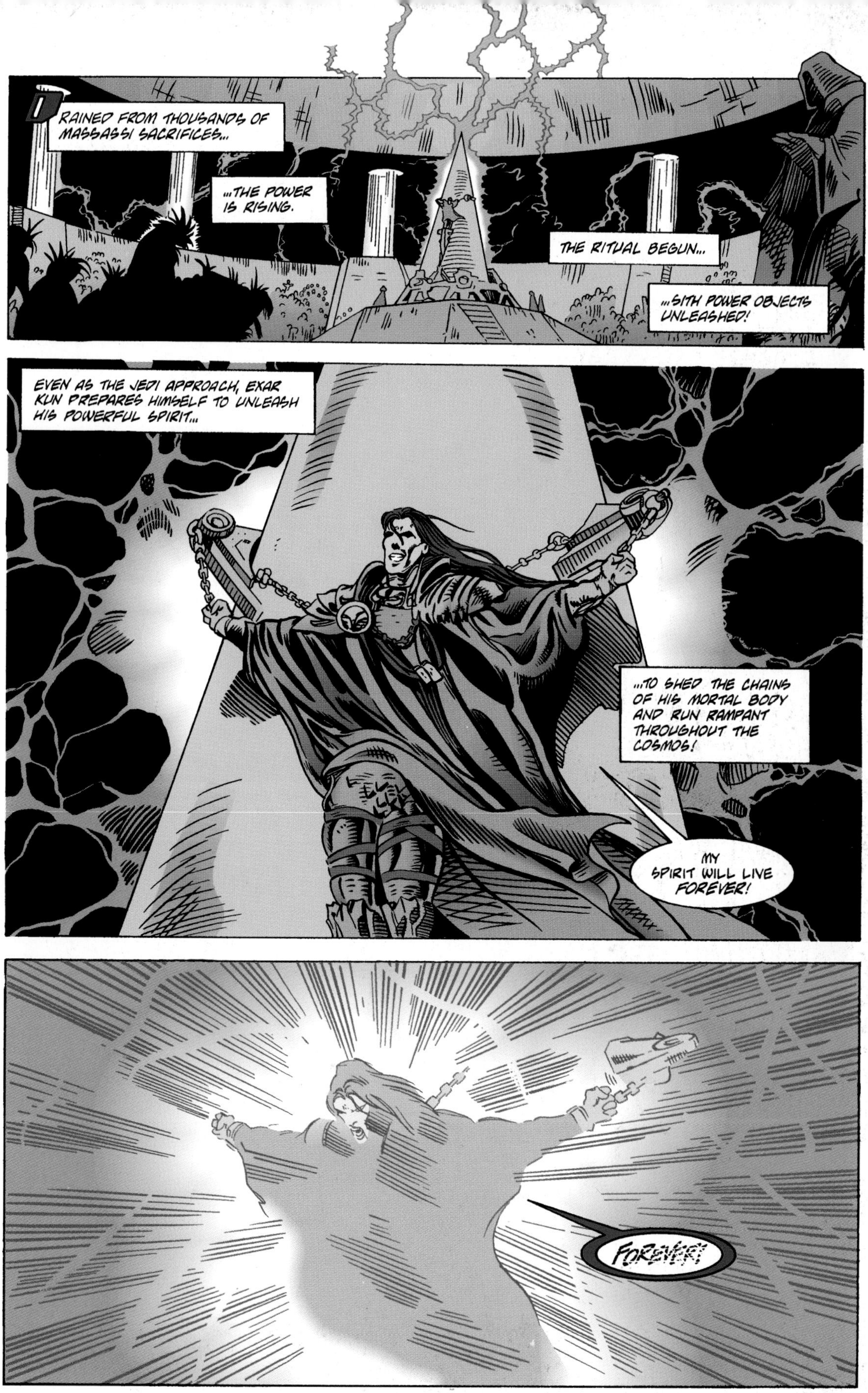
RAINED FROM THOUSANDS OF MASSASSI SACRIFICES...
...THE POWER IS RISING.
THE RITUAL BEGUN...
...SITH POWER OBJECTS UNLEASHED!
EVEN AS THE JEDI APPROACH, EXAR KUN PREPARES HIMSELF TO UNLEASH HIS POWERFUL SPIRIT...
...TO SHED THE CHAINS OF HIS MORTAL BODY AND RUN RAMPANT THROUGHOUT THE COSMOS!
MY SPIRIT WILL LIVE FOREVER!
FOREVER!

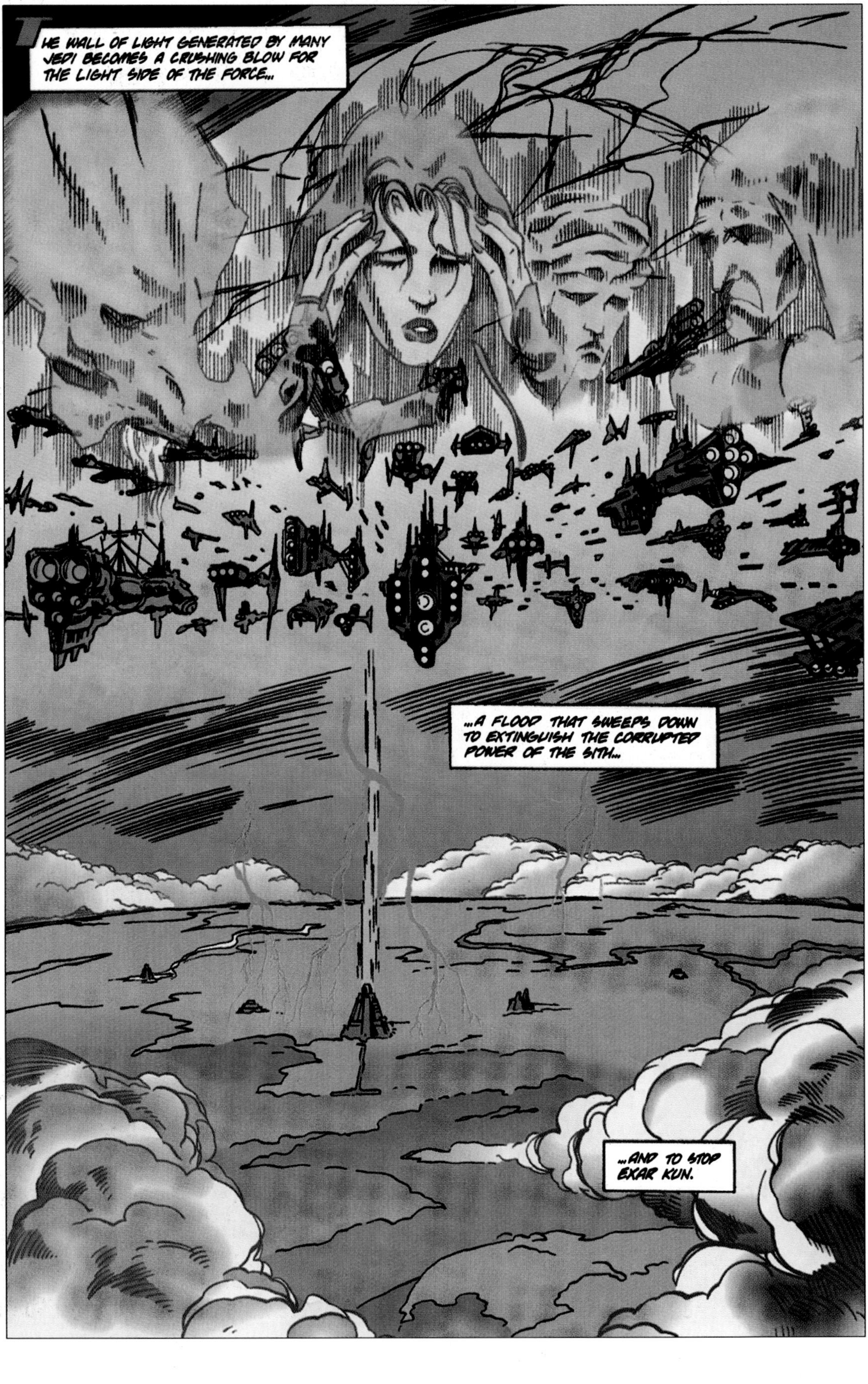
THE WALL OF LIGHT GENERATED BY MANY JEDI BECOMES A CRUSHING BLOW FOR THE LIGHT SIDE OF THE FORCE...
...A FLOOD THAT SWEEPS DOWN TO EXTINGUISH THE CORRUPTED POWER OF THE SITH...
...AND TO STOP EXAR KUN.

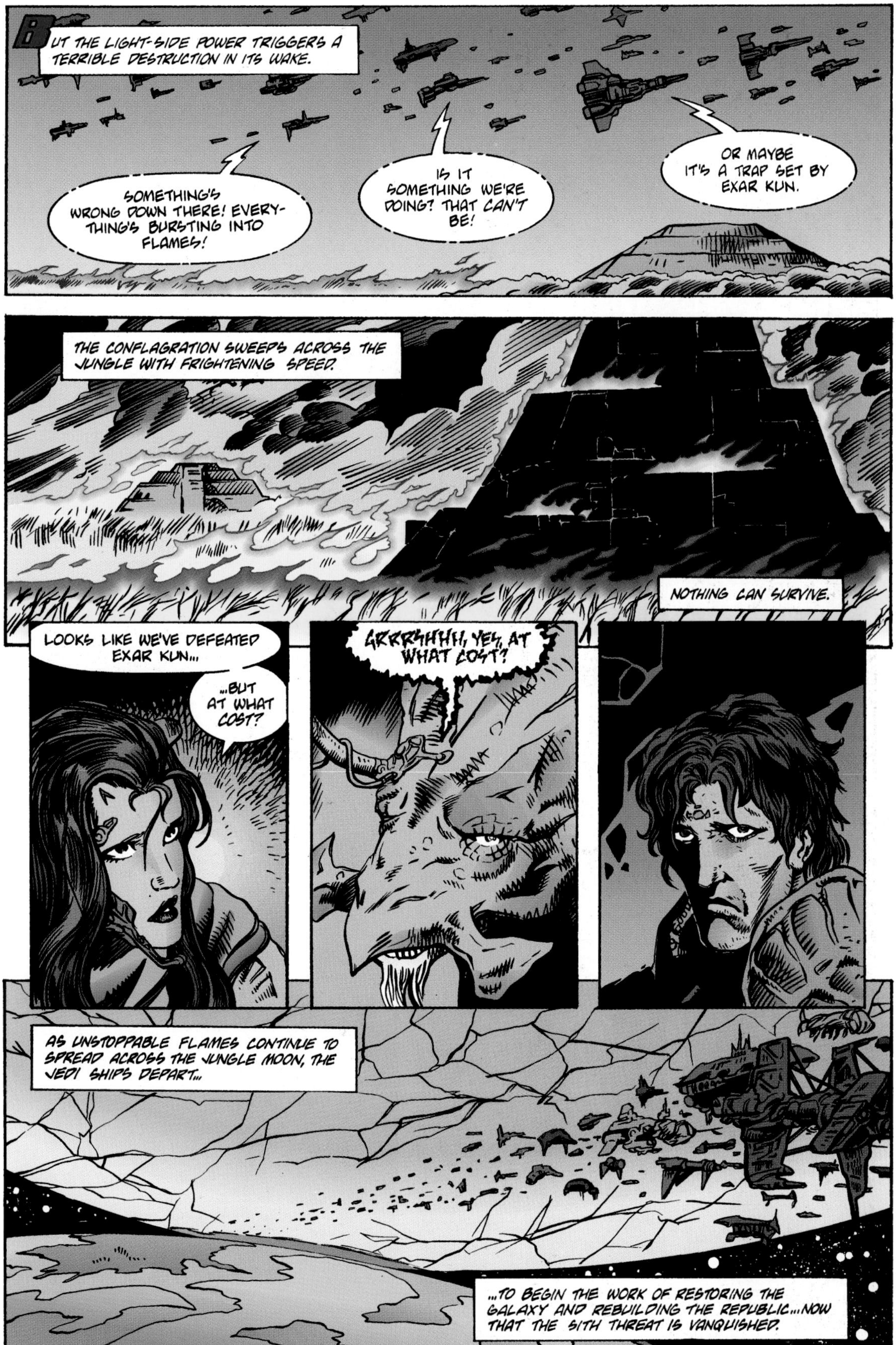
BUT THE LIGHT-SIDE POWER TRIGGERS A TERRIBLE DESTRUCTION IN ITS WAKE.
SOMETHING'S WRONG DOWN THERE! EVERYTHING'S BURSTING INTO FLAMES!
IS IT SOMETHING WE'RE DOING? THAT CAN'T BE!
OR MAYBE IT'S A TRAP SET BY EXAR KUN.
THE CONFLAGRATION SWEEPS ACROSS THE JUNGLE WITH FRIGHTENING SPEED.
NOTHING CAN SURVIVE.
LOOKS LIKE WE'VE DEFEATED EXAR KUN...
...BUT AT WHAT COST?
GRRRSHHH, YES, AT WHAT COST?
AS UNSTOPPABLE FLAMES CONTINUE TO SPREAD ACROSS THE JUNGLE MOON, THE JEDI SHIPS DEPART...
...TO BEGIN THE WORK OF RESTORING THE GALAXY AND REBUILDING THE REPUBLIC...NOW THAT THE SITH THREAT IS VANQUISHED.

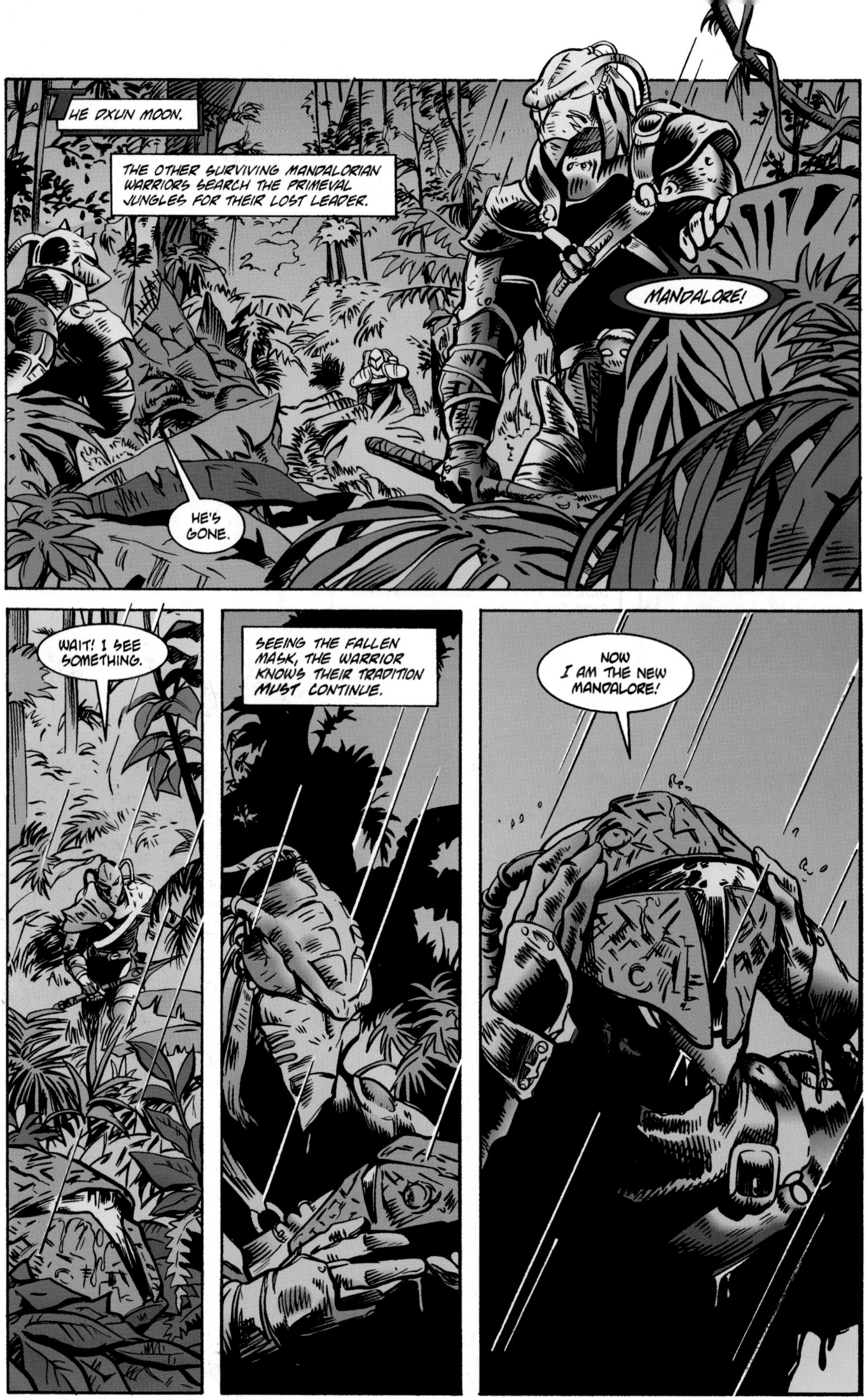
THE DXUN MOON.
THE OTHER SURVIVING MANDALORIAN WARRIORS SEARCH THE PRIMEVAL JUNGLES FOR THEIR LOST LEADER.
MANDALORE!
HE'S GONE.
WAIT! I SEE SOMETHING.
SEEING THE FALLEN MASK, THE WARRIOR KNOWS THEIR TRADITION MUST CONTINUE.
NOW I AM THE NEW MANDALORE!

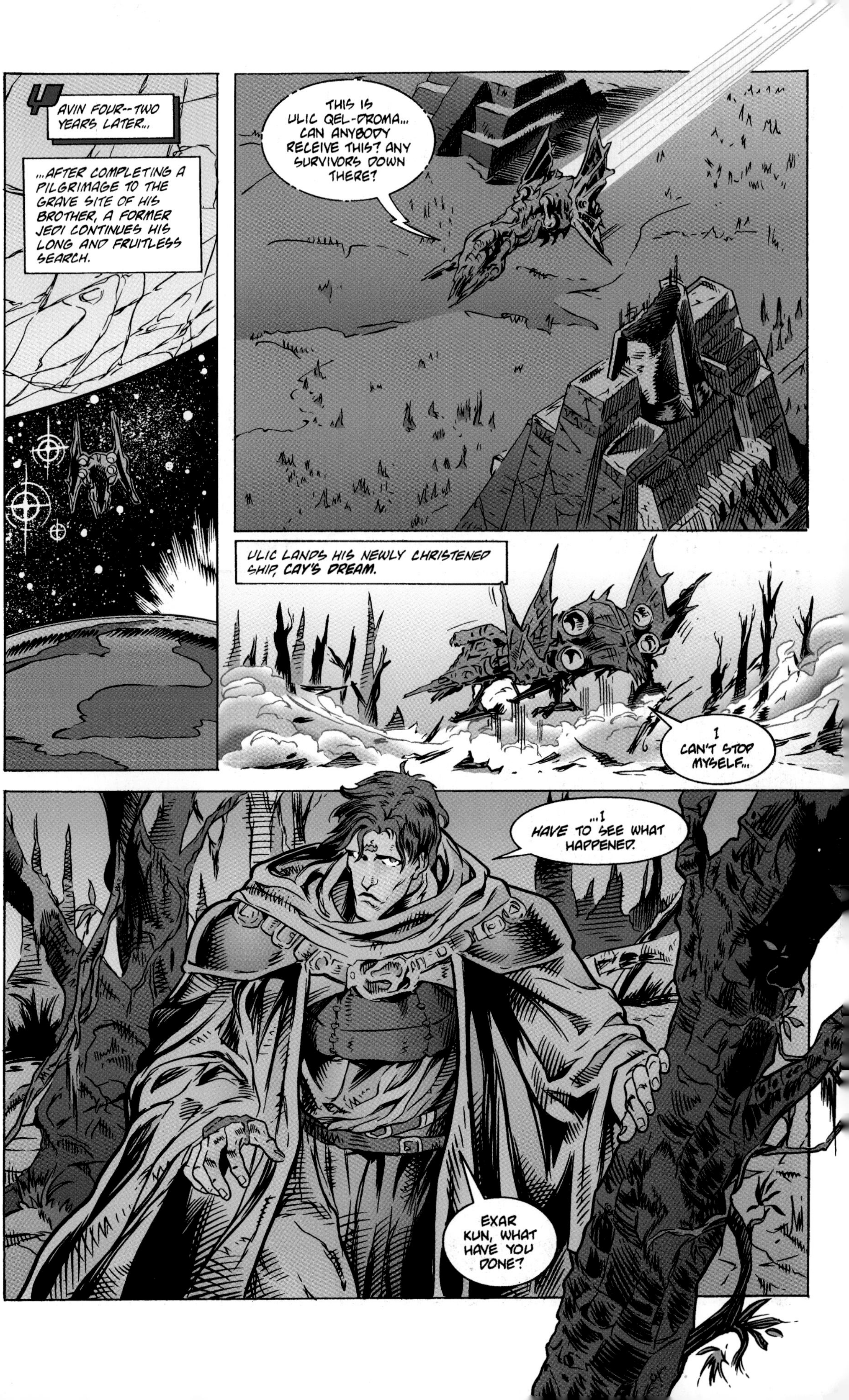
AVIN FOUR--TWO YEARS LATER...
...AFTER COMPLETING A PILGRIMAGE TO THE GRAVE SITE OF HIS BROTHER, A FORMER JEDI CONTINUES HIS LONG AND FRUITLESS SEARCH.
THIS IS ULIC QEL-DROMA... CAN ANYBODY RECEIVE THIS? ANY SURVIVORS DOWN THERE?
ULIC LANDS HIS NEWLY CHRISTENED SHIP, CAY'S DREAM.
I CAN'T STOP MYSELF...
...I HAVE TO SEE WHAT HAPPENED.
EXAR KUN, WHAT HAVE YOU DONE?

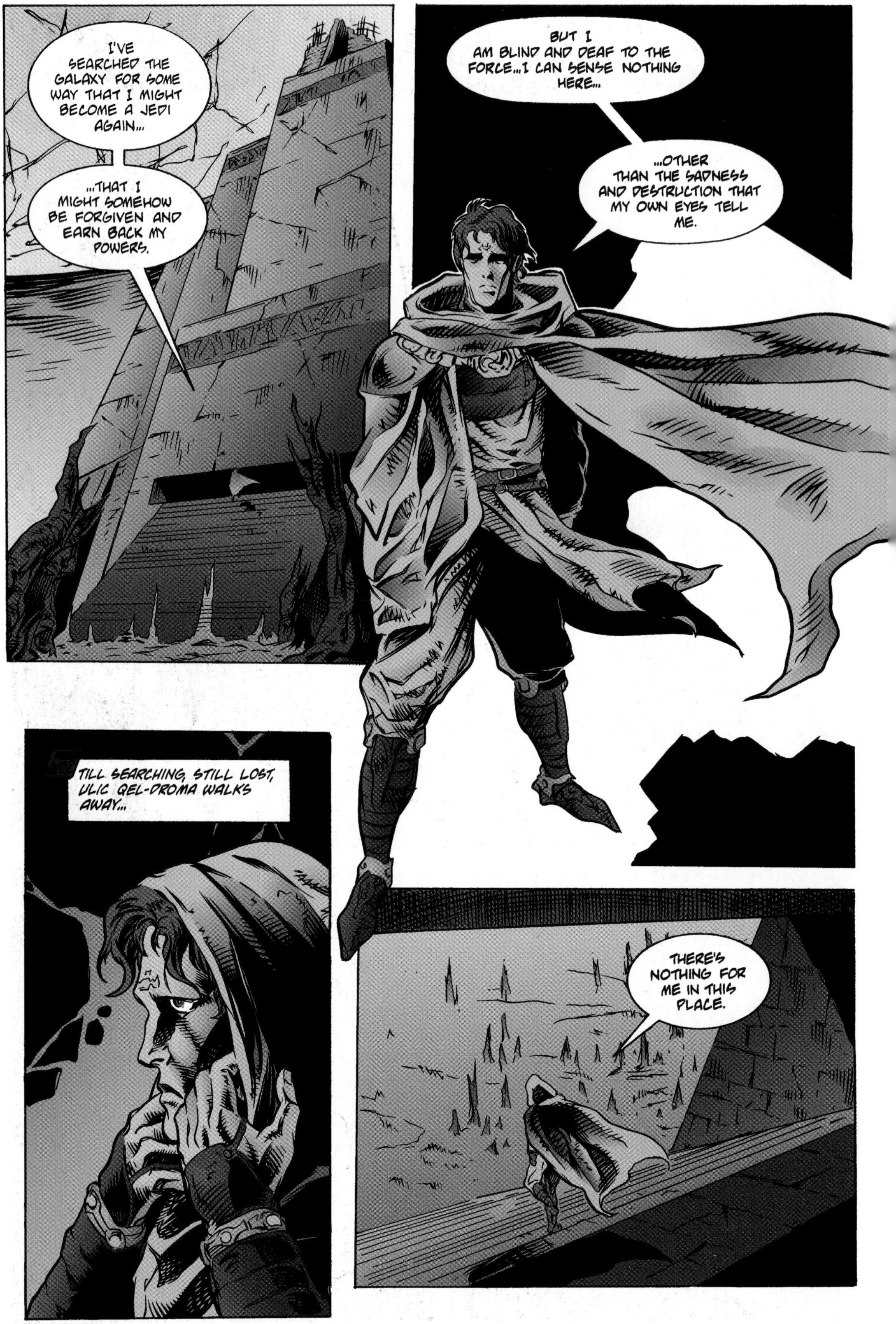
I'VE SEARCHED THE GALAXY FOR SOME WAY THAT I MIGHT BECOME A JEDI AGAIN...
...THAT I MIGHT SOMEHOW BE FORGIVEN AND EARN BACK MY POWERS.
BUT I AM BLIND AND DEAF TO THE FORCE...I CAN SENSE NOTHING HERE...
...OTHER THAN THE SADNESS AND DESTRUCTION THAT MY OWN EYES TELL ME.
STILL SEARCHING, STILL LOST, ULIC QEL-DROMA WALKS AWAY...
THERE'S NOTHING FOR ME IN THIS PLACE.

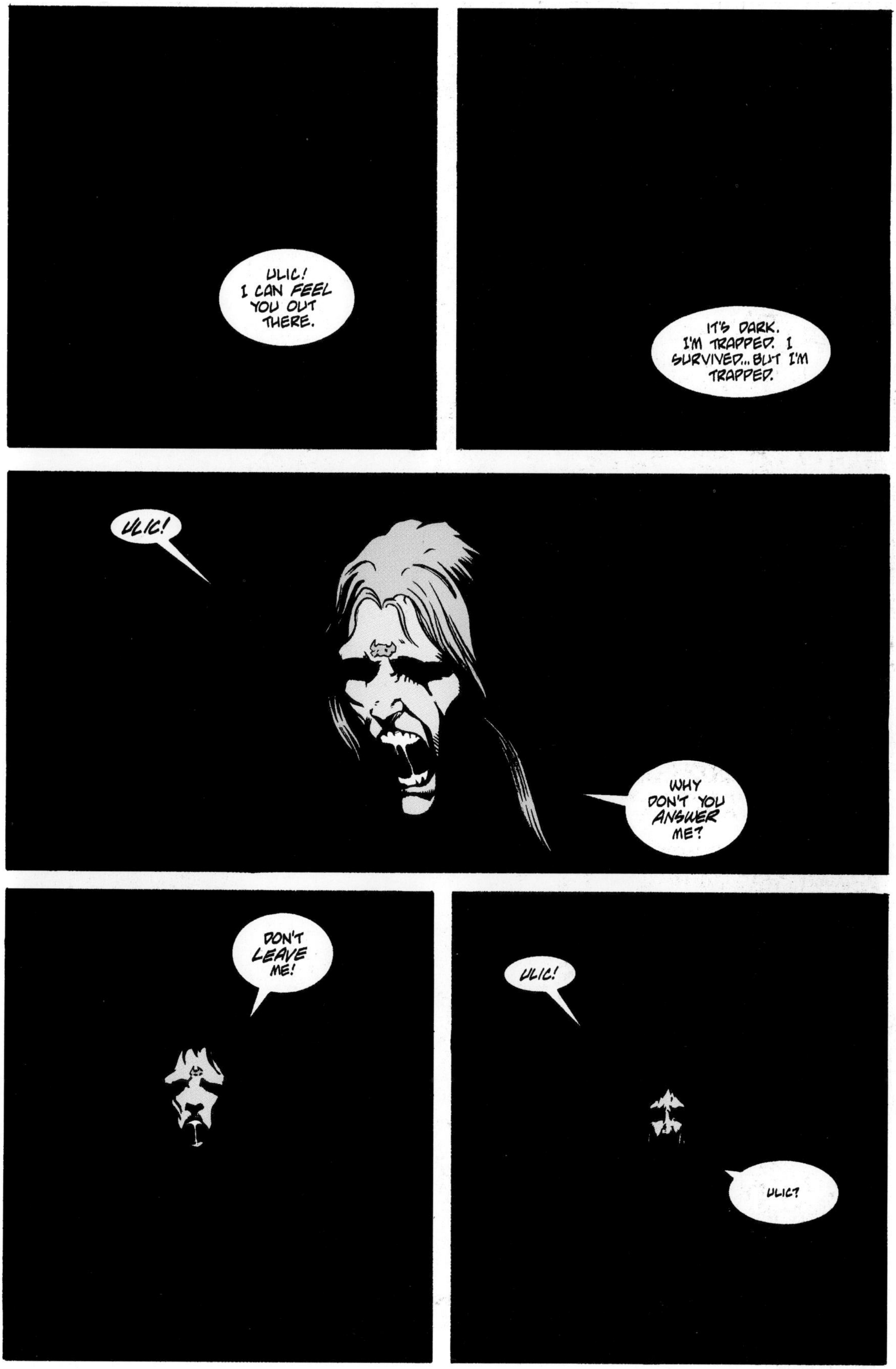
ULIC! I CAN FEEL YOU OUT THERE.
IT'S DARK. I'M TRAPPED. I SURVIVED... BUT I'M TRAPPED.
ULIC!
WHY DON'T YOU ANSWER ME?
DON'T LEAVE ME!
ULIC!
ULIC?
THE END

Gallery

Featuring the original comic-book series cover paintings by Hugh Fleming.

VDS

TALES OF THE SITH ERA ◄●► 25,000-1000 YEARS BEFORE STAR WARS: A NEW HOPE

TALES OF THE JEDI
THE GOLDEN AGE OF THE SITH
Anderson • Carrasco, Jr. • Gossett
ISBN: 1-56971-229-8 $16.95
FALL OF THE SITH EMPIRE
Anderson • Heike • Carrasco, Jr.
ISBN: 1-56971-320-0 $14 .95
KNIGHTS OF THE OLD REPUBLIC
Veitch • Gossett
ISBN: 1-56971-020-1 $14.95
THE FREEDON NADD UPRISING
Veitch • Akins • Rodier
ISBN: 1-56971-307-3 $5.95
DARK LORDS OF THE SITH
Veitch • Anderson • Gossett
ISBN: 1-56971-095-3 $17.95
THE SITH WAR
Anderson • Carrasco, Jr.
ISBN: 1-56971-173-9 $17.95
*REDEMPTION
Anderson • Gossett • Pepoy • McDaniel
ISBN: 1-56971-535-1 $14.95
*JEDI VS. SITH
Macan • Bachs • Fernandez
ISBN: 1-56971-649-8 $15.95

PREQUEL ERA ✦ 1000-0 YEARS BEFORE STAR WARS: A NEW HOPE

*JEDI COUNCIL
ACTS OF WAR
Stradley • Fabbri • Vecchia
ISBN: 1-56971-539-4 $12.95
*DARTH MAUL
Marz • Duursema • Magyar • Struzan
ISBN: 1-56971-542-4 $12.95
PRELUDE TO REBELLION
Strnad • Winn • Jones
ISBN: 1-56971-448-7 $14.95
OUTLANDER
Truman • Leonardi • Rio
ISBN: 1-56971-514-9 $14.95
*JEDI COUNCIL
EMMISSARIES TO MALASTARE
Truman • Duursema • Others
ISBN: 1-56971-545-9 $15.95
STAR WARS: TWILIGHT
Ostrander • Duursema • Magyar
ISBN: 1-56971-558-0 $12.95
EPISODE 1 —
THE PHANTOM MENACE
Gilroy • Damaggio • Williamson
ISBN: 1-56971-359-6 $12.95
EPISODE 1 —
THE PHANTOM MENACE ADVENTURES
ISBN: 1-56971-443-6 $12.95
MANGA EDITIONS
Translated into English
EPISODE 1 — THE PHANTOM MENACE
George Lucas • Kia Asamiya
VOLUME 1
ISBN: 1-56971-483-5 $9.95
VOLUME 2
ISBN: 1-56971-484-3 $9.95
*JANGO FETT
Marz • Fowler
ISBN: 1-56971-623-4 $5.95
*ZAM WESELL
Marz • Naifeh
ISBN: 1-56971-624-2 $5.95
EPISODE 2 —
ATTACK OF THE CLONES
Gilroy • Duursema • Kryssing • McCaig
ISBN: 1-56971-609-9 $17.95
DROIDS
THE KALARBA ADVENTURES
Thorsland • Windham • Gibson
ISBN: 1-56971-064-3 $17.95
REBELLION
Windham • Gibson
ISBN: 1-56971-224-7 $14.95
JABBA THE HUTT
THE ART OF THE DEAL
Woodring • Wetherell • Sheldon
ISBN: 1-56971-310-3 $9.95
*UNDERWORLD
THE YAVIN VASSILIKA
Kennedy • Meglia
ISBN: 1-56971-618-8 $14.95
CLASSIC STAR WARS
HAN SOLO AT STARS' END
Goodwin • Alcala
ISBN: 1-56971-254-0 $6.95
BOBA FETT
ENEMY OF THE EMPIRE
Wagner • Gibson • Nadeau • Ezquerra
ISBN: 1-56971-407-X $12.95

TRILOGY ERA ✪ 0-5 YEARS AFTER STAR WARS: A NEW HOPE

A NEW HOPE SPECIAL EDITION
Jones • Barreto • Williamson
ISBN: 1-56971-213-1 $9.95
MANGA EDITIONS
Translated into English
A NEW HOPE
George Lucas • Hisao Tamaki
VOLUME 1
ISBN: 1-56971-362-6 $9.95
VOLUME 2
ISBN: 1-56971-363-4 $9.95
VOLUME 3
ISBN: 1-56971-364-2 $9.95
VOLUME 4
ISBN: 1-56971-365-0 $9.95
VADER'S QUEST
Macan • Gibbons
ISBN: 1-56971-415-0 $11.95
CLASSIC STAR WARS
THE EARLY ADVENTURES
Manning • Hoberg
ISBN: 1-56971-178-X $19.95
SPLINTER OF THE MIND'S EYE
Austin • Sprouse
ISBN: 1-56971-223-9 $14.95
CLASSIC STAR WARS
IN DEADLY PURSUIT
Goodwin • Williamson
ISBN: 1-56971-109-7 $16.95
THE EMPIRE STRIKES BACK SPECIAL EDITION
Goodwin • Williamson
ISBN: 1-56971-234-4 $9.95
MANGA EDITIONS
Translated into English
THE EMPIRE STRIKES BACK
George Lucas • Toshiki Kudo
VOLUME 1
ISBN: 1-56971-390-1 $9.95
VOLUME 2
ISBN: 1-56971-391-X $9.95
VOLUME 3
ISBN: 1-56971-392-8 $9.95
VOLUME 4
ISBN: 1-56971-393-6 $9.95
CLASSIC STAR WARS
THE REBEL STORM
Goodwin • Williamson
ISBN: 1-56971-106-2 $16.95
CLASSIC STAR WARS
ESCAPE TO HOTH
Goodwin • Williamson
ISBN: 1-56971-093-7 $16.95
SHADOWS OF THE EMPIRE
SHADOWS OF THE EMPIRE
Wagner • Plunkett • Russell
ISBN: 1-56971-183-6 $17.95
RETURN OF THE JEDI SPECIAL EDITION
Goodwin • Williamson
ISBN: 1-56971-235-2 $9.95
MANGA EDITIONS
Translated into English
RETURN OF THE JEDI
George Lucas • Shin-ichi Hiromoto
VOLUME 1
ISBN: 1-56971-394-4 $9.95
VOLUME 2
ISBN: 1-56971-395-2 $9.95
VOLUME 3
ISBN: 1-56971-396-0 $9.95
VOLUME 4
ISBN: 1-56971-397-9 $9.95

CLASSIC SPIN-OFF ERA ♛ 5-25 YEARS AFTER STAR WARS: A NEW HOPE

MARA JADE
BY THE EMPEROR'S HAND
Zahn • Stackpole • Ezquerra
ISBN: 1-56971-401-0 $15.95
SHADOWS OF THE EMPIRE
EVOLUTION
Perry • Randall • Simmons
ISBN: 1-56971-441-X $14.95
X-WING ROGUE SQUADRON
THE PHANTOM AFFAIR
Stackpole • Macan • Biukovic
ISBN: 1-56971-251-4 $12.95
BATTLEGROUND: TATOOINE
Stackpole • Strnad • Nadeau • Ensign
ISBN: 1-56971-276-X $12.95
THE WARRIOR PRINCESS
Stackpole • Tolson • Nadeau • Ensign
ISBN: 1-56971-330-8 $12.95
REQUIEM FOR A ROGUE
Stackpole • Strnad • Barr • Erskine
ISBN: 1-56971-331-6 $12.95

IN THE EMPIRE'S SERVICE
Stackpole • Nadeau • Ensign
ISBN: 1-56971-383-9 $12.95
BLOOD AND HONOR
Stackpole • Crespo • Hall • Martin
ISBN: 1-56971-387-1 $12.95
MASQUERADE
Stackpole • Johnson • Martin
ISBN: 1-56971-487-8 $12.95
MANDATORY RETIREMENT
Stackpole • Crespo • Nadeau
ISBN: 1-56971-492-4 $12.95
THE THRAWN TRILOGY
HEIR TO THE EMPIRE
Baron • Vatine • Blanchard
ISBN: 1-56971-202-6 $19.95
DARK FORCE RISING
Baron • Dodson • Nowlan
ISBN: 1-56971-269-7 $17.95
THE LAST COMMAND
Baron • Biukovic • Shanower
ISBN: 1-56971-378-2 $17.95
DARK EMPIRE
DARK EMPIRE
Veitch • Kennedy
ISBN: 1-56971-073-2 $17.95
DARK EMPIRE II
Veitch • Kennedy
ISBN: 1-56971-119-4 $17.95
EMPIRE'S END
Veitch • Baikie
ISBN: 1-56971-306-5 $5.95
BOBA FETT
DEATH, LIES, & TREACHERY
Wagner • Kennedy
ISBN: 1-56971-311-1 $12.95
CRIMSON EMPIRE
CRIMSON EMPIRE
Richardson • Stradley • Gulacy • Russell
ISBN: 1-56971-355-3 $17.95
COUNCIL OF BLOOD
Richardson • Stradley • Gulacy • Emberlin
ISBN: 1-56971-410-X $17.95
JEDI ACADEMY
LEVIATHAN
Anderson • Carrasco • Heike
ISBN: 1-56971-456-8 $11.95

THE NEW JEDI ORDER ERA ◉ 25+ YEARS AFTER STAR WARS: A NEW HOPE

UNION
Stackpole • Teranishi • Chuckry
ISBN: 1-56971-464-9 $12.95
CHEWBACCA
Macan • Duursema • Others
ISBN: 1-56971-515-7 $12.95

INFINITIES — DOES NOT APPLY TO TIMELINE ⬢

*TALES VOLUME 1
Marz • Plunkett • Duursema • Others
ISBN: 1-56971-619-6 $19.95
*INFINITIES
A NEW HOPE
Warner • Johnson • Snyder • Rio • Nelson
ISBN: 1-56971-648-X $12.95
BATTLE OF THE BOUNTY HUNTERS POP-UP COMIC BOOK
Windham • Moeller
ISBN: 1-56971-129-1 $17.95
DARK FORCES
Prose novellas, heavily illustrated
SOLDIER FOR THE EMPIRE
Dietz • Williams
hardcover edition
ISBN: 1-56971-155-0 $24.95
paperback edition
ISBN: 1-56971-348-0 $14.95
REBEL AGENT
Dietz • Tucker
hardcover edition
ISBN: 1-56971-156-9 $24.95
paperback edition
ISBN: 1-56971-400-2 $14.95
JEDI KNIGHT
Dietz • Dorman
hardcover edition
ISBN: 1-56971-157-7 $24.95
paperback edition
ISBN: 1-56971-433-9 $14.95

SPANS MULTIPLE ERAS

BOUNTY HUNTERS
Truman • Schultz • Stradley • Mangels
ISBN: 1-56971-467-3 $12.95

* New
•Prices and availability subject to change without notice

Available from your local comics shop or bookstore!
To find a comics shop in your area, call 1-888-266-4226 • For more information or to order direct: •On the web: www.darkhorse.com • E-mail: mailorder@darkhorse.com
•Phone: 1-800-862-0052 or (503) 652-9701 • Mon.-Sat. 9 A.M. to 5 P.M. Pacific Time   *Prices and availability subject to change without notice